THE AGE OF
HERETICS

THE AGE OF HERETICS

HEROES, OUTLAWS, AND THE FORERUNNERS OF CORPORATE CHANGE

Art Kleiner

NICHOLAS BREALEY
PUBLISHING
LONDON

To Faith

First published in Great Britain by
Nicholas Brealey Publishing Limited in 1996
21 Bloomsbury Way
London WC1A 2TH

Published by arrangement with Doubleday, a division of Bantam Doubleday Dell Publishing Group, Inc.

ISBN 1-85788-157-5

British Library Cataloguing in Publication Data
A catalogue record for this book is available from the British Library.

Book Design by Chris Welch

CONTENTS

THE AGE OF HERETICS

EXECUTIVE SUMMARY

Executives, it is said, are too busy to read. Instead, they skim. They spend their precious reading time—on the train, on hold during a phone call, or under the porch light while their children sleep—sifting through hyped-up, ponderous management literature, searching relentlessly for any practical nuggets. Give them something they can *use,* on the shop floor or in a strategic plan. Give them something that can solve their problems, or make their efforts succeed, or let them go home early tonight.

This is not a book of nuggets, but a story of management history. To read it, if I've done my job correctly, is to drift down the broad stream of business thought and activity—particularly the rebellious and innovative parts—from the past fifty years. En route, you will relive the intellectual influences and emotionally charged controversies of managerial culture since World War II. If you are a manager, you might discover where your work and your thinking have come from, where they are going, and what forces have helped create them. You might get a feel for the influence that the ideas you work with today could have on the direction of civilization during the next century. Those who do not understand change are condemned to stay the same.

If (like me) you are not a manager, and never have been a manager, then you live in a world dominated by an alien culture. Nothing is created on a large scale without corporations. You may resent
the culture of business (so many people do). In fact, the culture you
resent is the culture of executive summaries, the culture that boils
stories down to a few choice nuggets, the culture that has no time
for the fable, but only time for morals (like these):

▼ "New truths," said Thomas Huxley, "begin as heresies." He was
defending Charles Darwin's theory of natural selection. He
might have added that new heresies also begin as truths. A heretic is someone who sees a truth that contradicts the conventional
wisdom of the institution—and remains loyal to both entities, to
the institution and the new truth. Heretics are not apostates;
they do not want to leave the "church." Instead, they want the
church to change, to meet the truths that they have seen halfway.

▼ Beginning in the late 1950s, a growing number of heretics
emerged in the dominant institutions of our time—mainstream,
publicly held, large multinational corporations. These were people within the firm who saw a truth that ran against its prevailing attitudes. They saw how, despite the power of corporate
practice, something desperately desirable had been lost in everyday corporate life: a sense of the value of human relationships
and community. They saw how, without that human spirit, corporations could not perform.

▼ Modern heretics are not burned at the stake. They are relegated
to backwaters or pressured to resign. They see their points of
view ignored or their efforts undermined. They see others get
credit for their ideas and work. Worst of all, they see the organization thrive as a by-product of their efforts, while the point of
their heresy, the truth they fought to bring to the surface, is lost.

▼ Despite all these frustrations, it is better to be a heretic than to
have one's soul wither through the denial of a truth.

▼ We can think of the 1950s, 1960s, and 1970s as the Age of
Heretics, not because heretics prospered, but because the idea of
valuing heresy gained currency. In earlier times, the leaders
of large institutions (like the church) never recognized the value

of dissent. Only now do we begin to understand how much there is to learn from dissent: how paying attention to it tempers the isolation, self-indulgence, and corruption of ordinary leadership.

▼ Corporate heretics built their work upon a body of intellectual work that emerged after the war. These ideas had roots in Western and Eastern spiritual traditions; in the new types of engineering and social science practice; in humanistic psychology and role-playing theory; in the experiences of anti-Nazi resistance fighters; in the models of systems engineers; and in the counter-culture of the 1960s.

▼ Corporate heretics were reviled from the left (as "ineffectually trying to work within the system when the system should be destroyed") and from the right (as "disloyal, effete, snobbish, and maybe Communistic"). Many corporate heretics were silly or pretentious: snake-oil salesmen (and saleswomen) of one sort or another. And yet corporate heretics may be the closest thing we have, in our self-contradictory time, to genuine heroes. They provide the unsung conscience of our civilization.

▼ They also represent an inevitable historical process. An institution, or a culture, sheds heretics as it matures.

▼ We cannot say, incontrovertibly, that any one corporation or organization has permanently changed for the better as a result of the events described in this book.

▼ But we can say that society as a whole has changed. Many of the tensions and revelations of society today, in 1995, represent the playing-out of forces that the heretics unveiled in the 1950s and 1960s.

▼ The skills all of us are going to need, as citizens and private individuals, have to do with learning to be responsible for large-scale endeavors, without being in control of them. Corporate heretics have pioneered the learning of these skills. And their heretical ideas have gradually moved into the mainstream, becoming key components of the operating premises of institutions worldwide:

   ▼ In the long run, nothing can be effectively controlled from the top of a hierarchy—or from any one perspective.

▼ People are basically trustworthy. Only workplaces that give their members the chance to learn and add value through their work will succeed in the long run.

▼ Industrial growth, when untempered by constant intelligent inquiry, leads to overshoot and collapse.

▼ No one can predict the future. All we can do is choose our contribution to the circumstances out of which the future will take its shape.[1]

▼ No one can make anything happen, in the long run, by commanding, programming, or regulating it. We can only change the world by taking part in it wholeheartedly, as if at any moment, our command may be upturned.

These themes have engaged dozens of people in complicated, controversial lifelong work, work to which they devoted themselves, and which often consumed them. This book is about those people. Behind every executive summary, there is a story . . .

TIMELINE

Benedictine monasteries demonstrate a prototype of self-contained corporate forms (4th–8th centuries A.D.)

Ecclesiastical universities (Paris and Oxford) develop the corporate form (13th–16th centuries)

New York State legislature develops blanket corporate charters (1811)

Corporate form evolves in battles between state legislatures (1820–1900)

"Divisional" corporate form emerges at Dupont and GM, managed by the use of numbers to compare performance at various corporate segments, and rapidly supersedes other forms of company governance (1920s)

Regulated merchant companies, chartered by the Crown, emerge to keep traders safe from liability (16th century)

Double-entry bookkeeping methods in Venice allow debt and equity to be recorded as part of commercial transactions (16th century)

Railroad, textile, steel, and explosives corporations develop more sophisticated forms of the "numbers" (1840–1910)

Frederick Taylor's "scientific management" establishes the "numbers" as the dominant method for drawing efficiency from people (1880–1930)

Donaldson Brown invents "return on investment" (1924)

A few corporate heretics begin to discover the tyranny of the "numbers" from within (1920s–1930s)

Chapter 1: Monastics ⟶

Vernacular life—the values of local community and family —governs commerce for millennia. Business represents a common resource for the local community

Industrial structures overwhelm vernacular culture, provoking a variety of forms of backlash and response

Buckminster Fuller's dymaxion car picked up, then dropped, by Chrysler (1934)

Countercultures emerge in the early industrial era

African-Irish-voodoo-slave-jazz counterculture roots

Kurt Lewin and Ron Lippitt study democracy in boys' clubs (1938)

Abelard (c. 1120)
"Free Spirits" (c. 1190)

Parzival written (c. 1210)
Reformists (c. 1250)

Social psychology begins to study organizational behavior (1920s–1930s)

Pelagius (c. 390)

de Molay executed (1314)
Mystics (c. 1350)

Galileo (1633)

Transaction time: as much as 11 years

Preindustrial   Industrial (1850+)

McKinsey and Harvard Business School emerge as avatars of "numbers wisdom" (1930s–1950s)

First big McKinsey European consulting job turns Shell into a worldwide decentralized company (1957)

Pierre Wack with G. I. Gurdjieff in occupied Paris during the war (1940s)

Pierre Wack studies the "art of seeing" (1950s)

Leo Rosten, Herman Kahn, and others at Rand Corporation develop scenario planning (1950s)

"Systems" disciplines, evolving in World War II, reshape engineering (1950s)

Engineering professor Willis Harman exposed to psychedelic drugs at Sequoia Seminars (1956–1961)

Chapter 6: Lovers of Faith and Reason ——⟶

Jay Forrester invents magnetic core memory (1955)

Counterculture is quiescent in 1950s . . .

Chapter 2: Pelagians ——⟶

Eric Trist studies coal mines in Haighmoor (1947)

Norwegian WWII resistance fighters develop "self-organizing" teams

First NTL-influenced "organization development" work, by Robert Blake and Herb Shepard at Esso's Bayway refinery (1958)

Lewin, Lippitt, Bradford, and Benne (the NTL founders) cross paths during the war

The Connecticut race-relations workshop (1946) leads to the invention of the T-Group and the founding of National Training Labs (1947)

NTL's thriving inventiveness period (1950s)

Ed Schein studies "brainwashing" in Korea (1954)

McGregor presents "Theory X and Theory Y" (1957)

Kurt Lewin and Ron Lippitt join Douglas McGregor at MIT, then Lewin dies. McGregor goes to Antioch, Lippitt to Michigan (1947–1948)

First corporate people, from Aramco/Esso, at T-Groups (early 1950s)

McGregor leaves Antioch, creates the "organizational studies" department at MIT (1955)

Chris Argyris publishes Personality and Organization (1957)

World War II

Transaction time: a few months to a few years

1940

1950

Heyday of Harold Geneen at ITT
(1960s, Chapter 1)

Pierre Wack goes to work for
Shell Française (1961)

Standard Oil executives ask Shell,
"What are you doing about the
future?" (1964)

Shell report on the year 2000; Ted
Newland and others at Shell begin
writing about the end of the
international oil system (1967)

Chapter 5: Mystics ⟶

Herman Kahn begins
courting corporate
clients, writes *The Year
2000* (1967)

Harman, Myron Stolaroff, and others
involved in psychedelics research at
private institute near Stanford
University (1960s)

Harman, Oliver Markley, and others
build "futures group" at Stanford
Research Institute, based on EEOC
assignment on the future of
education (1968)

Forrester develops Industrial
Dynamics concept and systems
modeling language (1956–1962)

Modern environmental
movement born (late 1960s)

Chapter 8: The Millenarian Meme ⟶

. . . but explosive
and vibrant in 1960s

Paul Hawken becomes manager
of Erewhon, natural foods
retailer/wholesaler (1966)

Counterculture businesses
and enterprises thrive,
grow, develop (1960s–
1970s)

Ralph Nader comes to
national attention when he
successfully sues GM for
harassment after his book
against the Corvair (1966)

GM chairman James Roche
earns $900,000 per year
(1967)

Chapter 4: Protesters ⟶

Riots in Rochester prompt
church activists to invite Saul
Alinsky; with a local black
community group, FIGHT, he
targets Eastman Kodak
(1964-1965)

Kodak manager John
Mulder agrees to a
compromise training
plan that is
immediately revoked
by his superiors (1966)

Antiwar protests begin to focus on
annual meetings at Dow Chemical,
Honeywell, and other companies (1969)

First politically motivated shareholder
protest, organized by Saul Alinsky
and community leader Franklin Florence
against Kodak (1968)

Michael Maccoby begins
"Gamesman" research at
Hewlett-Packard (1969)

Procter & Gamble's
first "technician
system" plant
(sociotech) at Augusta
(1962)

Trist, Emery, Thorsrud, and
others develop concepts of
"industrial democracy" and
"permanent turbulence"
(mid-1960s)

New P&G plants follow the
technician system; Charlie Krone
and others develop the Gurdjieff-inspired
Lima, Ohio, plant (1967)

Chapter 3: Reformists ⟶

Robert Blake and Jane Mouton
split from NTL and the U. of
Texas, develop the "Grid
System" (1962 onward)

Lyman Ketchum
and Ed Dulworth
go to T-Groups
(1965)

GF dog food plant managers
Ketchum and Dulworth,
chagrined by Kankakee's labor-
management malaise, seek a
better alternative (1966)

New dog food
plant approved for
Topeka: "You are
free to fail" (1969)

Argyris debate with
Odiorne brings T-Group
problems to light (1963)

Chapter 7: Parzival's Dilemma ⟶

NTL splits between East
Coast (research) and West
Coast (therapy) contingents

McGregor publishes
*The Human Use of
Human Beings* (1960),
dies in 1964

U.S. State
Department
organization
change-effort tests
NTL ideas in D.C.
(1965–1967)

Minority T-Group
participants stage
first race-oriented
confrontation at
Bethel (1968)

Warren Bennis
accepts, then
declines, NTL
presidency
(1969)

1960

Chapter 9: The Rapids

Boston Consulting Group carries the "numbers" concept into strategic decision-making "growth/share" rebus (1971)

Hayes and Abernathy from Harvard, and Peters and Waterman from McKinsey challenge conventional wisdom: American management may not have all the answers . . . (1977–1982)

Shell Group Planning scenario team forms (1971)

Pierre Wack presents the six "delta" scenarios, making it clear why oil companies must change assumptions (1972)

Yom Kippur War leads to oil embargo and price crisis (1973)

Shell planners consider "global environment" scenarios, invite Amory Lovins to quantify his ideas (1974-1975)

Lovins's "soft energy path" sets out an alternative direction for energy policy and corporate purpose (1976)

Herman Kahn, offended by Limits to Growth, develops "Belle Epoque" scenario of future prosperity (1970s)

SRI "Changing Images of Man" report sets out "new paradigm" for society, foreshadows New Age movement, and targets corporations as millennial agents (1974)

"Voluntary simplicity" project becomes SRI's most popular report (1977)

"Millenarian meme" develops its own identity and direction (late 1970s)

At Club of Rome invitation, Jay Forrester and the Meadowses apply system dynamics to global problematique, develop Limits to Growth model (1969-1972)

Owners and managers of Erewhon can't agree on how to manage growth; Hawken leaves business (1972)

Waiting in the wings, to emerge during the 1980s: the quality movement in the West (along with the "Japanese management" fad), self-managing work teams, the crisis of corporate governance, corporate environmentalism, reengineering, the impact of personal computers, and much more . . .

Campaign GM sparks national debate over "corporate social responsibility"(1970)

Saul Alinsky publishes Rules for Radicals, dies (1972)

Reverend Leon Sullivan, appointed to the GM board after the 1970 shareholder meeting, begins speaking out against corporate operations in South Africa (1971)

Quality of Working Life movement emerges from sociotech, focuses on redesign of plants in large corporations through labor-management agreements (1970s)

Ketchum and Dulworth forced out of General Foods (1975)

Krone leaves P&G, moves to Carmel to set up new type of consulting network (1977)

Topeka plant opens; Ketchum moves back to corporate GF (1971)

Trist and Ketchum meet, become friends; Topeka lionized outside GF, ignored within (1972-1973)

Chris Argyris (with Donald Schön) develops "theory of action," resolving Augustinianism and Pelagianism in organizational practice (1971-1979)

Bennis becomes president of U. of Cincinnati, bringing Hendrik Gideonse from EEOC to be education dean; for the first time, an NTLer will be at the helm of a large mainstream organization (1971)

Women's caucus emerges at NTL (1973)

"Four Horsepersons" reshape NTL with structure that forces diversity; Edie Seashore becomes president (1975)

While O.D. consultants grow independent, NTL declines (1970s)

Bennis faces crisis when faculty organizes union (1974-1976)

Bennis resigns from the U. of Cincinnati (1977)

After a heart attack, Bennis devotes himself to writing about leadership (1979)

"Great divide" economic shift

Transaction time: measured increasingly in weeks, days, minutes, seconds

1970

MONASTICS

The historian John P. Davis tells us that the great-great-grandfathers of today's large, mainstream corporations were the monasteries of the early Christian church. Organized during the dissolution of the Roman Empire, they were built as isolated communities, cut off from worldly villages and barbarian raids. Monks shared every aspect of their lives together; on a trip to town, they wore the community's best robes. When they came home, they returned the robes to the community's closet, exchanging them for everyday muslin. Rituals governed every moment of the monks' days. Uncertainties of the outside world, from the preparation of meals to their sense of life's purpose, were serenely controlled within.

Their knowledge of ritual gave the monasteries their power. Each monk lived a habitual regimen of fierce self-denial, chosen so that they could serve a purpose greater than *any individual's life could encompass. Monks were members of an elite; they often ignored commands from outside the cloister walls. Their nominal governors—not just the lords and political rulers, but the popes and bishops—let them be. Rome governed the church in principle, but the Franciscans and Dominicans fulfilled the church's mission in practice; they surged out into the medieval countryside as priests and counselors. They drew and held even people who felt repulsed by the corrupt papacies of the late Middle Ages.[1] Catholicism recovered from the blow of the Reformation only because the monasteries put their superior knowledge and support behind the church.*

Some monasteries evolved into great European ecclesiastical universities, the universities of Paris and Oxford, chartered by kings. These, in turn, became the models for mercantile stock companies. Expeditions across the Atlantic, or around the Cape of Good Hope, were too expensive for sea captains to finance themselves. If a ship failed to return, the owner would qualify for debtors' prison; if an owner died before a ship returned, his creditors might not be paid. Thus European kings and queens chartered corporations—creatures of legal sovereignty, named after the Latin word for "body." The stock company had no human body, but it was corporeal in every other sense. It was an engine for creating material. It could own property, outlive its human members, and borrow or lend money (a neat maneuver around the Christian law against usury). The monarchs had designed these new institu-

tions to carry out the policies that they found too risky to undertake themselves. To each successful corporate applicant the Crown said, as Isabella might have said to Columbus: *Go now. I judge you responsible to return with gold and spices. You are free to take a risk in our name.*

Corporations evolved further when the new American republic won its independence from England. The states took over the royal role of granting charters. In that era of budding industry, thousands of would-be railroad magnates and factory builders beleaguered the legislatures with applications to start companies. In 1811, the New York State legislature changed the rules of the game. Instead of tediously sorting through individual requests, they established a blanket corporate charter. Anyone who met the legal criteria was automatically granted the powers of a company: to own property, to outlive human members, and not to burden any individuals with their debts or liabilities. Nascent entrepreneurs flocked to the state, and then to other states such as Delaware and New Jersey, which strove to outdo the leniency of each other's laws.

Through the rest of the 1800s, the form of the corporation took shape in an elaborate dance of wills. Entrepreneurs, torn between building legacies and extracting cash, led the dance; state legislators, torn between attracting corporations and limiting their power, followed. Abuses of corporate will led to new prohibitions, which sent businessmen scurrying for new ways to get around them. New types of technological webs

bound the country: railroads, steamships, electric power, tele-
graph and telephone lines. The newly invented rotary press
enabled printers to put out 100,000 copies of a magazine; this,
in turn, allowed national advertising to sprout, which made it
profitable for consumer product giants to build brands.

By 1945—after a few decades of large-scale existence, after
134 years of legal life, after more than a millennium of craft-
ing its relationship with power—the commercial corporation
had come to dominate the culture of the world. Like patrons
of immense crystal gardens, industrial leaders had built up
great latticeworks of thrumming wires and churning high-
ways. They had cultivated, with indifference to any value but
the growth of their own enterprises, the banking empires
needed to finance those infrastructures. They had put forth
new packaging and refrigeration methods that had freed the
hungry from the tyranny of seasons—and then, to move that
food around the world, they had created a distribution and
transport system that would have boggled the imagination of
a Renaissance-era trader. Through broadcasting, they had
made real the age-old fantasy of seeing distant events reflected
through magic mirrors; through the aircraft industry, they had
allowed millions of people to take for granted the miracle of
flying. All of these boons, and many more, were commonplace
by the 1960s, to the point where no one praised them; it
would have meant voicing a self-evident cliché.

In a thousand different ways, the large mainstream firms of
the twentieth century reshaped the images of success and

achievement, of human worth and value. Decision makers at desks overlooking cityscapes plotted elaborate diagrams of authority, and signed off on allocating money, while secretaries brought coffee and the afternoon mail. Men measured themselves by the size of their paychecks and option plans, or by the number of tiles in the ceilings of their offices. Women judged their worth by the cumulative growth of their husbands' and fathers' careers.

Corporate culture was a vast wave, comforting to those whose natures fit with it, splashing across all competing desires for power and fulfillment, carrying progress and industry to every other culture. It struck with such immense, captivating grandeur that there seemed to be no escape.[2]

But the greater the wave, the stronger the undertow.

▼▼▼

This book is the story of that undertow. Like all heretical movements, the movement to reform corporations from the inside came into being because the prevailing institutions left a need unfulfilled. Something invaluable had been lost, and it had to be reclaimed. This lost quality, unnoticed and yet desperately needed, was the "vernacular" spirit of everyday life.

Or so we might call it. As writer Ivan Illich points out, there is no better word for the quality of relationships and culture that dominated community life before the advent of the industrial age—when most work was unpaid and the workplace was indistinguishable from the hearth and commons. People generally use the word "vernacular" to refer to untutored speech, but it originally came from the Latin word for "homespun" or "homegrown"—anything rooted in the places where people lived. Romans originally used it, during the early medieval years, to describe homemade goods and services, made not to be sold, but to be consumed by the maker.[3] A vernacular culture was often a preindustrial village culture, but it was really any culture where the best things in life *were* free; where livelihood and quality of life came to people because they belonged to a common place or family.

Vernacular life was the way of life that still exists in the villages of our dreams (and television programs and in a few preserves where indigenous cultures are maintained). In the vernacular world, work and life and family are all intermingled in a skein of human relationship. Every exchange of goods is not just an economic transaction but an expression of the community's spirit. A barn raising is a vernacular event, because the new building exists as an expression of the community's needs. It has not been *paid* for with money. Thus, it has not been distilled through the universality of the marketplace—which, after all, doesn't care where a building might be most needed, but reflects only the will of the person who can pay for it. In a vernacular culture, every tool used symbolizes the unwritten, heartfelt contract between the tool user and the community way of life. Every bit of work is paid for, not in money, but in the ability of individuals to belong, to give and receive, and most of all to be known, down to their core, by the people around them.

In the preindustrial world, before the advent of the giant corporation, mainstream business had been a vernacular affair. It was global, and currency was certainly involved; indeed, every merchant was part of a web of commerce that extended throughout Europe and the Near East, interlaced with markets, fairs, shopping districts, and sailing routes.[4] But commerce was also intensely personal, in a way that transcended any mere individual's personality or desires.

Transactions between preindustrial merchants were not conducted between individuals. They were conducted between families. The stakes were too high otherwise. To raise the money for a long voyage, an individual trader would have to use his children as collateral and risk their sale into slavery. The tools were too meager; medieval European merchants made all their calculations with Roman numerals. They couldn't manage long division, and their concept of "zero" was fuzzy.[5] And the time it took to manage the transaction, from start to finish, was too long. An import-export trip between, say, Portugal and Java might take eleven years or more, with stops along the way to lend and borrow more money and exchange goods en route. A trader might make the circuit only two or three times during his working lifetime. Even if all went well, and he returned to port a wealthy man, that return would take place a half generation later.

With that kind of rate of return, trust had to be based on something, and the most reliable foundation was the merchant's family. A family name was the individual's bond. At the same time the family took care of all the merchant's domestic concerns; it educated his children and cared for his elders. Work and family could not be separated. No one would have *thought* of separating them.[6] If you were the scion of a merchant family, you could not choose your mate or your career, because the family's line of succession, and all the people supported by its business, depended on your playing your part.

Then the world shifted; land began to be sold and enclosed, colonies created, labor paid for, bookkeeping spread, books published, and machinery built.[7] By the 1800s, thanks in part to the telegraph and the railroad engine, the feedback loop of commerce had been dramatically accelerated.[8] Now, if you borrowed money for a long-distance enterprise, you could return it within, perhaps, a quarter of a year. You did not need to buttress your credit with your personal relationship with a trader's family or guild.

Now individual capitalists could set out on their own, without being held back by their families. The bold entrepreneurs of the "robber baron" era—of whom some were unscrupulous extortionists, while others genuinely sought to create the legacy of a more civilized world[9]—could build larger, more comprehensive enterprises than had ever existed before, on an international scale. As they grew, they tried to swallow up rivals, suppliers, and large customers. They believed that the sheer size of their expanded enterprises would insulate them from the whims and vagaries of their customers and suppliers. The corporations they built became living monuments to their intent to control the uncontrollable marketplace.

The new form of the corporation evolved quickly, not just from its familial origins but from forms dominated by any single investor. By 1940, the age of the great monopolists like J. P. Morgan was over. The modern corporation was a hive of well-trained people (gradually labeled "managers"), with overlapping responsibilities and channels of command (these were called "matrices" and "objectives"), who all sat in judgment on each other (through a form of mutual persecution called a "performance appraisal"), acting together to comprise a single sentient entity, with powers and capabilities that the same number of trained people acting as individuals could never have equaled.

To outsiders, corporate leaders might have seemed like supremely powerful individuals, projecting their personalities on the global canvases of their companies. But with very few exceptions, chief executives tended to be unremarkable men. Most of them, as the economist John Kenneth Galbraith noted, tended to retire into "Stygian darkness." Their power stemmed from the power of the company and not the other way around.[10] As with the Franciscan and Dominican monasteries of another age, the power came from something innate in the enterprise, some understanding which was available only to people within the walls. It was as if every company were a living being, giant and invisible, offering great material rewards in exchange for fealty, seeking a kind of impersonal love and devotion that was all the more compelling because no one ever talked about it in public.

If no one controlled it—no entrepreneur, no robber baron, no banker, no investor, no legislator, and no king—then where had the power of the corporation come from? It came, in a very real sense, from magic. Magic, as the medievalist Jeffrey Burton Russell suggests, is a system of practice, uncanny to those who don't understand it, that attempts to manage, instead of simply accepting, the forces that shape human life.[11] Magic is a craft of rituals, often based on some scientifically provable truth, but expanded into assumptions that can never be tested.

Consider, for instance, the priests of the Nile in the time of the Pharaoh, who lived in a temple far upstream near the junction of its tributaries. Every spring, they would check the color of the water. If the water ran clear, the Nile would flood mildly that summer, and the crops would be meager. If it ran brown, there would be over-flooding; the country would be impoverished. But if it ran blue, there would be ample water to irrigate the fields; there would be prosperity, and the Pharaoh could raise taxes and go to war. The priests may or may not have known the reasons why the rituals worked each year; they may or may not have known that a different tributary, the Blue Nile or the White Nile or the brown Atbara River, controlled the river's flow each year.[12] It didn't matter. All that mattered was the ritual, and the lives of the priests depended on the fact that it continued to work, season after season. Certainly, they guarded the secrets of the temple as closely as they could.

In the industrial era, the secrets of the temple were, simply enough, the magic of the numbers. The everyday rituals of financial analysis and control used in large corporations were so effective at managing life on a large scale, and so impenetrable to outsiders, that in any other age the wielders of the numbers would have been known as sorcerers or priests.

The practices of this "magic" had emerged through years of trial and error throughout the nineteenth and early twentieth centuries. In the salad days of the industrial age, every company was a laboratory for new methods of counting and measuring work. From the New England textile firms of the early 1800s came the formulas of "cost per pound": a way to compare the speed and skill of every worker who spun cloth, rather than simply depending on observation.[13] From the early railroads came elaborate analyses of the costs per mile of track—a way, for the first time in history, to meaningfully compare one manager's overall performance with another.[14] From the great mail-order store Sears, Roebuck came a method for scheduling the paths of goods at a distribution center, as if they were railway cars in a freight yard; and from Henry Ford came an adaptation of the same inventive scheduling to the automobile assembly line.[15]

From Du Pont and Procter & Gamble came the innovation of diversification; when they produced a variety of products, managers were insulated from the inevitable ebbs and flows in the demand for any single item.[16] And from the gangsters of the 1930s, particularly Dutch Schultz's legendary financial handler, Otto Berman (whose nickname "Abbadabba" was derived from "abracadabra"), came a recognition of exactly how the numbers could be manipulated; Abbadaba used quadratic equations and probability formulas to rig his boss's illegal gambling rackets, increasing gross profits by more than 50 percent.[17]

One pivotal moment for the numbers came in the 1880s when Frederick Taylor, studying the movements of immigrants loading pig iron at a steel mill, began to calculate ways of pacing human labor, so that manual work could be handled more effectively. Eventually, these calculations were standardized down to the hundredth of a minute, covering the time it took to climb a ladder, walk to a desk, or read a gauge. A delusion took hold that the rigorous, formulaic approach of the "numbers" would yield boundless miracles in the "scientific management" of people.

Perhaps the most important single component was the invention of "return on investment." In the 1920s, a self-effacing Delaware farm boy turned management genius named Donaldson Brown moved up in the ranks at Du Pont, despite the fact that his family had been feuding with the Du Ponts for generations. He secretly married a Du Pont girl, and when the marriage was finally exposed, Brown was shunted off to a new Detroit company where Du Pont executives had an interest—a collection of formerly independent automotive firms, now combined under the name General Motors. There, working closely with GM's brilliantly practical CEO, Alfred Sloan, Brown hit upon a way of analyzing any business action according to the rate of return on the money invested in it. Brown's formulas allowed managers of vast enterprises like GM to think of all their far-flung divisions (Chevrolet, Cadillac, Buick) as components of a single system, instead of as defacto rivals within the firm.[18]

By the mid-1950s, nearly every large company had emulated Brown's formulas, Sloan's structures, Taylor's strictures, and most of the other management systems of the industrial era. At General Electric, AT&T, Procter & Gamble, and General Foods, encyclopedic manuals (sometimes called "blue books") dictated every aspect of workplace practice, from the layout of stamping machines to the format of quarterly reports to the placement of pencils on a secretary's desk. Formulas like these may have seemed rigorous and deadening to outsiders, but philosophically they represented nothing less than a breakthrough in human capability. Like incantations, the numbers gave names to elements of the world which had previously been vague, abstract entities; the value of human effort and the way that value might change over time could now be translated into "break-even points," "market sensitivities," "net present values," and the all-purpose measuring tool of "earnings per share."[19] A manager, through the numbers, could keep track of hundreds of people spending millions of dollars on dozens of thoroughly different projects. The marketer, through the numbers, could set a product's distribution and advertising patterns with the determination and strategic overview of a general plotting a war.[20] The financier, through the numbers, could build an explicit model of the forces of the future, forces which people from more traditional cultures could only comprehend through concepts like "karma," "hubris," and "destiny."

Most magical of all, perhaps, was the fact that the predictions from the numbers tended to come true—at least in the years before 1973. By applying a little numerical sophistication, managers could treat human effort, capital, and knowledge as commodities and *see* how those commodities would decrease or increase over time—on the scale of a community, a continent, or a civilization.

If there was any doubt about the power of the numbers, one need only look at what happened to the best graduates from Harvard and Stanford business schools. They went to work for McKinsey,

America's most successful consulting firm. McKinsey was founded in the 1930s, but it came into its own after World War II; its trail can be found winding sinuously through nearly any postwar story of large-scale corporate change.

During the 1950s in particular, it had an open field. There was very little popular management literature in those days, and even the most senior executives of many corporations had spent their entire working lives within one firm. These managers often had literally no idea how other companies had dealt with the problems that bedeviled them. McKinsey charged a typical client several hundred thousand dollars per job to tell them.

The service was delivered by young business school graduates earning salaries of $15,000 per year—a remarkable amount of money then for someone still in his twenties. The bright, clean-cut "associates," as they were called, were sent into client companies by the dozen. Like immaculate pilot fish, they swam around the sharks of management (whose infighting might have provoked the crisis that brought in McKinsey in the first place), scavenging details about the operation from every conceivable surface. Through phone calls and consultations back at the home office, the consultants could compare their findings with McKinsey's exclusive collection of in-depth case studies of the "numbers" in a hundred different organizations. Gradually, the senior McKinsey team would make a diagnosis, and eventually they presented it to the client— often literally reading from their report while the client company managers sat and listened, wondering what it would mean for them or how they would have to block its recommendations in order to protect their turf.

Finally, the moment of truth would come, when the most senior McKinsey consultant and the chief of the client company would uncork the client's bourbon together in private. "They're nice kids," the head consultant would say, referring to his own young tyros. "They'll go far. But here are the two or three things in the report that *I* would pay attention to, if I were you."

Of course, there were companies that didn't need McKinsey to convince them of the power of the numbers. One such company was International Telephone and Telegraph, presided over by the "living computer," Harold Geneen. Geneen used his genius for the numbers to build a diverse company that racked up profit growths of at least 10 percent per quarter. At ferocious staff meetings, he made his managers defend their performance measurement by measurement, picking apart the discrepancies he sensed with a kind of sixth sense for numbers that didn't fit the overall pattern.[21] Between meetings, Geneen kept fine-tuning the statistics in his head, as if they were all part of an intricate electric-train layout.[22]

As Geneen himself put it, the innate drudgery of numbers provided their central grace. Because they were mundane and unrelenting, the numbers could set you free:

> The very fact that you go over the progression of those numbers week after week, month after month, means that you have strengthened your memory and familiarity with them so that you retain in your mind a vivid, composite picture of what is going on in your company. . . . The self-confidence that you are in control, that you are aware of the significant variations from the expected, gives you the freedom to do things that you would not have been able to do otherwise. You can go ahead and build a new factory plant, finance risk-laden research, or go out and buy a company, and you can do it with assurance, because you are able to sit down and figure out what that new venture will do to the total picture of your balance sheet.[23]

To enforce their decisions, the Harold Geneens and Alfred Sloans of the mid-twentieth century did not give orders, as military men did; nor did they rely on family reputation and loyalty, as the traders of the past had done. Instead, they allocated cash. Profit itself, in this context, represented not the company's "gains" extracted from its workers' labor, but the firm's capacity to generate more projects, more investments . . . more magic. With this type of power inherent in it, the "magic" of corporate finance overwhelmed all other considerations. It no longer mattered that General Motors made cars, or General Electric made electric appliances, except as means to the end of maintaining desirable numbers.

It sounds incredible that managers believed in the numbers so wholeheartedly, at the expense of all other values. But they could not argue with results; and the rituals had their own compelling power. Managers, with their engineering and finance backgrounds, knew how treacherous words and emotions could be. (That might explain why they had gone into fields like engineering and finance in the first place.) But a number was inviolate. It could be misinterpreted, but given the right techniques, you could always ferret out subterfuge and misunderstanding. The best managers could read a table of costs, sales, profit margins, and earnings alongside a table of budget forecasts, and patterns would leap off the page to confront them, with the force of a villain's grimace in Kabuki theater. A great manager could almost smell difficulties and problems, in the same way that a great stock trader could smell when the market was about to rise or fall, on the basis of the rhythm of the tape. This was the skill that they taught in business school—the skill that made twenty-four-year-old MBAs so desirable as corporate minions.

Of course, whenever there has been a gain so great, then the loss is usually equally big—and generally invisible. The financial magic of corporations, when it took over the enterprise of a firm, bulldozed away the vernacular way of life. In a preindustrial town, if you had been a grain miller, you would not have conceived of selling your grain overseas for a better price than you could get at home—not while people in the village were hungry. But the practice of the numbers made it possible to sell that grain. Once you knew the numbers, you gave up your loyalty to the village for loyalty to an impersonal exchange that, you knew in the abstract, would better serve everyone in the long run—even if it seemed disloyal now.[24] (The same logic would later enable managers to shut down plants in rust-belt communities, where families had depended on their employment for decades.)

Admittedly, vernacular society had its bad points. It was unrelentingly local and parochial; it was slow and inefficient; it stultified ambitious people; and it condemned "worldliness." Yet the intolerance was even worse from the opposite direction. The builders of industrial culture didn't have to *reject* vernacular culture—they merely ignored it or destroyed it in passing, while the mobility made possible by the train, and then the automobile, and then the commercial airplane undermined the relationships that vernacular culture depended on.[25] Within corporations, there was just no room for vernacular spirit: The whole *point* of industrial management, after all, was to permit people to be more productive at work, without being held back by human ties. Armed with the knowledge that they gleaned from the numbers, industrial people could say in good conscience, yet using a slogan borrowed from gangsters like Abbadabba: "Don't feel bad that I won this round. It's just business. Nothing personal."

Outsiders never understood. They never saw the significance of the numbers. Factory workers, housewives, hipsters, and managers' own children—no matter what their walk of life and their intelligence, if they didn't get the right training (in math, for instance), they found the numbers counterintuitive. When ordinary people deposited a penny in a piggy bank, they felt they had accrued some cash. They didn't see how they had actually lost an opportunity to have that money grow through investment. They couldn't see how nothing remained static—how that penny, their time, their knowledge, and even their relationships would be worth either more or less in years to come depending on every action they took now.

Because noncorporate people and corporate people tended not to talk much to each other during those years, there were a lot of pundits, artists, politicians, and journalists who didn't "get" the magic of the numbers either. Instead, the educated people of the 1960s talked about how sick it felt to live in a world where every comfort depended on the kindness of experts. Seen from the vantage point of an outsider, the corporate world was a monstrous place—manicured, self-sealing, and vicious. The cartoonist Robert Crumb drew humans trapped like scared rabbits while crossing the street, paralyzed before the onslaught of brutal, malevolent Motor City trucks.[26] Women, black people, non-American-born people, aging people—in short, anyone who did not look, think, and act like bright, fresh-faced engineering college graduates—could never rise to the top. Or so the criticisms went. But who wanted to rise to the top anyway? Who wanted to work where you could not choose the focus of your work and where everyone around you continually sought to undermine your dreams?

From this perspective, business knowledge seemed like a fundamental evil—as usury had seemed evil to Christians for centuries. Look at all the frustration and suffering it caused. Politicians discovered during the 1960s, for the first time since World War II, that they could win votes by accusing giant corporations of villainy. People in the street increasingly *felt* how these giant companies, so visible in brand names and skyscrapers, had created the Vietnam War, the pollution, and the deadening squareness of modern life. The great French historian of economic life, Fernand Braudel, concurred. He closed his three-volume explication of civilization and capitalism in European history with a complaint: Big corporations, with their big production units, had squeezed out the small vibrant companies that represented the lifeblood of the marketplace. "Public hostility," he wrote, "is accurately and rightly directed at the top."[27]

Tragically enough, if corporate people had been truer to the lessons of the numbers, outsiders might have had less reason to complain. For the structures of corporate finance were based upon fundamental truths about the nature of human worth and the consequences of human action. But even within companies, many people did not know how to truly "think like a businessman," and those who knew were too busy to ponder the deeper implications of their work. Instead of understanding the meaning behind the rituals, people—from the CEO on down—fixed their attention on the trappings of the rituals instead: on the business plans, job descriptions, quarterly results, and performance appraisals, all of which had originally meant nothing in themselves.

Corporate decision makers had cornered the market on "know-how," said the architect/visionary Buckminster Fuller. But they lacked "know-why."[28] They had lost the awareness of their purpose, the reasons they were in business in the first place.

Fuller had plenty of stories to prove it. Again and again during his life, he had seen the numbers lead to corporate decisions that didn't make sense—decisions that screwed not just outsiders but the company's own long-term interest. In 1934, Fuller had interested auto magnate Walter Chrysler in financing his "dymaxion car," a durable, three-wheeled, aerodynamic land vehicle modeled after an airplane fuselage. Fuller had built three models that, whenever they appeared, drew enthusiastic crowds. Like all of Bucky Fuller's inventions (he was responsible for the dymaxion dome), it was inexpensive, durable, and energy-efficient, because Fuller worked diligently to cut back the amount of material and energy used by any product he designed. "You've produced the exact car I've always wanted to produce," the mechanically apt Chrysler told him. Then Chrysler noted ruefully that Fuller had taken one-third the time and one-fourth the money that Chrysler's company usually spent to produce prototypes—prototypes that Chrysler himself often hated in the end.

For a few brief months, it had seemed that Chrysler would go ahead and introduce Fuller's car. But the banks who financed Chrysler's wholesale distributors vetoed the move by threatening to call in their loans. The bankers were afraid (or so Fuller said decades later) that an advanced new design would diminish the value of the unsold motor vehicles in dealers' showrooms. In an era of mass production, for every new car sold, five used cars had to be sold to finance the distribution and production chain, and those old cars could not be sold if Fuller's invention made them obsolete.[29]

Fuller's story was just one instance of the perennial tragedy of corporate life when the numbers guided decision making. Every innovation was a risk; every change threatened the stability of the old corporate system. The bankers' reasoning was correct. It *wasn't* fair to force them to give up the profits from used cars. Nor was it fair to force that lost value on customers who had already bought cars (a logic which, years later, would force personal computer makers to shortchange their products by making them "backwards-compatible"). As long as the numbers provided corporations with their strongest sense of purpose, then decisions like the one that hamstrung Fuller would continue to be correct.

Yet, as a result of this noble rectitude, manufacturers had to routinely undermine the potential value of their own technologies. Managers held back their highest-quality technical work (and gave it the name "over-engineering," a synonym for extravagant waste), particularly when it meant greater up-front costs. Corporate decision makers denied the innovations and safety measures they knew would do most for the common good; they got in the habit of playing down genuine innovation or social responsibility. Instead, they tried to sell products based on styling details and the moods of the mass buying public, and anything that did not threaten their past success.

When there is no sense of purpose, the love of power and privilege rush eagerly to fill the void. In the 1950s and 1960s, the rewards of the corporate hierarchy grew out of proportion. James Roche, the chairman of General Motors, the highest-paid CEO in the country, made more than $900,000 per year in 1967—$200,000 plus bonus and stock options.[30] That wasn't bad for a guy with no university degree, who had worked his way up from a sixty-cent-per-hour statistical research job for Cadillac. A more typical salary for a chief executive was $450,000—enough, in effect, to establish an aristocratic dynasty.

The salaries, moreover, were supplemented by a wide variety of perks, most hidden from outside eyes. Many CEOs and senior managers went days without having to open their wallets; their meals, laundry, transportation, and entertainment simply arrived when needed. A retiring Royal Dutch/Shell chief executive was asked what he would miss most. "The man who meets me at the plane," he said, "and takes care of everything." Sometimes "taking care of everything" meant chauffeuring a customs official from, say, Kennedy Airport to a smaller private airport in White Plains or southern Connecticut—a two- or three-hour round trip—while the CEO and his guests sat inside the company's private plane drinking wine.[31] And even the largest capital expenses moved around at the top officers' convenience, as William H. Whyte (the author of *The Organization Man*) learned in the 1970s. Whyte studied corporations which had moved their headquarters out of New York. In *every* case, the new headquarters was located within eight miles of the CEO's home.[32]

With all of these rewards, was it any wonder that managers fought so bitterly over the chance to rise to the CEO position? Like a monarch's court, the structure of power in a corporation encouraged backbiting, sniping, and hiding information: Those strategies helped you rise. Every step up the ladder had the effect, intentional or not, of isolating the manager further from the immediate consequences of his or her actions. At many organizations, you weren't seen as powerful unless it was almost impossible to reach you by phone; unless you found a way to balkanize and bully your staff, or keep them spinning, always a bit off balance, for your favors and approval. After all, if they treated you as a colleague, or if they couldn't produce the right numbers on demand, that showed that they (and you) were "out of control." It showed you had no grasp on the magic, after all.

Most of all, managers focused on the numbers because it was so hard to accomplish anything else. If you worked to get the best scores you could, you did not have to think too carefully about the reasons underlying the choices you made. Nor did you have to think about the world outside the company. Like monks, the managers of corporations in the 1950s and 1960s had isolated themselves—cut themselves off from the world that their companies had created and that everyone else blamed them for creating.

* * *

Beginning in the 1950s, a few heretical managers saw how necessary it was to put back the vernacular into corporate culture. That
would mean taking the best from *both* worlds—corporate knowledge and vernacular concern for relationship—and fusing them into
some kind of ethic of service. This understanding could only have
existed against the backdrop of the counterculture. After all, the
counterculture was a revolt against all institutional priesthoods—
not just in corporations but anywhere where the vernacular had
been stripped away. To people in the counterculture, *everything*
was personal, even technology. And as the influence of the counterculture spread, a few managers began to question the prevailing
assumptions of the corporations they worked for.

Having bulldozed the vernacular, they keenly felt the loss, but
had no name to give to it. At first, it was simply an ache, vaguely
heard in the taunts that managers made to each other, or dimly seen
in the way that executives leaned down for the scotch bottles in
their bottom desk drawers. Every year, a few more managers felt
spurred to risk their jobs—to capture some kind of contact, some
feeling of being *in touch.* Every year, a few more managers ac-
quainted themselves with the ferment going on outside the walls of
their companies, the ferment of the counterculture. And gradually
corporations began to change.

The change has been slow in coming. It is far from complete
today; some observers argue that it will never be complete, beyond
a few pockets of "vernacular acolytes." But by the early 1970s, a
significant shift was already underway. It was far enough along that
companies were ready to let a man like Michael Maccoby in their
doors.

In the late 1960s, Michael Maccoby, a Harvard-educated American psychologist, began to investigate the personality of corporate
"winners." Maccoby had just returned from three years in Cuerna-
vaca, Mexico, where he had worked closely with the psychologist
Eric Fromm. Since Ivan Illich was a neighbor there, Maccoby had
been exposed in depth to Illich's theories about how professional-
ization and industrial development had destroyed vernacular cul-

ture. And Maccoby had seen evidence of that himself. For his research with Fromm, he had spent hours in Mexican villages where corporations were due to build a factory, getting to know the farmers who lived there. Before the factories came, they spent their free hours playing guitar, talking, and playing basketball. Then the factories opened. Suddenly the villagers turned into automobile assembly-line workers who did nothing during their time off except watch television.[33]

Maccoby began to wonder about the psychology of corporate people. What went on inside people who created and sold this devastating technology? And then, by extension, what went on inside people who designed technologies for mass warfare—bombs, missiles, and the computers that guided them? Did these technologists realize the impact they had upon the world? Did they care?

Maccoby got funding from Harvard in 1968 for a study to answer his question.[34] But he couldn't find a corporation that would let him in to talk freely to its people. Then, in 1969, Maccoby gave a talk near Stanford that eventually led to his introduction to John Young, a junior manager at Hewlett-Packard. "H-P," since its birth in 1934, had always been known as a quintessential engineers' firm. But Young, who would later become CEO of H-P, was interested in understanding the human effects of corporate work. He wanted to know how to hire people at H-P who would become entrepreneurial risk takers and not just corporate bureaucrats. Almost immediately, he approved Maccoby's study for H-P. He helped organize the study, even writing some of the survey questions. More importantly, he insisted that Maccoby include other companies as well, and arranged introductions to executives at Intel, Texas Instruments, and IBM.

During the next few years (from 1971 to 1974), Maccoby and a small research team visited ten different corporations, administering surveys and showing managers Rorschach blots. The managers, after all the times they had been forced to appraise their performance, were remarkably good at describing themselves and each other. They could dispassionately pick apart each others' strengths and weaknesses, attitudes toward work, sensitivities, goals, and the things that made them angry. In these interviews many of them felt fully recognized for the first time. "I have more people working under me than ninety percent of the mayors in America," one manager said, "but nobody has ever heard of me. This interview, for me, is like being on the cover of *Time* magazine."

At that time, there was a theory in the air, taken for granted by anyone who studied corporations, that most managers were primarily "organization men"—driven by the need to belong and conform, dedicating their lives to fitting into a hivelike whole. This theory came, in large measure, from the popular book *The Organization Man,* written in the mid-1950s by sociologist/journalist William H. Whyte.[35] Sponsored at first by *Fortune* magazine, Whyte had led a team of academic researchers who conducted dozens of interviews—with managers at companies like General Electric, American Telephone and Telegraph, Richardson-Vicks, and Ford, along with their wives, who were solidly entrenched in suburban enclaves. Organization man culture, Whyte argued, had pushed out the previous "Protestant ethic" culture of independent individualism; it had fostered an atmosphere where people chose to deny their own individuality because they didn't value it highly.

But Maccoby (fifteen years after Whyte) concluded that the organization man culture was dead—even in the corporate world. There were still "company men" (as Maccoby called them) in most firms, striving to fit into a bureaucratic mind-set. But they did not rise to the top of the hierarchy anymore. The dominant people were motivated primarily by the desire to *win*—not at someone else's expense, but in the sense of winning a game.[36] They had little interest in understanding the world or figuring out which game to play; getting a big quarterly result gave them more joy than producing a product. They were the natural aficionados of corporate magic, the people who delighted in making the numbers sing. Maccoby called these people "gamesmen."

Before his research had gotten underway, Maccoby had expected most managers to be "ambitious but neurotic failures," as he put it; "petty bureaucrats who have been so humiliated and discouraged by life . . . that they have chosen to use the little power they have to make others squirm." But the gamesmen Maccoby interviewed were likable people. Their companies might be ruthless places, but as individuals they had a strong sense of benevolence and justice toward the people around them. They drew enclaves around themselves, symbolized by the steel-and-glass structures which required visitors to run a gauntlet of old security guards and young secretaries. The atmosphere within these enclaves was hard-driving, and Las Vegas-ish, but also thoroughly warmhearted. Gamesmen looked after their own people at the same time that they relentlessly competed with each other.

The gamesmen were unconcerned with morality or with restrictions. They used the sexual revolution as a playing chip; the stylized attention of stylish young women was just one of the prizes in the office, one of the many ways to keep score. Miniskirted secretaries were encouraged to mildly flirt with the managers in their departments, creating an atmosphere where everyone felt a little bit charged up, a little bit pushed forward, a little bit high on the job. The bosses flattered the secretaries by telling them how they helped control the men's moods. One secretary at Hewlett-Packard took the day off when her fiancé broke their engagement. "I didn't want to make a lot of people feel down just because I wasn't smiling," she told Maccoby.[37]

Despite the low-level singles-bar atmosphere, there was something innocent about the places that gamesmen set up. Divorce rates were low; the managers obviously cared about their kids and families as much as they cared about their co-workers. "It felt to me like Santa Claus's workshop," recalled one of Maccoby's researchers. But in the end, there was something tragic about the gamesmen. After all, "there was something immature about it, as if playing to win was all that life was about."[38]

One of Maccoby's questions asked, "Is there any technology you would oppose on moral grounds?" At electronics companies, managers consistently replied, "We would never work for a chemical company. *They* produce napalm." Meanwhile, executives at Dow Chemical said, "We would never work for an electronics firm. They make bombs." And at both, managers (even the most senior managers) consistently underreported the percentage of their company's business that went to military contracting. At the same time, all of this self-justification was conducted on an intellectual level, close to the surface, with little feeling behind it. Few of the gamesmen cared much about the uses to which their work was put. Few of them felt much responsibility to the people outside the enclave, whoever they might be.

Outsiders were losers. They were "sick" or "weak," deserving of exploitation. They didn't have the knowledge that corporate people had, the knowledge of how the world works through the financial perspective. Indeed, Maccoby himself didn't have that knowledge. In the eyes of his own gamesmen, he too was an evolutionary failure—an intellectual operating outside of the magical business mainstream.

But Maccoby, with his psychoanalytic training, also saw images of shame, self-betrayal, guilt, and despair come up again and again in the gamesmen's dreams. One manager dreamed of being buried alive, with a telephone in his casket. Another dreamed of shattered test tubes (symbolic of an early dream of being a chemist, which wasn't a lucrative enough career). Another dreamed of wandering through a city of slimy skyscrapers, with corpses peering out of the windows. Many who did not remember their dreams saw bugs, worms, and rats in the Rorschach blots.[39]

One detail was so peculiarly disturbing that Maccoby left it out of his 1976 book on this research, a best-seller called *The Gamesman.* Yet this detail was evident at all ten companies, not just H-P, and for all managerial types. Maccoby's team had asked managers to name the historical figure they most admired. The answers, almost without exception, fit into a very short list: Abraham Lincoln, John F. Kennedy, Robert Kennedy, Martin Luther King, Jr. It was an odd list—why would predominantly white managers select King?—and it took a while to notice the one thing those heroes had in common. They had all been assassinated.

Did businesspeople feel betrayed in some fundamental way, as if they had given so much of their life to their jobs that they too had been murdered? Did they lack examples of heroic figures who had survived? Or did they believe that anyone who broke through the mold of conventional office politics, who actually managed to accomplish something within the system, would be slain?

PELAGIANS

"PEOPLE ARE BASICALLY WORTHY, AND YOU CANNOT UNDERSTAND A
SYSTEM UNLESS YOU TRY TO CHANGE IT."
NATIONAL TRAINING LABORATORIES, 1947–62

From the remote northern province of Britannia, around the year 390, came Pelagius: a fat, self-possessed cleric who called himself a monk (though he had never been ordained). He landed footloose in Rome, preaching about the human capacity for redemption. God did not choose who was saved, he said. Salvation was the result of human effort. If we could reach within ourselves and draw forth the core of natural purity that God had put there—for why would He create us without it?—we could remake the world during our lifetimes. The role of the church, Pelagius said, was to help its members fruitfully exercise the will to be good.

Followers gathered around the British monk. He often stood quietly on summer evenings as small groups of passionate would-be reformers of the church, including several of the younger bishops, talked excitedly about doing away with bap-

tism or encouraging good works. He attacked the nonsensical idea, as he called it, that Adam's sin had been transmitted to the rest of humanity. He argued that people were perfectible; that human actions and human will, guided by God, could create a kind of echo of heaven on earth. The prayer groups that gathered to hear Pelagius were like reflecting pools, in which the members could see their faith and aspiration echoed in the shape of the conversation.

Far away, in his cell outside Carthage, the solemn bishop Augustine of Hippo turned his attention to the Pelagian gatherings. He had spent his life branding and fighting heretics; Pelagius would be his last great opponent. He was a supreme logician, and he rested his argument against Pelagius on the innate corruption twined within the animal core of human nature. We are all fundamentally flawed—all tagged with our own limited view of the world. Every time we think that we have turned the corner and mastered our fate, our pride contains the seeds of its own collapse. How can we presume to declare that we will create heaven, when we can't even predict the effects of the everyday exercise of our will?

Saint Augustine won the ear of the emperor, of the Pope, and of the church leaders. Some say they found his doctrine more palatable because it legitimized their authority; if humans were innately damned, then they needed the church to intervene. Others say Augustine's strictures fit the spirit of the times. And still others say simply that Augustine was right. Fearing for his life, Pelagius fled to Jerusalem. Twenty years later, he was finally tried for heresy there. Despite Augustine's objections, he was acquitted, but he died shortly thereafter. His death inspired riots in Rome. All followers of Pelagianism were banished from Christian lands.

That was fifteen centuries ago. Ever since, Augustinians and Pelagians have battled for the soul of Western human beings. How arrogant, say the Augustinians, to presume that we can draw forth our full potential without God's direction. How hopeless, say the Pelagians, to deny our inner beauty and our capacity to help ourselves. ("There are no bad children, only bad parents," is a Pelagian sentiment.) The arguments echo in every sidelong glance that one human being gives another. Can our neighbors be trusted? Will they rise to meet our trust, or betray it? How much can we have faith in ourselves? Must all of our good works be rooted in evil?[1]

▼▼▼

In the years after World War II, businessmen were readier than anyone realized to be influenced by the Pelagian imperative. It quelled the ache that people felt when the vernacular spirit was dormant. It gave people a sense that they could come to work, achieve the performance required by the numbers, and still have a chance to realize their aspirations.

The promoters of this view didn't call it Pelagianism—they called it group dynamics first and later organization development and organizational learning.[2] In its earliest days, it was a stepchild of the panic people felt after the end of World War II. Even in the late 1930s, before the full story of the Holocaust was known, the example of Nazi Germany raised profoundly disturbing questions. Were its obscene atrocities rooted in some evil aspect of the German character? Was there some fundamental evil at the core of human nature? Or could there be something in the way that Nazi society was structured that allowed ordinary people to embrace tyranny and mass murder? Was there a way to organize people away from totalitarianism and toward democracy instead?

In the late 1930s and early 1940s, one of the key people concerned about these issues was a German-Jewish social psychology professor named Kurt Lewin. Lewin had left Germany in 1933 after a fortuitous teaching sabbatical in America the year before, and he settled into a teaching position at the University of Iowa. His mother, who remained in Germany, died in a Nazi gas chamber.[3] Photographs of him show a small, wiry, sharp-featured, witty man, with spectacles and a sardonic smile, looking a little like one of the Marx Brothers out of makeup. Though he couldn't speak English well at first, he was such a fervent, openhearted, good-natured, compelling teacher, and his ideas were so lofty and at the same time resonant with everyday experience, that he developed a circle of lifelong associates, many of whom were former students.

Kurt Lewin was never a businessman, and yet the distinctions and methods he taught (and the institute he inspired, the National Training Laboratories) have influenced thousands of organizations years after his death. Nearly every sincere effort to improve organizations from within can be traced back to him, often through a thicket of tangled, hidden influences. His work spread from mentor to student, from consultant to manager to colleague, always through the medium of small groups. He believed in the Pelagian ideal: that people have something innately valuable to offer the world. His work showed how this offering emerges, or is held back, depending on the groups in which people operate.

Lewin and his followers were social psychologists, but they abandoned conventional academic research methods, such as surveys and dispassionate interviews. Instead, they developed a concept that became central to organizational reform: You cannot know an institution until you try to change it, and you cannot change it without reflecting on its purpose. This meant studying companies with full immersion in their cultures, in partnership with those managers who wanted to make changes—typically managers of some pilot project within the firm.

The tricky part was persuading senior managers to support such unorthodox research. Lewin found only one workplace willing to experiment with his ideas in full—a pajama factory in North Carolina, where the manager was Alfred Marrow, one of Lewin's students. Marrow's experiments with shop-floor group meetings in the 1940s, with Lewin as a continual adviser, were unusual enough to inspire a Broadway musical and then a Hollywood movie, both called *The Pajama Game*.[4]

Lewin coined the now famous line: "Nothing is so practical as a good theory." He also developed a new theory of human personality. He believed, with the Freudians, that subconscious echoes of past traumas drive our deep feelings, and he also believed, with the behaviorists, that people could be programmed to respond predictably to stimuli. But Lewin argued that these were only two out of the many influences that could affect an individual's behavioral "forcefield" (as Lewin called a person's mental and emotional state at any given moment).[5] Other factors might include relationships with family members; perceptions of objects; aspirations (and the difficulties of realizing them); and social pressures.[6]

On blackboards, Lewin would sketch the topology of a given individual's "forcefield" as a big egglike oval, pressed by helpful and harmful forces from all directions—the person's marriage and family relationships, fears and hopes, neuroses and physical health, work situation and network of friends.[7] The diagram laid all these out in relation to the person's goals, to show *which* forces produced the most important resistance and which offered the most leverage for an individual to grow and learn.

Social groups, Lewin believed, were particularly high-leverage "forces" for influencing behavior.[8] In Iowa City, in the 1940s, he and his graduate student Ron Lippitt demonstrated how leaders of a group could dramatically affect the character of everyone within.[9] This work—which *still* provides powerful lessons for anyone trying to organize corporate teams—was conducted with boys' clubs, a venue in which Lippitt excelled. Starting as a teenager, he had worked with Boy Scouts, the YMCA, and a succession of summer camps and orphanages. His high forehead and glasses made him look cerebral and shy (which he was), but he was also savvy, inven-ᴛ e, and people-wise, in a tart midwestern way. For the experiments with Lewin, he (and a fellow researcher named Ralph White) organized some public school, middle-class eleven-year-olds into "G-Man Clubs," with five boys in each.

All the clubs were the same, except for the college man who supervised them. Some of these collegiate club leaders were told to become "autocratic." They gave detailed directions to the boys, telling them exactly how to paint their clubhouse signs or build model airplanes. Other, "laissez-faire" leaders stayed out of the way; and in the third group, "democratic" leaders helped the boys execute their *own* ideas, with as much noncoercive guidance as possible. While the boys played indoors, a group of researchers, haggard from intensive note taking, observed them from a darkened corner of the room, while Kurt Lewin filmed them with a movie camera. ("Those people are just interested in how a good club goes," Lippitt murmured to the boys. "They won't bother us, and we won't bother them."[10])

Laissez-faire leadership, letting the boys do whatever they wanted, bred frustrated cynicism. Under authoritarianism, some boys became extremely obedient ("unnaturally good," Lippitt wrote), while others fought, bullied each other, and destroyed their own toys. In the democratic groups, boys gradually became more conscientious, more tolerant of each other; less selfish; more adult. "Eddie really did a swell job on that, didn't he?" said one eleven-year-old about his former rival. "I couldn't do as good as that." Most intriguingly, when the democratic group switched to an authoritarian leader, or vice versa, after a day or two of transition, the boys changed their behavior to match the new dynamics. The structure of a group determined the character of its members at least as much as the members determined the values of the group.

This was not an easy message to get across in the individualistically minded United States. Lewin and Lippitt were still pondering it when the United States entered World War II. The war was generally an immense catalyst for social science in America (and England), because it pulled university researchers from their isolated posts. They worked together on real-world problems such as keeping up military morale, developing psychological warfare techniques, and studying foreign cultures.

During the war years, Lippitt's path regularly crossed with two other young psychologists from the Midwest. Their names were Ken Benne and Leland (Lee) Bradford, and eventually they would form the founding triumvirate of the National Training Laboratories. Benne was a charismatic young political theorist who had been one of John Dewey's last graduate students. He was the son of an old-time Kansas populist, from whom he inherited a steadfast mistrust of capitalist competition. He was equally mistrustful of Communism—or any system in which democratic principles were suspended, even temporarily. Social change had to be managed *intelligently*—not through force, manipulation, or greedy exploitation.[11]

Bradford was not a theorist but a natural organizer. Everywhere he went, even at temporary jobs, he brought people together into freewheeling volunteer discussion groups. Dedicated to the idea of adult education (and believing that learners, not an authoritarian teacher, should control the courses), he took a job at the National Education Association, the educators' professional and lobbying group. That concept of self-directed learning became an essential factor in his life after World War II, beginning with an event still known, in group dynamics circles, as the "Connecticut Workshop."

In 1946, amidst a flood of returning GIs and the winding down of defense industries, racial tensions began to flare in some northeastern cities. A Connecticut state agency, with sponsorship from the National Conference of Christians and Jews, called Kurt Lewin to ask for help. Together with Lippitt, Bradford, and Benne, he planned a two-week workshop in creating better ethnic relations, particularly between blacks and Jews.

It was held in July, in the small working-class city of Bridgeport, just west of New Haven. There were fifty participants: about fifteen schoolteachers, an equal number of social workers, a smattering of businesspeople and real estate dealers, a few volunteer housewives, several organizers from community groups, labor unions, and veterans' groups, and a few young men who had grown up in street gangs and then, in their late twenties, became community leaders. Most of the time was spent in small discussion groups, role-playing some of the troubling aspects of interracial life—like the tough time social workers had getting white and black teenagers to accept each other's company. This was an accepted therapeutic device: A white social worker might play herself trying to get a thirteen-year-old black girl to come to a mixed-race event: "Did you know we have a folk-dancing group every Wednesday night, Nancy?" Another white social worker would mimic the girl's reply: "My friends wouldn't want to come. It's not really their gang." Then the group would talk through the implications. It must have been a wrenching experience for some of the nervous social workers, whose *real* concern (it was obvious, when they repeated the dialogue back) was making sure everyone *appeared* to get along. Given that frame of mind, how could they reach *any* teenagers, let alone teenagers struggling with moving from a black to a white culture? These adults believed in rationality; they felt they had to instill, in their troubled charges, a respect for the orderly, rational life. But the role-play had suddenly confronted them with the huge wave of blocked feeling pent up within themselves, behind the wall of their stiff, well-meaning squareness.

The pivotal moment of the conference came one night during the second week. Four participants, wandering back to their hotel rooms, passed the open door of Lewin's room and asked to listen in as the trainers talked over that day's session. Lewin agreed. Sitting in the corner, one participant—a social worker named Mrs. Brown—began to recognize herself in Lippitt's description of a participant "who is customarily the most backward and hesitant" but who had suddenly become "a very active and verbal leader" in a role-play, even after the exercise ended. What did that mean? Was she unconsciously adapting the role-play personality into her own?

Before a social scientist jumps to a hypothesis, the observations must be verified. So Lippitt turned to a graduate student named Murray Horwitz, who concurred: Yes, Mrs. Brown *had* changed— and then he broke the frame. "I think she is here," he said, "so why don't we ask her if she noticed it too?" Lippitt agreed, and the attention of the group turned to Mrs. Brown. "Are we all off the beam here in our hunches?" Lippitt asked.

No, said Mrs. Brown. "I was aware too that I was much more in the swim of things this afternoon than I had been before." And then she started analyzing herself—a bit creakily at first, but the passion crept into her voice: "I surprised myself several times the way I spoke up and found myself enjoying it." She even complained— Lippitt had cut off the role-play before she was ready!—and the evening group broke into good-natured laughter.

Kurt Lewin, the elder statesman of participative psychology, was delighted. Here was a simple, obvious solution to an eternal experimental problem: trying to guess a subject's thoughts. Sure, you could ask them, but the interviewer's biases (and the subject's) made the answers unreliable. Now, in groups like this, answers would have much more validity. "We may be getting hold of a principle here," Lewin said, "[with] wide application in our work."[12]

Indeed, as the staff and participants continued their talk about the day's session, the barriers between them dissolved; they were all now just people, mutual participants in the inquiry, comparing notes and disagreeing, just like members of a vernacular community. When the social scientists got it wrong, the participants corrected them; when the participants lost sight of the larger perspective, the social scientists gently drew them back to equanimity.

Word spread fast; the next night, all fifty participants showed up for the evening critique. There at Bridgeport they had invented a powerful new kind of conversation, in which the flow of conversation is also the subject of the same conversation and in which people's understandings of themselves and each other seem to flow naturally to the surface. It wasn't a *therapy* group; its point was to understand social dynamics, not individual neuroses. Lewin, Lippitt, Bradford, and Benne called it the "T-Group" ("T" standing for training).

Within a few months, the Connecticut T-Group discovery was famous in psychology and education departments. Lippitt, Bradford, and Benne published their findings on it almost immediately, and made plans to convene a regular series of groups the following summer. The National Education Association (through Bradford) and the Office of Naval Research (through Lewin and Lippitt) granted them money to continue experimenting.[13] To submit the applications, the researchers needed to form an institute, and they chose a name in a hurry: "The National Training Laboratories for Group Dynamics."

Lewin suggested holding the T-Groups in a "cultural island," far from anyone's homes or daily cares, so participants could, in effect, enter into an isolated world together. After looking in Massachusetts, Bradford found the Gould Academy—a traditional New England school in Bethel, a small town in western Maine. They rented the classrooms for the summer and began looking for housing for the two hundred people—one-quarter of them staff—whom they expected to descend on Bethel.

In February, midway through this planning phase, Kurt Lewin abruptly died in his sleep during a heart attack. He was only forty-seven years old. The timing of his death gave NTL's birth a mythic stature. Lewin had been a prophet. He had articulated the theoretical foundations of social psychology. He had inspired a worldwide community of practitioners to use a new set of tools and methods. And then he had passed away just before reaching the promised land.

It was left to Lewin's disciples—especially to Lee Bradford, Ken Benne, and Ron Lippitt—to settle the new territory. At first, they had difficulty attracting participants. They almost got thrown out of Bethel the first year, when a party spilled out into the town streets after midnight—drinking (in a liquor-free town), singing, and driving one man's car around the Gould Academy's footrace track.[14] But by the mid-1950s a series of grants,[15] a solid business in training fees for nonprofit organizations, and an ongoing official existence as a division of the National Educational Association had given NTL a moderately stable financial existence.[16]

All three of the principals found influential winter jobs. Lippitt moved Lewin's Institute for Group Dynamics Research[17] from MIT to the University of Michigan. Benne got an appointment at Boston University. And Bradford maintained a permanent post coordinating adult education programs at the National Education Association. The NEA leaders barely tolerated the "labs," whose suspicious group methods threatened conventional teaching styles. Nonetheless, the melancholy but stubborn director made NTL his first priority. He became the labs' center of gravity, the person around whom the whole enterprise revolved.

As a child, while peddling newspapers on the Evanston-to-Chicago train, Lee Bradford had fallen off and broken his arm. It never healed right, and that, plus his thin drawl, gave him a lifelong quality of melancholy frailty, as if he were always about to burst into tears.[18] Bradford was proud of his unpretentiousness and his eagerness to help other people shine. In a way, he was proud of his lack of pride. He liked to tell the story about how, at the start of a conference he was leading, the audience waited patiently while a mumbling janitor fooled around with some microphone cables on the stage. Finally, the janitor turned around, announced he was Leland Bradford, and began to speak to the crowd.

This personality was perfect for the role Bradford had to play at NTL. In his mild-mannered way, he could get some of the most egocentric and self-aggrandizing people in the psychology and social work fields to return, year after year, to collaborate wholeheartedly. Thanks, perhaps, to his low-key gift for bringing out the best in people, NTL was never caught up in any cultlike episodes of charismatic leadership. Anyone who knew Bradford could see that leadership was supposed to emerge from within.

Throughout the 1950s a growing number of faculty members and graduate students—in social psychology, psychiatry, education, or social work programs from around the United States—came year after year to Bethel, giving T-Group "laboratory sessions" at the

Gould Academy.[19] The emphasis on "laboratories," with its re-search connotations, was deliberate. NTL was not governed by "partners," as in a typical consulting firm, but by "fellows"—about fifty of the leaders in the new academic field of "human relations." T-Groups were not going to be "management training" workshops; they would train "change agents": expert community leaders who would promote egalitarian, democratic, participatory organizations in communities across the country.

Making a significant alteration in an attitude or belief, Lewin had said, required three stages: an "unfreezing" process, to get rid of the old, outmoded beliefs; a "learning" process, to become famil-iar with the new idea; and a "refreezing" process, so that the new attitudes would stick and take root. The NTL people didn't quite understand how to refreeze, but T-Groups were clearly the most effective *un*freezing device anyone had ever seen. Anyone who had been through a T-Group could easily imagine city and country gov-ernments "unfreezing" out of their repressive, overly bureaucratic forms into collaborative "perfect communities."[20] Trainers began to show up at places like the United Nations, buttonholing dele-gates: "Don't you see? If we could just get the military leaders to sit down and do T-Groups, then there would be no war!" (Anna Freud had said the same thing about psychoanalysis, and years later the followers of W. Edwards Deming would say the same about Total Quality projects.) In their enthusiasm, who could blame them for losing sight, every now and then, of the fact that no one can force others to unfreeze their cherished beliefs?

T-Group sessions at Bethel typically began on Sunday night. Arriv-ing late that afternoon, participants would rush to the meeting room and would be seated at a big round oak table with ten or so other strangers, all with faces composed in a polite mask of atten-tiveness. The politeness wouldn't last long.

There would always be two trainers, typically psychology or so-ciology Ph.D.s or Ph.D. candidates. The trainers were sharp, ear-nest men who had developed the art of being *very good listeners*. They had a great deal of latitude in the design of their group; thus, only the opening moment was predictable. "We'll be together for many hours," a trainer would say to the people in the room. "We will learn by examining whatever happens as we meet together. And I won't be your leader." Then he would stop. Dead. Silent. And look impassively at the group.

"Could you repeat that, please?" someone might finally ask. The leader would offer the same few words. And again, silence.

"Well, what are we supposed to work on, then?" someone else might demand. "How are we supposed to get started?"

"You tell *us*," the second trainer might say. "These decisions will be made by the group."

Yet another silence. Then someone from the corner of the room might snap or growl. "This is a waste of time. Let's get started, so we can accomplish something. I propose we talk about the problems of communicating in a large bureaucracy, and we can vote to pick a group leader. Who wants to vote?"

More silence. The faces would still be polite, but tense and a bit agonized. Some hadn't been part of an unstructured group since they were children. Finally, they'd begin introducing themselves. They might make it all around the table, each person telling his or her title and organization's name, and then a trainer would break in: "Why are people introducing themselves in terms of their organizations? Don't you think it's safe enough to talk personally?"

A couple of people might make excuses, or muse about their own shyness, and then one of the group members might snap at the trainers: "You have given us no help. You've just let us drift. Either tell us what to do or stop criticizing us."

Now the atmosphere in the room would develop an enervated, stifling quality, as if the air were laden with ozone before a storm. Another member would jump in to defend the trainers: "That wasn't criticism; it was helpful." Others would chime in to describe the conversation the way *they* saw it, and the storm would break: the group would be off and running. For the next two weeks, as they continued talking, they would pause, every minute or two, to consider their own progress. "Why isn't John speaking?" someone might ask. Or "It seems to me that Sally answered a different question than the one Mike posed. Do others agree?" Or "We're now in three factions. How did *that* develop?"[21] It was wonderful and terrifying to see remarks and gestures held forth for study, as if frozen in the air, a few moments (or a few days) after they were made. The group members would pore over their memories of each other's remarks, interpreting and responding, and possibly critiquing tapes of their own sessions. (NTL had a cabinet full of audiovisual apparatus, rare and expensive in those pre-consumer-electronic years.)

Morning sessions would go on for three weeks, punctuated by other types of workshops in the afternoon. In "skill sessions," participants would learn techniques for leading their own groups. In "fishbowl" workshops, one group would watch another talk and then critique its openness and behavior. Participants might take part in a massive role-play session called "Regional City," lasting one or two days, in which all eighty or ninety people at Bethel would be given parts in mock unions, school boards, PTAs, chambers of commerce, and police departments. Through all of these exercises, they would see the value of experiential learning—how conducting their own experiments, and seeing the results, produced a much clearer understanding of human and organizational behavior than, say, listening to a lecture by an expert.

But there were lectures too: short ones, dubbed "lecturettes" by the trainers, about the dynamics of group behavior.[22] The T-Group participants would hear how their struggles over authority mirrored similar dynamics in workplaces and personal relationships everywhere. Meanwhile, in the groups, participants would begin asking each other to serve as their mirrors, offering what NTL trainers called "personal feedback"—reflections on how they came across, moment by moment. T-Group participants became extraordinarily sophisticated at seeing and hearing each other. They could now see how falsehood and doubt hung in the air sometimes—invisible problems, created by no one and everyone, forceful enough to block people from fulfilling their goals and dreams. They could tell each other why they came across as having a poor attitude or a self-pitying demeanor—and how to change it.[23]

There were also remarkably effective methods, available only at

NTL because they had been invented there, for redesigning meetings. These included one of the mainstays of meeting management: the use of flip-chart paper for notes. One story placed the genesis back at the Connecticut workshop; Kurt Lewin needed some paper for his egg-shaped "forcefield" diagrams, and someone (perhaps Ron Lippitt), looking in vain for a stationery store, passed a print-shop and bought some newsprint from the ends of the press rolls. With them taped to the wall, the room itself suddenly became a living memory for the group.[24] By the second week of a typical T-Group session, the rooms were a labyrinth of paper-covered walls, almost impenetrably dense with scribbled arrows, diagrams, and sentences.

Finally, toward the end of the two weeks (or three, or one), something wonderful and unfathomable would happen. It was rarely written down in the voluminous scholarly literature that NTLers created about T-Groups, but it kept drawing people back, session after session, and it prodded some participants to drop out of their management jobs to become educators and psychologists. After two or three weeks of soul-baring in a group of soul-barers, each person in the room would reach a moment when he or she discovered some core of redemption, some inner worth, deep within. The same feeling surged in those moments that, perhaps, surged when crowds gathered around Pelagius in Rome, and that surges whenever people gather to understand the deepest ties they hold in common.

Some of the NTL participants described the experience as "unconditional love"; others, as "pure joy"; others, as a kind of mystical breakthrough or peak experience. They returned, at least for a moment, to what Abraham Maslow described as the "childlike-easy-careless state of mind; to be simple, natural, spontaneous, fearless, anxiety-free . . ."[25] After you experienced that peak, you knew that the unconscious was not a Freudian cesspool spewing forth bitter legacies of childhood traumas. It was a source of Pelagian grace and hidden value, terrifying in its power and yet delightful in its beauty. It could only come forward when people learned, in a trusting, empathic environment like a T-Group, how to break free of their old ways of talking and thinking.

A few NTL participants never felt the Pelagian grace rise within them. They sat in their T-Groups, puzzled and mildly disappointed, while everyone around them was swept up in a contact conversational high.

NTL's researchers had inadvertently created an art form. Now they proceeded to dissect it. Like a newborn animal, each young laboratory group developed in distinct, but predictable ways, ripe for study and analysis. If you were a young social psychologist, Bethel was the most coveted place in America to spend your summer; and you could get in only through the recommendation of an NTL fellow. "It would be a lot easier to get into the Burning Tree Country Club," one former research associate reminisced years later. And that was only the beginning of years of exciting, but grueling apprenticeship. You would run T-Groups in collaboration with some of the best "process" facilitators in the world, gaining in skill year after year. Eventually, you might become a fellow yourself—*if* you were valued enough to be approved by the existing fellows, in a ballot so secret that nominees never knew they were being considered. Once you passed that hurdle, your income was probably assured, for NTL did not take most of the consultation work that came its way. Instead, it referred business to fellows, who also referred business to each other.

NTL trainers and academicians lived for the days *between* T-Groups, when the "customers" were gone and the really humming, inventive work took place. In the evening, associates and fellows alike would present their theories in the Gould Academy gym, while the whole NTL community sat up on the running track, passing judgment. Kurt Lewin had theorized, back during the Connecticut workshop, that the observations of an ordinary Mrs. Brown might be as significant as those of a trained social scientist. But Mrs. Brown could never have held her own in *this* crowd. "By God, you had to present good theory," one former associate recalled, "because it was thumbs up or thumbs down. Before my first big presentation one of the fellows took me aside and said, 'You see all of us acting spontaneous and unrehearsed. But we have gone over our presentations again and again before the mirror. So if I were you I'd get busy.' "

Toward the middle of the 1950s, as T-Groups became more popular, the balance swung back from research to helping individuals grow—or, as the trainers began to call it, "therapy for normals." This approach naturally lent itself to organizational consulting, and trainers began collaborating on a wide range of exercises, games, and workshop formats. They shared their ideas so freely, and in such a spirit of mutual invention, that nobody could ever quite remember who had created what. A few bits of credit are extant; Ron Lippitt, for instance, developed the idea of a "preferred vision" during his consultations with YMCA teams in Michigan. In a T-Group-like forum, he would ask them to brainstorm a list of the problems they faced. As the list grew longer, the vigor in the room deflated. People blamed each other or grew despondent. So Lippitt started asking teams to imagine a picture of the future they preferred. "Let's say it's twenty years from now, and you're flying over this region in a helicopter. What do you see down there?" The more detailed and sincere people were in envisioning a desired future, the more energized and excited they felt. Suddenly, they began coming up with mutual solutions to problems which had seemed insoluble before. All of the corporate "vision" and "mission-setting" consulting of the 1980s would later descend from this practice. Throughout NTL's history, attendees of its T-Groups had been teachers, academics, social workers, and church group members. A few executives had trickled in as Episcopal lay priests, but only now did a corporate audience emerge en masse. The reason was simple, and typical of corporate interventions; in short supply of funds, NTL went trolling.

In 1956, Lee Bradford invited a *Business Week* reporter to visit Bethel—over the objections of some staff members. Several large grants, which had sustained the labs for years, had run out. And NTL had bought a thirteen-room Victorian mansion in Bethel. Located at the end of a quiet cul-de-sac, surrounded by elegantly arranged trees and plants, the cream-colored headquarters added dramatically to the "labs'" cachet. But furnishing and maintaining it cost thousands of dollars each year—a significant part of the NTL overhead.

The *Business Week* article fulfilled most of Bradford's hopes: it was cheerful, it treated NTL as a research institution instead of a cult (the word that a journal for educational librarians had applied to NTL), and it mentioned that the labs were looking for industrial grants to conduct research on group dynamics.[26] Grants were not forthcoming, but business attendance began to increase dramatically in 1956, particularly as some of the trainers began tailoring "management work conferences" especially for them, where they would not have to mix with the other types of attendees—and where they could be charged higher rates. Since businesspeople couldn't generally spare three weeks, Bradford and some of the other senior fellows decided to cut the laboratories from three weeks to two. That decision was a baby step on the road away from innocence. Three weeks had once been called essential, so participants could experience all phases of group development. Now, it turned out, two weeks would have been optimal all along.[27]

Businessmen thronged to the two-week workshops—more than 20,000, at a fee of $800 each, by 1966.[28] They were interested in anything that would give them an edge in communicating and negotiating, and some signed up just because T-Groups were the latest, hottest management fad. (They were, in fact, the first major "human relations"-oriented management fad since the war, and the first to satisfy that invisible, yearning ache for the vernacular.) Rather than drag people up to Bethel, NTL's "industrial" session organizers generally held them at Arden House, an opulent castle in the Hudson Valley town of Harriman.

Upon arrival, business attendees often regarded the T-Group as an amusing, impractical diversion—a sort of summer camp with communication skills, paid for at company expense. The trainers didn't understand business, and their knowledge of organizations was limited to the bitter rivalries and occasional collegiality of uni-

versities. But as the T-Groups went on, managers came to exult in
the sheer freedom of speaking plainly and directly. Most of them
worked normally in an atmosphere of power politics that determined their every move, that they could not discuss openly. Some
managers talked freely at T-Groups for the first time since childhood, and that feeling alone—a feeling that humanities-oriented
people usually took for granted—was a revelation to them. Just as
business finance translated karma and hubris into numbers, the
T-Group translated the "just business, nothing personal" imperatives of the numbers back into the personal sphere. Moreover, to
some of the business attendees, the practices of NTL revealed an
entirely new way to think about the task of managing people.

The man who gave voice to that shift in attitude was Douglas
McGregor, who was the head of the Organizational Studies department at MIT's Sloan School (in the late 1940s he had brought
Lewin to MIT's faculty).[29] McGregor was a playful and charismatic
man, who had spent the early 1950s as the president of Antioch
University, a well-known experimental liberal arts college in Western Ohio, before returning to MIT. His original field had been industrial relations, and like many MIT business professors, he
moonlighted as an industrial consultant—in his case, often with oil
companies. At his suggestion, in the early 1950s some executives
had wandered into T-Groups from Standard Oil of New Jersey,
where McGregor held a position on the board for a while, and
where a subculture of second-layer managers had rebelled during
the 1930s against the legacy of unscrupulous harshness left by the
company's founder, John D. Rockefeller. McGregor was enthusiastic about T-Groups, but he didn't lead them frequently; he was
known at Bethel for pulling anyone he could find, eminences and
newcomers alike, over to the piano to sing gospel songs. And then
in the late 1950s he began to be known for his theories of human
behavior. In part through his experiences at NTL, he had discovered a relationship between the structure of organizations and their
managers' deepest attitudes.

Essentially, McGregor said (first in speeches during the late
1950s, and then in his 1960 book, *The Human Side of Manage-*

ment), there were two possible attitudes that a manager could hold about people. Whether or not they admitted or realized it, these attitudes affected managers' decisions in a thousand unseen ways, and colored the atmosphere of every conventional corporation. The first, and by far the more prevalent, was "Theory X." It was an Augustinian theory, professing that human nature is fundamentally corrupt—or that people are "gullible, not very bright, the dupe of the charlatan and the demagogue." Theory X said that people basically hate to work. They are motivated by fear and desire, and a manager's task is to force them to work, as if they were recalcitrant machines.

Unfortunately, McGregor said, Theory X was false. "The findings which are beginning to emerge from the social sciences challenge this whole set of beliefs about man and human nature." Yes, people might behave passively and selfishly on the job, but not because of their inner nature. Lack of productivity was an *effect*, not a cause, of the way that conventional management treated people.

So McGregor would ask his audiences to consider "Theory Y"— another way of looking at people, closer to the truth (as he saw it), but harder for most people to accept. Work, in its noblest sense, is built into human nature. People can't be goaded, cajoled, threatened, or even bribed with money into giving their hearts and souls to an enterprise. But if placed in a situation that honestly calls for a commitment, people will rise to the occasion. Or as McGregor put it: "The motivation, the potential for development, the capacity for assuming responsibility . . . are all present in people. Management does not put them there." Pelagius couldn't have said it any more strongly.

It was quite an article of faith, this Theory Y. Everything about the structure of corporations went against it: the perks and power structure of the hierarchy, the labor relations tradition, the curricula at most business schools (including MIT), and all those devices, like performance appraisals, that measured one person against another. Adopting Theory Y would mean giving up both the stick (threatening to fire people) and the carrot (bribing them or being paternalistic). Without those two weapons, what leverage did a manager have? Only the ability to spark other people's involvement and commitment, by giving them opportunities to do good work—hardly a strong incentive by conventional standards.

Yet McGregor had noticed, in a decade of corporate consultation, that *the most effective managers always seemed to hold Theory Y in their hearts.* Many of them had seen firsthand—and this was the factor that made some managers in the audience take McGregor seriously—the obvious bankruptcy of both the carrot and the stick. They could discipline workers and make them show up, but the old methods never managed to get people to act with care and commitment.

Unfortunately, if only one manager in a company believed in Theory Y, that manager would be impotent. No change could be put into practice until the large-scale systems of the company changed. Thus McGregor devoted more and more of his time to teaching a wide range of people about his concepts. He chose the names Theory X and Theory Y to avoid obvious bias, so managers could talk about their past attitudes without hearing them labeled as, say, "Theory Troglodyte." And he became more and more enthusiastic about T-Groups. Skeptical managers could simply be sent to a T-Group, where they'd feel their own intrinsic potential welling up inside them—and they could see firsthand how other people acted more powerful, free, and involved. They'd begin to think about harnessing a similar level of enthusiasm on the job, and suddenly Theory Y would feel right to them.

McGregor's father had been a midwestern reverend; he came out of the great American Protestant liberal tradition, the tradition of Quaker meetings, community barn raisings, and Ralph Waldo Emerson. Perhaps it was no coincidence that so many other NTLers—including Lee Bradford, Ken Benne, Ron Lippitt, and the eminent T-Group advocate Carl Rogers—had similar backgrounds.[30] Somehow, these ecumenical WASPs knew how to bring forth mutual understanding—which explained, perhaps, why the black and Jewish community leaders of the original Connecticut workshop had called in three of these white-bread characters. It also may have explained why NTLers seemed to feel responsible for developing a better world—perhaps from noblesse oblige, perhaps from a deeply inbred sense of populist egalitarianism, or perhaps simply because they didn't feel alive unless they were improving the world.

Whatever the source of that feeling, its force gave the NTLers a sense of confidence that bordered on hubris at times; they knew they had a set of answers to the paralysis that people felt when tough questions like racism came up. What they didn't know yet was *why* their technique was effective. Did it speak to a general condition within the human heart or was it merely well suited to tweak the spirit of a mid-twentieth-century American?

Or was it, as critics began to charge in the mid-1950s, a pernicious form of social control and brainwashing? That suspicion had been voiced every now and then by anti-Communists in the McCarthy era. T-Groups, like Communist cells, were small groups of people; they seemed deliberately designed to "unfreeze"—to break down the individual's will and resistance.[31]

Inside NTL, these accusations were taken seriously—but not in the way they were intended. NTLers believed that *all* controlled environments (including families, churches, and corporations) created the conditions for brainwashing.[32] People were *always* being manipulated; whether or not anyone *felt* manipulated depended on how angry they were about the content of the message. T-Groups provided an antidote by giving people a safe way to inquire: Did others feel the same pressures that they did? What did those pressures mean?

As it happened, there was an expert on brainwashing within the NTL community. A young psychologist named Edgar Schein, who came to McGregor's department at MIT in the late 1950s, had gone to Inchon at the end of the Korean War to help repatriate American prisoners of war. Many of these POWs had been in captivity for more than a year, and the U.S. Army leaders believed that the Chinese Communists in North Korea had brainwashed them. (The word "brainwashing," in fact, emerged from this episode, as a translation of a Chinese phrase meaning "to cleanse the mind"—in this case, of bourgeois concepts.) To an American audience in the

McCarthy era, there had to be some awfully powerful indoctrination at work to induce well-trained American soldiers to renounce their patriotism, inform on other soldiers, march in Communist parades, and make false confessions of germ warfare.

Stranded in Inchon for several weeks, Schein had interviewed some of the returning soldiers. They were relieved to talk about their time in captivity. The Chinese social control had taken place without drugs, hypnosis, Pavlovian conditioning, or even torture; all that was used was peer pressure. Just as in a T-Group, the Communists had put the POWs in a cultural island, cut off from all contact with outsiders, and surrounded them with friendly Chinese "big brothers" (who had been promised a reward for reforming their Western cellmates). There was always the threat of brutality and even death; the prisoners were continually reminded that collaborating with each other was the only way to survive. The "big brothers" harangued, insulted, reviled, humiliated, and pleaded the case of Communist values for days or months on end—an incredibly powerful "unfreezing" effort. Less than 10 percent of the soldiers held out, resisting to the end. Another 10 percent embraced the Communist line so fervently that it stuck with them. The vast majority fell in the middle. Their attitudes changed in Korea (after all, some of the Communist ideas resonated with their own populist feelings), but they changed back again without much stress once they returned to America. It's not hard to persuade someone, Schein ultimately concluded, "if you can physically constrain them to remain in a setting over which you have milieu control."[33]

That was the difference from the NTL experience; people came to Bethel freely and left of their own volition. But Schein *did* see an analogue to the Korean POW camps in America. He had visited some of the most influential management training centers in the country, such as GE's Crotonville and IBM's Sands Point. Isolated students in small groups analyzed "case studies," gave their guess about the correct answer, and were graded on how closely their answer matched the instructor's party line.[34] Most importantly, they couldn't leave without risking their jobs—which meant that if they entered the business world, T-Group leaders could have a kind of power they had never before enjoyed.

Or so it was thought. Then, in 1958, the techniques of NTL received their first full-scale test in a mainstream corporation.

New Jersey's factories and refineries tend to stand far from the roadways and truck routes, visible only distantly, like metallic castles half cloaked in the thick marshland mists. Perhaps the largest of these sites is the Bayway refinery. Its 700 labyrinthine acres of furnaces, tanker docks, and chemical processing plants, located on a small peninsula jutting out into the harbor from Elizabeth, comprised the largest provider of petroleum, natural gas, and related chemicals to the entire East Coast. In 1958 (when Exxon's East Coast operations were still called Esso[35]) a major labor contract was up for negotiation at Bayway. The independent union of refinery workers had demanded concessions worth three million dollars per year—enough, the managers felt, to put the refinery permanently into the red. Worse still, the union was flirting with joining a national affiliate—and not just any affiliate, but the national teamsters union, whose president was Jimmy Hoffa. To Esso's managers—and the executives of their parent company, Standard Oil of New Jersey—this would put a critical production facility, one that controlled much of the energy supply of the East Coast, under the control of organized crime. The memory of Bayway's unruly, militant strikes in the 1930s[36] still lingered in the viscera of both the managers and the union men. Each side routinely referred to the other's leader as "that son of a bitch." Anywhere the managers looked, they saw an unbridgeable impasse.

Except when they looked at NTL. As it happened, a few Bayway managers had been to T-Groups, thanks to Esso's long-standing involvement with Douglas McGregor. And in 1958 the Bayway general manager invited—or, rather, urged—two NTLers to join him at Bayway. They agreed, on the condition that they could keep all their conversations discreet; they didn't want anyone to open up to them and find themselves disciplined or fired as a result. The first NTLer was Herb Shepherd, an MIT professor of industrial economics, a McGregor protégé, and an elegant, theatrical man who loved to quote poetry. Shepherd had an insouciant grace that reminded people of Fred Astaire, and such an innate flair for T-Group dynamics that he could make them perform tricks. On the third day of a Shepherd-led T-Group, you could count on the members spontaneously throwing the leaders out so they could organize themselves, unaware that the previous half dozen Shepherd-led groups had done the same thing.

The other NTLer who came to Bayway, Robert Blake, was a professor of social psychology at the University of Texas at Austin. He and Shepherd were good friends, but they couldn't have been more different. Blake was dour, moody, cheerfully acerbic, and seemingly indifferent to people's opinions of him. The inner circle at Bethel considered him competent, but uninspired, pedantic, and guilty of the worst possible sin: he didn't know how to *listen* well. In the NTL pantheon, he seemed cast as a sort of peevish, saturnine figure, a Caliban to Shepherd's Ariel. "I'll hit 'em high," Shepherd once said to him. "You hit 'em low." Yet Blake's blunt manner belied a far-reaching intellectual background; he had studied or worked with some of the most eminent luminaries in social psychology and semantics research. He had spent a year and a half in London at the Tavistock Clinic, a British counterpart to NTL which was seen as more rigorous, more strictly organized, and more— well, more *serious*. At Tavistock, a group might last not three weeks, but a year and a half. The group's research would be rigorously channeled toward in-depth studies of its own power and authority patterns. Tavistock leaders didn't care, as NTL leaders did, about building "peak experiences" and helping people express themselves—or, as Blake put it scornfully, assuaging their feelings of "morale and cohesion."

NTL seemed to bring out Blake's bitter side. But at the Bayway refinery, he was a thoughtful adviser who could listen just fine and who managed to build confidence on both the labor and management sides. He ended up devoting two years of his life to the project, taking an unpaid leave of absence from his faculty position to do so. Shepherd came in as a consultant, and Blake also brought in a third person: his chief collaborator, Jane Srygley Mouton.

Mouton had been a mathematician and then one of Blake's graduate students at UT. Now she was a professor there and one of a handful of women in the 1950s to lead T-Groups. A fiercely intellectual woman, known for her composure, her devotion to work, and her outdoorsiness, she had married an investor named Jack Mouton. She and her husband lived on a ranch they owned outside Austin, where Mouton was an avid horsewoman. When she was working, she spent much of her time inventing and researching with Blake.[37] In their outpost far from the Bethel/Cambridge/Ann Arbor NTL axis, they had developed their own variation on the T-Group, and it would have enormous implications for the evolution of organizational change.

In ordinary T-Groups, Blake and Mouton realized, no matter how nondirective the facilitator tried to be, he or she was still subtly dictatorial, even more dictatorial (because of its subtlety) than the harshest CEO, because all of that control was hidden—as in Shepherd's manipulation of his T-Group's third day. But what if the T-Group were autonomous, without an assigned expert trainer? What if there were no change agents, but only participants ready to change themselves?

Blake and Mouton were well steeped in the techniques of devising "instruments" (as social scientists called them)—questionnaires which people could grade for themselves, which sparked conversation that led them to learn. (To get the flavor of these questionnaires, if you've never seen one, imagine the sorts of "self-assessment" tests which appear in magazines like *Cosmopolitan*. Now imagine one that was truly challenging, that measured your competence in a range of tough areas like business knowledge and ability to manage people. Imagine that you never had to show anyone else the results, but were told to use the group to talk through any of the issues that the questionnaire raised.) One year in the mid-1950s, when two hundred University of Texas undergraduates wanted to enroll in a course on T-Groups, Blake and Mouton tried breaking the course into sections and having each section more or less run itself. Remarkably enough, it worked. Students gleaned the same understandings of group power and authority, and even the same peak experiences, as if Blake and Mouton had led the groups themselves. So they tried it next with a group of Esso managers (on an off-site location in a Baptist church in Bella Vista, Arkansas). Instead of a leader, participants who walked into the room found a set of questions, beginning with "What is the ideal working relationship?" It turned out they all, unbeknownst to themselves, had a similar ideal. "Why then," asked the next question, "is it so hard to reach that ideal?"

While the managers deliberated, Bob and Jane sat in the next room worrying. What if the group exploded into a fight? Or, worse, what if they drifted into boredom? Every now and then, they sent in an undergrad on a pretext such as looking for a piece of paper. Then they grilled the student relentlessly: Was everything really okay in there? "No problem," the student would say. "They're doing great." In truth, hard as it was for an expert consultant to accept, the groups seemed more charged up, and yet more benign, when people could lead themselves.

When Blake, Mouton, and Shepherd began to work at the Bayway refinery in 1958, they planned on using similar "instrumented" groups. But the Esso leaders wanted in-depth counseling—most of which fell to Blake, because he had moved to New Jersey to work at Bayway full-time. Every night, he recorded his observations and field notes onto a tape, which he sent to Jane Mouton, who was pregnant that year, back in Austin. She would listen to the tapes, and the two of them would talk at length, once a week, about exactly what was going on at Bayway. Today, this would all seem commonplace, but in 1958 no corporation had ever invited a group dynamics expert so completely into its offices. The three NTLers recognized, almost from the beginning, that they were inventing a kind of therapeutic counseling that would not be aimed at helping *individuals* improve (or, if they did improve, it would only be a by-product). They were there to further the organization's development as a whole. Almost from the beginning, they referred to their work with a term that would soon become jargon: "organization development."

Blake had to be flown in by helicopter for some of his early meetings; the plant was on strike, and since he would have to talk in depth with the union, the managers didn't want him to be seen crossing the picket line. As one reads his journal (which was published in the mid-1970s), the impression comes through, again and again, of how squeezed everyone felt, on both the union and management sides.[38] More than once a manager made a promise to the unions in a meeting—for instance, a promise to name Bayway as a "union shop," in which workers were required to join the union—only to have it undone, or denied, in the most humiliating way possible, through a pronouncement from Houston.[39]

In his earliest sessions with managers, held off-site in hotels, Blake often posed the question "How can the union become an effective unit of the company?"

"They can't," was the first answer. The union leadership was composed of thugs, thieves, and crooks. "How could you cooperate with such a rat pack?" The only solution (other than "killing off the leaders," which some of the managers joked they wanted to do) was to secretly (and illegally) try to influence union politics to reveal the current elected officials "in the true phosphorescent light of their putridity, so that when the wage people come to ballot again, they'll do a better job."[40]

Gradually, as often happens in group dynamics, the managers' own attitudes came to light. They said they were open and fair, but they bullied and humiliated the union people constantly. They called meetings in midday, so "these bums will have to change in and out of their work clothes." They held last-minute meetings late, so the union reps would miss their car pools. They insisted on meeting in the administration building, where the union people felt uncomfortable. And they never said in advance what they wanted a meeting to achieve; instead, they sat, as stony-faced as poker players, giving in on each concession only at the last possible minute. Finally, after getting the venom out of their system, the managers realized, "We can only move forward by learning how to stop saying 'no.' That doesn't mean we say 'yes.' But when the union raises a point, we need to learn how to talk about it."

Meeting more informally with the union leaders, Blake asked about one of their biggest gripes: accidents and safety hazards. Here too there was a knee-jerk answer: It's management's fault. "Those penny-pinching bastards take away the safety inspectors, cut corners, and make us work faster. Pretty soon, they get accidents." Blake patiently heard them out—arguably the first time anyone from the management side had done so—and let them reach their own conclusions about what to do next. "I see somebody out on the platform," a union leader might say, "and he's walking through grease. I say to myself, 'He's gonna fall and bust a hip.' Sure enough, he falls, and I say to myself, 'I knew that would happen.' " In other words, they could only get the accidents under control if the hourly workers started speaking up ahead of time, instead of waiting for managers to handle it.

Over the next few months, the safety problems were cleaned up. The labor problems, albeit in fits and starts, began to diminish. The managers treated the union with respect; the union remained independent from the teamsters and organized crime. The next year, Bayway managers had to close down part of the refinery. Instead of clamming up and insisting on layoffs, they walked the union leaders through the rationale for the shutdown. "Now that you know why we're doing this," they asked, "what do you think of it?"

Flush with success, the Bayway executives sent 2,000 of their managers, from refinery foremen to market researchers, through instrumented groups—five teams of ten people each per session. During the summer of 1959, Esso took over part of the Thayer Hotel at West Point to handle the crowds. And to focus their attention, Blake and Mouton devised a framework which they called "The Managerial Grid."[41]

It looked like a nine-square-by-nine-square checkerboard, but actually it was a map of management attitudes with which people could identify their own behavior, or attitudes around them. Those who cared about production and efficiency fell further to the right (toward number 9). Those who cared greatly for people moved

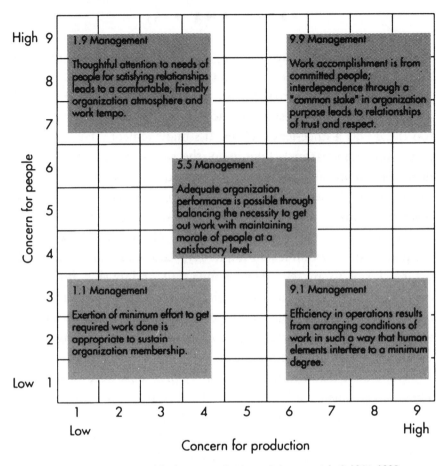

closer to the top (again, toward number 9). You could fit any managerial style onto this chart by putting the two numbers together. McGregor's Theory X covered the area around 9,1 ("Putting out strenuous effort," Blake would say, "and encouraging others to do the same"). Paternalistic "people-pleasers," who in Blake's view were just as destructive, ranged around 1,9. Most damaging of all (Blake and Mouton argued) were the people who spread themselves out around the chart, bouncing inconsistently between paternalistic benevolence and threatening autocracy. It was remarkable how many backstabbing, paternalistic, duplicitous types of behavior there were in organizations, behaviors that could be named, now, in a relatively safe way. "Martin's being awfully 5,5," you could say, instead of saying, "Martin cares only about covering his ass."

The Grid concept was very successful: managers loved it, and performance in the refinery noticeably improved. Yet the Bayway experiment ultimately ended ignominiously. The plant manager who had approved all the "organization development" training was recognized by being placed in charge of the Eastern Hemisphere at Esso operations. His successor was a more rational manager, who tried immediately to show how he could squeeze the union. Within twelve weeks, as one NTL observer later remembered it, the plant's union had signed on with the teamsters.[42] The NTL people would see this sort of thing happen again and again through the 1960s; it took months and years to develop positive change, and only a few weeks to kill it.

After Bayway, Bob Blake and Jane Mouton continued to develop the Grid system. They redesigned into a yearlong management development system, covering all the NTL group process skills—giving productive feedback, sharing a vision for the future, bringing hidden assumptions to the surface.[43] There were now six modules, blending NTL-style communication skills with a fine-grained business skills, over the course of a year or two. For business skills, Blake and Mouton used Alfred Sloan's just-then-published memoir, *My Years with General Motors,* as a mirror. Managers would compare their solutions to Sloan's, and discuss the differences in groups. The purpose was to create a company full of managers with Sloan's dual commitments—to people and business results simultaneously. And they would have succeeded, except that in many organizations, after the first couple of phases, the enthusiasm for the Grid dropped off somehow. Rare was the company that made it all the way to the Alfred Sloan material, partly because Blake and Mouton could never find enough program leaders who knew both the business and NTL material.

The more interested they became in implementing change throughout large companies, the more compelled they felt to leave the university. To academics, implementing change precluded "real" research. Blake and Mouton were too *busy,* enmeshed in the messy day-to-day life of thousands of people. They were too responsible for the careers of their well-meaning corporate patrons. This left them no time or attention for conducting the sorts of narrow, well-defined, self-contained management studies—"Measurement of a cognitive shift in how people perceive systems in a training process"—that would lead to a respectable journal article. The academics were great at diagnosis, but lousy at treatment. Blake and Mouton wanted to treat.

Before long, Blake and Mouton split with NTL as well. The NTLers could never reconcile themselves to Blake and Mouton's "T-Group in a box." To them, Bob Blake had finally decided to cash in on the techniques he had learned at Bethel. To make matters worse, managers in companies around the country began calling NTL and asking for the Grid system. But the staff in Washington had to sorrowfully say no, Blake and Mouton had broken the unwritten sharing code. Unlike Ron Lippitt, who also created instruments on paper, they had copyrighted their materials. No NTL trainer, and none of the new "OD" consultants, could use the Grid except by becoming a Blake franchiser. He had violated no overt NTL rule, but the trainers and faculty members were furious. They complained about the danger of letting managers lead their own T-Groups. The Grid gave a false impression, they said, that anyone could lead a T-Group by following a few simple recipe steps. "This will be the end of Bethel," Lee Bradford told Blake. "Why would people come here if they can transfer training into the organization?"[44] Blake excused himself early in the summer of 1960, and never returned to NTL.

Blake, of course, had his own interpretation of what happened. He had copyrighted the material only to keep it from being degraded by trainers who wanted to "borrow" an exercise or two, with no regard for its careful whole-system design. Moreover, he now believed, NTLers wanted managers to remain dependent on them. Maybe they even wanted organizations to remain sick, for that way they could keep their roles as vitally necessary therapists, with entire groups of people who needed their talents to remain healthy.

Robert Blake's system dealt a blow to NTL's spirit of freewheeling experimentation from which it never recovered. Once he had shown that it was feasible, and far more lucrative, to offer programs on your own—and probably better for the clients—everyone else realized, sooner or later, that they were foolish unless they followed his example. Bit by bit, the vitality drained out of the labs as trainers took their innovations into other venues.

In 1968, NTL's community spirit was tested still further, when trainers named Pfeiffer and Jones published a workbook of exercises that had been introduced at the labs. If Blake was seen as a black sheep, then Pfeiffer and Jones were out-and-out traitors in many eyes; but other NTL trainers reasoned, logically enough, that if they couldn't beat the copyrighters, they might as well join them. Instead of being researchers, engaged in mutual inquiry, they were now primarily paid consultants, looking for an edge over each other. Suddenly, you didn't want to show your best techniques up in Bethel, any more than a comedian will use the very best jokes when other comedians are in the room, ready to write them down.

More and more, NTL-based trainers eschewed the long trek to Bethel altogether. They still returned occasionally to Bethel, ostensibly to recharge their facilitation skills, or rekindle conversations with old colleagues. Mainly, they came to feel, even for a few hours, some of the old T-Group spirit. No one who had been exposed to that spirit in a T-Group or even a Grid session could forget it.

Nevertheless, Robert Blake was correct. The Pelagian spirit is not enough in itself to re-create an organization. Some structure or plan had to be designed that would carry that spirit into the fabric of the enterprise and the habits of the people who worked there. Arguably, the Grid system ultimately lost track of that elusive spirit, in the very process of capturing, distilling, and disseminating it. But could any other structure do better? Could anyone carry Pelagianism into an Augustinian society?

REFORMISTS

"THE ANSWER LIES IN GIVING PEOPLE SOME FORM OF
MEANINGFUL INVOLVEMENT":
PROCTER & GAMBLE AND GAINES DOG FOOD, 1961–73

Why does Galileo Galilei have the reputation of a heretic, whereas his seventeenth-century colleague Johannes Kepler is remembered only as a scientist? Because Kepler ignored the church. Galileo sought to change it. The professor from Pisa spent the last third of his life arguing, with increasing fervor, that the Catholic church leaders should rewrite their doctrines and even their Bibles. Many of the cardinals and church officials who censured and imprisoned him recognized the validity of the new cosmology and physics that Galileo championed. Some didn't want to shake up their system too quickly. Too many monks and small-village priests clung to Ptolemy and Aristotle. The "people" would rebel at any sudden revision of the "truth."

Galileo didn't care. Like many heretics, past and present, he thought at first that changing the institution would be feasi-

ble. He only had to show people what he had seen and they would naturally adapt. When people doubted observations that, to him, were obvious, he lost his tact. He made enemies (some said needlessly) of the Jesuits, who fought bitterly to see him condemned; and he closed one of his notorious tracts, the Dialogue on the Great World Systems, *with a snide lampoon of the views of Pope Urban VIII. Until then, Urban had been his patron and champion. Ten months after publication, in 1633, Galileo was on trial in Rome.*

Even under house imprisonment, Galileo continued researching and writing, developing and articulating his theories of physics and the heavens. Perhaps he was comforted by the knowledge that people outside the church hierarchy had carried forward his research, and were building upon his theories. Or perhaps he spent much of his time in his cell in mourning for the institution of the church and the beacon that it might have been—if only he could have found a way to get the point across.

▼▼▼

Why, in fact, do the Galileos of the world get so *disappointed* when the institution doesn't come across? Why don't they expect resistance, and prepare for it? Perhaps because they're blinded by the brilliance of the truth they see.

Consider the plight of Eric Trist. In the mid-1940s he saw a better way of managing the workplace, a democratic approach that would clearly lead to unparalleled performance. He spent his life testing and preaching his vision, building a worldwide network of devoted associates (including Kurt Lewin and Douglas McGregor, along with many others) whose work laid the groundwork for the management innovations of the 1980s. The movement inspired some successes, including a series of secret but dramatic workplace design reforms at Procter & Gamble, and a passionate experiment at a dog-food plant in Topeka, Kansas. But it never got mainstream acceptance. Like Galileo and many other reformists throughout history, Trist was mournfully aware that the prevailing organizations did not live up to the great destiny he saw for them.

Trist was a small, almost frail man, with a shy smile, prone to bouts of depression and long periods of melancholy, and yet thoroughly gregarious. Although he made his living as an academic, and wrote in impenetrable academese, he talked like a British laborer— with working-class outrage, sly irony, and quiet profanity. His morose spirit stemmed in part from his background at the Tavistock Institute, the British home of group dynamics research. While National Training Labs took its cue from sunny Pelagianism, Tavistock was guided by the brooding Augustinian spirit of psychoanalysis.[1] Tavistock's practitioners were well aware of the dark side of human nature, the visceral "death instinct" of primordial envy and hatred that could crop up in even the most idealistic personality. They knew that group dynamics, in itself, could not deal effectively with the hidden rage, frustration, and viciousness that inevitably emerged when people began to work together. It would take a redesign of the channels of power. In the numbers-ridden industrial age, there was no persuasive model for how that redesign might look.

Until Eric Trist stumbled into one—almost literally. In 1947, a post-doctoral student at Tavistock casually invited him to visit a British coal mine at Haighmoor. Nearly all British coal mines had been industrialized into an assembly-line approach since the nineteenth century, but this mine was an exception; it was based in a rich seam that assembly-line-style equipment couldn't reach. Therefore, the miners had developed their own system. It was part-vernacular, part-industrial; a hybrid of mining traditions from generations past and new postwar technologies. Instead of being set up as interchangeable parts, cogs on the assembly line of the mine, these miners worked in teams they organized themselves. Each miner might handle a half-dozen jobs. The teams ran the job and sold the coal—even taking care of their members' families if someone were hurt or killed.[2] They also competed vigorously against each other—to the point where fights sometimes broke out between members of rival teams.[3]

The results, as Trist discovered, were remarkable. Haighmoor was far safer, and far more productive, than any other mine. In fact, since the rewards were based on tonnage-per-cycle, and the miners felt some influence over their work, they all continually added innovations to the work. They had no incentive, as long-wall miners did, to "screw the next shift" by cutting corners on maintenance or safety. To Trist, Haighmoor provided a glimpse of how the best of vernacular and business culture could be designed to fit together—anywhere.

The British government agency that managed the mine let Trist study it at first—until Trist, following Lewin's tradition of "learning through experimentation," wanted to see if some of the same techniques might help the beleaguered workers at other mines. Then the managers balked. Why try to instill freedom, when mines were becoming even more controlled and mechanized? Why set up false expectations? They even forbade Trist to include the name "Haighmoor" in his reports.

So Trist devoted himself to conducting workplace experiments and seeking ways to broaden the intellectual base of his insights. A key group of his colleagues were Norwegian, with roots in the resistance movement of World War II. Norway had beaten back the Nazis through small groups of eight to ten people, somewhat like the teams of Haighmoor. There was no central command. Each group chose its own immediate objectives and tactics, acting with greater persistence, commitment, and skill than they would ever have gained by taking orders. When the Nazis captured a team, the members could reveal no one's plans but their own. During the 1950s and 1960s, the resistance veterans spread through Norway, gradually becoming directors of its state-owned industries and government agencies, helping each other set up self-managing teams at wire companies, lumber mills, the electric utility Nørsk Hydro, and elsewhere.[4]

Trist and his closest colleagues—particularly the Australian researcher Fred Emery—adopted several terms for their work: "Industrial democracy," "open systems," and "sociotechnical systems." They believed that corporations were analogous to eco-systems, subject to the same sorts of interrelationships that governed prosperity and survival in the wild. As business environments became more turbulent, top-down hierarchies would cease to be effective, just as they were ineffective amid the disorder of nature. (Emery and Trist had hit on this theory during a turbulent plane trip to Norway, when Trist was forced repeatedly to use the air-sickness bag, and realized that his feeling was an analogue for the way managers often felt.[5]) Living systems coped with turbulence by *generating their own order* from the bottom up. A living creature can take its shape even from a damaged fetus or ovum (this had been proved with sea urchins), without any external control. In fact, attempts to control a living creature's growth too harshly would make it wither and die. Why shouldn't the same be true for organizations?[6]

Nearly all factories of that time were, like the British coal mines, set up as elaborate machines. Work was broken up into as many disparate tasks as possible. Workers were programmed, through stringent rules and elaborate pay scales, to specialize in those tasks. Expert engineers designed the jobs, controlled the work, and inspected the products. Workers who followed the rules got pensions. Workers who slackened or faltered got disciplined or fired, unless their unions, explicitly or implicitly, arranged to protect them.[7]

The overall approach, often dubbed "scientific management," owed its compelling power to the systematic practices devised by Frederick Taylor, the first industrial-era management consultant. In the early 1880s, Taylor began clocking the movements of workers—from burly immigrant steelworkers to young girls inspecting ball bearings—hoping to establish, once and for all, the most efficient methods of working. The productivity gains in the short run were enormous. One ball bearing factory, following Taylor's advice, cut the number of inspectors from 120 to 35, nearly doubled wages, dropped two hours from the workday, tripled production, and improved accuracy by two-thirds.[8] But Taylor's methods also ossified industrial work in the long run. Living inside a machine ultimately leads to deep, inbred malaise and resentment, a thorough atrophying of creativity, and the propensity to sabotage.

What if, like Eric Trist and his colleagues, you saw the dangers of the machine approach and wanted to try an alternative? Then you would have to establish your factory as a community. Every part of the assembly line would be managed by self-governing teams of, say, seven to twelve people. The teams would have a task at hand—a product to get out—and they would care about the results of their labors, because they would see how they belonged to the system as a whole. If they found a way to improve the work, they would have the power *and* the interest to bring that improvement to life, without going through a lot of bureaucratic approval; and they would be rewarded in ways which touched their wallets *and* their pride. Despite the seeming lack of control, the community as a whole would run itself much more smoothly than any machine—through the interplay of dozens of teams of people, all acting in synch, with everything from the machine setup to the maintenance schedule designed to reinforce their collegiality.

Only one American company in the early 1960s took these ideas seriously. That company was Procter & Gamble, the Cincinnati-based manufacturers of soap, detergent, toilet paper, and other household products. For them, "open systems" was a kind of magic formula, as precious as a patented cleansing formula, and they wanted to get the most they could from it.[9]

In 1962, Procter & Gamble had just celebrated its 125th birthday. There was much to celebrate. It was the predominant company in American marketing; P&G managers had originated not just the packaged soap and the laundry detergent but the structure of the advertising business (including its mainstay, brand management), the soap opera, the profit-sharing plan, and (just the previous year) the disposable diaper. P&G (or "Procter," as its managers routinely called it) had also consistently doubled its annual sales every ten years since it had started—an operational mission the company had held since its beginnings.

At the same time, some of P&G's manufacturing people were beginning to discover firsthand the problems of scientific management. Workers were rigorously measured, sometimes in hundredths of a minute, against the optimum time that the rule books said it should take to climb a ladder, walk to a tank, or read a gauge. Maintaining this tangle of rules took so much time and caused so much frustration that a group of quiet rebels began to gather in the upper echelons of the manufacturing functions. Led by David Swanson, the manufacturing manager for the paper division, the rebels were determined to find a way out from under Procter's rigid constraints. They knew it would mean fighting the P&G corporate hierarchy, whose members were deeply committed to scientific management; they would have to hide their innovations from their own corporate chiefs.

Fortuitously, they began by bringing in Douglas McGregor from MIT.[10] McGregor had just published his book *The Human Side of Enterprise,* and his visits represented the first time anyone in manufacturing at P&G had been allowed to "examine our navels," as one plant manager later put it.[11] This was a major shift for managers at Procter, who had always been pressed relentlessly not just to perform but to expect high performance from themselves and everyone around them. In the Procter lexicon, the worst thing you could be called was a "tinkerer" or an "experimenter"; that meant you weren't sure about your results.

At the same time, paradoxically, P&G was well suited to hear McGregor's message. Unlike many "organization men," Procterites valued the plainspeaking, brutally frank, fiercely engaged meeting style that McGregor championed. They particularly appreciated what he told them about Eric Trist's work. They used those ideas when developing a new Tide detergent plant in Augusta, Georgia, in 1963. In Augusta, P&G managers abandoned some of P&G's most cherished practices. They banned the incentive pay scheme, production quotas, and job classifications. There would be no more operators who ran the lines, mechanics who fixed them, electricians who handled the wiring, or machinists who tooled new parts. There would be only "technicians," working in teams, setting their own goals, rewarded not for the boundaries of their jobs but for the skills they possessed. If the packing insulation around pipes leaked out, the operators wouldn't have to wait around for a mechanic who was allowed to carry a wrench. The operators would carry wrenches, blueprints, and slide rules or calculators. Together, the technicians would gradually develop all the expertise they needed to keep the plant going and improve it. They spent an unprecedented four hours per week in training; and two more hours per week meeting together to solve problems. The idea of these technicians was so central to the new design that manufacturing manager Dave Swanson dubbed the plants "high-performance technician systems."

Augusta and its successors were so successful that by 1967 every new P&G plant was required to operate under the technician system. Since no one was allowed to see the plants—not even people at Procter outside of their own manufacturing groups—they acquired a mythic, legendary air, bolstered by the exotic names of the prosaic places where they had been located. There was Mehoopany, located in rural Pennsylvania; Modesto, in central California; and Albany, in Georgia, which made paper products like toilet tissue and disposable diapers. Most important, there was Lima, Ohio, which made Downy fabric softener and Biz detergent[12]—the first plant designed from the ground up, from day one, to incorporate the technician system, instead of having the new structures merely grafted onto an existing factory design. Twenty years later, the management writer Robert Waterman would hold up Lima as the primary example of "what America does right" on the factory floor, and probably the best-managed plant in the United States.[13] It was a wonderful place to work, and not just because wages were high (so high that P&G managers from corporate grumbled about "giving away the store"). Yet production costs were said to be half the costs of a conventional plant, and the true ratio was even lower;

the Lima managers assumed that nobody would believe the real figures.[14]

Lima was a philosophical crown jewel for the technician system, and perhaps the single place in the world where sociotechnical ideas and practices had been given full rein. The chief philosopher there, the man who pushed Lima into its legendary status, was one of the great charismatic leaders in the history of American organizational change. He hadn't yet garnered the notoriety he would have in the 1980s, when he would become (unfairly) labeled by San Francisco newspapers as a Rasputin-like New Age management consultant with a cadre of manipulative change agents who had plotted to take over California's premier telephone company. In 1967, the "Kroning of Pacific Bell" (as the San Francisco *Chronicle* called it) was twenty years in this man's future. He was simply a middle manager, not very high in the Procter hierarchy, with a strong following among some of his P&G associates. They liked the way his conversation mixed nuts-and-bolts shop-floor data with cosmological theories about the purpose of human life. His name was Charles Krone.

Charlie Krone was not a typical Procter production executive. Raised in Kansas, he had graduated from an experimental high school run by the psychologist Karl Menninger, a school where students were taught to study the process of their own learning. He had an engineering degree from the University of Kansas and he had done postdoctoral work in the philosophy of law at Northwestern. In the Navy, he had been part of a group that rewrote the code of military justice. He had started his P&G career as an engineer at a fatty-alcohol plant, but as the technician system took hold, he had become increasingly committed to it. He was one of the first P&G people to attend a workshop at NTL in the early 1960s, in the days when Douglas McGregor was still consulting for Procter. Then, after McGregor's death, he had become one of twelve "organization development consultants" within P&G sent for in-depth training at the University of California at Los Angeles, where they studied with eminent NTLers, sociotechnical researchers, and Eric Trist himself.[15]

But Krone also pursued his own studies. During one of his visits to UCLA, he had been introduced to some of the teachings of the spiritual leader G. I. Gurdjieff. Gurdjieff was perhaps the first twentieth-century figure to expound Tibetan and Sufi mysticism in the West—certainly, of all mystic leaders, he has been the most influential in business circles. (Later, in Chapter 5, we will see his influence on the scenario planners of Royal Dutch/Shell.) Gurdjieff and his followers, who lived together in Paris from the 1920s through his death in 1957, developed a worldwide community composed of small groups of people who practiced and studied self-observation, group dynamics, and reflective dances.

Mankind, according to Gurdjieff, had gone astray.[16] The "old world," the materialist and nationalist global civilization that had created wars and suffering, was on the point of dying. Either it would extinguish itself and humanity would perish, or it would be replaced by a more highly evolved epoch. To prevent the former, Gurdjieffians took on the mission of a lifelong "war against sleep," a constant battle against the numbing complacency of everyday existence. Gurdjieff had discovered that an immense personal power was available through increasing awareness—not just through study and discussion, but through dancing, movement, theater, and meditation. Like the NTLers, Gurdjieffians used small groups as mirrors, which brought to the surface the behavior and thoughts of people in the room.

Most of all, in order to follow Gurdjieff's path, you had to learn to give up your habitual, knee-jerk reliance on your own gut feelings about right or wrong. Gurdjieff told a mythic story about the "kundabuffer"—an organ planted in the bodies of the earliest human ancestors, blocking them from fully experiencing reality. Though that organ had disappeared long ago, humans still carry the vestigial emotions that it spawned: self-love, vanity, swagger, pride, and arrogance. Any human being can be convinced of anything, Gurdjieff wrote. All you need to do is find a way to resonate with one of those vestigial misperceptions, buried so deeply within us that we are unaware of them. But if you could find a way to eliminate the automatic, learned, ego-driven responses within yourself, a void would be created, into which your "true self" could flow.

Charlie tended to inspire an intense loyalty in his friends at Procter, as if he were not just their friend and colleague, but a kind of in-house spiritual teacher. At meetings, he was a huge meditative presence; he stood six feet six, with sharp features and shrewd, heavy-lidded eyes, and he weighed a rangy two hundred pounds. He would hover silently in the corner of a meeting like a benign giant, almost invisible to the group, injecting questions every now and then that seemed to put everything into perspective. He avoided corporate rituals and the trappings of authority, talking as easily to factory floor workers as to managers. Charlie was the kind of guy who would sit down at a tense, confrontational union-management meeting and say, "Let me tell you how things would be if we could just work together as one system."

But some Procterites didn't care for him. They resented his cavalier approach to Procter's schedules, rules, and boundaries. In that tight, close-knit corporate culture, where people were expected to keep their promises, Krone would schedule two or three meetings at once. Then, seemingly at the last minute, he would decide which one to show up at. Was he just being arbitrary and self-indulgent, or (as his friends professed) was he deliberately acting as a trickster, to spur groups into learning to think for themselves?

In 1966, Procter & Gamble chose Krone to form a team to plan a new demonstration factory. They selected a site at Lima, a half day's drive north of Cincinnati, just far enough away to escape the pull from headquarters. Krone recognized that they would need to go audaciously beyond the achievements of previous plants at Augusta and Mehoopany; they would need to go beyond what anyone, even sociotechnical leaders like Eric Trist, thought was possible. They would deal directly with the emotional and psychological issues—the spiritual issues, really—that these plant organizations raised. Borrowing from all the schools of thought they knew—

Gurdjieff, Trist, NTL, systems design, and Tibetan and Sufi mysticism—he and the other Lima designers argued that the whole plant should be an "open system." It would never be "finished"; it would never stop learning and evolving during its lifetime. In addition, the plant would be conceived as a coherent whole. Not only would most people at the plant work at a variety of tasks (as in Augusta) but everyone in the plant would be aware of all the stages of the work. As commonsensical as this approach seems today, it was the opposite of the conventional plant design process, in which each stage was treated separately, and often designed separately, with components imported from different places.[17] This new approach was to be a perennial theme in an industrial renaissance that would eventually spread out from America and Japan under the name of the quality movement.

Here's how Lima worked. Suppose you were a technician with an idea for a machine that would place empty plastic bottles onto the conveyor belt, instead of having someone place them arduously by hand. You would raise it in your own team, knowing that nobody else would steal it, take credit for it, or dismiss it as dumb. Instead, they would challenge it: if they liked the idea, some would champion it with you, adding features of their own. The members would then take it to their other teams, and gradually the idea would filter through the plant.

If interest lasted long enough, a team of enthusiasts might form around this project; since you had proposed it, you might lead the team. You would rotate between time on the assembly line and time in this special project. All your fellow team members (including some engineers) would get an education available nowhere else, because your investigations would not be bound by the preconceptions of professionals. According to established engineers, for instance, a bottle-placing machine was technically impossible. But one team at Lima invented one. Procter ordered it, an industrial supplier built it (after meeting with various key participants in the plant), and it runs in Lima today.

Lima (and the other technician-based plants at P&G) soon became famous for the speed with which they handled difficult problems. In 1969, for instance, the state of Michigan outlawed phosphates in detergent. Ordinarily, P&G's product development engineers would have turned that change into an expensive, time-consuming, bureaucratic endeavor. But for Biz, the technicians handled the challenge. They sent a delegation to the supplier's plant site to help develop a new material that could fit their process. They managed the changeover of formulation and packaging, and ended up producing the only detergent that replaced phosphates without jacking up costs, reducing quality, affecting performance, or facing shortages of supplies.

And the rewards the technicians got? They were not paid as highly as managers, but the salary structure was the same—the amount of pay was based on the number of "qualified blocks of skills" that a technician mastered. There was very little overtime at Lima; teams managed their own weekly schedule, and pay rates were high enough that they never got in the habit of sacrificing weekends for extra pay. Unlike at other plants, though, pay was not the only incentive at Lima. There was also an intangible kind of satisfaction, from both the process of creation and the fact that Lima had no team leaders; everyone rotated in and out of the leadership positions, so that everyone had a stake in the whole operation. Krone dubbed this approach the "flowering organization," and drew an organization chart on the wall composed of interlocking circles, like an unfolding flower. Power rested not at the top, but at the center, in each individual's core leadership, and filtered out to related areas of interest as they were needed.[18]

In this model, there was no consensus or "democracy" in any traditional sense. Initiatives were carried out when someone championed them and nobody else came up with good reasons to get in the way. Real authority should be based, Krone would say, not on who had the highest rank, the best skills, or the most charisma, but on who cared the most about that particular initiative and could act most effectively on it. To make the organization live up to that notion, the salaried managers had to take on a leadership role that was unfamiliar to most of them. Did they have enough "faith in the process" to let a problem go *un*solved, as long as it took for someone to step forward to assume leadership? And would they have enough self-awareness—and this was the truly hard part—to recognize when it was appropriate for *them* to be the leader, because they cared more than anyone else?

Hard as it was for the Lima managers, it would have been even tougher if they'd had to buck headquarters at the same time. Therefore, Lima—and all the "technician" plants—operated under a strict veil of secrecy. Even other P&G managers couldn't find out about them; some were subtly threatened with being fired when they tried to find out. On the outside, labor leaders and sociotechnical experts would only hear vague, whispered rumors about the experiments going on. For all the value of P&G's experiments, and all the lessons they had to offer America, they were invisible. It fell to another renegade plant, at another company, to introduce sociotechnical practice to the public eye.

One morning in 1966, in an isolated warehouse at a dog food plant in Kankakee, Illinois, a twenty-year-old night-shift worker was discovered bound to a column with packaging tape. He was unhurt, but he could not get free. He furiously kicked against the tape because his shouting could not be heard. Once found, he was easily cut down, but figuring out what to do with him, or with the workers who had hung him up, was not so simple.

At that time, this plant (which made Gainesburgers and Gravy Train) belonged to the grocery conglomerate General Foods—one of the largest and most influential consumer products companies in the world. That did not mean that its managers felt powerful. For instance, they were bound by strict regulations for hourly workers that had been negotiated with GF's unions over the previous thirty years. At the Gaines dog food plant, a manager couldn't sack workers outright without triggering a grievance from the Federated Grain Millers local. Depending on how hard the union fought, the manager might win the right to hire a replacement—but the manager might also find himself in a long-drawn-out arbitration dispute. Even for an offense like taping a twenty-year-old boy to a pole, firing or disciplining people was hardly worth the trouble. A manager who cared would have to find some other way of preventing that problem from happening again.

In this case, that task fell to the third most senior person at the plant, engineering manager Ed Dulworth. He was thirty-one years old, a burly, boyish man with wavy blond hair and a genial, plain-spoken style. He had a volatile temperament and was prone to both enthusiasm and anger, but he also had a knack for making people feel comfortable. Of all the managers at Kankakee, Dulworth had the best rapport with hourly workers (which was why he was often tapped to deal with these sorts of problems). He stayed late the next night and called the boy's co-workers together in an impromptu meeting. Why had they taped this kid to the pole? "We didn't," one of them said. "We found him there. We were trying to get him down." Dulworth just stared at them. Amiably, but persistently, he drew the truth out of them.

The kid, who had just been hired a few days before, was working too hard. If he kept up his pace on the line, the rest of them would have had to speed up. They tried to warn him to slow down, but he couldn't stop. He was too charged with nervous energy. So they taped him up there.

Dulworth had been through dozens of similar situations (indeed, they were endemic to American factories), and he knew what would happen: nothing. He was damned if he disciplined them harshly; they would just ignore any punishment he was allowed to give them. And yet he was damned if he laughed it off and let them go back to work. Unofficially, he knew who was guilty, but officially, he couldn't hold a hearing. Nobody, not even the kid, would testify. He couldn't even move the kid to another locale or shift. Like everything else in the plant, the kid would just stay put.

That burned him. In a sense, Ed Dulworth had been running away from systems that "just stayed put" all his life. He had grown up in rural Michigan, and then been trained as a production engineer at General Motors. He had left GM when he saw that, no matter how well he performed, he would have to "sit in the god-damn chair," as they called the low-level supervising jobs, until he paid his dues as a manager. So in 1961 he'd come to this Gaines plant, and he'd advanced to become the youngest engineering manager in the entire General Foods system. He'd fulfilled his dream, or so he felt, of working in a place where people were judged on their performance, not on company politics. And his performance, in turn, depended on his geniality and open-mindedness. He had gotten in the habit, years before, of asking for help and advice from people who worked on the assembly lines he designed, and his systems tended to work better than those of engineers who thought they knew all the answers themselves.

Over the years, he'd also come to realize the value of looking at things from the other person's point of view. The line workers who strapped up that kid, for instance, were reacting to the pressure that the whole plant felt. "Semi-moist" dog foods, the generic name for cellophane-wrapped, pressed-together, semi-dry pellets like Gaines-burgers, had surged in popularity during the last year or two. The new Gaines dry dog food, Gravy Train, was also extremely popular. Demand for both had grown fourfold in four years.

But at the GF headquarters in White Plains, New York (thirty miles north of New York City, a thousand miles from Kankakee), Gaines pet food was a low-prestige product. GF was a conglomerate, formed through a half century's worth of mergers. There was continual, bitter turf conflict among the divisions, or (as managers called them) "mafias": glamorous Maxwell House versus Jell-O (the Jack Benny sponsor), versus technologically innovative Birds Eye (inventors of frozen foods), versus the profit center of Post cereals. Meanwhile, there was also an ongoing cross-divisional battle between the old-time production and sales people—gritty, matter-of-fact engineers and salesmen trained at municipal New York colleges—and the younger newcomers in marketing—aggressive Ivy League MBAs. Nobody ever talked about that rivalry publicly, which made it all the more deadly. Since most managers shifted jobs every three years, anyone might land under a boss from another faction, who could block his advancement or fire him.

For the moment, a production man named Tex Cook was CEO, so the production guys had the upper hand. But the war had made both sides hunker down, avoid mistakes, and play things strictly by the rules and procedures. Occasionally managers rebelled in small ways; one used footage of the GF corporate hallways in a mock-horror film: "Here is where the brain-dead sleep."

Gaines, with its little dog food business, was not even a full division. None of the experts at headquarters expected it to develop a miracle product. When Gainesburgers took off, they didn't quite believe it. They called it a "fad," continually underestimating demand and underbudgeting investment, while the Kankakee facility struggled to keep up with its mushrooming orders.

Only a few years before, 500 people had worked at Kankakee. Now, 1,700 were packed into their spots on the assembly line. Supervisors were under constant pressure to boost production, which meant haranguing the workers to move faster, in a plant that was crowded, damp, and prone to temperature extremes. (Part of the plant, converted from a warehouse, had never been insulated.) People had to struggle with new equipment designed for a complex Gainesburger packaging process that was still being broken in. More than half the plant's workforce was under twenty-eight; they'd been hired right out of high school, and acted angry to be there at all. Sensing the hostility of the supervisors, they retaliated with inarticulate, frustrated, and sometimes dangerous pranks. Some workers, for instance, nearly killed one unpopular manager by dumping a bucket of water on him while he was a hundred feet in the air, holding on to a vertical chain-link conveyor belt called a "man-lift."

Dulworth also understood the resentment felt by the supervisors and managers who wanted to "kick ass and take names"—to find and weed out the troublemakers. Most of the production managers, like the workers, were in their late twenties; the plant sometimes looked like a dank, subterranean city full of men just past their teenage years. The young managers usually came to Kankakee just out of business school, where they had studied the formulas for financial analysis and operations control. But they never learned the more crucial skills (as Dulworth saw them): how to listen to people or how to think on their feet. Those who learned these vernacular skills on the job soon got promoted elsewhere; Kankakee was a development arena, feeding managers to other plants in General Foods.[19] The more inept managers stayed put. They complained regularly to Dulworth and the other senior managers about not being backed up when there was "trouble in the ranks." They wanted Dulworth to pull rank, give orders, and punish the worst offenders.

Maybe that approach would have worked in the past, but at that time, in the mid-1960s, Dulworth thought it would create more bitterness and trouble than it solved. The answer to all these disciplinary problems lay not with punishment, but somehow giving people some form of meaningful involvement.

In the 1960s, the impulse to give people meaningful involvement was as grounded in evidence as Galilean astronomy; and it was just as threatening to the status quo. Like Galileo, managers such as Dulworth couldn't stop themselves from trying to push the institution forward, even after they'd been warned to ease off, no matter how much difficulty and pain that added to their lives.

Unlike Galileo, however, Ed Dulworth did not face the Inquisition alone. In 1966, a new plant manager arrived at Kankakee.[20] His name was Lyman Ketchum, but people called him Ketch. In his late forties, bespectacled and grizzled-haired, he liked Dulworth and soon came to regard him as a favored nephew. Ketchum understood both the hourly workers and the low-level managers. He was the son of a fervent union man—his father, a carman for the Santa Fe Railroad, had lost his job when he led a bitter, violent railroad strike in the early 1920s. Ketch had gone to the University of Kansas on a football scholarship and then put himself through engineering school, determined never to feel the resentment of the system that he saw in his father. He had worked at a variety of jobs in the grocery and food industry, including plant management for Quaker and other companies.[21] Like Dulworth, he knew how capable and motivated factory workers could be, and he had been somewhat influenced by the few management professors who pushed, during the 1940s and early 1950s, for what they called "participative management"—giving workers influence over their work.[22]

But while he remained convinced of the value of worker participation, he hadn't thought much about it for several years. Beginning in the late 1950s, Ketchum had begun to work his way successfully out of the production track at General Foods and into
marketing and regional sales. Then he had been tapped in 1965 for
a dream job, the first that would really use his intellectual gifts:
strategic planning for Gaines pet food. His first project had been a
major report on the future of American consumers, influenced by a
few farsighted people in the market research department. The mass
audience was going to fragment into dozens of smaller, less homo-
geneous audiences, with vastly different tastes. Subcultures would
appear among pet owners; for instance, there would be "anthropo-
morphists," who treated their animals like people and relied on
them for companionship. Ketchum argued that GF should produce
multiple-flavors for dogs whose owners thought they craved variety.

As far as Ketchum ever heard, the study was well received at GF.
But his sympathizers in marketing learned differently; the Ivy
Leaguers who ran that function mocked them. "Treating a dog like
people? That's sick!"[23] A plan to redesign Gaines Biscuits and Bits
packages to emphasize companionship was turned down, simply
because the corporate plan said it wasn't time yet to change the
package. (The marketing man who proposed the plan left the company in disgust; when his redesign finally went through two years
later, it received the Pet Food Institute's Package of the Year award
and probably quadrupled sales.)[24]

Ketchum, meanwhile, spent only four months in planning. A
reshuffling at the top had led to a battle over who would head the
Kankakee plant. As the only candidate acceptable to both sides, he
was drafted. This was seen as a great career break. "Going to Kankakee is like going to the bank," one GF executive told him. If he
could run the plant effectively, he was slated to become general
manager of the pet food business.

But Lyman, from the moment he got to Kankakee, could see the
Gaines problems all too clearly—and their roots in the corporate
investment policies. During his many visits to White Plains (for he

had purchasing, inventory, manufacturing, and engineering responsibilities for all of Gaines), he began to speak out about the stresses
on the plant. Salespeople would ask him to fill new orders, and he
would say, "All right, but which of our old customers do you want
to ask to wait?"

In the early 1960s, General Foods' human resource staff began promoting NTL T-Groups to help ease tensions between "mafias."
Ketchum's turn to go came up, as it happened, a month before he
left for Kankakee. A year later, after hearing about it from
Ketchum, Ed Dulworth signed up.

Both men were impressed with T-Groups, but Dulworth in particular felt an awakening within himself. One man in his session (in
a hotel on the Jersey shore) convincingly portrayed himself as an
outstanding management expert. But the group's conversation
broke through the man's veneer and revealed him to be (as Dulworth later recalled it) "the biggest schmuck in the group." The
"schmuck" finally confessed that his marriage was falling apart and
he was in danger of losing his job because he kept fighting with his
fellow managers. Seeing this man's defenses, Dulworth understood
a little better what drove the many self-appointed experts at GF,
whose arbitrary-seeming judgments had stymied him throughout
his career.

When he saw his wife after the session, he began raving about
the fabulous insights he'd felt and about what it meant to be a more
open person. She stiffened, so he began to probe into her responses,
to draw her out as the T-Group leaders did. She burst into tears. He
saw, then and there, how threatening all this talk about "being
remade" could be to someone who wasn't prepared for it with two
weeks of camaraderie, and he resolved to keep a low profile around
the plant about this group dynamics stuff.

Nonetheless, the T-Group experience left him with a more philosophical perspective. He still had to deal with rigorous paperwork,
but it no longer made him fume. It was just a symptom of deeper
problems in the system, and he began to talk more freely with
Ketchum (and a few other managers at Kankakee) about perfor-

mance and sabotage problems: "There's something wrong here. What on earth is going on?" They could admit they had no answers, at least to each other, without the constant fear most managers have—appearing not to be in control of the situation. They thought more coherently about the welfare of everyone in the plant, as if everyone were part of a single community. Ketchum would catch himself, as he drove to work, musing about the other people who worked there. "What is each one of them thinking right now?"

The two men began to treat people more judiciously, to set up opportunities to talk through problems, and to invite involvement, to some small degree, from workers.[25]

By 1967, behavior had begun to change a little. First-line supervisors were a little less likely to blame the workers; workers were a little less likely to sabotage their work. Ketchum had time to put together a long-range facility plan, a project most GF managers never got to because they were too busy dealing with crises. Yet when he looked at the Kankakee plant as a whole, he despaired. There were too many people, too entrenched, with too many constituencies at White Plains or in the union, to change just because a senior manager was promoting a new crusade. Ketchum wished he could just start Kankakee over from scratch.

That fall, when senior executives at General Foods began to talk about expanding Kankakee, Ketchum argued instead for designing a new plant. Typically, launching a new factory was a cumbersome, rushed process in which cadres of construction engineers, financial controllers, and personnel managers battled with the specs and regulations. The plant manager and his staff, let alone the workers, were never asked for advice about the building in which they would spend their days. This time, Ketchum said, let us "unlearn" every traditional practice and design the plant as a single effort. We'll spend six months researching how the most farsighted, high-performance plants in the world are organized. Then we'll develop a plan for the site, the management, the adaptation of machinery from Kankakee, and the labor force all simultaneously, all working together, as if we were creating them all from scratch on a "blank sheet of paper."

Ketchum knew vaguely, from people he had met at NTL, that dramatic innovations were taking place in factories at Procter & Gamble, at Westinghouse, at AT&T, and in Sweden. He began to think that his little dog food division could learn from these examples, design a plant where people treated each other with grace and civility, and thus, in turn, set an example for others. It would be a daring deed for General Foods—a mission into uncharted territory. Nothing like this had ever been written into a rule book. He and Dulworth knew already, for example, that they would have to organize the factory's work around collaborative teams. But they had no idea how to compose the teams, how to set up pay scales, or how to fulfill a thousand other needs and details. They would have to figure all this out as they went along, while still creating a profitable dog food factory.

For more than a year, the division managers of Gaines pet food, as well as the GF corporate executives, resisted Ketchum's idea. They relented only after a strike erupted in October, and another was narrowly averted the following August. The grievances in both cases were the same: intolerable working conditions and long hours. By the end of the summer of 1968, Ketch had preliminary approval to look for a new site for a $12 million facility. Looking near Kansas City, to be close to freight lines and sources of grain, they finally found a site a few miles outside Topeka—on a desolate, windswept stretch of prairie next to the railroad tracks.

Dulworth, in addition to his job at Kankakee, worked nights developing a technical design for this new plant in Topeka. He continued that work even after January, when Lyman appointed him manufacturing and engineering manager—the second-highest post at Kankakee. Lyman, meanwhile, persistently battled with senior executives at the Post division, where Gaines had been subsumed during a reorganization. The Post corporate engineer demanded engineers in every senior position; the division president suggested for plant manager an advertising/merchandising veteran who had never run a plant before. When he heard that, Ketchum could barely control his temper. He still didn't know many of the details of this new plant, but he knew that it would require far more invention and sensitivity than an ordinary start-up. If it didn't have experienced and enthusiastic managers of people at the helm, it wouldn't fly. Unfortunately, Ketchum didn't have any suitable candidates of his own to suggest for plant manager.

Finally, one night early in 1969 at a bar in Kankakee, Ketch confessed his despair to Ed. "Look," Ed said, "if you want me to, I'll take the job." Both of them knew that Dulworth was one of few candidates whom Ketchum and the White Plains executives could agree on. Nonetheless, Lyman said no at first; he was reluctant to gut Kankakee by removing Ed, and he wasn't sure it was Ed's best possible career move. Dulworth had to convince him that Topeka had become his baby, too.

In April 1969, Ketchum and Dulworth were allowed to assemble a planning team. They felt some urgency, because Kankakee was already overburdened, and the new Topeka plant was overdue. But they took a few months to educate themselves. They read management books; they visited consultants to ask about pay systems, facilities, and motivation studies; and they tracked down every facility they could find that had tried something better than the conventional authoritarian approach.

Ketchum and Dulworth didn't realize that they were about to create the first major factory showplace of the postindustrial era. Nor could they foresee that their own careers would become a visible warning of how large corporations can martyr their visionaries. All that was still in the future. For the moment, they were simply asking: Had anyone, anywhere in America or around the world, ever created a plant like the one that Lyman and Ed imagined in their hearts?

Here they were extraordinarily lucky. One of their long-standing consultants was the Purdue University professor Richard Walton, who was moving that year to the Harvard Business School. Walton had been a trainer at NTL, a labor negotiation specialist, and an expert on conflict resolution. He already saw that his own reputation could be bound up with this new General Foods project. He spent many hours helping with the plans for the new plant and began writing about it for management journals before the plant opened. Walton had also spent some time at UCLA, where he had gotten to know Charlie Krone. He offered to introduce the Gaines people to the seer from Procter & Gamble.

The General Foods people flew to meet Krone in his Cincinnati office, and came away impressed on several levels. "He talked about Augusta, Lima, and Mehoopany," Dulworth later recalled. "Jeez! These were big-time, total designs, committed to a radically different approach." It was also noteworthy how the Lima designers balanced their commitments to the new management philosophy and the old attitudes back at P&G headquarters.

Almost unwittingly, Krone and Dulworth slipped under the Procter "soapsud curtain" into one of the most hidden arenas in the company. Charlie grandly dismissed all concerns about secrecy. "Procter has a social responsibility to share what we're doing with others," he told Ketchum and Dulworth. They assumed that he meant openness was Procter's policy; they didn't know he was speaking only about his *own* policy. Krone was also helping managers at the British chemical company ICI and at Du Pont. He believed that open systems, in general, had more to gain by sharing their techniques than bottling them up. True, he forswore writing or speaking publicly about Lima, but only because he thought no one could do the concept justice except through in-depth consultations. He had a Zen-like belief that seekers should only find masters when they were ready to learn in depth; not when they wanted a quick answer. And Ketchum and Dulworth were clearly eager to learn in depth.

They learned that the rest of Procter was not so open when they tried to verify what Krone told them. Somehow, they obtained the design document for the Mehoopany plant. They figured they would follow up by going to Mehoopany, but no one let them inside. Instead, they hung around the town's bars and bowling alleys, collaring plant workers to ask them what was going on. "It was a major learning experience," Dulworth said later, "to hear that it was alive, and not just words. It gave us lots of confidence."

*   *   *

Meanwhile, the Topeka project continued to ruffle feathers back at White Plains. Ketchum deliberately asked nobody from the Post engineering and financial staffs to join the five-person Topeka planning group.[26] He had enough trouble with staff people as it was. Someone from personnel would pull out a policies and procedures book, and Ketchum would drawl, "Well, we're not going to have one." What about a controller? A personnel department? A quality control department? "No, we don't need any of those either."

They had also decided not to invite a union to organize the plant. This was, in part, a selling point at White Plains; and it meant they could experiment with shifting work rules far more easily. Later, this would be a key point of criticism against the plant. It wasn't an exercise in "workplace democracy," critics would charge, but an impossible showplace whose successes could never be duplicated in, say, Kankakee. For their part, Dulworth and Ketchum felt very little of the visceral, venomous resentment of unions that colored many managers' attitudes. Ketchum still maintained a close relationship with his labor-organizer father, and one of Dulworth's most disturbing moments, during the research phase, was a visit to work redesigners at Westinghouse who only went into action when they got wind of a union organizing campaign.

To help ensure that Topeka would be different, Dulworth invited onto the design team an hourly worker named Don Lafond, a maintenance craft foreman from the Kankakee shop floor. Lafond was insightful and thoughtful; he was an unofficial counselor to other workers in the plant, and he had put himself through night school to learn electrician skills. He had also been a union shop steward and local president, which made him indispensable for understanding potential grievances that the design team would otherwise miss.

At first, the rest of the team had trouble getting used to him. Lafond wasn't articulate in the way a college-educated, General Foods-assimilated manager would be. He didn't know how to prepare and package his thoughts before he spoke. He would see something in the Topeka plans that didn't make sense, and he

would shyly raise his hand and launch into an interminable pream-
ble about how he was just a farm boy and people on farms learned
to be jacks-of-all-trades. That would all be a warm-up for his main
point: "You guys are trying to make everything idiot-proof again. I
don't want there to be only one person in the plant who knows
how to program the line."

In December, the design team faced its biggest test: a series of
presentations of the detailed Topeka plan to Headquarters. One
presentation stuck in Dulworth's mind for years. It came at a tough
moment: The president of the Post division had recently told Lyman
Ketchum that he would never be promoted again. Apparently Ketch
had ruffled too many feathers in assembling the Topeka team. "This
was at the height," he later recalled, "of the most creative work I
had ever done in my life. Once I realized that my career was in
jeopardy, that made me all the more determined. If I was going to
go down in flames, I would go down my own way." He had
reached the point that Galileo reached after accusations against him
began: where making the church see the truth is more important
than getting along with the cardinals.

Dulworth had not yet been tagged with a negative label, and he
handled most of the presentation. The pitch was based on the point
that workers, even assembly-line workers, aren't in it just for the
money. "People have 'ego' needs," Dulworth argued, "they want
self-esteem, a sense of accomplishment, autonomy, increasing
knowledge, and skill and data on their performance. People invest
more when they have these things."[27]

The new plant would be designed to capitalize on that aspect of
human nature, he said. It would have a minimum workforce, in
which teams measured their own work and set their own goals. The
managers, without the need to watch over people so closely, would
be free to develop innovations. Dulworth and Ketchum estimated,
on the basis of their research, that the new factory might expect
productivity gains of 50 percent.

Sitting at the end of the table that winter morning was Jim
Stone, the vice president of operations for all of General Foods.[28]
Despite the lofty title, Stone's was a staff position; he advised,

rather than controlled, the divisional managers of the GF "mafias." But he was powerful enough to speak for the organization as a whole, not just for the pet food division. To move forward, they needed his support. And Stone was sympathetic: he had long been interested in finding ways of making manufacturing more efficient and using insights from people on the assembly lines.[29] He saw that the Topeka plant would give General Foods an opportunity to experiment firsthand.

But in the carefully orchestrated corporate meetings of the mid-1960s, senior managers did not speculate or join in any presenter's enthusiasm. Instead, Stone sat there—not antagonistically, but impassively, as if marking time—while Ed Dulworth grew progressively more nervous. Finally, the vice president for operations gave his judgment. "I don't think this is going to work." He added a benediction that Dulworth had never heard before during his professional life: "But you are free to fail."

Being "free to fail" seemed to make Lyman promotable, after all. In early 1970, he became the first operations manager for the Gaines pet food business. He interpreted the appointment as a vote of confidence in the new Topeka approach, and as an unofficial opportunity to become an organizational change agent for all of General Foods, helping plants convert to the team system. Ketchum's move was a blow for Dulworth, however; he hadn't imagined life at Topeka without Ketchum as a mentor, and now he had to run interference with headquarters. Instead of being protected, he was now the buffer.

Meanwhile, the first skeleton members of the Topeka crew moved into the plant—including Don Lafond and several people slated to be leaders of the Topeka teams when it opened. They were deliberately chosen to be diverse: a recent college graduate, a former auto plant supervisor from Ford, a college coach, a graduate of the U.S. Naval Academy, a former personnel staffer from another company, and an FDA inspector who also owned and ran a farm. Topeka was originally due to open in September of that year, but construction delays pushed the date back to January 1971. In the meantime, from a makeshift office in a storefront, the team leaders hired sixty-three plant staffers. At first, they ran applicants through an elaborate set of tests, but after a while they realized that they only needed to give them a plant tour. "We don't know exactly what this job is going to be," Dulworth would tell the applicants, "but you can pretty much make it what you want. The more you want to do, the more you'll be able to do." People who responded eagerly were probably Topeka material.

Within a few months of opening, the plant began to show the same kind of results that had been so impressive at Lima. Production costs were 40 percent below Kankakee's, and absenteeism held at a remarkable 2 percent rate (Kankakee's was 15 percent). Total production rose to 300 tons of dog food per day, the plant's target, and never fell below.

The plant found its first in-depth critic that year. A doctoral student of Dick Walton's named Mike Brimm, researching his dissertation for the Harvard Business School, spent the summer of 1971 on the shop floor; Dulworth wouldn't admit him unless he agreed to work all summer. Brimm took on the job wholeheartedly. He didn't just *interview* his subjects; he worked with them, went swimming with them, and drank with them at 7 A.M. (Night-shift crew members often gathered in a field outside for a sunrise after-work beer.) Afterward, Brimm would hurry home to dictate what he remembered into a tape recorder. Trained in Marxist theory, Brimm had deliberately set up his dissertation to look at the plant from two perspectives. To a sociotechnical theorist, it was an unqualified success. To a socialist, it was a failed attempt to mollify the working class within a capitalist framework. Yet he had to admit that the feeling of democracy was palpable, particularly when compared to his earlier visit to Kankakee.

For one thing, the plant was modern and temperature-controlled. The square, grooved, five-story, gleaming white tower at the plant's center rose from the stark Kansas fields like the last rook on a giant chessboard. Inside (like every pet food plant) it stank of tallow and grain, but in every other respect it was a comfortable place to work. Most factories are laid out horizontally, but Topeka was designed as a living silo. Starting in bins at the top of the building, grain dropped through the floors, propelled by gravity, traveling through successive stages of production as it fell. Sections of the plant were painted bright colors that showed the flow of work; meeting rooms became natural centers where teams gravitated to compare notes or argue. Instead of supervisors (the Kankakee word for "foreman"), there were "team members" and "team leaders" (the GF designers had decided against importing the sterile term "technician" from Procter & Gamble). Unlike Kankakee, the Topeka plant had no reserved parking places for managers, and only one lunchroom, where everybody ate together at large round tables. The break rooms had carpeting, Ping-Pong tables, and (most incomprehensible of all to GF headquarters) a television set. There was no bathroom on the first floor, so managers and workers had to use the same facility; and only one entrance, so everyone used the same door. There were no fences, no guards, and no locks on the lockers. When large quantities of dog food were found missing, the teams of workers laid a trap and caught the thief in the act.

Pay scales, instead of being based on seniority or the boss's favor, were based on knowledge. Team members decided when their fellow team members were ready for more pay, simply by trusting them to handle a particular task.[30] (The design team had considered hiring everyone on a salary basis, as at Lima, but Ketchum knew he couldn't sell that to the executives at White Plains. He didn't even try.) Teams also set their hours and breaks, and dealt with their own problems in meetings. If you were regularly late, the people who had to cover for you might ask you to cut them some slack. All this felt controlling and cliquish at times, but it gave the factory a barn-raising atmosphere. When railroad boxcars showed up full of hundreds of hundred-pound packages of dog food ingredients, every team member (including the team leaders) dropped what they were doing and pitched in to unload it.[31]

Brimm himself worked at nearly every job in the plant, sometimes in teams that processed the dog food and sometimes in teams that packaged it. He examined railroad car-loads of incoming grain for infestation by insects ("a job for neither acrophobes nor those with queasy stomachs"[32]); he worked the assembly line where dog food was injected into bags; and he was a "humper" at the end of the line, piling fifty-pound packages onto wooden pallets. Normally everyone took two-hour turns as humpers, but there was a six-hour first-day initiation that Mike, like all his fellow team members, endured. "When I first saw you come in the door," one of his co-workers told him that day, "I said, 'Here comes Joe College to snoop around and keep clean. Now, I see that you're a regular guy.'"[33]

Most of all, Brimm was impressed with the ways in which team members learned the work from each other. In Kankakee, workers had deliberately tried to keep production down, for that was their only weapon against the system. Here, Brimm wrote, "it was not uncommon for a passing fork-lift operator to stop and offer me tips on an easier way to pack bales." Despite his many years as a student, he added, "I have encountered few teachers and colleagues who exhibit the patience, skill, and sensitivity which I observed and experienced among this work force. . . . My successes were rewarded with smiles and slaps on the back; my failures, with compassionate concern and assistance."[34]

Other workers were also impressed with the place. Many referred to Topeka as "us," and internalized the corporate goals: "Trucking the product to market will cost us $5,000 more a day," or "Our product has to have a rich, red color or the consumer will buy Purina next time."[35] Comments like that brought out Brimm's Marxist suspicions. After all, the plant did not belong to these workers, no matter how much they felt they owned it. Suppose they insisted on replacing that backbreaking "humping" job with expensive machinery, which the accountants had already rejected because the payback period was too long?[36] Suppose they wanted to stop making dog food and produce something else? Suppose they wanted to use the increased profits from the plant to raise their own pay or hire more workers? They'd soon see that they were free to make decisions only "as long as these yielded the same outcomes that the higher-level authority would have chosen (had he been there)."[37] The managers set the goals; the workers merely had a bigger voice in how to implement them.

And, indeed, when Brimm returned for follow-up interviews the next summer, in 1972, many of the workers had discovered the limits of the system. The feeling of being pioneers had leveled off. Ketchum had lobbied to have a second plant (to make canned dog food) built on the site, and now there were disputes about who would be team leaders in the new plant. Most telling of all, the people who had talked about utopian dreams the previous years now said to Brimm, in effect: Don't get me wrong. My job here is the best I could find anywhere in Kansas—maybe anywhere at all. But it's still just a job.

"We were all in the clouds for a long time," one worker told him. "Sometimes I think the people out in the office still are. But 300 tons of dog food a day, every day, can bring you down to earth in a hurry—particularly if you're the one who's making it. Some of the guys really crashed down when they realized this."[38]

You might think just "having a job" is not that awful a fate, particularly when American manufacturers were beginning a twenty-five-year period of downsizing and shifting jobs overseas. But Ketchum and Dulworth, like Eric Trist and Charlie Krone before them, began to feel a bit messianic about their system. At the same time, back in White Plains, Ketchum encountered the sort of nonchalant skepticism that must have dogged Galileo in Rome.

Staff people calling from White Plains knew nothing of improved performance; they knew only that when they called Topeka for the quality control or pricing data they needed, fast, they had to wait on line, fuming, until someone rounded up Ed Dulworth or Don Lafond. "Well, we can get that data," Lafond might say. "But not within twenty-four hours. We have to get it from the teams."

"Well, who can I talk to right now?" the staff member would snap.

"Anybody in Team A might be doing quality this week. We'll have to find out. Team B doesn't come on until eleven. Are you sure I can't call you back?"

A plant manager not knowing who was "doing quality" was like a commanding officer not knowing the name of his quartermaster. But when the staff member went to complain to Ketchum, he would simply say, "You don't need those measures in the first place. They don't really help production, do they?" Ketchum may have been right, but the word began to get around in White Plains that performance at Topeka was out of control. The plant couldn't even make its numbers. And Ketchum himself was becoming a "missionary."

This sort of flak hit practically everyone at some time in their career. But it worried Ketchum. He called Charlie Krone, asking, "Where can I find an expert to help me talk to these engineers . . . ?" Krone referred him to Eric Trist, whom Lyman invited to speak to a conference of General Foods manufacturing managers. The two men, who had only been vaguely aware of each other, became lifelong friends that night; eventually they collaborated on a book together.

Trist, as part of his research, had studied the diffusion of pilot projects like Topeka. He had concluded that they represented a losing game. They almost never influenced organizations like General Foods, which were set up, almost as if by design, to discourage any single division from learning from any of the others. "Don't get stuck," Trist told Ketchum, "on changing General Foods." Topeka's success, he predicted, would eventually stimulate other projects around the world.

It was a prescient remark. In the early 1970s, academic hand-wringing over American worker discontent—"blue-collar blues," as it had come to be called—was percolating through the federal government. The executive branch—particularly the Department of Health, Education, and Welfare—was full of well-meaning policy makers left over from the Great Society. Under Nixon's HEW Secretary, Elliot Richardson, they were shifting their focus "from community development and civil rights to productivity and workplace reform."[39] Starting in 1971, Ed Dulworth, Lyman Ketchum, and their adviser Dick Walton were invited, more and more, to make presentations about the fundamental industrial shift going on at

Topeka. The Topeka story was big news. It was dramatic, it took place under the aegis of one of America's most visible corporations (unlike Trist's work), and it provided a built-in warning. If corporations continued to set up their plants in the traditional manner, workers might erupt as blacks had in the early 1960s.

In November 1972, Richard Walton published an article in the *Harvard Business Review* that echoed this theme and presented Topeka as an industrial solution.[40] The following February, the New York *Times* ran a front-page story on Topeka. Then NBC-TV covered it; then *Newsweek, Business Week,* and *Reader's Digest.* The articles tended to mention experiments going on at other companies (there were projects at about a dozen U.S. firms by then)[41] and then single out the Gaines plant as the prime example of the next generation of industrialism. "We fit with the times," Dulworth said later. "We had a demonstration of a different kind of working life, one that valued individuals and wasn't highly structured. You could wear a beard and tennis shoes."

Spurred by the news reports, other companies began sending emissaries to visit Topeka. The Japanese Productivity Institute sent forty people; they endured three days of intensive study amid the stench of dog food. Eventually, tours became so numerous that Dulworth charged fees. The most senior General Foods executives blessed the idea of making Topeka a public example. (Unrelated to Topeka, GF had just had to publicly write off a series of large losses and bad investments—the first such write-off in its history. Topeka provided welcome publicity.) After the NBC broadcast about Topeka, Dick Walton ran into General Foods president Arthur Larkin at a party at the Harvard Club in New York. "Art, do you really understand what you've got in that plant?" he asked the president. Shortly afterward, Ketchum's appointment to his internal consulting job was approved. He would now be able to work full-time helping other plants follow Topeka's example. A community of people involved in this type of work design was emerging, and General Foods would be at the forefront.

*   *   *

The short happy life of Topeka's influence at General Foods ended in April 1973. That month, *The Atlantic Monthly* published excerpts from a forthcoming book called *Job Power* by a writer named David Jenkins, who described both Topeka and Lima. It was the first time Procter & Gamble's Lima plant had been mentioned in print. Jenkins wrote, inaccurately, that teams at Lima, without any direction from management, hired their own people and set their own salaries. He found, and quoted, the elusive Charlie Krone: "The plant was designed from the ground up to be democratic. The technology—the location of instruments, for example— was designed to stimulate relationships between people, to bring about autonomous group behavior, and to allow people to affect their own environment." No doubt Charlie had said something like this, but for his career it was the worst possible quote. In the tough-minded P&G culture, "democracy on the shop floor," no matter how much it helped performance, was not a plus.

Meanwhile, Tex Cook, the chairman of General Foods, made a formal visit to Topeka. At lunch, Ketchum mentioned all the help Charlie Krone had given. Cook had once been a star executive at Procter & Gamble; he had left for General Foods in 1950. "I still know the chairman of P&G," he said. "Would you like me to mention this to him?" Ketchum eagerly said yes, thinking it would help his friend. But it was the worst possible help he could have given Krone. First, it revealed that Krone had broken the secrecy barrier and the *Atlantic* leaks were not a fluke. Worse still, General Foods and Procter & Gamble were competitors; both companies, for instance, made coffee. Perhaps worst of all, Tex Cook was not a credible source at P&G. He had committed one of the company's most heinous unwritten sins—not just leaving the company but doing well elsewhere.

Krone was put under a form of house arrest, limited (as best as he could be limited) to Ivorydale (P&G's oldest plant, in Cincinnati) and Lima, and especially forbidden to work with other companies. Surreptitiously, however, he continued to bring outside managers into his consulting meetings. The first visitors, from the British chemical company ICI, were grudgingly accepted at

Ivorydale because ICI was a Procter supplier and customer. Then Krone began to visit Du Pont, whose managers showed up occasionally at the informal breakfast meetings he conducted in Cincinnati. From them, he began to get an idea of how much he could earn as an independent consultant.

The group of Procter and Gamble managers who had built the Lima plant, along with their wives, were coalescing into a tightly knit group of friends during the 1970s, a kind of Midwestern Bloomsbury. They spent weekends together in impromptu study groups, instigated by Charlie's wife Bonnie, in which they talked about Gurdjieff's ideas and the ramifications of their new workplace philosophy. They were creating a new type of community, they decided: a habitat that could raise the awareness and capability of the community's members. They read up on the great communal experiments of nineteenth-century America: Robert Owen's New Harmony, Indiana, and the Transcendentalists' Brook Farm. Ultimately, they even chipped in to buy and restore a run-down cattle farm in southern Indiana. By hassling through the knotty questions that come up when people share a common property, they would more fully understand the new system they were creating at Lima. Meanwhile, Krone gradually became more and more remote at Procter & Gamble. With an entrée through some of his UCLA contacts, he had begun to spend time on the West Coast. One day Krone's boss dropped in at the office of Charlie Eberle, another long-standing champion of the technician approach. "You know," said the visitor, "Charlie Krone is going into business for himself."

"I hadn't heard," Eberle said.

They were going to let him go, the visitor said matter-of-factly. "He'll make a hell of a lot more than we can pay him. We're really stretching now to keep his compensation where it is."

Years later Eberle remembered that exchange as an early signal of how Charlie Krone's style was changing. A second signal came in 1977. At the suggestion of some of his UCLA contacts, the Krones moved away from Cincinnati to Carmel, California—to a house on the ocean in which Carl Rogers had once lived. Rumors began to circulate back at the conservative Cincinnati Procter & Gamble headquarters: Charlie was living in an ashram on a cliff. He conducted meetings in white robes, burning incense, while devotees in the audience chanted ritualistic hymns.

The reality was more prosaic. Starting with several faculty members and students from Stanford and UCLA, as well as some disenchanted managers, Charlie Krone had begun to assemble a core group of consultants and convene training sessions for them every six weeks. He opened the sessions by putting up abstract drawings, like the flower diagram, that he called "frameworks." Each one described a relationship between the structure of power, authority, or process flow at a workplace and the attitudes and goals of the people in the situation. And then everyone would talk through the frameworks.

Krone wore sweaters and jeans, not robes, to his meetings, which he conducted with the same friendly, bemused, matter-of-fact approach that had served him well at P&G. He talked of mysticism, but combined it with practical stories of results achieved at Lima and elsewhere. He talked frequently, with admiration, about the achievements at Topeka. But pilot programs, limited to a single workplace or factory, would always fall short of the ideal. With his small group of colleagues, Krone was beginning to tackle the same problem that had inspired Robert Blake and Jane Mouton's package of "Managerial Grid" instruments. Any significant change in the corporate world would have to take place on a large scale, involving the organization as a whole. It would have to be planned with the breadth of a political campaign and the depth of a personal epiphany. This challenge represented the central problem of corporate change, and it looked as if Charlie Krone's group, with its blend of systems understanding, spiritual practice, work design, and practical engineering theory, might have more of a chance of solving it than anyone else.

But there was, indeed, a disturbing, almost cultlike aspect to Krone's practice. Although he no longer had to follow P&G's policy of compulsive secrecy, he created his own. Everyone who came to his workshops, and everyone who worked with him, was required to sign a nondisclosure agreement. People who flouted the agreement were banished from the group. The papers that Krone handed out, with the frameworks photocopied onto them, were rigorously embargoed from outside eyes. A manager could not go hear Charlie Krone give a keynote address at a conference or read a Charlie Krone interview in *Business Week* or *Fortune.*

Krone's rationale for this made sense to his close associates. He believed that publishing articles or making speeches simply misled people. To have a meaningful effect, he said, he had to tailor the message to each student's ability to accept it. This could only be accomplished in small, face-to-face groups, small enough for him to see participants and match his message to their eyes. Krone, who had never had much faith in the conventional ways of reaching people, now began to feel that, like Gurdjieff, he would have to develop his own. He was determined to keep as much control as possible over every aspect of his method and wisdom as they went out into the world, so they wouldn't get misused, corrupted, or simply dismissed by people who might say, "There's nothing special here."

But his followers had to admit that his methods, closed off to public view, were denied an important feedback loop—the feedback of public criticism. The Krone method was protected, but it was no longer an open system.

Ketchum and Dulworth had the more truly open system, and it made them vulnerable. In 1973, Ketchum's most prominent protectors disappeared. (Jim Stone, for instance, was promoted to run GF's Latin America/Far East division.) Repercussions began to move against Ketchum as inexorably as the denouement of a Greek tragedy. One time he returned to find that his horizons had literally shrunk—he had been moved into a smaller office. Instead of directing new plants, his job was reduced to advising the new plant managers. He set up a network of sympathetic managers from different plants, to compare techniques, but managers were discouraged from attending by their bosses. Plant managers were not supposed to talk regularly across channels. The corporate industrial engineering group conducted a major performance analysis and discredited Topeka's breakthroughs. (Years later it was recognized that the study was biased against Topeka and flawed in its accounting—for instance, the way it amortized the costs of new equipment.)

The worst blow to Ketchum's credibility came when he was told to report to Betty Duval, the vice president in charge of organization development and compensation. Ten years earlier, Betty Duval and Ketchum might have been allies. As one of the first vice president-level women in the Fortune 500, she had come up through the training department. In the 1960s, she had brought T-Groups to General Foods—in effect, helping start Ketchum on the path that led him to the Topeka work. She still saw her role as changing the GF culture by putting the managers through communications training, to help them work together better across the barricades of the General Foods "mafias." To Betty Duval, Ketchum's ideas were applicable strictly to the shop floor, with no broader interest. He, meanwhile, saw her as a politically motivated meddler without real power. It was as if they had been brought together to undermine each other.

It was true that Ketchum could never explain clearly enough what he was trying to do. When he tried, all Duval heard was jargon. He'd talk about a "total systems approach," or he'd offer comments like "This is the only way." It came across as too academic, too theoretical, too mysterious. Finally, he began to talk about the "Topeka phobia" at General Foods. People were afraid, he said, of opening their minds to see what Topeka had accomplished. Now senior managers began to complain to Duval: Couldn't she do anything about this missionary guy?

Resolved to prove everyone wrong, Ketchum teamed up with the amenable manager of a coffee plant in Hoboken, a plant with all the problems of Kankakee, plus a union said to be controlled by organized crime. They were just starting to make progress when the Maxwell House operations manager pulled Ketchum out of Hoboken and told him to focus instead on a new Jell-O plant in Lafayette, Indiana, with one of the most authoritarian managers in the corporation. "If you can make this plant work under him,"

Ketchum was told, "then I believe your strategy could work anywhere." Ketchum gamely set out, returning to Hoboken in his spare
time, and achieved some minor success at both plants. But he had
no freedom to redesign the work processes from scratch, and he
bitterly missed the collaboration he had enjoyed with the people at
Topeka.

Other members of the team were, if anything, worse off. The
team leaders at Topeka were eligible for promotions elsewhere, but
nobody else in GF wanted them. Instead of being sought after, they
seemed to have a kind of intellectual virus which no one else
wanted to catch. Ed Dulworth was profoundly disillusioned with
General Foods. When he talked privately with other General Foods
managers—men he respected—about the performance gains, they
were apathetic. "My boss isn't really interested in performance,"
they would say. He turned down a promotion to product manager
in White Plains, preferring the autonomy of being a plant manager
in the outpost that he had come to think of as their little monastery.
Inside, its halls rang with hope and laughter, but it stood forlornly
alone in the fierce wind of the Kansas prairie.

Ketchum quietly lost his job at age fifty-seven, in 1975. He retired
on a minimal pension, and opened a consulting business of his own.
His first years of consulting were melancholy. Ketch was used to
being considered an expert. Now he had to sell himself, like dozens
of other organizational consultants, and without the faculty posts
that many of them used to bolster their credibility. Back at General
Foods headquarters, he had lost his close contact with Topeka, so
he didn't fully realize how people there regarded him as a George
Washington figure: the father of their new system. But he did expect
Topeka's notoriety to guarantee him a steady stream of consulting
business. It didn't happen. A recession was raging. Few plant managers were interested in experimenting right then, thank you, particularly when it meant up-front investments. They had all they
could handle trying to meet their quarterly targets.

That same year, at a meeting with the top management of the
Post division, Dulworth's boss asked him to make a five-minute

presentation. It was a routine request. In the political context of General Foods, it was a compliment, an invitation to make Topeka palatable to the brass. Any normal manager would have eagerly assented. But Dulworth was sick of the "usual bullshit." In front of the entire senior management, he told his boss that it was a "dumb idea." Five minutes wouldn't be enough time to present the Topeka concept in any way that made sense. "If they're interested," he said, "they can read about it."

Four weeks later, he was summoned to White Plains again and told he would be demoted to second-in-command at another plant, where someone else could supervise him. He just hadn't delivered the results at Topeka, they said, and he wasn't trustworthy. Then they mentioned that people said he was drinking too much. "I lived in a corporate culture where there was lots of drinking," he recalled later. "If I had a problem, then I knew a great number of people with the same problem, including some of my bosses. They used it as a crutch to get me, and shame me. We all knew that drinking was not the issue here."

Dulworth asked if he had any other options. They said he could resign, although his salary might continue for a while. None of his supporters felt able, or willing, to help. Ketchum was already gone. Jim Stone, out in Latin America, was thinking about retirement. "It's too bad," he told Dulworth, "but I'm not involved." Dick Walton, the sociotechnical consultant at Harvard, continued to write about Topeka; it defined his career thereafter. But he had no influence on the senior management of General Foods; he barely knew anyone higher up than Ketchum. His interest turned to other companies.

So Dulworth resigned, and other Topeka managers also left. Soon, of the original team, only Don Lafond, the former union rep, remained. Perhaps because Lafond had started as an hourly worker, his reputation remained unscathed.

Every year thereafter, through the 1970s and 1980s, Topeka was the most productive plant in the General Foods system—according to just about every measurement, including the satisfaction of people on the line. Today, the corporate parent, General Foods, no longer exists. It was taken over by Philip Morris, and its components have been spun out to various corporate parents. Even so, the "sociotechnical" system continued to thrive at Topeka, under several corporate parents, until March 1995. Then Quaker Foods sold the plant to Heinz.

Since then, the new managers have shut down half the plant, suspended team meetings and ongoing training, and laid off 150 people. Ironically, Heinz did this at the moment in history when technician systems were finally becoming recognized. Heinz's managers could have had a showplace. Instead, they locked up the system they bought, put it behind bars, and are apparently waiting for it to die. Perhaps it will eventually be revived. Even the Roman Catholic Church eventually admitted that Galileo's cosmology was correct—after 359 years.

PROTESTERS

"A COMPANY CAN ONLY MOVE ITSELF FORWARD BY MOVING ITS
COMMUNITY FORWARD":
SHAREHOLDER ACTIVISTS AND CORPORATE SOCIAL RESPONSIBILITY ORGANIZERS,
1964–71

Into a twelfth-century village in Poland, or France, or the
Low Countries, a protester against the church would stride.
He would find a high spot not far from the church's outer
wall. He would position himself so that members of a gathering crowd could turn their eyes from his face to the spire, and
back to his face.

"We propose to recount some testimony from the Holy
Scriptures," he would say, "to give knowledge and understanding of the true church of God." And they would fall
silent: they knew he was drawing a contrast, as audaciously as
he dared, between the church of God and the building before
them. "This church," he would say, "is not made of stones or
wood, or of anything made by hand, for it is written in the
Acts of the Apostles that the Most High dwelleth not in
houses made by hands." As they listened, men in the crowd

could feel the calluses on their fingers, or hear again the stories of calluses on their fathers' hands—hands that carried stones to this building.

"This church refrains from adultery and all uncleanness," the man would say, and one or two women in the crowd would feel their lips tighten as they remembered a piece of gossip they had heard about the rector—or a glance from him. "This church refrains from theft or robbery," the protester would say, and the wine merchant would think of the triplefold tithe that he had paid, while others thought of the gold rings that the cardinals wore. "This church refrains from lying and from bearing false witness," the man would say. "This church refrains from oaths. This church refrains from killing." With every line bitter memories would disturb the faces in the crowd. And finally, in a reference to himself: "This church suffers persecutions and tribulations and martyrdom in the name of Christ."[1]

By then the priest would have had time to hear of the protester's presence. An angry force of three or four men might arrive, ready to seize him for a trial. Or perhaps the speaker would merely slink away, his speech incomplete. In evenings in someone's home, in the privacy of a more ardent group, he would add to the sermon. The sacraments were not real, and did not count, he would say, if they were performed by immoral priests. The "ravening wolves in sheep's clothing" whom Rome had ordained could not rightly preside over baptism or communion.[2] The people should take back their church.

"Are you saying," a voice might inject from the back of the room, "that the sacraments are so weak that a mere priest can corrupt them?" Augustine had used this question against the Donatists eight hundred years before. Authority, after all, does not come from the priests. It comes from the church as a whole. If your priest, or any local administrator, is corrupt, then you need not fear: for the system is stronger than the abuses of any of its members. The system will take care of you.

On the other hand, if your argument is with the authority as a whole, it is senseless to criticize the priest. The priest is just a tiny reflection of corrupt authority. Having come this far, you must take the next step. You must criticize the establishment that put the priest in place and the sacraments that were given to him. But that is unfathomable and unthinkable, because those foundations come from God. To question them is to move into exile. You and anyone who befriends you will be considered enemies—even if you are correct.[3]

▼▼▼

To whom should a corporation be responsible? In the mainstream business world, there is only one self-evident answer to that question. A corporation exists to return profits on shareholders' investments. But that leaves an enormous amount of discretion to managers. When should those profits be returned? Every quarter? Every year? Any manager continually balances the value that may come from a long-term investment against the time it takes to receive the returns.[4] Moreover, the responsibility of profit says nothing about the vagaries of fate. Is it acceptable to invest heavily on a risky future? And in the process of returning profits, does the company owe anything to the rest of the public, even if paying off that more evanescent debt makes the bottom line suffer in the short run?

A manager who thinks seriously about these issues will recognize after a while that defining a corporate purpose means balancing a *group* of loyalties.[5] True, the shareholder is guaranteed profit and control. But the corporate manager has also signed a contract with government—the corporate charter, dating back to the European monarchs—in which the manager agrees not just to respect public laws but to *contribute to public welfare,* in exchange for protections against legal liability. There are also contracts, implicit or explicit, with unions (which are organized to bargain for stable employment) and with customers (who want the cheapest, best product, without hidden hazards).

Finally, there is an implicit contract, vaguest of all, with the community. It is much like the implicit contract in medieval times between a church and its village. The church had the power of its far-flung organization, its Inquisitorial police, and its accepted link with God. There could be no greater power. But if there were visible simony, lechery, or corruption among the priests, then in the long run protests would overwhelm the church. Similarly, today, the community wants the corporation to act in an exalted fashion: to be a delightful neighbor, to refrain from polluting, to contribute to the common good, and to employ people in good faith. In exchange, the community will act neighborly itself. It will meet corporate initiatives halfway—to improve the schools, for instance, or to reconstruct regulations. It will hold protest in abeyance.

This bargain works, of course, as long as the corporation and the community coexist with the same basic values. But in the 1960s, the values of the community changed, and it demanded that the corporations change to keep up with it. It happened first in the civil rights movement, which redefined the boundaries of community. Civic responsibility no longer meant paying attention to the needs of the "nice" part of the city alone; rather, the demands of the whole had to be met. Corporations didn't immediately follow suit, and the contract between corporation and community fragmented.

* * *

Consider, for example, the fragmentation that overtook the Kodak Corporation in the mid-1960s. If ever a neighborly company existed, that was Eastman Kodak. It was founded by a nineteenth-century bachelor named George Eastman, who lived with his mother all his life in the city of Rochester, New York, and who deliberately promoted civic responsibility. Eastman founded the city's Community Chest, along with a renowned school of music and a community theater. Under his guidance, and after his death, Kodak always contributed generously to the city's hospitals, schools, and charities—$22 million between 1954 and 1964. As far as civil rights were concerned, Kodak's boosters could imagine no reason for complaint; the company sponsored a fellowship program for black schoolteachers and contributed generously to the United Negro College Fund. Kodak had been an early participant in John F. Kennedy's Equal Employment Opportunity Plan for Progress program, and in 1964 it had recently expanded its recruitment efforts to include black colleges.

Internally, the company was also benevolent. Kodak people participated in the rewards of the company's success (the Instamatic cartridge-film camera, a marketing triumph, had come out only a few years before). They were paid high salaries and generous annual bonuses averaging $2,000 per employee—most of whom took for granted that once they were in the door they were employees for life. The senior managers of the firm were all well educated and straitlaced. The president, William Vaughn (he was about to become CEO), maintained the same strict rules of propriety that had existed since George Eastman's day. Executives who kept secretaries after 5 P.M. had to call in a chaperone; no one was reimbursed for liquor on a Kodak expense account.[6]

But if people felt well rewarded and well protected, they also tended to feel disoriented, at least when they worked on the factory floor. The old joke about traditional management practice being like mushroom farming ("Keep them in the dark and feed them manure") was bittersweet at Kodak, where light-sensitive film was manufactured in total darkness. As if to add to their disorientation, the plant had staggered schedules; workers alternated between the day shift, the night shift, and the graveyard shift, always without light. (A union would never have permitted that, which was one reason why Kodak's senior managers felt so phobic about organized labor.)

And to those outside the company, particularly the black people of Rochester, the company was an object of seething resentment. It was the largest employer in Rochester, and it had never let them into the family. In 1964, there were 20,000 blacks in Rochester, crowded into a few neighborhoods where landlords rented to them. Most of them had come up from the southern states in search of jobs; now they lived in tenements with twenty-four or twenty-eight families squeezed into houses designed for two. Their unemployment rate reached almost 15 percent (three times as great as the white neighborhoods).[7] Churches were weak; only 3,000 residents of the area went to church regularly. Street gangs were strong and growing stronger. The major employer in the neighborhood, the Rochester Institute of Technology, was already making its plans to move to the suburbs.[8]

The leaders of "old, monied, Episcopalian, upper-class Rochester"[9] tended to pooh-pooh the city's racial problems. Frederick Douglass had published his papers on the abolition of slavery there. It had been one of the key stops on the Underground Railroad. It had no machine politics, a strong tradition of Jane Addams-style settlement houses, and high average salaries.

Why had prosperity not reached the city's black underclass? No doubt all the familiar factors were responsible: white racism, the inherent erosion of self-esteem built into an underclass lifestyle, the suburban exodus of the middle class, and the pitiless barriers built into Rochester's educational system, banking habits, and hiring structures. In Rochester, community groups blamed Kodak—which controlled (they felt) the school board, community chest, and other civic institutions. Automation had also begun to play a part; opportunities for high-paying unskilled factory work, which had been seen for thirty years as an essential part of upward mobility, were increasingly scarce. A contingent from Rochester took part in the

1963 March on Washington for civil rights, where 300,000 people shouted not just "Freedom Now!" but also "Jobs Now!"[10]

Rochester's riots took place in July 1964. They started, as riots often did, when white police entered a black neighborhood. One Friday night, a canine squad came in to answer a call about a disruptive man at a neighborhood block party dance. Many people in that neighborhood believed that the Rochester police deliberately used dogs to harass blacks, and a group of men who had been at the dance began throwing rocks at them. As the violence escalated, the police were rapidly forced to retreat. Within three days, four people had been killed and hundreds hurt; scores of stores had been damaged and looted; nearly a thousand people were arrested; and the governor, Nelson Rockefeller, had sent in the National Guard.[11]

The riot paralyzed Rochester's aristocracy; they could no longer feel that they had one of the most benevolent cities in the North. Into the void came Rochester's Third Presbyterian Church. Before the federal War on Poverty began, churches in northern cities had often bankrolled independent community organizing efforts—generally with tacit support from all of a city's varied interest groups, from businesses to unions to the ghetto. With 2,500 members, Third Presbyterian was one of the largest, most established churches in the city. Faced with a shortage of pastors, it had recently hired a thirty-two-year-old (white) minister named Paul Long, a slim, brash man with a disc jockey's voice. Long had been arrested and jailed during civil rights demonstrations in Mississippi the previous summer, one of thousands of Northerners arrested in southern protests in 1963. Now, in the wake of the riot, he convened a six-week study group, meeting Thursday nights, to talk about a book by *Fortune* magazine writer Charles Silberman. Called *Crisis in Black and White,* it traced the history of racism in the northern American cities, said the cities could explode in riots (a few months before they did), and featured, as the best hope for fighting poverty and forestalling turmoil, a community organizer named Saul Alinsky.

Saul Alinsky's organization, the Industrial Arts Foundation, had an unparalleled track record in teaching slum dwellers to improve their own neighborhood conditions, often beginning by winning over the neighborhood's delinquent gangs. In most Alinsky campaigns, a figurehead leader (often Alinsky himself) would berate established leaders in speeches and in newspaper articles. Meanwhile, organizers would fan out into the neighborhoods, ringing doorbells, starting block clubs, and building trust through gatherings in churches and people's homes. They shared information (about which landlords, for instance, were the most negligent), planned tactics (about how to picket the landlords' homes), and provided day-to-day advice on coping with government services or cutting down electric bills. The central idea was to build up the savvy and self-esteem of leaders from the communities themselves. Within a few months of an Alinsky campaign, the "dumb people," with their high school educations, knew how to track down obscure public hearings, show up at those hearings en masse, and ask the expert lawyers and planners whether they'd remembered to get the right approvals for, say, a freeway they wanted to build through a poor neighborhood.

Alinsky himself cultivated flamboyance. The son of a Russian Jewish tailor who had emigrated to Chicago, he had an immediately recognizable warmth, set within an acerbic, brassy bluntness. He cheerfully walked a tightrope between the wealthy patrons whose grants he courted and the impoverished people whom his organizations had to galvanize. Many of his speeches were built around comedy routines. Arguing with the political leaders of a city, Alinsky would compare himself to Moses arguing with God about destroying the Jewish people:

Look, God, you're God. You're holding all the cards. Whatever you want to do, you can do and nobody can stop you. . . . What do you care if people are going to say, "There goes God. You can't believe anything he tells you. You can't make a deal with him. His word isn't even worth the stone it's written on."[12]

Paul Long, the young Presbyterian minister from Rochester, brought five white and three black Rochester church leaders to Alinsky's office in Chicago that November. He had met Alinsky once before, when he spent a summer with a Chicago community organizing group. But to the other Rochester people, Alinsky was a third choice; Martin Luther King's Southern Christian Leadership Conference and Whitney Young's Urban League had turned them down. Alinsky had offers from two other communities, and he put them through a screening. Were they *sure* that they wanted him to get the attention of their smug city leaders? Once he began, he said, life in Rochester would never be the same.

While they thought about it, he made them take him to lunch at an elegant restaurant in Chicago, where the church leaders had trouble flagging their waitress. Alinsky smiled at them. "Do you really want her attention?" he asked. They nodded. "No, listen to what I'm saying," he said. "Do you *really* want her attention?" They assented again. Alinsky took up a plate from the table, held it high for a moment, and smashed it on the floor. The waitress came running, flushed with anger, while the church leaders sat aghast, looking at him. "We got her attention," Alinsky said.

He finally offered to bring his organization to Rochester for two years, for the extraordinary sum of $100,000—up front, with no strings attached. He and the organization would account for it, but they would spend it as they saw fit. Finally, he wouldn't come into the black community, he said, unless churches and organizations *there* invited him, not just their white counterparts. He began to muse about possible tactics to make the Rochester ghetto problems impossible to ignore. They could buy four hundred tickets to the Rochester Symphony for blacks, hold a giant baked-bean dinner just before the event, "and then fart the symphony out of existence. How would that go over in Rochester? Wouldn't people love that?"[13] To make sure the farting incident never happened again, he explained, the city leaders would agree to anything that the churches wanted. People in power would only make the right choices, he said, for the wrong reasons.

Despite their reservations—would he make the community

placid again or would he just incite the violence further?—the church leaders raised the money. To this day, the Reverend Long isn't quite sure what convinced some of the donors, especially since public opposition to Alinsky was mounting fast among Rochester conservatives. Almost immediately upon signing the contract, Alinsky polarized things further, casting himself as a lightning rod of resentment and outrageousness. Reporters quoted him calling the city a "little Congo" and a "huge southern plantation transported North." Privately, he cheerfully admitted that his accusations were unfair. "The one thing that is certain to get your enemy to react," he said, "is to laugh at him."[14] The white establishment wasn't laughing. Alinsky had soon collected many of the most prominent Rochester citizens as his enemies, including many members of the Presbyterian church where Paul Long gave impassioned sermons on Alinsky's behalf on Sundays.

Meanwhile, Alinsky and his organizers moved into the black wards. Their first step was to cultivate black leaders, who were frankly suspicious of him. ("I don't know if you can trust me," Alinsky agreed. "You'd better watch me."[15]) A stocky minister at the Church of Christ named Franklin Delano Roosevelt Florence— a friend of Malcolm X's who had marched in Selma, Alabama, and spoken out against the arrest of Black Muslims in Rochester— emerged as the president of a new organization, which they christened FIGHT, to show that they *expected* battles.[16] (It was an acronym for "Freedom, Integration, God, Honor, Today.") Following Alinsky's methods, FIGHT was set up as a coalition of smaller groups, based in social clubs, churches, pool halls, beauty salons, each with its own leaders—a community equivalent to the self-organizing teams of Topeka and Lima. Florence was a naturally gifted, albeit inflammatory leader, who showed up at most meetings wearing bib overalls and who routinely kept his white supporters waiting two hours or more at appointments. "Why do you put up with that?" Paul Long's friends would ask him. But as he later put it, the encounters were cathartic and exciting: "All of a sudden, a black guy was rubbing our nose in what we'd been rubbing his nose in for three hundred years."

Florence also attacked middle-class blacks, the Urban League, and (foreshadowing the racial crises of the late 1980s) FIGHT's Jewish supporters. In a public argument with a Jewish superintendent of schools, Florence snapped, "That's the trouble with you Jews when you get your color up." In the mini-furor that followed, Alinsky tried to defend him by arguing that Negroes were hostile to *all* whites. Jews were simply more visible in the ghettos.[17] Somehow, the ugliness got smoothed over, but Florence always had to battle against the discomfort that many white citizens of Rochester felt around him.

His hard-liner's attitude served him, however, in the black wards. These were the years of nascent Black Power. To be black and young in the early 1960s was to feel completely, irredeemably, and undeservedly shut out of American opportunity. As the first large-scale coalition to be organized by blacks in Rochester, FIGHT was only credible when it gave voice to that resentment. Thus, white sympathizers were not allowed to join FIGHT—not even the whites who had hired Alinsky, or Alinsky himself. The white churches, Alinsky agreed, were not supposed to be like colonial powers, "sending in missionaries whether they're invited or not."[18] To provide a place for the whites, Florence and the Alinsky co-organizers hurriedly set up an auxiliary called Friends of FIGHT. The Reverend Long was one of its first presidents. Florence took over the central role, and Alinsky stepped a bit into the background, to act as his adviser.

During the next two years, there were no riots. FIGHT's leaders lobbied for, and won, a city-funded public housing corporation, mandated to build housing on undeveloped land. They trained blacks to pass civil service examinations and developed job-training programs with Xerox, the second-largest Rochester company. Despite their inflammatory rhetoric (at their first major meeting, Florence refused to shake any of the Xerox executives' hands), the Xerox people felt that FIGHT's people acted with integrity. FIGHT leaders didn't leak, for instance, any of Xerox's confidential information.[19] And they followed through on their promise to be responsible for the trainees; "to prepare them for the world of work," as Florence said, "getting up on time, making sure they had transportation, following them on Friday to make sure they didn't drink all weekend."[20] While other cities were mired in rioting, FIGHT (and Alinsky) got much of the credit for Rochester's peace.

All along, Alinsky wanted FIGHT to go after Eastman Kodak. The company employed 13 percent of the city's labor force—but its 40,000 employees included only 1,400 blacks. More importantly, Alinsky said, Rochester was under Kodak's thumb. The company was *more* powerful than the government, particularly when you factored in its influence. "If we can get Kodak in line," the Minister Florence preached, "every other business would follow."

Thus, on September 2, 1966, Franklin Florence walked into the company headquarters with fifteen other members of FIGHT and demanded to speak with "the top man." They were taken to meet the three highest officials of the company, including the president, William Vaughn, a tall, patrician man, originally from Tennessee. Florence gave an impromptu speech about the problems of blacks in Rochester's ghetto and asked the Kodak leaders to set up a job-training program for people who couldn't meet the regular Kodak recruitment standards. Vaughn replied that Kodak already had one. But Alinsky and Florence kept returning with new proposals, which they couched as demands.[21] Over an eighteen-month period, Kodak would hire and train between 500 and 600 black people for entry-level positions. FIGHT (as the only mass organization of poor people in the area) would recruit them. Kodak resisted. Alinsky and Florence organized a letter-writing and publicity campaign. Kodak announced an end run—expanding their training programs through another organization, a competitor to FIGHT. Florence was enraged; he and Alinsky stepped up the media pressure.

In principle, Kodak executives agreed that opportunities for blacks should be increased. But they didn't see that this was Kodak's responsibility. Let the blacks pull themselves up, as every ethnic group in America had done, to the point where Kodak would want to hire them. The blacks had rioted; they had destroyed their own neighborhood. Why should a private company like Kodak assume any greater share of their burden? Florence replied that Kodak already had the burden, like it or not, because of its size and influence. FIGHT would not stop the pressure, he insisted. Anyone who looked at both organizations could see that an impasse was inevitable. You could see it in their buildings: "FIGHT's shabby storefront," one writer put it, "versus Kodak's carpeted tower on State Street."[22]

Then, that December, a miracle took place. With startling suddenness, Kodak agreed to hire 600 people referred by FIGHT. The FIGHT trainers agreed, in turn, to provide counseling and support. A joint Kodak-FIGHT committee would nail down "job openings, specifications, and hourly rates"—as well as make announcements to the press. It was a groundbreaking agreement, and a dramatic boost to FIGHT's credibility. It might have made a significant difference to the future of Kodak. But it lasted less than a day.

A heretic within Kodak named John T. Mulder engineered the agreement of December 1966. Like Ed Dulworth of the Gaines dog food plant in Topeka, he was an operations guy—assistant vice president of operations, in charge of the company's largest Rochester plant, which manufactured film. Mulder was a sandy-haired, quiet, good-natured man with thirty years of service to Kodak behind him and a genuine affection for his company. He had a large house on Lake Ontario, one of the first to have a swimming pool. He and his wife, who taught Sunday school at the Third Presbyterian Church, were among the most dedicated, meticulous people that the Reverend Long had ever met.

Mulder was also one of a growing group of people within Kodak who were sympathetic to FIGHT's ideas. He and his wife were veteran settlement house volunteers. His wife was a member of Friends of FIGHT, and the Mulders had both belonged to the discussion group for *Crisis in Black and White*—the group which had been instrumental in contacting Alinsky in the first place. As a longstanding plant manager, Mulder had a visceral sense of the ways in which the company's doors were unofficially closed to black workers. And he had an innate understanding of how race made no difference to an assembly line—particularly one where the workers couldn't even see each other.

One night during the months when FIGHT was waging its publicity campaign against Kodak, Mulder met with a friend who was a FIGHT leader, a reverend named Marvin Chandler. Together they developed a plan, which Mulder drafted and submitted to his superiors. It suggested that, instead of talking with senior leaders, the FIGHT team should negotiate with the operations managers, who were, after all, directly responsible for hiring and training. With a sense of genteel relief (we may imagine), Vaughn agreed. He deputized John Mulder to head the Kodak delegation and authorized him to agree on a program with FIGHT. Mulder and Florence began meeting on December 19 in a room at the Downtowner Motor Inn.

Mulder had a pragmatic, problem solver's mind. When he heard what FIGHT wanted—jobs for a large number of people, with the community organization involved in recruitment—his response was simple: "We can handle that." In fact, the idea sounded like an enlightened operations manager's boon: a chance to open the doors of the plant and learn from FIGHT's community leaders, while they, in turn, gained a hands-on understanding of what Kodak really needed from its workforce. Perhaps they could find a way to convert uneducated people into high-quality Kodak workers en masse. If so, Mulder must have reasoned, then they would have a huge jump on competitors—particularly in those years, when the supply of young workers had begun to dwindle (thanks, in part, to the Vietnam draft). During his meeting with Florence, Mulder kept calling Vaughn's office. Each time he got approval to increase the number of trainees. On the second day, they settled on 600. The number seemed so large that the Reverend Florence repeatedly asked Mulder, "Are you sure you are authorized to sign this?" Mulder insisted that he was.

Around three o'clock that afternoon, a high-level Kodak manager called Dr. Louis Eilers, the incoming Kodak president: "Mulder has signed an agreement with FIGHT." The manager had heard about it on the radio. It had been billed as a great victory for the black organization.

"The hell he has!" Eilers snapped. He sent for Mulder and the agreement and sharply dressed him down. The next day, the executive committee met and repudiated the agreement. They knew it would be awful to renege in public. They believed it would be more awful to let the deal go through.[23] Officially, as William Vaughn related it to *Fortune* later, Mulder had misunderstood his charter. Kodak could not enter into a direct relationship with FIGHT "and still be fair to the more than 60,000 people who apply each year."

Unofficially, there were several problems. Mulder had misunderstood his charter. They had expected him to negotiate some cosmetic settlement, not give away the company's sovereignty. The company's chief counsel, summoned to Eilers' office, had taken one look at the agreement and said, "This is a hiring law. We're involved with the National Labor Relations Board if we agree to this." That would be outrageous, particularly for a nonunion company which had successfully repelled several labor-organizing attempts. It could even open the doors to a fierce battle with organized labor.

Moreover, FIGHT was (in their view) a rabble-rousing group. Its leaders were interested in power, not constructive change. They made inflammatory speeches; they embarrassed and threatened their white supporters, and they could do the same to Kodak at any time. Saul Alinsky admitted as much: "It's only when the other party feels threatened that he will listen," he would say. FIGHT also, in Kodak's eyes, inflated the size of their constituency. (FIGHT claimed, through 110 community groups, to have 75 percent of the black population of Rochester among their membership.[24]) But the Kodak leaders didn't understand that the "power" they feared was grounded in the mass of ghetto residents and nonghetto admirers who gave FIGHT their time and money. Interest groups were still relatively new in the United States, and most people did not yet understand the truth about interest-group power. At any time it could be taken away when members withdrew their membership. Even if there *were* manipulators at the top, the fundamental power rested in the group.

Mulder's friend Marvin Chandler had planned a Christmas party that night, with Franklin Florence as one of the guests. Around ten-thirty, Mulder showed up, pale and distraught, announcing that Kodak was repudiating the agreement. "He looked," Florence said later, "like he'd been in the hands of the KGB." Eilers lost no time making a public statement; the partygoers saw it on the eleven o'clock news. Alinsky was out of town, but his associate Ed Chambers and Florence immediately called a community meeting the next morning, if only to forestall a riot. There, Florence preached to an overflow crowd, excoriating the whites for not backing FIGHT enough. It was getting harder and harder, he said, to convince his ghetto constituents that they had a chance for a better life. Tensions were so high that one white preacher hung himself that afternoon, convinced that the city would go up in flames. But it didn't. Being organized into small groups, people apparently didn't feel the need to riot. Florence met with Kodak's President Eilers three times in the next few days, offering new concessions each time. For the first time, the FIGHT leader agreed not to call their agreement a contract. Or Kodak leaders could dispense with the agreement altogether if they would appear with Florence on television, promising joint cooperation. Florence knew that if he didn't get Kodak to keep their word, his own credibility in black Rochester was in jeopardy. Perhaps Eilers had exactly that in mind when he refused.

Florence took the only course left that would give him political survival. He stiffened. He began to hold public press conferences, calling Kodak "institutionally racist" and saying that the company's dishonesty would produce "troubled times, grave times, for the total community."[25] Eilers, meanwhile, held his own press conferences, where he accused FIGHT of running a continuing war on Rochester's Community Chest and schools. During the next few months, whenever Kodak had a training or recruiting session, FIGHT members were there, protesting.

Publicly, Eilers said there would be no change in John Mulder's job, but within the company Mulder's future was destroyed. He was stripped not just of his negotiating role but of his vice presidency. Then he was moved into a backwater position at Kodak Park. In retrospect, he might have expected the reaction. Another Kodak manager had been stripped of his security clearance simply for standing up in a church and voicing support for Alinsky. But Mulder had such an exemplary record that it took him by surprise; he hadn't known he would be branded as a heretic. He refused to speak to the press and bowed out of the public eye. He would remain at Kodak, a quietly tragic figure, until his retirement. Within a few days, the negotiations ceased.

In mid-January, 1967, Stokely Carmichael arrived in Rochester, threatening a national Black Power boycott of Kodak. Alinsky was impatient with the idea. "You couldn't ask the country to stop taking pictures," he said. But they needed some vehicle to carry the battle further, outside of Rochester. Alinsky toyed with the idea of bringing Kodak up on antitrust charges, and then stumbled across a much better idea: he didn't fully understand its implications, but it clearly had immense possibilities. They would hold a demonstration at Kodak's annual meeting of shareholders.

Kodak's annual meeting was scheduled for April 23, 1967, in a public school auditorium in Flemington, New Jersey, about fifteen miles northwest of Princeton. Like many corporate annual meetings, it would be held in a remote village to discourage casual participation by minority shareholders. FIGHT spent $1,442.65 to buy ten shares, which meant that ten people could enter and raise objections from the floor. But Alinsky had something else in mind. He wanted thousands of protesters to descend on that annual meeting, and he was prepared to use the next two months to lobby with Kodak's existing shareholders, to let some FIGHT member attend in their place and cast their votes for management. "Remember, these are not hippies," he insisted, "but American citizens in the most establishment sense—stockholders! What could be more American than that?"[26]

Protests at annual meetings were rare events, limited to financial matters.[27] But the time was ripe for a shift. Since the early 1950s, the predominant ownership of corporate stock had shifted from investment banks to new types of shareholding institutions.[28] A typical company had 40 percent of its stock owned by pension funds, and pension funds (through bonds) typically controlled 40 percent of most companies' debts.[29] After a stock slowdown in 1966, the pension fund managers began to compare notes on their investments' performance more carefully.

"I don't think anybody really knew," an AT&T pension fund manager named John English recollected years later, "how well or how poorly funds were doing until 1967."[30] But now that they knew, they began to impose more pressure on managers of companies whose shares they held. They demanded meetings with senior officials, wrote letters asking for better share performance, and even made timid threats to vote against the management's proxies—the officially approved candidates for the company's board of directors.[31] Since some of the largest pension funds were for public employees, such as teachers or social workers, their managers often had political backgrounds. These funds, as well as church groups, were attuned to Alinsky's idea: using the power of their position to pressure Kodak, in this case, to reach a settlement with FIGHT.

There was no resolution about the FIGHT dispute before the Kodak shareholders. But that didn't matter. Alinsky embarked on a six-week campaign, calling as many people as he could reach, to get Kodak shareholders to sign their proxy ballots over to FIGHT's name. Within a few weeks, the national representatives of Presbyterians, Episcopalians, the National Church of Christ, and Unitarians all announced publicly (albeit hesitantly) that they were withholding their Kodak stock proxies from management.

Before, the Kodak senior executives had been irritated. Now, they were shocked. William Vaughn and a Kodak in-house lawyer traveled to New York to try to dissuade (without success) two church groups from giving Alinsky their support. At first glance, the Kodak managers' distress seems out of proportion; after all, Alinsky's allies controlled only 40,000 shares out of 80 million—barely half a percent in a real vote.[32] However, the announcement of the proxy fight piqued the curiosity of both news reporters and politicians. New York's Republican senator, Jacob Javits, contacted Kodak with an offer to help mediate, while the Democratic senator, Robert Kennedy, offered to engineer a Senate subcommittee hearing if Alinsky gave the word.[33] Kodak's managers could see themselves hauled before Congress, or permanently pilloried, at least in business circles, as the executives who could not keep their own shareholders under control.

Still, nobody gave in. By early April, Alinsky, Florence, and the FIGHT leaders had organized buses to Flemington from Rochester, New York, and from several universities: Cornell, Dartmouth, Princeton, and Yale. Kodak bused in its own employees, apparently enough to fill the auditorium. On April 23, the night before the meeting, William Vaughn (who had just succeeded Eilers as company president) went down on his knees at the Princeton Inn, where he was staying, and prayed that everything would come out right. ("If Saul Alinsky had only known that he had, so to speak, brought Kodak to its knees," wrote Alinsky's biographer, Sanford Horwitt, "he would have been a very happy man."[34]) Alinsky spent the evening talking to reporters, chortling about the Kodak security guards in his motel: "Kodak's afraid that if somebody knocks me off, they'll get blamed for it." The town braced itself: streets were lined with a hundred state troopers along with local police officers, most of them expecting a riot. Many stores in Flemington were closed.

Seven hundred FIGHT supporters marched to the auditorium the next morning. Ten people, including Alinsky and Florence, were admitted, while a few shareholders in the audience murmured, "Throw the niggers out!" Taking the measure of the room, Alinsky decided that they should make a quick statement and leave. So as soon as Vaughn's gavel hit the podium, Florence stood up and cried for a point of order. "We'll give you until two o'clock to honor that agreement," he shouted, and then walked out with Alinsky, the rest of the FIGHT delegation, and about twenty other sympathetic shareholders.

They remained outside the rest of the day, surrounded by television cameras and demonstrators. Inside, Vaughn gently suggested that "FIGHT deserves credit for putting pressure on us." All of the officers supported by Kodak's management won their ballots. No one within raised a question about the demonstration. At two o'clock, the reverend reentered and asked Vaughn, again, whether he would honor the agreement with FIGHT. Vaughn simply said, "No." Florence marched out, back to the TV cameras, to denounce the company.

The meeting ended with that stalemate intact. When FIGHT's buses and Vaughn's limousines left the village, both sides must have wondered whether they had won or lost. And both sides had reason to wonder. Alinsky's church groups were shaky; they had never used their stock proxies as a political weapon before, and they weren't sure they liked the feeling of confrontation. Kodak's leaders saw summer coming. Franklin Florence warned there would be more protests. A candlelight march on the anniversary of the 1964 riots was planned. Alinsky threatened them with another, better-organized stock proxy battle the following year. When Daniel Patrick Moynihan, then at the Joint Center for Urban Studies at MIT and Harvard, offered to mediate a settlement, both sides jumped at the opportunity. Alinsky and Florence knew they wouldn't get Kodak to agree to a contract. Instead, after a week of secret meetings, Florence accepted a mutual "settlement" (Louis Eilers called it an "understanding") that allowed both sides to begin a long-standing mutual plan.[35]

Within a year, several new job development programs existed in Rochester. None were controlled by FIGHT, but Florence was mollified, because the "understanding" included Kodak guarantees to order parts from a new subcontracting company, which FIGHT could control. They called the company FIGHTON, and located it in an old textile factory in one of the black wards. It made electronic and vacuum-cleaning equipment and took advantage of offers of management advice from Xerox. It was a triumph, and it continues to be solvent today, as the largest minority-owned business in Rochester (although it has undergone a reorganization and a name change to the less inflammatory Eltrex Corporation).

Alinsky's organization moved out of Rochester in 1968; by then

FIGHT didn't need (or want to pay for) his help anymore. Florence remained as the organization's leader; with Stokely Carmichael, he continued to press for national demonstrations against Kodak. As he became more militant, he began to lose the support of local churches. In mid-1967, the Rochester Area Council of Churches, which had supported FIGHT until then, passed a resolution criticizing FIGHT for "intemperance."

The Reverend Long, the man who had first suggested recruiting Alinsky, was pressured to leave the Third Presbyterian Church around that time—its conservative elders could no longer ignore his dual role as pastor and activist. He escaped to a Presbyterian church in Cincinnati. Alinsky, meanwhile, would never organize another ghetto area again. He was captivated by what he called his "Wall Street Wonderland" technique. He told his friends that he had never seen the establishment so uptight. Shareholder activism was a whole new handle with which to get a chief executive's attention. Moreover, it was based on the principle of democracy: one share, one vote. It opened a crack in the facade of the impermeable corporation. And it bred instant notoriety, of the kind he found both useful and exhilarating.[36] He began to spell out these thoughts in speeches and conversation, hoping to spark a new type of social activist movement.

Antiwar organizers in the New Left began to use Saul Alinsky's technique in 1969 and 1970. They showed up at Dow Chemical annual meetings protesting napalm, at United Aircraft of Hartford meetings protesting warplanes, and at the Bank of America annual meetings arguing that the bank should close its Saigon branch. In Minneapolis, Honeywell's chairman shut down the 1970 annual meeting after only fourteen minutes, after demonstrators, who had bought stock to protest the company's weapons production, began to shout *"Sieg heil!"* from the floor.[37]

Even sympathetic executives fiercely resisted these protests, because they did not want to seem to give away any of their power to outsiders. Dow's managers, for instance, had grown weary of the napalm business. The returns weren't worth the aggravation. But

Robert McNamara had publicly praised them. Their senior managers were not going to demonstrate to customers, shareholders, managers (and unions!) that they could be pushovers for a few campus radicals and church groups. If you want to stop the use of napalm against civilians, Dow managers told the press, then stop the government, not us. Meanwhile, they quietly bid high on the next napalm contract and did not squawk when another company's bid was chosen.

The arbitrariness of the protests always seemed peculiar to managers. Certainly, the protesters selected large, visible companies—but why Dow and not Du Pont or American Electric? Why Bank of America and not Chase Manhattan? The truth was, some targets had more mythic power than others. The larger the target, the better, because the provocation for the protest, the death of vernacular values, was so large and ill-defined. In 1970 and 1971, the anti-corporation protests coalesced in a shareholder action against the largest, most mythic target of all: the giant defense contractor and motor vehicle manufacturer, General Motors.

Four young District of Columbia lawyers had decided, late in 1969, to carry Saul Alinsky's shareholder proxy tactics to a national arena. Their names were Philip Moore, Joseph Onek, Geoffrey Cowan, and John Esposito. Three of them had been active in civil rights; one of them, Jeff Cowan, had worked with Alinsky in Rochester. They chose GM not because it was particularly pernicious, but because it was big. You could not live in America and be unaffected by the company. "We want corporate leaders," their first press statement read, "to be accountable to all people affected by corporate decisions." Corporate leaders, they added, "could do more to eliminate job discrimination or air pollution than any U.S. senator." If turning Kodak might mean turning Rochester, then turning GM could turn the entire country.

They started by buying twelve shares of stock in General Motors. They incorporated themselves as the Campaign to Make General Motors Responsible, or Campaign GM for short. At the press conference they held in February 1970, they announced they were introducing nine shareholder resolutions for a vote at GM's annual meeting in May. One was rhetorical: adding language to GM's certificate of incorporation stating that no policy would be "detrimental to the public health, safety, or welfare." Another challenged GM's management control: establishing a shareholders' committee on corporate responsibility, which would make an independent, annual, public report on the company's behavior. Another resolution demanded that GM allot more car dealerships to minority owners; a fourth demanded support for public transportation. Two of the resolutions focused on safety: that all GM vehicles be designed so that a crash at 60 miles per hour would not injure passengers wearing shoulder straps, and that GM offer a five-year warranty on its cars and a lifetime warranty on defective parts.[38] Two other resolutions would commit GM to doing something about air pollution: designing, for example, a pollution-free car over the next five years.

Interestingly, none of the resolutions dealt with the most difficult crisis going on at that moment within the company. At a GM assembly plant in Lordstown, Ohio, outside Akron, some of the younger workers on the line had developed their own team-based style, akin to the sociotechnical systems of the Gaines Topeka plant or Procter & Gamble. Instead of having a manager champion their efforts, they'd simply "doubled up" themselves—working the shift in pairs, covering for each other, and redesigning the layout of their stations. This was a matter of survival: The plant had been recently opened. It was designed as an automated "factory of the future," to produce the Chevrolet Vega, the much ballyhooed GM small car of the moment. But a state-of-the-art factory in 1970 was a brutal place to work. Jobs had been divided, for efficiency's sake, into the smallest possible units. In some cases, workers were driven to handle two cars a minute on jobs so depressingly simple and numbing that they were literally beyond human endurance. Meanwhile, supervisors tracked every detail of their performance, particularly speed. The workers had a choice: redesign the work themselves or take out their frustration in sabotage and absenteeism.[39]

When General Motors cracked down on "doubling up" in 1970, and the national United Auto Workers refused to defend the workers, the plant had entered a state of siege. The local assemblers had initiated one of the worst strikes of the decade. It was a strike staged almost entirely by young workers in their twenties.[40] But the Campaign GM organizers had not heard of Lordstown or the problems involved in introducing state-of-the-art assembly-line technology that ignored the people on the line.

A final resolution expanded GM's board of directors by three members. The purpose of this resolution, which made no mention of the public interest, was to allow Campaign GM to nominate three symbolic people for election to GM's board if the resolution passed. They knew it probably wouldn't pass, but they chose their nominees carefully: a world-renowned environmentalist and author named René Dubos, a black minister and politician named Channing Phillips, and Betty Furness, who had been New York City's consumer adviser. The lawyers formally asked GM to include their resolutions in the shareholders' proxy mailing. Finally, as a stake in the ground, they also invited GM's most visible public enemy, Ralph Nader, to join them before the press. Nader wasn't directly involved in Campaign GM, except as an occasional spokesman, but he became the most prominent figure of the campaign. The organizers spent the next two years in his shadow.

General Motors had made Ralph Nader famous, in the same way that the popes had made the success of Martin Luther inevitable.[41] By fighting him antagonistically, and trying to discredit him before they understood his criticisms, they had boosted his credibility at the expense of their own. Even Ford's outspoken CEO, Henry Ford II, understood that. "If this industry of ours had been on its feet instead of its ass," he said scornfully, "Nader would never have surfaced."[42]

In the early 1960s, after graduating from law school and a few years of law practice, Nader had drifted into a career as a freelance writer/researcher on auto safety. Already he was an anomaly in leftist circles: a crusader against corporations, yet a man who seemed to have no feel for labor issues. ("He is a believer in the marketplace," an associate of his said years later, "not in some worker-run socialist state. But he believes that the marketplace is so totally skewed away from consumers that it requires some rather radical government intervention.") In other words, Nader had seen something that Alinsky hadn't seen—that corporations weren't delivering what they had implicitly promised, even to their own constituents. They were supposed to deliver good products, high quality of life, and concern for the safety and well-being of their customers. Instead, the top managers seemed to think of their customers as serfs, and the biggest feudal-minded lords were the leaders of the auto industry.

Nader worked as a behind-the-scenes technical adviser to Abraham Ribicoff, the Democratic senator from Connecticut, when Ribicoff questioned GM's CEO, James Roche, about the company's investments in traffic safety. Then, in 1964, Nader published a book called *Unsafe at Any Speed,* about the hazardous Chevrolet Corvair, a small GM car with its engine mounted in the rear. The book accused GM of deliberately shortchanging the car's safety; instead of padded dashboards, shoulder belts, and collapsible steering wheel columns, the company had spent its research money on flaring tail fins, a faux-Porsche design, and "creative obsolescence"[43]—the cavalier, almost deliberate policy of making the cars more shoddy than they had to be, because quality cost money.

GM's managers literally couldn't imagine that someone like Nader existed. So they hired a private detective, who in turn devised some startlingly clumsy efforts at entrapment.[44] Young women walked up to Ralph Nader in stores and tried to lure him back to their apartments. (He stiffly walked away.) People who said they were prospective employers called his old acquaintances, asking if he was homosexual or had a drinking problem.[45] Ultimately, they figured that he had to be a shill for ambulance-chasing liability lawyers (an accusation that would dog Nader throughout his career).

Nader sued GM for harassment the following year. He also brought the matter back to Ribicoff's attention. On March 22, 1966, the Senate subcommittee on government functions, which Ribicoff chaired, subpoenaed James Roche again. The tall, reticent chairman, whose voice rarely rose above a whisper and who looked like an absentminded college professor, was forced to admit that his company had hired the detectives (though without the knowledge of top management, he claimed, and without any of the sexual entrapment attempts). Roche then took the unprecedented step of apologizing to Nader before television cameras at the hearing. It was the most ignominious moment for a large American company since General Electric and Westinghouse executives had been called before Congress during a price-fixing scandal several years before.

Now, Nader was broadening his inquiries to corporate practice in all arenas. He never expected corporations to become ethical through their own volition. He thought them incapable of self-control. Instead, he said government should keep watch over companies, and be the source of their accountability—and the consumer movement, of which he was now a leader, would be the watchdog over government.

Throughout his career, Nader would rely on a network of whistle-blowers within companies for much of his corporate data. But he did not convert many executives. Businesspeople didn't understand him, nor he them. He shared none of their appetites or needs. To people who worked for companies, who wanted to know how they could improve the corporate product, he offered only one implicit answer: "Leave the company, blow the whistle, and devote your life to public service."

It was easy for Nader. He had no children (let alone children in college), no mortgage, and no love for creature comforts. He maintained the austere life of a perpetual graduate student, in a small apartment, wearing cheap suits as a badge of pride or, more likely, disinterest. His social life revolved around work; he was so intensely shy with strangers, in any case, that he came off, at first, as brusque. Only after aides knew him a while did he reveal his natural, almost childlike warmth. All of this made him insensitive to the burden of keeping profits high; insensitive to the seduction of perks and salaries. (The failed investigators who had worked for GM back in 1966 had tried unsuccessfully to find some personal weakness of Nader's that they could exploit.)

In Detroit, engineers ended up mistrusting Nader, which was a shame, because many of them had originally looked on him as a potential savior. He was making some of the same points about auto safety that they had tried, and failed, to foist up the chain of command. For instance, the Corvairs had been produced over the objections of a number of senior GM engineers; the dissenters had been told to "get on the team or find someplace else to work." To them, Nader's critiques missed some of the Corvair's worst defects: its tendency to snap in two when hit in the side (this had killed the comedian Ernie Kovacs) and its shoddy engine blocks that slowly disintegrated under fast driving conditions. (One Ford engineer, driving behind a Corvair on a freeway, saw its engine pop out of the bottom of the car, strike the pavement, and explode.)

Even when Nader included these points in his criticisms, he got the technical nuances wrong—an inevitable mistake, perhaps, because of his own visceral dislike for automobiles. He was hypersensitive to the fragility of those hurtling metal boxes, and the engineers could tell. Anyone who "came out of the closet" at Ford or GM and said something like "You know, this guy Nader has a point" would be immediately hooted at by the other car guys. "Gee," the head engineer of that function might say, "I thought you knew more about cars than to agree with that asshole."

Worse still, from the point of view of the managers in the companies he fought, Nader didn't play the game of confrontation fairly. Instead of trying to negotiate directly with GM, he leaked his criticisms to the press. Saul Alinsky admired him for this; in Alinsky's eyes, Nader knew how to go for the jugular. But managers felt about him the way they felt about the industry reporters from local newspapers, who always got key business details wrong because they hadn't worked inside for twenty years.

Nader, for instance, didn't seem to know that Detroit had already *tried* safety. In the early 1950s, Ford designers had put out a line of cars with a range of super-safe features. The cars had bombed. Detroit managers had concluded that Americans didn't want safe cars; they wanted styling. As a result, as the management writer Peter Drucker wrote in 1967, "the automobile manufacturers bitterly resent as rank ingratitude that they are being blamed for unsafe cars, subjected to punitive legislation, and held up for public scorn."

And yet, Drucker had written, nobody should feel sorry for managers of large firms like GM:

> They are indeed not to blame for unsafe cars [or] polluted air in the sense that they caused it. Theirs is a greater blame: They have not lived up to the demands of leadership. It is the task of the leader to anticipate . . . to find the right way and to lead the crowd.[46]

Originally, the Campaign GM organizers had planned to run Ralph Nader for the company's board of directors. An enormous and gripping public relations carnival would have ensued if they'd gone through with it, and Nader flirted with the idea for several months before declining.[47] He was still enmeshed in his invasion-of-privacy lawsuit against GM (he was now claiming damages of $17 million), but he did not decline for legal reasons. Years later, he told a social investing historian that he saw the whole shareholder election process as rigged; after all, management controlled large blocks of institutional shares, and support for the management position was too entrenched to shift. He didn't want to invest that much of himself in a symbolic effort, where the dissent level would be "not much larger than a Kremlin-style election."[48] But he threw his support behind the Campaign. So did Alinsky, who praised it to his colleagues and who introduced Nader to one of his own benefactors: Gordon Sherman, the liberal Chicagoan who had inherited ownership of the Midas Muffler company and made himself president.

Other notables joined the Campaign GM effort. The antiwar activist and Nobel Prize–winning biologist George Wald made speeches on its behalf; so did a housewife and self-taught economics gadfly named Hazel Henderson, who ran a group called Citizens for Clean Air from her New York City kitchen table. So did Robert Townsend, the former president of the Avis car-rental company and author of the best-selling business book *Up the Organization,* an antibureaucracy screed in which he recommended that every manager do his own secretarial work. Townsend argued that Roche should cut GM's advertising budget from $240 million per year to $40 million and spend that on one message about what they would do with the savings: "General Motors is going to spend four hundred million dollars in two years to wipe out pollution."[49]

The young lawyers used a Securities and Exchange Commission ruling to force GM to include two of their resolutions in its mailing to all shareholders. The actual mailing, of course, mattered less to the Campaign GM strategists than the press coverage they got when they announced that GM would include their proxy forms. Then they set about trying to mobilize church and student support groups, hoping that these would, in turn, influence big institutional and pension fund trustees to turn their proxies over to the Campaign. At MIT these efforts led the school to hold a debate between Joe Onek, one of the Campaign's organizers, and a senior GM official. The official happened to be the treasurer—a shy, bespectacled finance man named Roger B. Smith. Onek was a better debater, but the MIT trustees voted their proxies to GM management anyway. Nonetheless, Campaign GM did get proxy support from Amherst, Antioch, Tufts, Boston University, and Iowa State; and from pension funds in San Francisco, Iowa, Wisconsin, and New York City.[50]

In May, three thousand people showed up at the GM annual meeting in Detroit's Cobo Hall. Roche presided over its full six and a half hours. This happened to come in the midst of the company's most turbulent year since World War II. First quarter earnings per share were down; they'd fallen from $1.82 to $1.21. The stock price had fallen to the lowest point since 1963. The president of the United Auto Workers, Walter Reuther, had died in a plane crash just a few days before—which threatened the company's stable relationship with the UAW. Coincidentally, the UAW was poised to strike over cost-of-living wage increases, which—even if the union lost its demands—would cost the company twenty-six cents more per person/hour.

If Roche felt extra pressure, he didn't show it. Instead, he lifted his gavel at 2 P.M. to begin, and continued stolidly and even-temperedly through an afternoon of nominations, motions, countermotions, and impromptu speeches about General Motors' air pollution and racial hiring policies. His voice hardly rose above its customary whisper, even when a black UCLA law student named Barbara Williams confronted him: "You have failed not only the shareholders but the country. Why are there no blacks and women on the board?"

To many observers, the most irritating comments came not from the Campaign GM protesters, but from their opposition—longtime, eccentric gadfly shareholders who had been protesting for years that GM's managers wasted their money. One of them wore a black bathing suit and a sash reading "Miss Air Pollution." Another made rambling speeches about (for instance) how GM's "splendid" cars would be involved in fewer accidents if only Ralph Nader's followers would stop taking drugs.

To all these disparate curmudgeons, James Roche responded courteously. (The New Yorker called him "gallantry personified.") The Campaign GM people were equally polite. Donald Schwartz, the Campaign GM counsel, gave the organization's closing statement for the day. He finished by saying, "Mr. Roche, we look forward to seeing you next year."

By the standards of corporate social responsibility efforts, Campaign GM was a remarkable success. It produced results. Within the next three months, General Motors had put into effect several new policies intended, in one way or another, to satisfy Campaign GM's concerns. The company instituted a public policy committee, delegating five of their existing board members to make a report to shareholders. They added a post of vice president of environmental matters, and hired a University of California professor named Ernest Starkman, whose specialization was air pollution, to fill the post. They also formed a committee of scientists to study the environmental effects of GM cars. All of this, ultimately, was window dressing; none of it had much effect on the practices of the corporation.

But a final response was more significant. GM added a slot on the board and filled it with the Reverend Leon Sullivan. Sullivan was a black minister from Philadelphia and an outspoken civil rights activist; he had co-founded a black-owned aerospace parts manufacturing company in Philadelphia and pressured other Philadelphia companies to adopt open employment policies.[51] Like Rochester's Franklin Florence, he was skeptical of managers' motives, although he was somewhat less confrontational. When he accepted the job, he explicitly told Roche that he wouldn't be tied down to a traditional board role. "I'm more interested in human terms than capital terms. My main concern is helping to improve the position of black people in America. I want to be a voice from the outside on the inside."

At that time, few people in corporate circles knew much about Sullivan, but he would become one of the key figures of corporate change during the 1970s and 1980s. He made his presence known publicly the following year, at the 1971 annual meeting, when Campaign GM returned with three new shareholder resolutions. This time, although they'd done much more legwork and gotten more proxies dedicated to them up front, they ended up with far fewer votes. Apparently, in its shareholders' eyes GM had already done enough to change. But alongside Campaign GM, the U.S. Episcopal Church filed a proxy resolution of its own: that General Motors should shut down its manufacturing facilities in the apartheid-dominated country of South Africa.

The resolution was voted down, but not before Leon Sullivan asked for the floor. He made a dramatic speech about U.S. corporations in South Africa, how they had essentially underwritten the continuing presence of apartheid there. "American industry can't morally continue to do business," he said, "in a country that so blatantly, ruthlessly, and clearly maintains such dehumanizing practices against such large numbers of people."[52] It was the first time a GM director had ever spoken out against the board's position at an annual meeting.

* * *

The person angriest about Campaign GM, at least to judge by the tone of his prose, was not associated with General Motors at all. He was the economist and writer Milton Friedman. Unlike most economists, Friedman was a well-known figure, mainly because of the clearly written, acerbic columns that he had written for *Newsweek* since 1966. His bespectacled, smiling face appeared every three weeks above a page of text in the magazine.[53]

One of the most famous articles of his career appeared in *The New York Times Magazine* in the fall of 1970. It was titled "The Social Responsibility of Business Is to Increase Its Profits,"[54] and in case readers missed its topical significance, the editors illustrated it with photographs of Jim Roche, faced off against the Campaign GM leaders at GM's annual meeting. Corporations could only hurt society, Friedman argued in the text, if they tried to tackle social problems. Executives were too "short-sighted and muddle-headed" about matters outside their own business purview; what if their well-intentioned efforts went wrong? Specifically, Friedman was fuming about wage and price controls that Nixon had not yet put into effect but which a number of large American corporations were lobbying the President to adopt. But he had a point. Some very public but halfhearted efforts toward training minorities for jobs had arguably made things *worse* in cities like Detroit. They raised expectations, failed to meet them, and then claimed (through the numbers) that they *had* met them, making managers and trainees more cynical about further job efforts down the pike. Even the best-designed effort was now more likely to fail, because it would exist in an environment where people didn't believe in it.

Even if a social program effectively created jobs or curbed pollution, Friedman said, it constituted fraud. Executives on company time were the agents of shareholders. Shareholders, by definition, had only one goal: higher value for their stock. That could come only from higher profits. Those who wanted to make a social contribution should act through individual charities, or through their vote—not by trying to sneak past the fact that most Americans were not interested in social goals, he said. In that context, he wrote, corporate social responsibility was an unseen tax without representation—the exact form of tyranny that had prodded America into revolution almost two hundred years before. And the message to managers, in effect, was simple: "Forget about institutional social responsibility, just make profits. If your conscience troubles you, give more to charities yourself." And there the debate sat, thoroughly missing the point that John Mulder had seen: an effective program, working with social forces, would serve shareholders by making the corporation thrive in the long run.

Ever since the 1960s, a small group of heretics have struggled to maintain the movement for corporate social responsibility. They haven't succeeded, but in the process they've opened up a debate over corporate governance that is still being argued today.

They began, once again, with Saul Alinsky. In 1971, Alinsky finished writing a book of tactics for community organizers called *Rules for Radicals*. He had been working on it, on and off between campaigns, for ten years. It was, as befit its author, a cheerful, flamboyant book. Alinsky had been buoyed by the success of Campaign GM, whose progress he had followed closely. The FIGHT campaign against Kodak had convinced him that the future of organizing lay with the middle class. In addition, as his biographer Sanford Horwitt notes, Alinsky had nowhere else to go. With the rise of Black Power, there was no place for him, or any other white organizer, in black ghettos.[55]

But consider the opportunities for making a difference! The lower middle class, wrote Alinsky, felt threatened from all sides; their future pressed by inflation, their jobs threatened by cutbacks (and competition from the black labor force), their daily life victimized by interest on installment payments and misinformation about their choices in advertising. They were potential fodder for demagogues—unless smart, rebellious organizers could find a way to reach them. The upper middle class, better educated and more secure in their employment, thought that they only needed "a split-level house in the suburbs, two cars, two color TVs, country club membership, a bank account, children in good prep schools and then in college, and they had it made. They got it—only to discover that they didn't have it." He exhorted the activists reading his book to "return to the suburban scene of your middle class with its variety of organizations from PTAs to League of Women Voters . . ." Find areas of common agreement, he told them. Excite their imaginations. Introduce drama and adventure into their lives. Pitch major battles around the quality and prices of consumer goods.

And then there were opportunities within corporations themselves: "The corporations must forget their nonsense about 'private sectors.' Every American individual or corporation is public as well as private; public in that we are Americans and concerned about our national welfare. We have a double commitment and corporations had better recognize this for the sake of their own survival." Organizing executives around this principle, Alinsky suggested, would give them "a reason for what they are doing—a chance for a meaningful life."

To show how citizens could apply outside pressure in the meantime, Alinsky sketched out some ideas for brash, large-scale proxy campaigns: Instead of a few thousand shareholders, bring 50,000 to a town like Flemington, New Jersey. Force corporations to ask for the National Guard to control their own shareholders! Or force them to hold their meetings in venues like Yankee Stadium! Set up computerized operations to coordinate study groups on corporate policies, so people could learn which corporations were worth investing in and which corporations needed to be pressured. He wrote that he expected to be with this campaign "full time, for its launching and its setting out to sea."[56]

Alinsky didn't live to see it happen. About nine months after his book was published, he died of a sudden heart attack. He had been a key figure, though he probably never knew it, in three separate aspects of the movement to improve corporations. First, the corporate social responsibility movement still had years of life in it. There were managers within firms who believed that a policy of, for instance, training the uneducated did more than simply serve a political or social agenda. It served the company's own economic interest. This wasn't because social policies would attract customers.

Very few customers, it turns out, buy products because of what a company does or does not do. (Very few people stopped buying Dow's Saran Wrap because of napalm.) But when a company started thinking seriously about social responsibility, people all through the organization seem to wake up. Suddenly they have to pay attention to the organization's purpose. It would take another fifteen years for this fact to bear fruit—in the form of corporate environmentalism.

Second, Alinsky had sketched out the basic ideas behind the social investing movement. Fueled by church investment groups, it would gather steam during the 1970s. By the mid-1980s, proxy battles—modeled, in part, on Campaign GM, with Louis Sullivan as one of the most significant participants—would be a major component of the fight to keep multinationals out of South Africa and to push for better environmental policies.

Most powerful of all, however, was Alinsky's third legacy to corporations. This showed up only in the hearts of a few people who had seen him at work, or heard about the way he worked, or worked with people who worked with him. Community organizers like Alinsky and his confederates knew how to work with the vernacular, and they did so in dozens of settings—not just in urban neighborhoods but with (for example) the United Farm Workers, during the grape boycott campaigns led by Cesar Chavez. Community organizers brought skills and tactics to the campaigns. They coordinated theatrical performances that dramatized people's aspirations and anger. ("At Friday night meetings," recalls a community organizer who worked with Chavez, "the grandparents, parents and children would watch with rapt attention as El Teatro, with only masks, small placards, a pair of sunglasses, a crude picket sign, or a red bandanna, served as midwives to the birth of hope . . ."[57]) They ran group conversations, specifically designed to bridge gaps between ethnic groups that had traditionally mistrusted each other. They made a point of publicly honoring people's contributions. And they set up community suppers, sometimes over meals as simple as beans, where people could contribute just by bringing food, even if they didn't talk.[58]

All of these skills would be remarkably useful for the heretics within corporations who were bold enough to use them. Suppose, for example, that you are one of the few people at your company who understands a piece of its potential to exalt the world. Suppose you see a way to serve the people, inside and outside the company, and have some fun and make some profit in the process. Chances are, there are few venues inside the firm where you can mention your idea without being shunned or made irrelevant. But consider the effect you would have if you felt charged with a mission and you could summon up Alinsky's verve, acumen, care for people, and willingness to dance on the edge of tolerance.

You could bring people together over impromptu meals. You could convene study groups to teach each other the ins and outs of bureaucratic regulations. You could challenge authorities within the company by publicly holding them accountable for the promises they have made. You could find a way to talk to the William Vaughns and James Roches of the world, to make them see themselves more clearly. You could, from time to time, drop plates of food on the floor. If you found a way to survive and if your attitude was openhearted, you might become the most valuable member that the organization ever had.

YSTICS

"THE FUTURE CANNOT BE PREDICTED; IT CAN ONLY BE SEEN":
ROYAL DUTCH/SHELL'S SCENARIO PLANNERS, 1967–73

To be a mystic in fourteenth-century Europe was to be more devout than the faithful. You would embrace ritual and ceremony with a fierce, scrupulous, almost unworldly joy. But your goal would not be devotion or sacrament. You would seek, above all, awareness. You would want to see more deeply into the world; more thoroughly into reality. In that time, this meant learning to see God directly, finding your way to the direct divine presence.

The journey would begin with the control and suppression of worldly desires. Through meditation, prayer, and strict observance, you would cultivate the spiritual self. After going as far as possible on your own, it was said, you might reach a point, like a stopping place on a journey, where you could pause and wait, alone. Then God would come and lift you the rest of the way.

Eventually, you would have to return from the meditative journey, with a travel-weariness that would inevitably be perceived as smugness. You would present yourself to the local abbot and villagers—to tell them about what they too could see if only they found the discipline to look past the blinders of their daily thoughts. As a mystic, you would have the desire—what human coming down from your journey would not have it?—to see your own new comprehension of reality ripple out into the community around you. People needed that comprehension, you would know, to live more effectively. If only you could find the words to describe it . . .

It is said that mystics never find the words. And yet communities ardently remember the mystics who live within them. Ordinary people, nontravelers, have changed their lives, then as now, because of what a mystic said to them. Some ability to see more clearly, it turns out, can be drawn from within an attentive listener by an experienced traveler if the conditions are right and external forces are propitious.

The church establishment did not admire the mystics, who made them appear weak or irresolute. But they recognized that they needed them. The mystics, for their part, had to be careful not to undermine the church. It sheltered them and made their journeys possible. For centuries, the priests and the mystics lived in this uneasy truce.[1]

▼▼▼

On the south bank of the Thames, just across the river from the tower of Westminster Abbey, stands the tower of Shell Centre: a twenty-four-story, boxy-windowed, sand-colored skyscraper. When it opened in 1963, Queen Elizabeth dedicated it,[2] while Prince Philip remarked privately that it looked like a Chinese flophouse. Tourists sometimes idly wonder which country has positioned its embassy so prominently near the Houses of Parliament—until the flags on the roof unfurl in the snapping wind and reveal the symbol of the Royal Dutch/Shell Group of Companies, a yellow stylized scallop, outlined in a frame of red.

In 1964, one of the senior directors of Standard Oil of New Jersey—Shell's greatest and oldest competitor—visited Shell Centre. Sometime during the visit, he casually asked, "What is Shell doing about the long-term future?" A few years before, he added, Standard had put together a long-range planning group to consider the Far East. Their investments in marketing to Japan and Korea were beginning to pay off, and their futures group was working on a twenty-five-year plan.[3]

The executives of Standard Oil of New Jersey and Shell probably never talked to each other again about the future. Twenty-four years later, in 1988—after Jersey's name had changed to Exxon; after the once-stable price of oil had ricocheted through shocking gains and losses; after several giant oil companies had disappeared, and Exxon itself had endured the worst round of layoffs in its history; and a few months before Exxon's Valdez oil spill would become an international symbol of negligence and corporate arrogance—an Exxon manager would hear about that now-legendary plan and ask to see it. When it was finally unearthed, the Exxon manager would discover that it said very little, except: "We will meet every eventuality." This was the blind confidence with which companies like Jersey greeted the future, back in 1964.

Shell managers, however, could not afford that blind confidence, and some of them knew it back then. At that time, Shell was the weakest of the "Seven Sisters"—the major oil companies that dominated the international petroleum business.[4] (Forbes had called it the "ugly sister."[5]) Shell had neither the huge reserves nor the exclusive relationships with Arab nations that other major oil companies enjoyed. Its traders had to be more canny than the competition, because Shell bought more oil than it drilled. Thus, the Jersey man's casual remark lingered with one or two members of Shell's Committee of Managing Directors (which was, in effect, a chief executive committee for the Shell Group). They decided that Shell should have its own in-house studies on the long-term future.

One of those studies was assigned to a manager named Ted Newland. He was newly assigned to the international Group's planning department, recently transferred from Nigeria, where he had been the administration manager—in effect, the de facto mayor of the compound where 500 expatriate families lived near a Shell tanker station. Now, back in London, Newland found himself given a couple of assistants, a tiny budget, and the task of "looking at the long-term future." Unofficially, and unexpectedly, he had been assigned to the only job in the world that he could ever excel at and love. It was the job of pundit.

At that time, most large companies, particularly in the oil business, employed large forecasting departments to help their managers make day-to-day decisions. The very name of Shell's forecasting technique, the Unified Planning Machinery, reflected confidence in its mechanistic process. Under the UPM system, Shell's managers around the world fed in estimates of the next year's sales and costs, based on the performance of the previous year. Then armies of analysts in the planning department, armed with calculators and ledger pads (for spreadsheets had not yet been invented), reshaped the estimates into intricate predictions of the expected price of crude oil and the growth of demand for new oil. With that data, or so it was believed, Shell executives could plan their next moves—how much to invest in a refinery or a tanker, or how much to bid when they traded. If a contrarian like Newland tried to talk about any of the long-term issues that gave the figures meaning, the operating managers would typically cut him off: "I don't need to know that. Just give me the price."

The price, as it happened, was stable in those years. It had hovered (wholesale) around $2 per barrel since World War II—longer than most Shell executives' careers. (A barrel was 42 U.S. gallons, or about two tankfuls of gas in, say, a 1968 Buick.) As for the worldwide demand for oil, it rose steadily but surely. When plotted on paper, it produced a graph of easy growth, always a little bit better than the planners anticipated. At Shell, they called this the "horse's tail" graph, because it arced up like the tail of a cantering horse, from the past to the optimistic future.[6]

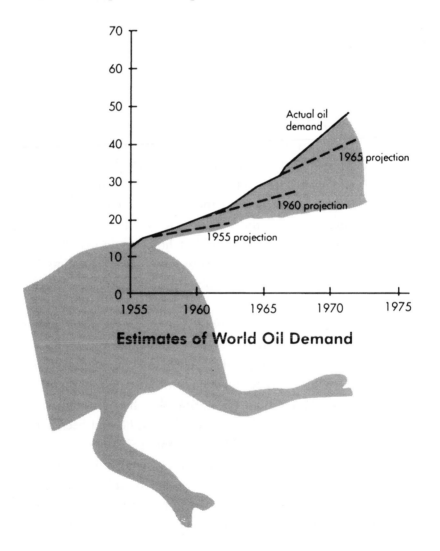

Estimates of World Oil Demand

The smoothness of the graphed lines did not mean the flow of oil was stable. The source of most petroleum, the Middle East, had staggered for decades from one volatile political squabble to another. But none of the squabbles ever disrupted the oil supply for long. A peculiar structure of checks and balances had evolved out of World War II, composed of rivalries, treaties, arrangements, and alliances among oil companies, countries with large oil fields (Saudi Arabia, Iraq, Iran, Kuwait, Libya, and Venezuela), and major industrial powers (the United States, the Soviet Union, Britain, Japan, and Europe). The system was like a giant, invisible, global-sized apparatus of pipes and pumps, controlled by the largest oil companies (the Seven Sisters). When pressure built up in one part of the system (as in 1967 when the Saudis cut world oil supplies to protest Israel's victory in the Six-Day War), the Seven Sisters could relieve the pressure by turning a valve somewhere else (in that case, boosting production in Iran, Venezuela, and Texas).

By the late 1960s, the leaders of most oil companies and nearly all the governments of the industrialized West behaved as if this machine could go on forever.[7] The Unified Planning Machinery forecasts concurred, almost as if they were specifically designed to tell oil managers around the world exactly what they wanted to hear. It was just one more example of how a numbers-based system, even when derived from a powerful way of looking at the world, would sooner or later devolve into meaningless, dangerous ritual.

Ted Newland was one of several people in the Shell planning department who suspected, as early as 1967, that the stable petroleum system was *not* going to last. UPM was hurting. A tall and reedy man, Newland was Anglo-Argentine by origin and still spent vacations on an Argentinian plantation that he had inherited. He had never earned a university degree; instead, he had been a Royal Air Force pilot in World War II before joining Shell in Venezuela. In Nigeria, he had been known for his iconoclastic style: he had integrated Shell's private hospital and made its subsidized housing available, for the first time, to locally born managers. He was also cheerfully pessimistic about human nature. During a 1964 strike, when a mob of Nigerians gathered nearby, Newland suggested turning an unfinished canal into a moat around the compound. The rioters, someone replied, would simply swim across. "Well," said Newland, "we can always put crocodiles in."

He was now going to have an opportunity, at corporate expense, to explore Shell's environment with unprecedented depth and sensibility. He wouldn't do it alone. He would be part of a team of people. Like mystics, they would devote themselves to developing a new method for seeing the patterns around them more clearly. Like mystics, they would then have to communicate what they had seen, in a way that would make the rest of the managers pay attention. If not, the corporation could face debilitating losses. Some Shell veterans still believe today that the survival of the enterprise depended, in those years of crisis, on its ability to cultivate its mystics.

Unlike other oil companies, Royal Dutch/Shell belongs to no nation in particular. Its London headquarters are to England (or, some British politicians might say, *aspire* to be to England) what the United Nations building is to New York or the Vatican to Italy: a neutral zone, its fate intertwined with all the world. Though Shell men come from every continent and background, they all seem to be imbued with the same understated, pragmatic intellectualism. (They also tend to be men; Shell's culture quietly resists giving responsibility to women.) You would not find them taking target practice from their hot tubs on weekends, like the oil cowboys of Larry McMurtry's *Texasville*. Instead, they cultivate orchids and lead chamber music ensembles. One managing director, during the years of his tenure, published well-received histories of Nigeria and Turkey.

To outsiders, Shell seems uncommonly close-knit and insular. An observer of several meetings between the British government and oil company representatives during the 1970s noticed that men from Exxon, Texaco, BP, and Gulf tended to blurt out angry reactions on the spot. The Shell man would wait quietly, watchful and attentive, his position prepared. He would have talked over Shell's stance several times that week with colleagues back at the office. If he had to denounce someone or block a plan, he struck "not with a bludgeon, but with a rapier," the observer recalled. Shell men were like representatives of a secret service, he had decided—not people to oppose lightly.

Most oil companies (such as Exxon) are strict hierarchies, run from the top man's hip pocket. But at Shell there is no hip pocket. Instead, more than 270 separate firms (called "operating companies") exist as sovereign entities, most centered in a particular country, each making its own decisions about (for instance) where to buy oil or how to set up a gas station franchise. The central operations, based in The Hague (in a building that looks like a palace) and London (in the embassy-like Shell Centre), are often described by Shell managers as mere service providers, sources of such amenities as technical research, trading coordination, and the Shell gasoline brand name.

Yet London and The Hague, these ostensible "service providers," are still the only places from which a voice can speak for Shell with worldwide authority. An investor can't buy stock in Dänske Shell or Shell du Laos, or even in the holding companies that own them, but only in *their* owners, the Royal Dutch and Shell Transport and Trading companies at the top. As a result of this peculiar structure, authority at Shell comes not just from the top but from all directions; it filters through the management by means of a kind of gravitational force, partly collegial, partly rigidly hierarchical, and partly based on the fact that sooner or later, if you work there, you will work at enough far-flung operating companies to become loyal to the Group of companies as a whole, and a citizen of the world.[8]

At its birth, this most collective of firms was dominated by two of the most individualist businessmen of the late nineteenth century. Marcus Samuel was the son of a London-based Jewish importer of fashionable boxes made of seashells. He converted his father's company into Shell Transport and Trading, an oil-importing firm. Henri Deterding, an energetic financial prodigy from the Netherlands with a remarkable gift for mental mathematics and another gift for strategy, was president of the Royal Dutch Company, which imported kerosene from Sumatra. Deterding formed an alliance with the Rothschild family, the famous Jewish financiers of France and England; then, in 1907, he went face to face with Samuel, jockeying over the terms of a merger between their firms.[9] When the dust cleared, 60 percent of the new combined stock went to Royal Dutch shareholders, and Deterding won the post of managing director. Samuel gained a fortune and spent the rest of his life as Lord Bearsted, a newly entered member of the British aristocracy.

In the 1920s and 1930s, Deterding evolved from a fervent anti-Communist into a fervent Nazi supporter. It was an ironic stance for a man whose most prominent partners had been Jewish financiers and a Jewish trader. Fortunately for the Allies, and for the company, Deterding retired (or was eased out of the firm) before World War II started. His controlling shares passed to other directors (which meant the Nazis could not use them to take control of Shell's oil business). When he died in Germany in 1939, Hitler and Göring sent wreaths to his funeral.

Having learned the perils of entrusting power to one man, Shell's managers after Deterding established a tradition of rule by committee. The new Committee of Managing Directors (or CMD) was put in charge of the company, with a membership that varied over the years from four to eight people. The committee never voted on major issues; when there was a disagreement, they tried to come to a consensus on it, and if the disagreement persisted, they did not proceed. Other Shell teams imitated that style; the result was a culture in which Shell managers sometimes had to work by consensus, sometimes to obey orders, and sometimes to act alone. Other companies would have given managers a thick handbook of regulations for sorting through the resulting conflicts; at Shell, they followed unwritten rituals and unspoken hints, which they had learned to understand either at Cambridge and Oxford (where many of the British had gone to university) or in the equally close-knit Dutch university cultures of Delft and Leyden. (It has been called a company of "Scottish accountants and Delft engineers.")

Governed by a centralized bureaucracy, Shell's management ossified after World War II. In one celebrated case, Gerrit Wagner, the president of Shell Venezuela, had to fly to The Hague to argue for building a new storage tank. The CMD members irritatedly heard the arguments over this dispute, which seemed far too local to require their attention. They granted Wagner his storage tank, but they had realized by then that they needed an organizational equivalent of spring cleaning.

Thus in 1957, around the time Shell laid the cornerstone for its tower on the Thames, McKinsey & Company was hired to study Shell's corporate structure. The scale of Shell's problem was so huge that McKinsey took more than a year to research and write their report.[10] McKinsey's young MBAs shrewdly picked up on the hunger within Shell for local autonomy; no national group, especially the Dutch and British, wanted to feel dominated by any other. They divided the Group system two ways; each activity was now part of a "function" and a "region," and every major request had to be approved by both chains of appeal.[11] McKinsey's young men had borrowed this matrix concept from General Electric, whose "scientific management" wizards had adapted the concept from General Motors, which had learned to diversify from Du Pont, which had more or less invented the idea in the 1920s. (In fact, some companies were growing tired of it; another McKinsey team, at this same time, helped Mobil return to a centralized form. "They sold us Mobil's organization," Shell managers joked, "and Mobil bought ours.")

Thanks to this structure, anyone like Ted Newland, with an idea that the future might change, could never simply convince one top boss or another to adopt the appropriate policies. Anyone who wanted Shell to change would have to find a way to make the future clearly visible, so a wide range of people within the company could see it coming.

Newland's assignment to look at the future was a minor task, one of many prospective papers and projects handed to the planning department during the course of a year. But Newland took it seriously. He immediately began to look around for people who had found ways to think coherently about the future. The most interesting man he found was Herman Kahn, the founder-director of a freewheeling think tank called the Hudson Institute. Located north of New York City, the Hudson Institute specialized in a type of future stories that Kahn called "scenarios." These stories about the future aimed at helping people break past their mental blocks and consider the "unthinkable" futures, which would take them by surprise if they weren't prepared.

In those years, Kahn was best known for an idea that many people considered heretical: that the best way to prevent nuclear war was to think soberly and in full detail about what would happen if that war occurred. In lectures and books, he had described dozens of ways in which the nuclear powers might move into global confrontation. There was one tit-for-tat exchange scenario, for instance, in which the United States devastated Moscow after the Soviets destroyed New York. In nearly all these potential futures, society survived and had to cope with the results.

Kahn did sound detached, even jovial, when talking about these prospects; his acquaintance, director Stanley Kubrick, used him as part of the model for the title character in *Dr. Strangelove*. He appropriated his trademark phrase, "thinking the unthinkable," from a bitter exchange of letters with the editor of *Scientific American,* after the magazine published an article condemning his approach.[12]

Kahn first began to "think the unthinkable" in the late 1940s, when he forsook an academic career in physics to go to work at a military-oriented think tank called the RAND Corporation ("Research and Development"). RAND was set up to employ physicists, mathematicians, and (later) policy analysts to research new forms of weapons technology; its first report, published in 1946, foresaw the launching of the Sputnik satellite fourteen years later.[13] RAND gave Kahn his first exposure to the war games of military strategy, which he began applying to technological prospects: "If a new weapon is developed, how will people respond to it?" He'd cloister a half dozen RAND staff members in a weeklong meeting,[14] and at the end they would emerge with a scenario about, say, India, written as if from a vantage point ten years hence: "In 1965, there was an uprising in Bengal . . ."

The term "scenario" for these types of stories was suggested by the sociologist, novelist, and screenwriter Leo Rosten (author of *The Education of H*Y*M*A*N K*A*P*L*A*N).* One night Rosten (who freelanced on RAND documents) poked his nose in on a group of physicists who were hunting for a name for alternative descriptions of how satellites might behave. "You should call them scenarios," he said. "In the movies, a scenario is a detailed outline of a future movie." Actually, Rosten knew that the word "scenario" was already outdated in Hollywood; it harked back to the silent era. But to the RAND scientists, it sounded more dignified than "screenplay."[15] Herman Kahn particularly loved the word, including its literary connotations. Scenarios, as Herman Kahn saw them, were supposed to be fictional and playful, not some sort of rigorous forecast. The point was not to make accurate predictions (although, like all futurists, he gleefully loved being right), but to come up with a mythic story that brought the point home. That mythic quality was one of the things that impressed Ted Newland, one of the things he saw that he could bring back to Shell.

By the mid-1960s, Kahn had left RAND to found the Hudson Institute, where he and his staff of twenty-odd people began to actively court a broader range of clients. Military scenarios had become boring and repetitive for them; they wanted to look at culture and the economy. Kahn began by taking an assignment for the American Academy of Arts and Sciences, to prepare background material for a series of inquiries on possible futures in the year 2000. Typically, when Kahn was interested in something, he didn't let trivialities like the boundaries of an assignment stop him, and his small role quickly expanded into a full-scale set of scenarios for the world at the turn of the century. Most of them were variations on one full-scale, inexorable future: worldwide peace and financial boom. In the United States, prosperity would produce a permanent upper middle class, taking on many of the habits and attitudes of the landed gentry of nineteenth-century Europe.[16] Kahn predicted that

Communism would collapse within twenty years under the pressure of its own economic failures. He called this the "surprise-free" future—if it came to pass, it would not surprise anybody very much ("or at least not *me*," he said).[17]

Kahn himself made an impressive mythic figure. Over six feet tall and 300 pounds heavy, he moved through his days with relentless energy. Colleagues remember him striding through airports at top speed, bearing two shopping bags full of books he had bought en route, while a harried assistant scrambled frantically to keep up and passersby leapt out of his path to avoid collision. He spoke often, striding around stages in his shirtsleeves, cracking jokes and sweating with the exertion of getting his words out. He charmed audiences, who could feel their place in the grand scheme of history as he talked about the promise of the industrial revolution, and how it was still in its infancy. But they also recognized that his cosmic timeframes made him treat facts loosely. Kahn didn't hide the point. It's not that he forgot facts; indeed, he had a photographic memory, and could talk extemporaneously (and accurately) about subjects that ranged from the trajectory of ballistic missiles to the variations between translations of the *Rubaiyat* of Omar Khayyam. Nonetheless, he didn't think the specifics of the details were all that important. "I just made up this data," he would tell an audience, chuckling. "But it's really *good* data."

Kahn tended to organize his thoughts in lists, and his list of the 100 most probable scientific breakthroughs by the year 2000 included artificial moons, designed to light large areas of the earth at night; individual flying platforms; human control of weather and climate; and extensive use of robot household slaves. (To be fair, he also predicted personal computers and superconductivity.) Because he was so willing to scatter hypotheticals, he was the first to hit some targets. For instance, Kahn was the first pundit to alert American corporate leaders about the need to watch Japan. "What will the Japanese do when they overtake the West?" he would ask. "I can't imagine a Japanese without a goal. Can they find one in organizing the political economy of Asia? Or, in the absence of a new fashion, will they turn to an old one—imperialism?"[18] He deflated one War Gaming Agency scenario, in which the United States emerged out of a nuclear skirmish victorious over the U.S.S.R. and with no other enemies, simply by asking, "If the U.S. massacres the Soviets that way, whose side will Japan be on?"

Beginning in 1966, pressed by the chronic financial straits which the Hudson Institute often landed in, Kahn began to hold meetings for corporate sponsors. Newland began to attend them regularly, jetting to New York as many as ten times a year, one of thirty corporate managers at a briefing. (The others tended to be executive vice presidents and CEOs from companies like Corning, IBM, and General Motors—to Newland, the "top people of the world." But few of them seemed to take Kahn's material as seriously as he did.) By 1968, when preliminary versions of Kahn's book *The Year 2000* began to circulate within Shell, Newland had become a friend of Kahn's. He saw that if economic growth continued to accelerate (as Kahn seemed sure it would),[19] then demand for oil would reach astronomical figures. Newland figured a demand somewhere around 110 million barrels a day by the year 2000. The world would need ten or twelve Saudi Arabias, all pumping full tilt, to keep up. But when Newland mentioned the possibility to some of his colleagues in Shell's planning department, even as a straw man, they shrugged it off: "We'll meet that need when we get to it."

A colleague from this era remembers Newland stopping him in the corridor to say, "I've just had an idea. What if the United States tried to close off the Western Hemisphere to the rest of the world? To corner the market on Venezuelan oil, for example?" The colleague spent a day or two researching the idea, and then dropped into Newland's office to lay out the reasons why it wasn't plausible. Newland waved him aside. "You've shown that won't work. Let's look at something else, then."

This was unusual at Shell. As at most companies, people were expected to act like they always had the answers. But Newland was protected by two influential advocates. The first was his boss, planning coordinator Jimmy Davidson. Davidson was a feisty former fighter pilot with a rakish mustache, who, like Newland, had worked in both Venezuela and Nigeria. Then he had directed the economics and planning function for exploration and production. When the Royal Dutch/Shell planning department was reorganized, Davidson was appointed its head. He became one of several voices arguing, as early as 1967, against the use of the Unified Planning Machinery. In 1968, Newland introduced him to Herman Kahn's scenario method, which Davidson saw as a possible alternative to UPM. It took several years, but by the end of 1969 the majority of the Committee of Managing Directors became convinced, and they commissioned Davidson to manage the shift to a new set of planning methods.

Newland's other advocate was Lord Rothschild (Victor Rothschild), Shell's research coordinator and a member of the family that had bankrolled Henri Deterding. Rothschild was also a Cambridge-trained biophysicist with a background in military intelligence from World War II.[20] He was impressed by Newland's first look at the future, and in 1970 he asked for an expansion, with a focus on the Middle East. This was controversial because Shell's exploration and production engineers, the most influential function in the Group, considered the Arab world their territory. Newland had never been there. As if that was not bad enough, the news he had to report was grim. The Western oil companies, including Shell, were about to lose control of their business. The Unified Planning Machinery on which Shell men based their predictions gave no hint of the crisis to come.[21]

Yet anyone with a halfway sophisticated background in the industry could, if they cared to look, see the strain on the invisible pipes and pumps. The unthinkable, as Herman Kahn might put it, was about to happen. The balance of power in the Middle East was about to shift. At the same time, demand was beginning to outstrip the ability of the non-Arab oil fields to meet it. In the past, 75 percent of the oil produced in Texas had gone into strategic reserves, as a hedge for use during shortages. Now, only 10 percent of the oil was saved for reserves. Exxon, Texaco, and Chevron executives knew this very well and were, in fact, pleased about it: "Thank goodness we're getting more of this oil out into the market." They didn't imagine any reason why they should build up more reserves as a safety net.

The Japanese policy makers saw the danger of severe shortage; in 1968, they began to wean themselves from their oil dependencies, beginning an energy-efficiency improvement effort with a twenty-five-year deadline. Americans overseas saw it. From Riyadh to Tripoli, local oil company office managers would send back cables to their home offices saying, "This free ride is not going to last. Let's do something." They were ignored.

At Shell, Ted Newland was not alone in recognizing that a crisis was brewing. But he was not in the majority either. He sent a preliminary draft of his report to some Shell exploration and production managers, expressing his concerns. They returned it with a comment scribbled in the margin: "Arabs will never get together."[22] Of course they won't, Newland thought to himself. They would compete with each other to see who could press the price of oil highest.

In 1970, Libya's shrewd new dictator, Muammar al-Qaddafi, threatened to cut off supplies from his country. This forced the price of Libyan oil up 30 percent, and forced Occidental Petroleum, which was locked into a contract there, to give Qaddafi 55 percent of its Libyan profits, instead of the standard 50 percent. When the news broke publicly about Libya's deal, all the other Arab countries insisted on similar terms. The balance of power had already shifted away from the oil companies.

Gerrit Wagner—the former general manager of Shell Venezuela, who had once had to petition the CMD for a storage tank—was now a managing director himself, and slated to become chairman. Wagner was an avuncular, genial amateur historian, and a Dutchman who spoke five languages fluently (CMD business was always conducted in English). With planning finally slated to move away from its mechanistic system, he felt that it should take on a new mission: to articulate the danger that might lurk in the Middle East. Shell managers needed to understand the forces that had *produced* the turbulence around them. They needed an intellectual maverick who could speak to Shell managers throughout the world, to help them learn how to be prepared *before* the crisis struck.

Ted Newland was too crusty and erratic to be the communicator that Wagner and Jimmy Davidson were looking for. But they knew of someone who would fit the job quite well. He worked in Paris as the director of economics research for Shell Française, the French operating company. He was unique within Shell—a former magazine publisher, trained in spiritual disciplines and government administration, familiar with Japan and India, and knowledgeable about Shell's business problems. He was also a very magnetic man—the sort of man whom people intuitively feel can understand them. His name was Pierre Wack.

Pierre Wack was then forty-eight years old; he had been with Shell ten years. He had heavy-lidded eyes, a professorial air, a resonant voice with a thick French accent, and the cosmopolitan quality of having grown up in two cultures at once. (He was from Alsace-Lorraine, the borderland where France and Germany meet.) He had graduated first in his class from the most prominent French university of public administration, L'Ecole des Sciences Politiques. Then he had taken a job helping Alsace-Lorraine to rebuild after the war. After growing disgusted with the bureaucratic mind-set of his government office, he had moved to Paris to become the editor of *Occident,* a magazine of current affairs. Meanwhile, beginning with his college days during World War II, he had become part of the circle of G. I. Gurdjieff, the philosopher/mystic whose ideas Charles Krone would study so assiduously in Cincinnati.

Gurdjieff, then in his late seventies, lived in Paris during most of the war years. Wack, still in his early twenties, was a student at Sciences Politiques in Lyons, from which he sneaked into Paris regularly, sometimes across German lines. Years later, he recalled his introduction to Gurdjieff:

A friend of mine in Lyons told me, "Look, I met a very interesting chap, and I have an appointment at this address [in Paris] at four o'clock Friday, and you go in my place." So at four o'clock I rang the bell. I didn't know where I was or who I was seeing. I opened the door, and I saw the back of some armchairs in which a dozen people were sitting. I heard the voice of a woman speaking. This was Mme. Jeanne de Salzmann, a key associate of Mr. Gurdjieff's, and I was abruptly put in a quite advanced group.

Very soon afterward—I think within four or five months—I was presented to Mr. Gurdjieff, alongside a quite famous man, Lanza del Vasto, who had written a best-selling book about walking across India. Happily, Gurdjieff started with him first. He really agonized del Vasto. We came back afterward through the Metro, and del Vasto was so shattered [by Gurdjieff's gibes and questions] that he could hardly walk. I got a few tough remarks too, but after what I had witnessed, it was not much.

Throughout the war, Wack showed up at Gurdjieff's salons at least once a week. At times, the communal meals Gurdjieff cooked up from black market supplies were Wack's only source of food. Although Gurdjieff's ideas did not directly influence Wack, it was in his house that Wack began a lifelong preoccupation with the art of what he called "seeing." To *see,* Wack would later say, meant not merely being aware of an element of your environment, but seeing through it, with full consciousness.

In 1953, for example, Wack spent several weeks in Japan with a premier garden designer. Garden design is held in as much esteem in Japan as painting and sculpture are in the West, but the most renowned Japanese gardens have no exotic plants; rather, they are arranged to pull a visitor's mind past everyday mental chatter, and past the expectations of what a garden should be, toward a more intense sense of being present. Instead of comparing the garden with other gardens, trying to learn the names of plants, or admiring the work that went into the horticulture, "you see a branch, or a rock, or a leaf, very intensely. And when you see this way, you have an extraordinary feeling, that this is how I always should see." Wack sometimes told the story of his last day with the garden designer, who took him to a corner where vegetable brush had been piled. " 'Look here,' he said. 'Look at it really. This is real. It *is*. And it is much more important than to be beautiful. Never forget. What is, is.' It was my first feeling of really seeing."

This preoccupation with seeing led Wack to travel regularly throughout the world, particularly in India and Japan, always seeking "remarkable people" (as he called them). That phrase would eventually become common idiom at Shell. Acquaintances often wondered if it had been borrowed from Gurdjieff, who had written a book called *Meetings with Remarkable Men*[23] and who defined a "remarkable man" as someone who "stands out from those around him by the resourcefulness of his mind, and knows how to be restrained in the manifestations which proceed from his nature, at the same time conducting himself justly and tolerantly towards the weakness of others"—someone, in other words, who was relatively free from corrupting influences like the "kundabuffer."

But Wack meant something quite different. He sought out acute observers with keen, unending curiosity. These people devoted themselves to *seeing:* to constant attention to the ways the world worked. Meeting with them became, as Wack put it, "an addiction; my own luxury." When *Occident* folded, he became a consultant, specializing in marketing and economic policy studies; he arranged many of his assignments to take him overseas for months at a time, to Japan, Guatemala, Sri Lanka, Burma: "You find that a remarkable person usually has remarkable friends. It was a good preparation for what I had afterwards to do at Shell."

In the years that followed, Wack developed an ongoing relationship with a teacher in India whom he visited once a year—a man whom he referred to, simply, as "a wise man I know." In Sanskrit, the word for wise man *(rishi)* literally means "seer," and this teacher suggested to Wack that his work should become a test of his perceptiveness. "If your seeing is complete and perfect, at the right state of observation, then there should be immediate understanding." The task of a seer was to regard the world from as many perspectives as possible—aware, all the while, of what message each perspective on a problem had to offer.

* * *

Under French law, people who began working for an organization after age thirty-nine were not guaranteed a pension. Thus, when he reached age thirty-eight, Wack decided to take a full-time job. "My two favorite customers [as an economics consultant] were Shell and Michelin," he later recalled. "And I knew Michelin better than Shell. But [at Michelin] I heard to my amazement that I had to take my holiday when the whole company shuts its door—in August." In August, Japan and India are unbearably hot and humid, and Japan is overrun with insects. When Wack learned that he could schedule his own holidays at Shell Française, he agreed to join them.

This was typical of Wack's style. To his colleagues, he routinely seemed to extract extravagant perks where others didn't even dare ask, somehow bending the system to his will—not because he was manipulative, but because he knew his own priorities. Wack had a distaste for small talk and pettiness; and he was a master at snubbing people whom he considered lightweight. But he was also a gifted listener, with the ability to remember, word for word, conversations that had taken place years earlier. Most of all, he was self-possessed; even in his moments of indignation, he seemed aware of details around him.

After a few years as a marketing planner, Wack became the director of economics at Shell Française. At this time, a few operating companies had been asked to experiment with new planning approaches, as part of the CMD's drift away from the Unified Planning Machinery. Wack leaped to the bait. Like Ted Newland, he had gotten to know Herman Kahn ("an enormously stimulating man," he later said); and he experimented with Kahn's approach in looking at the future of Shell's heating oil business in France. How ample would supplies of the primary competitor, natural gas, be? And how restrictive the government? "Only an idiot," Wack said, "or a god would pretend to know the answer."

Wack generated four obvious futures for heating oil. Then a hapless member of his staff spent weeks calculating projected forecasts for each future—figuring, for example, the expected number of oil-heated homes in each of France's regions. It took enormous effort to crunch the numbers, and the results, Wack realized, merely confirmed the strategies which Shell Française already followed. But the process of coming up with these unimpressive futures had begun to open up a more complete understanding of "the forces behind the system." Why had the natural gas business evolved this way? How were French attitudes about heating fuel changing? These questions needed serious investigation. "Forget about this year's work," he told André Bénard, the chief executive of Shell Française. "Let me start again next year, and we'll do it correctly."

But Bénard was promoted the next year, in 1970, to become the Royal Dutch/Shell coordinator for Europe (roughly equivalent to an executive vice president for the region). The following year, he moved up again, to become a managing director.[24] Even before leaving France, Bénard had already begun to tell people in Shell Centre of this man at Shell Française with the gift of sparking people's imaginations, of making them see the world as he had seen it. Thus, for at least a year, Jimmy Davidson avidly courted Pierre Wack to join Group Planning. But Wack refused Davidson's first offers to move. He enjoyed his position in France, and he did not want to subject his dog to England's six-month quarantine for immigrant pets. When his dog died, early in 1970, he agreed to take the job. But first, he said, Bénard had once promised him a year's sabbatical in Japan, and he wanted to take it now. "It will be the reverse of the trip the Japanese make when they come to the West to learn from us."

Thus, Pierre Wack spent much of 1970 in Japan. It was a rare opportunity for a Westerner. Knowing that the hardest task would be gaining entrée to Japanese companies, he acquired a series of letters of introduction to the *keidanren,* the most powerful association of Japanese manufacturers. A vice president of the *keidanren* agreed to act as Wack's "godfather," and Wack was granted time with senior executives at such companies as Sony, Matsushita, Nippon Steel, and Honda. Even then, he didn't approach them directly. In many cases, he wrote out thirty or more questions, submitted them in a respectful letter, and returned two months later to discuss the answers.

Wack found Japanese firms surprisingly vulnerable to external shocks and surprisingly unconcerned with predicting future events. "We do not share your enthusiasm in the West for planning," a Sony executive told Wack, smiling with satisfaction. "We merely have a clear vision of what company we want to be." All the companies he visited had decided which strengths they wanted their company to have in the future ("strengths they would rely on as an animal relies on its claws, its beak, or its capacity to hide," Wack later said), and had set out to build that strength in themselves. Sony's leaders, for instance, had chosen to become *ichiban* (excellent) in three technologies: color video, solid-state electronics, and magnetic tape recording. "Other companies may be better in one of those three," the executive told Wack, "but no one will be as good in all of them together." Indeed, Sony held on to this long-range goal for more than a decade—until they had achieved it and outgrown it.

When Pierre returned to Shell Centre in early 1971, the rest of the scenario planning team began to work out a strategy for using their method to inform decision makers. Jimmy Davidson devoted himself to creating an atmosphere not only in which people like Pierre and Ted could thrive but from which they could be heard. He knew how to soothe ruffled feathers, to mediate when tempers flared, and to maintain good relations with people throughout the Shell system.[25]

Newland, meanwhile, formed a bond with Wack. Their talents were intensely complementary. "I think I was much stronger in intuition," Newland would say. "He was much stronger in intellect." Newland would later compare the two of them to Tweedledum and Tweedledee; Wack saw them as two pieces of jade, which, by rubbing against each other, became polished. Pierre reminded some Shell people of Agatha Christie's detective Hercule Poirot, methodically deducing the psychological and social factors that had produced a seemingly impossible set of events. Then he would describe them in metaphors and parables, which he delivered with the otherworldly mien of a stage magician. Ted was more like Sherlock Holmes. As he mulled over the facts, he would mumble darkly, lost in his thoughts. Then, suddenly, he would leap to an insight and his voice would grow more and more emphatic, until (as one Shell planner put it) "you couldn't help but feel that his warnings were terribly important."

Both Newland and Wack believed that Kahn's scenario methods needed a full overhaul, but they did not quite know how to invent one. In 1971, they developed four new "exploratory" scenarios, images of the world as it might look in 1976, using a Kahn-style matrix to generate them. There was a "surprise-free" world, for instance, in which the shocks that everyone dreaded simply never came to pass. There was a "high-take" scenario, in which the Arab countries demanded more money and received it from a desperate world starving for oil, and a "low-demand" scenario, in which economic depression deflated the need for oil. Finally, there was a scenario in which the energy picture switched from oil to nuclear, coal, and other "alternative" sources.

As with the scenarios that Wack had done for Shell Française, these were lavishly fleshed out with numerical forecasts: Worldwide oil demand would rise by the mid-1970s, they said, to somewhere between 56 and 62 million barrels per day. But the planning staffers understood that the scenarios had little value except for their own education. Wack said as much privately to André Bénard: "Look, this is not the real stuff yet," he said. "These are just our own learning tools, which we are using to leap into the jungles."

The directors were suitably unimpressed by the presentation. Frank McFadzean, who had once been responsible for planning (and a partisan of the Unified Planning Machinery), grumbled that he could have done as well on the back of an envelope. Newland assumed this was their last chance. He was relieved when he and Wack learned that their job was still on. Both men knew that they could do much better next time.

It might seem surprising that the task was so difficult. By now, in mid-1972, everyone at Shell—and in the other oil companies—

knew that the old oil game was falling apart. The OPEC governments, in the gentle voice of their new spokesman (the Cheshire
Cat-like Saudi oil minister Sheikh Zhaki Ahmed Yamani), were asking for "participation." They were no longer content to rent their
land to oil companies; they wanted stock in the companies that
drilled the wells. The major oil companies thus found themselves
threatened with the possibility that they might lose their holdings.
To the oil executives (and to most American citizens), it was as if a
gang of belligerent street thugs had suddenly gained the power to
dominate the world. (Of course, the Arabs, seeing the West through
the light of their Islamic faith, felt the same way, except that in *their*
view the thugs had been in charge since the end of the Ottoman
Empire.)[26]

The managing directors at Shell recognized the danger. If industrial growth depended on oil, then an oil crisis could soon lead to
global shortages and even economic collapse. The chairman of the
CMD, Sir David Barran—an erudite Cambridge alumnus who wore
a monocle in public—began to say in speeches that the industrial
world was "peering down the muzzle of a gun." André Bénard
visited his European contacts, including Henri Simonet, the Common Market energy commissioner in Brussels. He warned of the
impending crisis, and explained some possible remedies, including
setting up an oil reserves storage system for Europe. Simonet was a
socialist, suspicious of multinational corporations in general and
Shell in particular. "I'll be damned," he responded, "if I understand
why a representative of one of the most capitalistic companies in
the world should come and explain this to me."

"Listen, it's very simple," Bénard replied. "Until now, I had this
on my conscience. Now *you* have it."

Yet Shell's *own* policies had not changed. The organization,
from managing directors on down, was still buying the same types
of drilling equipment, refineries, and tankers, and making the same
trading arrangements, as if nothing was going to happen. It's not
that the managing directors lacked capability. In fact, they were
among the most sophisticated people alive, particularly in dealing
with uncertainty. They had worked in the oil industry all their lives.

They had an innate gut feel, a tangible sense of judgment, for the geological realities and the markets of the oil business. They could easily handle a question of whether to invest $200 million in Greenland looking for oil or to drill in offshore Brazil instead.

But when told, by these first scenarios, about a future potential oil market that might be either 56 or 87 million barrels per day, the managing directors seemed to become paralyzed. They lacked the necessary gut feel for the new world which Wack and Newland were trying to describe. They did not clearly see its geopolitics, changing markets, and inconstant cultures. And without that gut feel, they could not act. If the planners wanted the company to succeed, then they would have to make this new world tangible somehow. That, in turn, would mean somehow reaching the part of the managers' minds that harbored their perceptions. In late 1971, after Wack was ensconced in London, he, Newland, and the team of planners began to figure out how to design scenarios to accomplish this goal.

First, the planners focused on what Wack called "breathing in"—gathering intelligence from the outside world. With his background in magazine publishing, Wack knew the first rule of information gathering: you cannot take in without giving something back. Most corporations, including Shell, conducted their research in strict secrecy, which meant they could not share information. They had to buy it from consultants like Herman Kahn and McKinsey. But Wack hated to spend money on information. Moreover, the most successful oil industry consultants were constrained by conventional views.

Instead, Wack and the planners cultivated their own network of "remarkable people." Wherever Wack traveled, making presentations to Shell offices, he sought out people, inside and outside the company, who had some depth of understanding. When other planners asked how he recognized remarkable people, he would say, "You know very well who they are when you meet them." Sometimes, a remarkable person from outside Shell might stumble into a scenario presentation, as an Iranian physician did in the early

1970s, looking for stimulating conversation. ("You know," Wack recalled, "it's rather boring to be in a Middle Eastern country.") The two men became close friends. Each year Pierre would visit and ask how his perception had changed.

Wack's reliance on "remarkable people" was not universally popular at Shell. Some reasoned that if they weren't chosen as "remarkable," that must make them *un*remarkable. More significantly, the idea contradicted an unwritten axiom of postwar management: that any manager would be "remarkable" enough to step into any role. Wack, therefore, played down his research methods at Shell Centre, where he focused on the other half of the task. For following "breathing in," an organism must "breathe out."

The twenty-odd members of the scenario team spent much of 1972 plotting out the elements of six stories about the future, weighing them according to what would "really make a difference." They overlaid these scenarios with a "triangle," as they called it, of the most significant energy actors: the oil-producing countries of the Middle East, the oil-consuming countries of the West, and the oil companies. They picked the most promising combinations and then they role-played them—taking the part of every significant player on the scene. What would the Shah of Iran do? How would Richard Nixon react? How about Qaddafi? And Exxon? As they played out the results, sometimes shouting at each other in character across the conference room table, they listened for contradictions.

For their first great exhalation, scheduled for September 1972, Wack asked for an unprecedented half day to talk before the managing directors. "They can leave if they are not interested," he said. "But if they *are* interested, they must be able to stay the whole morning." He had spoken to some of the managing directors ahead of time, dropping hints. He knew that they would stay.

Twenty years later, after they had retired, at least three of the managing directors would vividly remember the way Wack talked to them that September.[27] With the directors seated at a semicircular table before him, and a screen for slides behind him, he began with a quiet, but still heretical, statement about forecasts. Trying to predict the future was not just impossible, he said, but dangerous. The most perilous forecasts to listen to are those, like the UPM, which have recently been correct, "because probably they have been right for the wrong reasons, and you are tempted to believe them. Sooner or later their forecasts will fail when you need them most."[28]

However, in some cases, he said, the forces that create the future have already shown themselves. He asked them to consider the Ganges River, which he knew well because his Indian teacher lived near its source. "From spring to mouth," he said, "it is an extraordinary river, some fifteen hundred miles long. If you notice extraordinarily heavy monsoon rains at the upper part of the basin, you can anticipate *with certainty* that within two days something extraordinary is going to happen at Rishikesh, at the foothills of the Himalayas." Three days later, there would be a flood at Allahabad, which is southeast of Delhi, and five days later in Benares. "Now the people down here in Benares don't know that this flood is on its way," he said, "but I do. Because I've been at the spring where it comes from. I've seen it! This is not fortune telling. This is not crystal-ball gazing. This is merely describing future implications of something that has already happened."

What predetermined events, then, were rolling down like monsoon water to flood the world? To start with, Wack said, Westerners had always thought of Arab countries as a common bloc. Shell, for example, had an expert whose function was to analyze OPEC, but his analyses always lumped all the Arab countries together. Henceforth, he would need to look at each of the Arab nations separately. For example, the Shah of Iran had been the West's most eager and compliant oil supplier. But Iran had only fifteen or twenty years' worth of oil reserves left, and it desperately needed revenues. Its impoverished population was continuing to grow—a seedbed, though most of the world didn't know it yet, of the most virulent Islamic fundamentalism. The Shell planners had role-played the Shah of Iran in a variety of situations. He was like a chess player with only one feasible move left on the board; no matter how he felt personally, he would push for higher oil prices and cut supplies. "If we were Iran, we would do the same," Wack said.

Saudi Arabia, on the other hand, was so sparsely populated and rich in oil that the ruling Saudi family members had more money than they could invest. They could open up more reserves, but that excess oil was worth more to them under the ground, without the expense of pulling it out. (Saudi officials had been saying as much for months.)[29] If you looked at pressures like these, you could see that—after twenty years of enmity—the oil-producing countries would now find it irresistible to act in concert. They would unite against their former Western allies. If any oil-producing country had had large oil reserves, and the need for more investment capital, OPEC would have collapsed immediately. But there was no such country.

That was why, Wack said, the fears of the managing directors were correct. Instead of OPEC, the governing structure of international oil production would collapse. This would inevitably change the underlying balance of power in the industrial world. It would begin with an "energy crisis," the break in the apparent availability of oil—certainly in the short-term availability of oil. This would probably happen before 1975, when the existing Teheran Agreement between OPEC and the oil companies was set to expire. The exact moment of collapse was unpredictable, but the collapse itself was unavoidable—and imminent.

So was another apparently "predetermined element," the expanding need for oil in the West. At that time, energy profligacy in the United States was accelerating. People were driving more, air-conditioning their homes, embracing air travel. Europe and Japan were rapidly building roads and electrifying (which would drive up fuel costs generally); and the nations of the "developing world," the independent former colonies of the Far East, South America, and Africa, were all hungry for fuel. Oil exports would probably grow at a rate between 3.5 and 4 million barrels a day per year—four times the annual increase of the 1950s. Thus, a shortage seemed unavoidable. What he did *not* know, Wack said, was how each of these governments would react to the pressure of a shortage. The

Americans would be angry, the Japanese anxious—but would they panic? Would they muddle their way into a depression? Was it possible to tell?

At this point, if not sooner, members of the CMD interrupted with questions. Wack handled them as he always would: "I'm coming to that!" he said, and then hurried on ("very politely," Gerrit Wagner remembered). He now projected a chart on the screen behind him. The planning people who had prepared it called it the "delta" chart, because it looked like a river delta, with the flow of time split into six separate forks, each one a different scenario describing an alternative future. In the bottom three tributaries, the crisis was averted somehow, and oil remained plentiful throughout the world. In the top three, an oil shortage took place, but with different types of political response.

Only one of the forks, A2, led to crisis. The other five represented the hidden hopes of the people in the room. Thus, there was a moment of relief, until Wack began to describe each of the alternatives and the CMD members could hear how absurd they sounded.

The *Private Enterprise Solution* (A1) suggested that free-market forces would solve the problem in the form of higher prices charged by oil companies. This future, however, depended on governments recognizing the crisis *before it happened*—in time to undo their oil company regulations in advance. Shell's managers knew they could not count on this future.

In the *Dirigiste* scenario (A3), the industrial governments would similarly anticipate the crisis. This time, they would take the role of strategists. They would act together ahead of time: collaborating on policies to control prices, allocate the flow of oil among themselves, and negotiate as a bloc with the Arab world. This future, to anyone who knew the governments, was even more unlikely.

The *Successful Muddling Through* scenario (B2) was Wack's response to a comment from one of the British planners: "Look, you are French. You guillotine your kings. But here in England, we tend to muddle through these crises and come out the other end. Why couldn't that happen with the oil crisis?" A muddling-through sce-

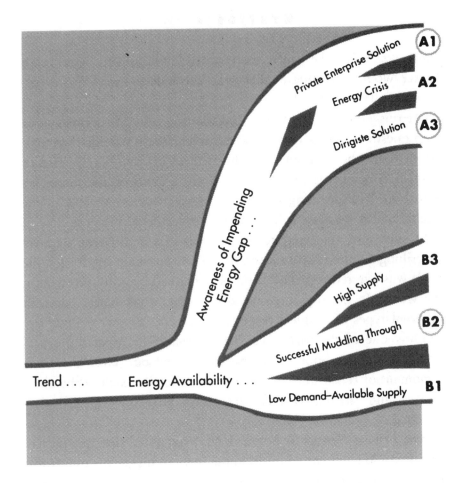

nario was reasonable, Wack said, "as long as we do not probe too deeply into current forces." In order to successfully muddle through, the West would have to encourage energy saving ahead of time (reducing the demand for oil) and find some leverage with which to get the OPEC countries to back down. (In some respects, the events Wack described for this scenario *did* take place—but it required twenty years.)

A *Low Demand* scenario (B1) posited that new countercultural values (or, as the planning people called them, "the change in social attitudes toward work and achievement"[30]) would abort the rat race of industrial expansion. People would voluntarily consume less, corporations would produce less, governments would promote energy efficiency, and the need for oil would decrease. The idea had seemed plausible during the European recession of 1971, but the recession had ended. The stoutly successful businessmen of the CMD had little trouble dismissing *this* scenario.

Finally, that left what Wack called the "Three Miracles" scenario—the image of the future that some of the CMD men still held dear. On the chart, it was labeled *High Supply* (B3): it said that through the heroic efforts of oil companies, the West would develop enough new oil to keep on top of the world's demand. Mild shortages might take place temporarily, but they would simply reinforce the instincts of most oil executives—to explore, drill, refine, ship, and market oil even more aggressively than they had in the past. In this scenario, the crisis would be merely an opportunity to show what they could do.[31]

"But let us see," Wack said dryly, "what would have to come to pass." This future would require not just one, but three simultaneous miraculous events. First, oil companies would have to find and retrieve new reserves incredibly quickly—including 13 million barrels from Africa, and 6 million from Alaska and Canada.[32] These regions were all unprepared for new drilling, and, in some cases, closed to it. Second, the OPEC countries would have to undergo a change of heart and become willing to sell as much oil as they could produce, happier with massive amounts of money in the bank ("exposed to erosion by inflation") than with oil in the ground. And, finally, there would have to be no extra strain on oil production capabilities—no wars, no extra-cold winters or sudden demand for off-road vehicles, and no natural disasters. Most daunting of all, there could be no more oil spills or refinery fires that would waste oil. "Any single small accident could upset the whole system. Again," continued Wack, brandishing a pointer at the screen, "nothing short of miraculous."

Most of the managing directors could see that now. The mood of the room rapidly deflated. They already knew that the easy years were over, that they could no longer count on the financial cushion of a steady, unwavering stream of oil supply money. ("We sensed it more than we knew it," Gerrit Wagner would later recall.[33]) They could no longer build unneeded refineries, just to preempt a competitor in some region; they could no longer buy unneeded tankers.

For the first time, they had a visceral sense of what type of age was coming. It was represented by the only scenario left on the chart: the *Energy Crisis* (A2). The price of oil might jump fivefold within a few years: from $1.90 per barrel, where it was now, to $10.[34] Shell would now have to work much harder at weighing its investments, and every other major oil company would be in the same position.

Toward the end of the session, one of the managing directors asked Pierre Wack a question that scenario presenters are always asked. Which scenario was most probable? Which should they choose to prepare for? Wack refused to answer directly. "Look," he said. "Each of these scenarios is serious. You should weigh the probability against the seriousness of the consequence—if it happens and you are not prepared for it." Probabilities, he said, were subjective. People tended, despite themselves, to assume that the scenario which felt most familiar was the most probable. "These scenarios," he said, "help you not to prepare for the last war. Sometimes you have to prepare for a nuclear war and a guerrilla war, two wars that are completely different, and you have to do it at the same time because both may come."

At this point, we may imagine, he clicked off the projector and stood impassively for a moment. And then discussion began.

When Pierre Wack and Jimmy Davidson walked out of the room a couple of hours later, they had two new assignments. First, they must present the scenarios to Shell managers around the world; henceforth, Shell managers would have to justify their decisions in light of the scenarios. Second, Shell would make a concerted effort to describe the forthcoming world to government officials and try to persuade them to act. There was one sticking point: even the worst "energy crisis" scenario, said the managing directors, should only predict a price of $6 per barrel, in constant dollars. Ten dollars was too outrageous; no one would accept it.[35] (Within a year, the real price would rise above $13, and by 1979, after another oil price shock, it would soar to $40.)

A sense of urgency overtook the scenario team. Late in 1972, they produced a small "white book," with their estimates of every Middle Eastern country's oil reserves. In January, the "eggshell-blue book" appeared. This one, for Shell eyes only, laid out the six scenarios that Pierre Wack had shown the managing directors three months before. Meanwhile, Wack and Newland found themselves on tour. Wack made more than fifty presentations that year. First, he laid out the scenarios before the "coordinators" of functions and regions. They were a blunter, more skeptical group than the managing directors, and they walked into the room without preparation, expecting a barrage of standard UPM-style projections and figures. When Wack finished, they applauded him—a gesture they had never made for any speaker before.

The operating company managers were far less receptive—but, of course, the message for them was more difficult. In Shell, as in nearly all major oil companies, there are two separate cultures: upstream (exploration and production) and downstream (refining and marketing). To upstream managers, Wack and Newland offered a new "unthinkable" to think about: "You are going to lose your mining rents." In the oil industry, "mining rents"—an economic term for the revenues from low-cost oil fields—represented the most lucrative aspect of the upstream business.[36] Now Wack said, "They're finished. You had better find new sources of profitability."

To the downstream people, there was the equally frightening warning that they would now become a low-growth company. "No longer," Wack told them, "will the normal growth of the market make [a poor investment] all better in a year or two. You're going to have to be fully responsible for what you do. You cannot trust your normal reflexes."

Many Shell managers walked away from the presentations angry. "Just give me a number," they pleaded. Capital-intensive businesses like Shell Marine, with its need to plan for buying tanker ships, could not move forward without a number to plug into their calculations. But the scenarios offered no single number, so the managers chose one. Many of them took the projections from the "Three Miracles" future, which felt the most reasonable, and plugged that into their formulas. Never mind that the results were a recommendation to buy more tankers than a crisis would support.

"We were in a new dimension," one of the staff members, Napier Collyns, would later recall. "We were imagining things which were unimaginable—chief among them this impending shortage. And I think we all knew that it would be rejected by the rest of the Group. Ted and Pierre weren't too involved with our colleagues in operations, but I was much closer to some of them; I counted them among my close friends. And now I had to put up with them regarding our ideas as mad. I was reminded of the myth of Cassandra—you tell the truth about the future but no one believes you—over and over and over and over again."

Government officials were even less receptive. Wack flew around Europe and North America handing out what the scenario planners called the "pink book"—the scenarios, edited for non-Shell eyes. Like many documents that must navigate a balance between two sets of constituents, it was extraordinarily difficult to produce; but even Frank McFadzean, the UPM promoter, praised it as one of Shell's most effective publications. But at best government officials listened politely without paying attention. The Americans refused to make time for Wack, whom they perceived as a middle-level Shell planner—a particular disappointment because the United States was the world's greatest waster of energy and could have done the most to avert the crisis in advance. At that time, the Americans were doing exactly the opposite of what was prudent: depleting their reserves of oil, instead of building them up. There was no political support for petroleum taxes, or even for encouraging energy efficiency. The American government was like a man who, hearing a warning that he may lose his job, goes on a spending spree; and the American oil companies were like an investment counselor who advises him to do exactly that.[37]

"We thought naively at the time," Wack recalled, "that governments would be wise enough to see what we told them, and act immediately on it. Instead, everybody thought we exaggerated. There was the same first reaction everywhere: 'Why does Shell tell us these horrible stories?' They tried to find out what interest we had. And obviously we had no interest; after all, we were predicting that our property would be nationalized. Second, they said, 'Oh, you exaggerate. It will not come in 1975. It may come in 1980.' Finally, the government officials would ask, 'How can I take advantage of this?' " One high-level politician from Alaska, for instance, wondered out loud whether an impending oil crisis meant they would be in a much better bargaining position for putting through the Alaska pipeline. No one ever seemed to hear Wack's main point: that by acting wisely, in concert, the developed nations could anticipate the crisis and stop it.

As bleak as things seemed, change did begin at the Royal Dutch/ Shell Group—lurchingly, arbitrarily, and almost unconsciously. In some operating companies, managers began to alter their land purchases; parcels slated for refineries were also designed to be suitable for chemical plants, in case the refineries became impractical. A few Shell engineers began designing refineries that could switch from Kuwait crude to Saudi or Iranian (all of which had different technical requirements), depending on what was available. In refining, they increasingly used a technique called "cracking" to upgrade more of the less valuable "heavy oil" and convert it into lighter, more valuable gasoline. The worldwide manufacturing coordinator, Jan Choufoer, had proposed these improvements in the past, but they had been considered too expensive under the old planning requirements. Now scenarios gave them a broader base of support and Shell moved, in oil company parlance, to the "highest-technology barrel." (Later, Choufoer would advance to managing director.)

Bit by bit, Shell executives began to put in place many of the commonsense, mundane frugalities which had been lost amid the frenetic growth of the 1950s and 1960s, but which all oil companies would have to learn to practice during the following years. The managers who made these decisions were, in effect, trapped by the scenarios; if they continued the old profligate policies, and the crisis indeed came to pass, they would not be able to claim now that they hadn't seen it coming.

"We had too long acted," Gerrit Wagner later wrote to Wack, "on the implicit assumption that the energy world revolved around Shell together with some other companies, without realizing that we were approaching the end of the oil era. We now had to observe a much larger scene and also consider a wider time horizon."[38]

By the following summer, Group Planning had begun to prepare the final version of a new, crisper set of three scenarios, designed to give managers a more intuitive, almost visceral understanding of their choices in the new world. These were scheduled to be presented to Wack's most cherished audience, the CMD, in October 1973. But there was never a chance to learn what the new approach might achieve. By the date of the presentation, the crisis had arrived, three years ahead of schedule, with its own existential imperative.

Through the summer of 1973 and into September, Saudi Arabia's King Faisal gave a series of interviews on American and British television. He wanted America to cut off all its aid to Israel. "It makes it extremely difficult," he said, "for us to continue to supply the United States with oil." He hinted that, if Arab nations got into a war with Israel, the Saudis would be tempted to wield their "oil weapon" and cut off supplies.[39]

The Saudis modeled their oil weapon wielding after the United States' own use of economic sanctions.[40] The next step, for instance, was to brandish the weapon by bringing it out into the open. Thus, in mid-September, OPEC's ministers told the oil companies that their current contracts, which were supposedly valid for another three years, were no good. They agreed to meet in Vienna on October 6 to negotiate new contracts. This happened to be set on Yom Kippur, the Jewish Day of Atonement, as well as during the Muslim feast of Ramadan.

The night before the Vienna conference was to begin, warplanes left Cairo and Damascus—bound, respectively, for the Sinai Peninsula and the Golan Heights. The first reports about the attacks implied that Israel's military had been devastated. It was a shocking moment for the West, and it startled the oilmen who represented the industry at the conference. Gradually over the next six days, the advantage shifted back to Israel's armies. The war added stress and agitation to both sides in the negotiations, and on October 12 the Vienna talks broke down completely. OPEC and the oil companies could not agree on a price.

That night, Gerrit Wagner was having dinner with his daughter, a college student who lived in a houseboat on a canal in The Hague. Midway through the meal, the phone rang; when his daughter handed him the receiver, he heard André Bénard's voice. Bénard was the Shell representative on the oil industry's negotiating team. "These guys are crazy," he said. The OPEC leaders were demanding a doubling in the price of oil—to the outlandish sum of $5 per barrel.

Wagner told him what all the oilmen already knew: the stakes were too great for the companies to negotiate on their own. They would have to check with the governments of Western nations, which would take at least two weeks. But Sheikh Yamani had no time for that. He would have to set a new price immediately, or else the Arab leaders would break off their deals entirely. They were too enraged by the war to wait. The Iraqis, in particular, were pressing to nationalize all the oil fields and cut off all shipments to America.[41]

Yamani himself did not want this to happen. He believed that the retaliatory climate from the West would be awful for Saudi Arabia, which depended on U.S. military protection. He wanted the Arabs to raise the price incrementally. That night, after midnight, he received Bénard in his suite, along with George Piercy from Exxon and two other oilmen. They asked once again for two weeks so they could get approval from their governments. He again insisted that a deal was necessary that night. He kept stalling them, doing anything possible to get them to agree before leaving the room. He offered them soft drinks, and when Piercy accepted a Coke, Yamani cut open a lime to squeeze into it. He passed around a plate of dates. "I always bring my own dates from Saudi Arabia," he said. "They're the best in the world." As evidence of good faith, he called another negotiator at the hotel, a delegate from Kuwait, who arrived in his pajamas. He called Baghdad, talking vigorously in Arabic, and then, when he got off the phone, he told the oilmen, "They're mad at you." He scrambled around looking for airline timetables, hoping to find the oilmen later flights. But finally, in the very early morning, he let them leave with no deal struck. "If you want to know what happens next," Yamani said, "listen to the radio."[42]

During the next few days, government officials crowded into the offices of oil company officials. Everyone wanted to make sure their country would not be shortchanged in relation to the others. Each country put pressure where it could; while the British enlisted Lord Rothschild to lobby Royal Dutch/Shell, the French threatened to tax or seize Shell's assets in France. "All right," said Wagner to each of them, "we'll do as you wish, provided you go and explain why they will get so much less oil in Bonn or Zurich or Barcelona." In the end, he felt that none of the countries had been prepared. "Nobody was ready. The whole thing was put back into our lap and we had to just make the best of it." The "best" of it was a provisional agreement, between the oil companies, to meet the Arabs' terms.

Meanwhile, the radio carried news of war. Israel pressed its military advantage against Syria and Egypt. The United States sent contradictory signals about whether it would join in. Arab leaders teetered between their fear of United States reprisal and their fear of Islamic popular rage. Then, on October 16, they finally struck with the oil weapon they had been brandishing. The OPEC leaders announced that, hereafter, they would set the price of crude oil themselves. The oil companies could take the arrangement . . . or leave it, and the Arabs would find other commercial partners. At this moment, the oil companies finally lost their domination of the international labyrinth of pipes and pumps, or so it seemed. Ironically, lack of control would make them richer, but they didn't see that yet.

A second blow to the West came on October 20, when the Arab oil ministers announced that they would punish "Western supporters of Israel" with an embargo. Only a limited number of barrels would flow to consuming countries. They would deal particularly harshly with the United States. This happened to come during the same week as Richard Nixon's "Saturday Night Massacre"—the firing of Archibald Cox, the prosecutor who had subpoenaed his Watergate tapes. If Nixon was distracted by Watergate, so was the rest of the nation; the embargo was thoroughly unexpected, not just by the government and public but even by many of the executives of American oil companies. They had assumed that the Arab nations would nationalize their oil production companies; an embargo had not occurred to them.

The embargo decision and the price decision had been made independently, by two separate bodies of OPEC ministers. Nonetheless, together the two had a devastating impact. The oil company representatives heard about the details of the embargo at another meeting with Sheikh Yamani, this one in early November. "Forget for a moment that you are representatives of oil companies," Yamani said, "and just put yourselves in our shoes."

Bénard, on behalf of the oil companies, found himself making a speech in reply. "I can very well understand that the temptation of increasing prices is irresistible for you," he said. "But if you act in a totally irrational way, you will have killed your clients. They will find a way to no longer need what you supply. So you have to think a little bit about how you treat them." It was a lecture that every leader in the industrialized world, corporate or government, could have benefited from hearing; the nuclear industry, the oil industry, the chemical industry, the automobile industry, the food industry— and the Arabs—would all fall prey to hubris during the following fifteen years.

Shell, as it happened, was the only major oil company that had taken measures before the shock. It would never again be thought of as the "ugly sister"; indeed, it would become Exxon's greatest rival. That was far in the future, but even in the short run, the October War and its catastrophic aftermath provided an enormous boost to the morale of scenario planners at Royal Dutch/Shell. "Having told everybody that the unthinkable would happen,"

Napier Collyns later remembered, "and then having it confirmed so incredibly quickly, gave us unbelievable self-confidence." Hard-boiled managers from Shell U.K. or Shell Malaysia could actually be observed wandering through the corridors at Shell Centre, saying, "Perhaps we should have listened to these guys."

Within ten days after the war started, the planners had put out a written scenario package that explained what was happening. Their speed was particularly impressive because they were also busy making presentations. Managers from most of the 270 operating companies were called in to hear Pierre Wack and Ted Newland. Then, while the planners took notes, each of the major operating companies—Shell Japan, Shell Oil/U.S., Shell Française, Deutsche Shell, and others—described how the supply system looked from their end. This meeting was a crucial strategic move, because Shell, like all the oil companies, was about to be placed in the uncomfortable position of allocating oil among all of its consumer countries, and at times there would not be enough to go around.

But the morale boost was short-lived. The operating companies and the departments of Shell Centre were still slow to change their behavior. They could intellectually see the forces at play, but they still felt committed to old habits. Wack began to think of his scenario method as a loud and ineffective machine, like a vacuum cleaner—wasting 40 percent of its energy in producing heat and noise. What was missing, he would later say, was "existential effectiveness," which he defined by quoting a Japanese proverb: "When there is no break, not even the thickness of a hair, between a man's vision and his action."

Despite all their unheeded warnings to public officials, the Shell managers still had their own "microcosms"—Wack's term for the inner views of the world that, contrary to whatever they espoused, would govern their actions. As long as they felt in their hearts, for instance, that the best policies were to "explore and drill, build refineries, order tankers, and expand markets," then they could not help perceiving evidence in support of those policies wherever they looked. Wack remembered visiting Nippon Steel in Japan. They had a completely different investment strategy than their French counterpart, the Usinor steel company. This was not a matter of one company being more rational or intelligent than the other; both acted rationally, according to their "mental maps" of the steel market. Those different perceptions, in turn, governed their actions and their justifications for those actions. To affect behavior in a useful way, he decided, the task was not just to argue with managers, or to lay out facts before them, but to change the "mental maps" they held of their world.

More than one planning staffer, for instance, vividly remembers his visits with Pierre Wack to Shell Marine, the international company that bought and managed Shell oil tankers and sea transport. Wack would conclude his presentation by saying, "Look, under every scenario we will need fewer tankers." There was, after all, no oil to carry in them. He would ask them to reconsider their current purchasing plans. In reply, some Marine people would tell him to come back in three months: "The boss is away in Japan, ordering ships, and the number two man is ordering some ships in Finland." Others would burst out in frustration: "I don't know whether to hire or build more tankers, or get rid of the whole fleet! I thought your job as planners was to tell me what the future would be." And yet others would say, "Well, we've looked at all these scenarios, and even if we believe them, we have such marvelous advantages with our superior ship designs that we don't need to stop ordering." Wack began to grumble that the scenarios had been like "water on a stone"; nothing was more difficult, he said, than changing the mind of a Dutch engineer.

In the meantime, the scenario writers had to start thinking about what to say next. The oil price crisis, they suspected, would open the world up to far more turbulent changes. Companies like Shell would have to pay attention to many things that had never concerned them before. There were obvious concerns, like environmentalism—which one of the planners, a Dutch enthusiast named Hans Dumoulin, had suggested they look into—or energy efficiency, which another planner, Gareth Price, was beginning to champion. And there were less obvious concerns, like the legal and public relations barriers that would keep Shell (and other companies) from being trusted in the future. Shell's policy in South Africa, for instance, would become a source of great controversy a decade later.

The planners didn't know most of the details yet, but they knew (along with a growing number of people) that relationships between corporations, governments, and the rest of society were about to change fundamentally. A time of shaking-up was coming, a bottleneck of trends in which all assumptions would be up for grabs. This period would last for years before things settled into a new equilibrium. Gareth Price had given the period to come the name "The Rapids," and Pierre Wack began incorporating the image in his talks. The Royal Dutch/Shell group of companies, and implicitly society as a whole, were like white-water rafters who hear the sound of the rapids they are approaching, just around the bend.

LOVERS OF FAITH AND REASON

"THE MECHANISTIC WAY OF THINKING CANNOT SUSTAIN ITSELF":
HERETICAL ENGINEERS AT THE STANFORD RESEARCH INSTITUTE AND MIT,
1955–71

The great professor and lover Peter Abélard was thirty-seven when he fell in love with a Parisian schoolgirl named Héloïse. He schemed to become her tutor, she gave her heart to him, and they married secretly. At that moment, early in the twelfth century, they became one of the first medieval couples (that we know of) to break the precedent of prearranged marriage in the name of romantic passion. Because professors at the University of Paris lost their privileges when they married, Abélard hid Héloïse in a convent after she became pregnant. Her uncle, after this insult, hired men to assault and castrate Abélard. For the rest of their lives, he and Héloïse lived married but apart. As a nun, she mourned for the passion they once felt. He retreated from his adoration for her and returned to philosophy. In that process, he became a heretic himself.[1]

A passionate lover seeks to know everything that can be

learned about the beloved. The lover dreams of understanding every mood and fulfilling the beloved's whims and vanities as no one else ever could. Abélard, caught up in the love of his church, used his classrooms and colloquiums to peer deeply into the motives and habits of Christian faith. He held the doctrines of the church up to examine them in the light of dialectic inquiry. Which, he asked his students, was more fundamental: the universality of God or the trinity of the church? He invited his students to express their doubts and reasoning, quoting from the sayings of Jesus Sirach: "He who believes quickly is frivolous." In an age when miracles were no longer commonplace, what other buttress could exist for faith except the understanding that comes from open reasoning and logical debate?

This passion became his crime. His teachings and writings became evidence of heresy; Abélard was forced to recant and was imprisoned. His books were burned. His sentence was pronounced by a group of drunken bishops at a bacchanalian feast. They fell asleep, one by one, below the table while Abélard wept, hearing his work read aloud and condemned.

When Abélard died of a skin disease six months into his imprisonment, Héloïse requested his body. It was sent to her convent for burial. She lived for another twenty years, and then was buried with her husband. Eventually, Abélard's students, and other people trained in logical discourse, developed much of Europe's scientific tradition. Abélard may not have inspired or trained all of them (though he had many students), but he exemplified their sense of purpose. Through their faith they discovered the gripping joy of reason.

▼▼▼

Nine hundred years later, in the 1960s, there was a man in California who lived his life as a sort of Abélard in reverse: through reason he discovered the compelling force of faith. His official profession was "futurist," an occupation that had not existed a few years before. His background included teaching circuitry design and philosophy to engineering students at Stanford University; a key role in an alternative religious movement; and another leading role in psychedelic drug and parapsychology research. The same drive that had led him into engineering, the drive to take apart and understand the world, had pushed him into mysticism.

This man was known in some business circles for his gift of engaging people in casual, but deep, conversation. An executive would stumble across his path, perhaps after a speech or in an airport bar between planes. Half an hour later, everything in the executive's life would be changed. Goals would shift. Possibilities would feel more open. The petty rules and formal procedures that seemed so confining before now seemed irrelevant. Spiritual growth was no longer something to be sneered at. It was a tool to be used, a part of daily life inside and outside the organization. It could be pursued *without* having to give up a job selling Coca-Cola or designing plastic components. Eventually, dozens of people in corporations throughout the world would carry fond memories of their brief but pivotal chat with this fellow from Stanford named Bill Harman.

Willis Harman was a part of the small, but long-standing, tradition of visionary engineers. This is the tradition of Nikola Tesla and Alexander Graham Bell, of Claude Shannon and Charles Kettering. They all built and crafted machines, often making fortunes by doing so, but then—in the process of building and designing—found themselves facing broader, more complex questions than they had

ever imagined when they began their careers. They devoted their
lives to a rational way of thinking, and suddenly came up against
problems that could not be explained rationally: human emotion,
aspiration, and ineffable purpose. Willis Harman, when that happened to him, embraced the extrarational qualities of life with an
Abélard's devotion. He spent his life trying to understand them—so
wholeheartedly that he renounced the value of rationality. In the
process, he "engineered" the beginning of the New Age movement.

Another visionary engineer, Jay Forrester, a very different man,
took his understanding from the construction of models. All machines can be used as analogues of deeper things; Sigmund Freud
had based his psychology on the analogy of the hydraulic pump.
Forrester built a modeling language on the example of
servomechanism motors. He used that language to describe and
predict feedback—the way that a circuit, an ecological niche, a human body, an organization, a culture, or any other system will regulate itself, growing or seeking stability over time. Some experts
said that these systemic behaviors were too complex to diagnose;
humans would never understand them.[2] But Jay Forrester's language seemed to apply in every sort of system—even the future of
the world as a whole.

Forrester's models were deeply rational—but they led their users
through rationality into an experience of faith. The most famous of
his models, the model of the world's future known as "Limits to
Growth," diagnosed a potential for global calamity inherent in the
rationalistic mind-set of the industrial age. To produce a worthwhile future (this model suggested), the policy makers of the present would have to develop a less mechanistic way of thinking about
population, economic growth, the environment, technology, and
human aspiration. These were all related; they could not be considered apart from each other. Faith and reason were part of one system, and somehow they would have to be reconciled.

It's worth noting the background against which Willis Harman and
Jay Forrester lived. World War II had been an extraordinary catalyst for the study of complex systems. Just as the war had mingled

social scientists in unprecedented numbers, leading to the invention of the T-Group, it had also assembled physicists, mathematicians, logicians, game theorists, and physiologists to work on problems beyond the range of any individual discipline. These were not engineers, but "operations researchers"—students of the nature of complex systems and developers of ways to manage them more effectively by translating them into mathematical models.

First in Britain and then in the United States, operations researchers helped military leaders set up complex radar mechanisms, calculate how the fewest boats could patrol the most water, and predict the casualties from bombing raids. Then, after the war, they adopted similar game theory and decision analysis techniques to the business arena, building mathematical models of advertising campaigns, factory openings, or procurement efforts.[3] Ordinary engineers solved problems in the time-honored Cartesian manner—breaking them into manageable parts and dealing with the pieces individually, and then reassembling them. But operations research problems couldn't be solved that way. An operations researcher had to look at the whole problem, the probabilities inherent in it, and the attitudes of the human beings involved.

Then engineers developed their own counterpart. Called "systems engineering," it was also inspired in part by the information theory and telephone network design ideas that had emerged at technical research centers like Bell Laboratories. By 1961, it was a well-established field. This was particularly wonderful for disaffected electrical engineers who felt, in their hearts, that building computers and designing chips were somehow trivial. Building an automated refinery, or installing a complex grid of traffic lights in an urban downtown, required new *types* of thinking, unprecedented in their complexity, blending computer science, civil engineering, aerospace technology, ergonomics, and servomechanism mechanics.[4] At last, engineers had a discipline where they couldn't be pigeonholed and where philosophy was an inherent part of the craft.

*   *   *

Despite the esoteric travels that consumed most of his adult life, there was always something a bit rumpled and down-to-earth, a bit prosaic, about Willis W. Harman. He had unusually penetrating eyes, set in a face like that of a middle-aged policeman: bushy eyebrows, a thick nose and jowls, and a quick, uneven smile. He talked a little out of the side of his mouth, like Buddy Hackett. His voice was sonorous and soothing; his words tended to be matter-of-fact. The most interesting thing about him, perhaps, was the way he pursued his philosophical quest with an engineer's deliberation.

Harman grew up in a rural town in Washington State during the Depression. After World War II, he moved to California and became a professor of electrical engineering. "I was minding my own business, with no thought of changing anything," he would later say. But in 1954, while teaching at Stanford University, his life changed when a Stanford business law professor named Harry Rathbun, a man Willis knew casually and liked, invited him to an informal off-campus seminar. The subject of the seminar was "values."

Willis expected an intellectual discussion group. Instead, he found himself in a sort of secular church. Its members studied scripture and spoke of Jesus Christ as a teacher, but they also studied Jungian psychology and mysticism. They sat in circles and described their own feelings and what they wanted most deeply for their lives. They meditated, as a group, to music; they painted with their left hands, trying to release locked-up creativity.[5] Rathbun, smiling benignly, was suddenly transformed into a spiritual leader. Willis signed up for a two-week program that Rathbun called a "Sequoia Seminar," held at a modest lodge in the hills above San Jose.

"The seminar was an upending experience for me," he would say years later. "It hit below the belt. I was aware of thinking about value issues and so on, but on the last day I started to report to the group what I felt I had learned and I burst into tears. I wasn't sad. They might have been tears of joy, except that I didn't know what I was joyful about either. I had no intellectual comprehension."

Richard Rathbun, the group's leader, had been an electrical engineer (like Harman) before going to law school. He was one of the most popular professors on campus, but he had never risen far in Stanford's academic circles. Instead, he spent most of his time, together with his wife, Emilia, producing their Sequoia Seminars, named after the nearby redwoods, in which people studied the life of the historical Jesus Christ as a model for how to live.[6] Like T-Groups, or like Saul Alinsky's community organizing groups, the Sequoia Seminars gave people a chance to delve below surface conversation. Members stood up and talked, often for the first time in public, about the unseen patterns in their lives, their fears and angers, and how they perceived each other. Repressed, hidden rage would burst forth, to be replaced by cathartic sobbing or fierce, unexplainable joy. In California in 1954, there were not many opportunities for this, especially if you wanted to keep your job as an electrical engineering professor.

Like many engineers, Willis had held an image of himself as a supremely rational person, a person who kept his emotions sternly in control. This way of living made people neurotic: it made you afraid of other people, yet desperately eager for their approval, and bursting with bottled-up rage. In the Seminars, Willis saw that his feelings had power and validity. Years later, remembering his sobbing, he decided that those were tears of gratitude. "At last I had gotten off dead center and was starting on some sort of path. But at that time it didn't mean anything to me, except that I was impelled to go and look into areas I had never looked into before—comparative religion, parapsychology, mysticism, the whole works."

Harman was a dogged researcher, and Stanford had an excellent library on mysticism and religion. For two years, he spent every on-campus moment in the stacks, ducking out just long enough to give his engineering classes. At night, after his wife and three children had gone to bed, he hit the books. He continued taking seminars, and gradually became part of the group's inner circle. Things might have ended there, except that in 1956 the group introduced him to another type of catalytic agent.

*　　*　　*

The Rathbuns knew a British-born philosopher and mystic named Gerald Heard, who lived in a Los Angeles canyon, and whose worries about atomic war had influenced them. Heard was also a close friend of Aldous Huxley—the British author who had written *Brave New World* and, more recently, *The Doors of Perception,* a book about his experiences with psychedelic drugs. When, thanks to the Sequoia Seminars connection, Heard came up from his Los Angeles home to give a lecture at Stanford, someone in the audience asked him about his experiences with mescaline and lysergic acid diethylamide (LSD). Heard gave a ten-minute reply, describing what it felt like to take a mind-altering drug. Listening, Harman suddenly felt that this was what he had been searching for.

Today, in a time when the word "psychedelics" conjures sensationalistic images of ruined lives or spent morals, it is difficult to convey—especially to businesspeople—the great value that people found in the drug LSD-25. In the early years of its existence, many psychologists hoped that LSD would become part of their everyday tool kit. Clinicians used it successfully to treat psychotics, alcoholics, and other psychiatric patients, and psychological researchers saw it as a way to learn about the workings and potential of the human brain. In the early 1960s, when the FDA banned the drug's casual use and strictly limited its use in research, a significant number of experimental psychologists felt deflated.

Thereafter, LSD's supporters tended to keep a low profile. For every Timothy Leary—thrown out of Harvard, discredited, and arrested—[7] there was at least one Willis Harman, who spoke of the drug openly throughout his career, but never as a missionary. He never proselytized or insisted. He never even lost a job over it.

When in 1957 he asked Gerald Heard for more information about the psychedelics, Heard referred him to Captain Alfred M. Hubbard—a man who would eventually be known as the Johnny Appleseed of LSD. A boisterous, coarse, crafty man who loved uniforms, drank rum, and took long meditation trips out in the desert, "Cappy" Hubbard was one of the first people to conceive of using LSD as therapy. At three Canadian hospitals, he had used it to help alcoholics make the first step in an Alcoholics Anonymous program.

When Cappy Hubbard talked about his past, his friends never quite knew what to believe. He said that he was a World War II veteran of the Office of Strategic Services (which had become the Central Intelligence Agency), and that the CIA still owed him back pay. He and J. Edgar Hoover were close friends. He had designed and built a nuclear-powered motorboat, which he piloted around Lake Union in Seattle. (According to Harman, he disassembled his motor and buried the pieces on an island in the Vancouver Gulf, to prevent any government from misusing it.) After the war, he had become a millionaire by running a small northwestern airline—and then he had walked away from his business (he said) after having a mystical experience in a forest. An angel appeared before him and told him that he could play a role in the birth of something very important to humankind. Shortly thereafter, he heard of a psychologist at the University of British Columbia who was experimenting with rats and LSD. Hubbard wandered in, introduced himself, took the drug, and thereafter devoted the rest of his life to it.

American LSD research was closely linked with the Central Intelligence Agency's "truth serum" experiments of the early 1950s. CIA agents not only took LSD themselves but doped their unsuspecting peers and monitored the results.[8] Hubbard, however, hated the CIA, not just because of the way he claimed they'd mistreated him but also because he disapproved of their purpose. LSD was for enhancing awareness, not for manipulation.

Meanwhile, however, the gentle people of 1950s suburbia "didn't have the vaguest fuck of an idea of what's going on out there," he'd say. "Most people are walking in their sleep," he told Willis Harman. A dose of LSD would wake them up. If enough people took the drug, Hubbard felt, it would free the world.[9]

With Hubbard visiting increasingly often, the inner circle of the Sequoia movement began to experiment with LSD—generally at their retreat, with one member taking the drug and the rest watching. LSD was still legal at that time (the late 1950s), but it was hard to obtain and was never taken casually. Fearful, intrepid, like a traveler pushing aside branches in an unexplored forest, the user in the center would call out every sensation, so the others could monitor his (or her) progress. Having taken the drug, there was no going back: it took an hour or two before the effects took hold, and they lasted eight hours or more. Always, an experienced veteran sat nearby, ready to calm the tripper in case of panic (Captain Hubbard took this role whenever he visited), but the Sequoia trippers rarely panicked, no more than a trained sky diver would panic, during a normal jump, halfway to the ground.

Harman took his first "trip" at a Sequoia member's home, with a half dozen members in a circle around him. Before long, he began to feel as if he had a jug inside himself, into which he had spent his life stuffing emotions. Now someone had pulled the plug. He saw the emotions, beaming glorious light, spill out and cascade around him. Then he grew light-bodied, and floated above the rest of them, looking down. He tried to test his perceptions, seeing how many different corners he could look down from, and trying to remember, so he could describe it later, how his inert body looked when seen from above. He could also see, he discovered, through the wall into the next room. Then he was overtaken with the sensation that he didn't belong up there. "And right on the heels of *that* was the reaction that I was not my body. I was not the gray stuff inside my cranium. I was something else that's not in the world of space and time. Finally, I understood why people spend their time praying."

After an hour or two, he fell back into his body, moved his limbs, and began, while still under the drug's influence, to describe to the Sequoians what had happened. They had, of course, only seen his physical form lying in front of them. And they had never heard anything like what he described. Driving home with him that night, his wife said, "If you keep getting mixed up with this sort of thing, we're going to have to get divorced, because it's all too frightening." But within a couple of months she had taken the drug too and forgotten her qualms.

The group dynamics of the Sequoia Seminars had shown Bill Harman that a world of strong feeling lay beyond the dogmatically rational worldview of his engineering training. Now he began to use LSD regularly to explore those new dimensions. It was thrilling to see the form of a face or a house or a tree shift, to turn into a creature of imagination that also revealed, somehow, its essential self. It enthralled him to peel away layer after layer of his own temperament, drawing continually closer to the primal heartbeat that he shared with every vertebrate on the planet. Sometimes he saw links between himself and other people, hanging like sparkling circuitry patterns in the air. Later, when he came down, he could remember those patterns and theorize about them—did they exist only in his mind, or were they always present, but the LSD made them visible? The drug started Harman into his lifelong fascination with the nonrational—an engineer's fascination, driven by the need to pin down the essence of the nonrational, name its parts, and try to spell out how it worked. He felt he had a special role to play, because he still had credibility in the engineering and technology world. Somebody needed to introduce the two worlds to each other.

There were already a few sympathetic people in the business world. One of the first was Myron Stolaroff, an executive with the Ampex Corporation, the foremost manufacturer of magnetic tape recording equipment. Ampex was also a military contractor, specializing in telemetry and monitoring equipment. In 1958, when Stolaroff was in his late thirties, he began to explore the use of LSD as a management tool. Like Willis Harman, he was both an engineer by training and a long-standing member of the Sequoia Seminars. He was good friends with both Gerald Heard and Al Hubbard, and his job—assistant to Ampex's president, with particular responsibilities for long-range planning—included the task of keeping track of new esoteric fields.

In using the drug, he had come to states where the mind was unusually clear, where new perspectives and ideas burst through. "Such heightened perceptions," he argued to the management committee, "could be valuable in improving business operations," and he urged them to sponsor a series of experiments with the drug. However, the management committee of the company vetoed the idea, and he acted alone instead. He brought a group of friends, all engineers, to a cabin in the Sierra Nevadas, with Captain Al administering the drug. He found the results fruitful enough to keep conducting experiments and recruiting more engineers, until finally, in 1961, he resigned from Ampex and founded his own nonprofit corporation for psychedelics research, which he called the Institute for Advanced Study (IAS).

From the beginning, Willis Harman was an enthusiastic volunteer consultant and a board member. So was Captain Hubbard, who arranged to have the LSD shipped in from Canada and also apparently leaned on some of his Washington connections to protect the institute from the increasingly strict LSD research bans.[10] Hubbard had also made an arrangement (with some of the National Park Service rangers, he claimed) to conduct LSD trips at Death Valley National Monument. He called the monument his "laboratory," and he regularly drove friends down there for weekend sessions. Meanwhile, at the Menlo Park offices of the institute, with a clinical psychiatrist on hand, Hubbard, Harman, and Stolaroff conducted trips for executives from firms like Ampex or Teledyne, a Los Angeles-based defense conglomerate.

"We were meticulous in *not* suggesting the kind of experience a person should have," Harman later recalled. "We put them in a room with light pop music in the beginning, which would shift after two or three hours to some deeply spiritual classical music, perhaps Bach. In the room there would be a red rose and other objects with spiritual significance. A mirror was always very important. One person, who was fairly controlled and obsessive, looked in the mirror and saw his face made of stone, with faint cracks. He was profoundly moved. You can call it a hallucination, but it was very creative—the psychedelic experience as a new concept in psychotherapy. Instead of going back and examining all your past traumas, you could have a conscious experience which set you off on a different course in your life."

Engineers, it turned out, were particularly good candidates for LSD research. They were often emotionally sensitive men with painful early lives. "This [had] resulted," Stolaroff later wrote, "in the choice of a vocation that dealt with inanimate objects, sparing further emotional pain. LSD was a marvelous tool for discovering and releasing buried feelings."

There were a wide range of responses, from the mundane to the mystical. Some alcoholics stopped drinking; some engineers found themselves capable of solving technical problems that had bedeviled them. There were measurable improvements in scores, related to rigidity and neurosis, on personality inventories. Managers became more poised; they handled disputes among people more effectively. Under the direction of some LSD experimenters high in the company, Teledyne began to treat its largely Mexican workforce with more respect and to invest more in educating and paying them. Stolaroff himself found that his ability to play the piano improved remarkably.

And there were uncanny cases, like that of a Teledyne engineer, who later became one of the company's most senior officers. He took a walk in the desert on LSD with Captain Hubbard and Hubbard's Pomeranian puppy. Along the way, the engineer conceived the notion that he and the dog had a mental link, that they could sense each other's "higher mind." All through the car trip home, the engineer kept trying to think up an experiment that could prove or disprove whether the mind link actually existed. Then, at a restaurant where he and Hubbard stopped for coffee, he looked up and said, "Al, we'd better check on the dog. He's in pain." He persuaded Hubbard to step out to the car. From the outside, the dog looked fine; but when they opened the car door, they could see the puppy had jammed its paw between the seats and broken its leg.

Cases like that showed why LSD research met with such resistance. How could you talk about paranormal phenomena in any rational way among a community of engineers without triggering distaste? And yet, those were the experiences that kept people returning to the drug; how could you *keep* from talking about them? There was also resistance from people who worried that "nonrational" experiences were evidence of insanity. Finally, although LSD was still legal, being a psychedelics enthusiast was not a terrific career enhancer, particularly if you worked for a defense contractor that had to put its people through security clearance checks. For all these reasons, the experimenters who visited the IAS tended to keep their enthusiasm to themselves.

One other factor made it difficult to talk openly about the LSD use; it disturbed the faith that the engineers had in technology itself as a panacea for social problems. After a week with Hubbard in the desert, one middle-aged Teledyne engineer described to Willis Harman a vision he had seen of the industrialized future. The world was like a train barreling down a technological track, but the tracks were about to bend sharply. The engineer didn't know where the new direction would lead. Nor could he tell whether the train would go off the tracks entirely. If they took their visions seriously, then men like this engineer—and men like Hubbard—would have to think seriously about how to keep civilization from derailing. After all, they had laid the track.

In the early 1960s, after the Rathbuns shrank back from using LSD in the Sequoia Seminars,[11] Harman drifted away from the Seminars. Stanford was spinning off a new systems engineering department, a potentially congenial place for him. No one would look *too* much askance if he began to raise general philosophical issues, or even spirituality, as part of his courses. Soon he was teaching a course on "the human potentiality," funded by a Ford Foundation grant for interdisciplinary studies. Because he was an engineering professor, Stanford's administrators assumed that his course wouldn't be too flaky. It would have practical relevance. But Harman focused it on Eastern religious traditions, "which we Westerners have neglected through the supreme arrogance of our belief system." He included material on indigenous North Americans, some Greek philosophy and European poetry, encounter group sessions modeled after the Sequoia Seminars (but without psychedelics), and books by the two psychologists who had been so important to the National Training Laboratories: Carl Rogers and Abraham Maslow. They were now becoming known as the founders of humanistic psychology.

The students in the course were young business majors, educators, and social scientists. Some were there on the earliest Vietnam War draft deferments for graduate students. Others had wives and young children. Most of them had never been asked to reveal their thoughts in a classroom before. But Harman was skilled enough to keep from threatening them. One of his 1963 students, a young man named Oliver "Mark" Markley, recalled Willis handing out a one-page poem by W. H. Auden, about an archetypal man ("Anthropos apteros," Auden called him, meaning "wingless man"), lost in a British garden maze:

> No question can be asked unless
> It has an answer, so I can
> Assume this maze has got a plan.[12]

Each of the stanzas that followed was like a rung on a theological ladder. A plan implied that God designed the maze. That, in turn, implied that a path existed out of it. But how could Anthropos find the path? Through his senses? Through logic? Through the dictates of feeling, or some form of spiritual renunciation? Then Auden parodied the idea that we create our own fate:

> I'm only lost until I see
> I'm lost because I want to be.

Auden had set the last stanza of the poem in italics:

> *Anthropos apteros, perplexed*
> *To know which turning to take next,*
> *Looked up and wished he were the bird*
> *To whom such doubts must seem absurd.*

"What do you make of this?" Harman said in class when they began to discuss the poem.

Nobody replied. Eventually, Markley inched up his hand. He was in his mid-twenties, a gangly sandy-haired youth raised in Kansas by fundamentalist Christian parents. He had come to Stanford for a bachelor's in engineering, on a fellowship designed for people with strict religious values. The course had been a disturbing initiation into esoteric mysticism for him. "I think it has to do with something transcendental," he said.

Harman smiled. "What do you mean by that, Mark?"

"I haven't the vaguest idea in hell," Markley blurted out. Harman smiled and moved on to the next student.

Markley felt his own mind racing; Harman had not answered him, but accepted him. That was typical of Harman. Male students from repressive backgrounds, in particular, tended to come away from his classes understanding that Harman accepted them with all their blocks and stiffnesses intact. "You didn't have to go all the way," another of his students would remember. "He didn't make judgments about you being good or bad, and, as a result, he was very supportive."

Late in the course each semester, Harman described his LSD research, and then told the mesmerized class that there was still a little such research going on, in a private center in Menlo Park, where he was a volunteer consultant. Any student with five hundred dollars could buy their way into the project. That would pay for the rigorous testing and counseling which led up to the trip and for a male and female sitter, who would accompany you through an all-day experience.

Markley lost no time signing up. For his first trip, Willis was the male sitter, and Markley's hallucinations foreshadowed the career both men would soon share. He saw the stream of history flowing as if it were a river between two banks: one side of fear and one of love. The two banks existed in perpetual balance: when torture, tyranny, and cruelty had risen in the Middle Ages, Markley saw them being balanced by the prayers of the Cathars and other heretical monastic orders. ("I could taste the personality venues of the different medieval orders, and say to myself, 'Oh, and here's what *they* contributed.' It was all visible in a synthesized realm.") When he came down, he and Willis both agreed that they had heard something calling them. "It seems like there's something new that's wanting to emerge," Willis said. "We can take part in helping the birth if we choose—or not if we choose."

Markley instantly changed the direction of his life. He had been pursuing a graduate degree in design engineering, but now he switched to social psychology, the field of people like Kurt Lewin and Robert Blake. He didn't want to be a psychologist. He dreamed of being a "social engineer." He wanted to be the bird flying over the hedge in Auden's poem. He wanted to see, and then help shape, the pattern of the labyrinth.

Markley spent another year in graduate school, now in psychology, before returning to the Institute for Advanced Study. This time, he joined Harman (and some other Stanford instructors) for a one-day experiment with mescaline: would the drug make people do better or worse on tests of creativity? After acing the creativity tests, the men spent the rest of the day experimenting with extrasensory perception, in which Harman's interest was increasing. He also knew that it had been a hot topic at the CIA during the 1950s. The spies had tried to view faraway missile bases through some form of drug-enhanced imagination.[13]

During the next couple of years, Markley sought out, and began to study with, the psychologists whose work had been so pivotal to Willis' class: Abraham Maslow and Carl Rogers. By mid-1967, he had a postdoctorate fellowship at the Western Behavioral Sciences Institute in La Jolla, near San Diego—the institute which Carl Rogers had co-founded, whose leaders aspired to build it into a West Coast counterpart of NTL. Meanwhile, Willis had been invited to leave Stanford University and join a group of technological researchers assembling at the Stanford Research Institute (SRI), the commercial research firm associated with the university. There was a growing trend in social science research; under the label of "technological forecasting," engineers and technologists were increasingly being asked to identify the social and political implications of the tools they built. Policy makers wanted to know, for instance, whether they should plan in advance for the advent of communications satellites or new types of rail links.

For Willis, the timing couldn't have been better. The FDA was about to ban LSD research entirely. Here was an opportunity not just to conduct research on broad social and philosophical issues, but to be influential.

They even had a potentially permanent client with deep pockets: the U.S. Office of Education, part of the Department of Health, Education, and Welfare. As part of the Great Society agenda of the 1960s, the education bureaucrats wanted someone to study how to design schools with an eye toward the future. What sorts of people would be needed in the year 2000, and how could they be educated now to meet those needs? This was a chance to look at the culture of the United States in the year 2000, and to express what they thought it *should* become. Was Markley interested in signing on?

The Stanford Research Institute, where Oliver Markley joined Willis Harman in mid-1968, was a hybrid institution: part commercial and part academic, part liberal and part deeply conservative. Its founding fathers included Herbert Hoover. An ardent alumnus of Stanford University (the Hoover Institute at Stanford is named for him), Hoover had pressed the university for years to create a research institute.[14] Ohio's industrial corridor had Battelle; the East had Arthur D. Little; New York had Bell Labs and General Electric's "Works" up in Schenectady. But there was no place where industrialists on the West Coast could hire academic scientists on a contract basis. Many Stanford professors loved the idea; they taught on the quarter system, which gave them several months per year of free time. But they had no venue through which to peddle themselves.

The Depression and World War II delayed the birth of SRI. It opened in 1947, just in time to take advantage of the great postwar economic boom, SRI's bread-and-butter work in the early years came from oil companies. But thanks in part to persistent lobbying from Hoover,[15] it also became one of the two primary outside research groups advising the U.S. military. (The other was the RAND Corporation, where Herman Kahn was involved in developing the scenario method.) SRI's first military projects included a Navy-funded search for a domestically grown rubber tree and a study for the Air Force: with the war over, could that branch of the military switch to handling domestic emergencies?[16] Perhaps because of projects like these, SRI became the first university-related think tank to include long-range planning for business, incorporating operations research, economics, and political strategy alongside its hard-science and military consulting.[17]

Around 1967, as the Vietnam War drained military budgets, government support for technology, hard science, and military research dwindled. (Herman Kahn had felt the same pinch.) At SRI, the futures research and other "soft" social science programs (which charged clients as much as 110 percent overhead, compared with the 50 to 80 percent a university might charge) were needed to pick up the slack.[18] Hence, the SRI administrators welcomed projects like Willis Harman's—which must first have seemed like it would be confined to the innocuous domain of education research. No one knew that Harman and Markley—and their client, a thirty-two-year-old U.S. Office of Education researcher named Hendrik Gideonse—were already talking about reshaping society.

Gideonse's small planning office had a budget of about one million dollars per year, and he was encouraged to use it in the most visionary fashion. Studies showed that it took fifty years for new education ideas to percolate into actual schools, and Gideonse thought ("with the hubris of youth," he later remarked) that this time could be halved to twenty-five years. To shape the schools now, the federal agencies needed to know everything they could about the social context of the year 2000. With the advice of Herman Kahn (who appreciated the opportunity to get out of the military rut), Gideonse funded five ongoing projects in 1967 on the future of education.[19] Harman and Markley won a contract for SRI, because of the way they proposed to combine hardheaded engineering approaches with the softer, values-oriented concerns of humanistic psychology. In early 1968 the SRI "futures group" (as Harman and Markley called it) began their research. They spun themselves through a variety of future-gazing methods, from straight-line numeric forecasts to literature searches on utopias and dystopias from science fiction. They pored through forecasts, coded trends onto punch cards, fed them into an SRI mainframe, and sorted through the resulting printouts of hundreds of alternative futures.[20]

The most daunting aspect of scenario work is complexity. Unless the boundaries of concern are drawn narrowly—as the Royal Dutch/Shell planners drew theirs around OPEC—it's easy to get overwhelmed with details. To help sort through the data, the SRI consultants called in a group of consultants who had helped Douglas Aircraft conduct similar "alternative futures" planning efforts by grouping possible events into "fields" and then assigning values based on their relative plausibilities.[21] For the education project, there were two key dimensions of uncertainty. One was the degree of "Faustianness"—how inept or adept would society as a whole be at controlling its destiny? The other dimension was "openness"— would society be flexible, open, tolerant, and civil or authoritarian, violent, and efficient? Plotting the possible futures on this scale, the SRI group ended up with a tree of destinies that split into five main trunks, each representing another path that America might travel.[22]

The SRI planners dramatized the full range of possible futures by walking into Hendrik Gideonse's office with a miniature tree which they had commissioned a sculptor to make from clear Lucite. This diagram shows not just the tree but the variations on the main trunks (in dotted lines) and a couple of rogue scenarios that Harman and Markley felt lay outside the "cone of plausibility"— for instance, a Soviet-controlled dictatorship in the United States was too improbable to worry about.

Anyway, the *plausible* futures were dire enough. They ranged from bureaucratic stultification and a raging recession (future #3, "Imprudent Optimism") to an apocalyptic future of pandemic violence and brutal police crackdowns in response (future #5, "Violence Escalated"). Schools would become armed camps taken over by street gangs. Terrorism, in the United States and abroad, would increase, and armies would mobilize against it. It seemed all too plausible in 1969, only a year or two after the U.S. Civil Rights Commission had implied that nothing could be done to avoid ur-

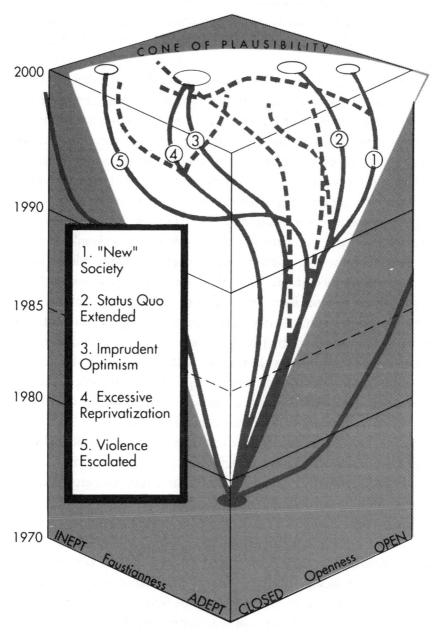

**Five SRI Scenarios for the Future
of American Society**

ban violence. Some of the details that Harman spelled out, in story form, to the Education Office bureaucrats, were startlingly similar to the way that the Symbionese Liberation Army/Patty Hearst saga would unfold five years later. One scenario (#2, the centermost branch of the Lucite tree) portrayed the optimistic "official future" of prevailing conventional wisdom. On the Lucite tree, that scenario was called "Status Quo Extended." Such problems as population growth, dissent, race relations, ecological destruction, and urban problems would simply take care of themselves. This was Herman Kahn's projected future, but neither Harman nor Markley nor any of the other SRI staffers believed it could happen. Wealth was concentrating too much in the hands of the wealthy; the American middle class, the path of social mobility, was shrinking.[23]

The SRI researchers only found one path through which a desirable future could unfold. They called this the "New Society" (future #1), notable for its high levels of openness *and* adeptness. But, realistically, this couldn't happen under prevailing government policies and the prevailing corporate structure. In fact, it couldn't happen unless the cultural values of industrialization shifted. People would have to learn to stop keeping up with the Joneses, or buying a new car each year, or filling their lives with junk. Government would have to learn to adopt an ecological ethic.

In 1971, Willis Harman took that message to Hendrik Gideonse and Gideonse's bosses, the directors of the U.S. Education Office. As officials of the U.S. government, he said, they had an important mission before them. Never mind the fact that they could lose their jobs next year if a new President was elected. Never mind that the scenarios had been commissioned as guides for school planning, not as a blueprint for large-scale social change. As the developers of educational policy for the next twenty-five years, said Harman, the bureaucrats of the U.S. Education Office would be the perfect people to lead a transformation into a postindustrial way of thinking.

Sure they would.

Gideonse's superiors at the Education Office listened blandly to Harman, Markley, and other SRI staffers talk of terrorists and ecological values, and then said that there was nothing to fear. The government was conducting raids on the New Left and expected to collect all its weaponry and explosives before long. The economy was in stable condition. All this talk of paradigm shifts seemed "so far out and touchy-feely and irrelevant," as Gideonse would later recall, "that they felt public money shouldn't support it."

Another factor made it inevitable that the project would peter out. Even before SRI's researchers had finished their first report or commissioned their Lucite sculpture, the Great Society had begun to grind to a halt. Nixon's election accelerated the dwindling of the Office of Education's budget, and the shrinking of its horizons to simple projects—curriculum guidelines and school construction support programs. Gideonse tried valiantly to protect the last vestiges of long-range planning. Like many idealists in government agencies during those years, he felt deeply betrayed by the way that events in Washington undermined the sense of possibility he had felt for long-term social change. He left in 1971. Meanwhile, Harman's group began looking for new clients: corporations and private foundations. Willis didn't mourn. Education, as these bureaucrats saw it, bored him. "The really exciting stuff," he would later say, "was going on outside the educational system. And still is."

This was the period when extrasensory perception experiments swung into high gear at SRI. First NASA and then the military began funding a small group of SRI researchers to experiment with remote viewing: spying on faraway sites using psychic means. Even within the institute, there was disagreement about whether or not remote viewing "worked," and if so, whether it was ethically justifiable. But in those years the futures group members were enthusiastic supporters, and occasional research subjects.

To Harman, the ESP work was significant because it demonstrated a giant flaw in the existing rationalist mind-set. He did not see it as a renunciation of science. Indeed, he had arrived at ESP *through* science. He was trying to portray the ineffable as a tangible thing, a component of the world that science and engineering must describe. It was difficult, because ESP work, no matter how vivid, confounded all attempts to measure or replicate it. Yet some experiences (they felt) couldn't be dismissed. In one SRI-sponsored session in group self-hypnosis, the researchers mentally followed the Apollo 13 moon flight, and (as Markley later wrote), got a distinct impression that something spherical was leaking. The next morning's news was filled with the emergency caused by leakage of the Apollo 13 tanks."[24]

Admittedly, there wasn't much that Harman and Markley could *do* with experiences like this. They couldn't write about it in SRI reports, or sell it in consultation. Nonetheless, the implications of the psychic work saturated their thoughts. If other people at SRI felt skepticism, well, that was just more evidence of the old, materialistic Western mindset embedded within people's tacit points of view. As that mindset fell away, as people left the attitudes of industrialized society behind, they would become more aware of the most exciting prospect of their time: designing a postindustrial, participative society no longer hamstrung by the tired values of the industrial era.

Around that same time, as it happened, the values of the industrial era were distinctly questioned, loudly and publicly, through the computer modeling work of another engineer—Jay W. Forrester, a fifty-two-year-old professor at the Massachusetts Institute of Technology. While people like Harman might be ignored, Forrester could not, because he was one of the most accomplished engineers alive. He had invented the addressing system for digital computer memory.

Forrester had grown up on a cattle ranch in the Nebraska Sandhills region.[25] After getting a graduate degree at MIT, he designed servomechanisms (mechanical automatic control devices), radar controls, and flight-training computers for the Navy. That led him, during the early 1950s, to a job managing Project Whirlwind, a team at MIT that built one of the first digital computers.[26] At Whirlwind, he figured out a way to organize into a grid the magnetic cores that stored information so that the contents of their memory could be retrieved.[27] "It took us about seven years to convince industry that random-access magnetic-core memory was the solution to a missing link in computer technology," he later said. "Then we spent the following seven years in the patent courts convincing them that they had not all thought of it first."

In 1956, while still in his thirties, Forrester had walked away from computer design, feeling that the exciting pioneer days were over. He joined the School of Management at MIT, looking for a way to use his intellect in the study of real-world problems. Soon after he arrived, a few managers from General Electric's household appliance division found their way to his office with a problem endemic to any manufacturing business.[28] Some months, the factories had so many orders they couldn't keep up, even with massive amounts of overtime. Other months, they wanted to lay off half their people. Why couldn't they develop a steady production flow? Why did orders rise and fall?

Traditionally, managers blamed these types of fluctuations on business cycles. Sometimes consumers bought more, sometimes they bought less, and there was nothing one could do about it. But that explanation didn't sit right with Forrester. The dynamics reminded him too much of servomechanism controllers. A servomechanism is a mechanical device hooked to a sensor, like a thermostat on a building's automated heating unit. The first signals to come in from temperature sensors often report that the building is still too cold. Thus, the thermostat may continue dispensing heat, and the building becomes too hot. The thermostat signals for cooling but, once again, it takes time to change the temperature. The building becomes too cold. The fluctuation has nothing to do with the actual outside temperatures, but with the disparate rhythms of the heating versus the measuring devices. It seemed to Forrester that the General Electric managers were faced with a similar problem— and if so, they could fix it.

A few economists had used servomechanism theory to develop models of business cycles during the 1930s and 1940s.[29] Those system models incorporated the principle of feedback: the idea that influence is cyclical. You turn a faucet to produce a stream of water and fill a glass, but the volume of water in the glass is also controlling your hand, by influencing it to stop when the glass gets full. Feedback relationships in business could interact for years, with various management policies pushing each other in intricate patterns, producing complex results that would seem thoroughly mysterious unless you understood the dynamics of their interrelationships over time.

In the first quarter of GE's data that Forrester studied, for instance, retail appliance sales increased by 10 percent.[30] Retailers then ordered more appliances to refill their inventories. But it took weeks for orders to work their way through the wholesaling channels and for the GE factories to ship their products. While they waited, retailers tended to panic—and to pile on more orders than they needed. This, in turn, caused distributors and wholesalers to pile on their orders, and that, in turn, added pressure at the factory, where orders jumped by 51 percent.

After six months, when all the orders had finally arrived, there was a glut at appliance stores, so they cut orders and returned their

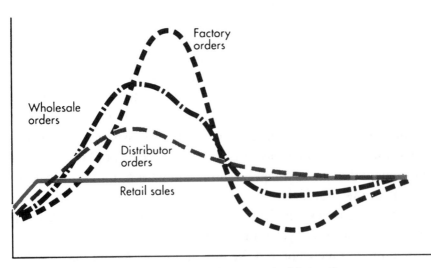

**Production Fluctuations in Household Appliances,
(as described by Jay Forrester)**

extra stock to the warehouses. Distributors, in turn, sent them back to GE. Factory production eventually dropped to 3 percent below where it had started—a disaster. The result was a series of curves that rose and crashed in succession.[31]

That tiny 10 percent jump in sales had been amplified again and again as it worked its way back and forth along the distribution chain, until it resulted in hundreds of thousands of dollars' worth of excess toasters on warehouse skids. It was all exacerbated by the managers' reactions to what they perceived as outside problems— like seasonal demand or competitors' actions—because they had no understanding, Forrester said, of how the system worked. If they really wanted to smooth out the fluctuation, he suggested, they could eliminate a level of distributors or react more slowly to surges of orders. That's where the leverage existed.[32]

Soon, Forrester developed a computer model of GE's supply chain, which some of his MIT students turned into a board game for team play in the early 1960s. As college students, they found beer more appealing than toasters, and they called it the "MIT Beer Game." It is still played frequently in corporate training programs. But there was a lot more to Forrester's method than streamlining the production-distribution cycle. Concepts from engineering, such as noise (irrelevant signals) and the use of non-linear equations, all had implications for his managerial models. Determined to develop a professional field of system dynamics, Forrester wrote a computer modeling language (called DYNAMO) that represented managers' decisions in terms of the vessels and pipeline valves ("stocks and flows") of fluid dynamics.

Forrester believed that managers' intuitive "mental models" (as he called the theories that most of us have about the nature of the situations around us) were ill-suited for anticipating the future behavior of systems.[33] In one celebrated case, he advised the Digital Equipment Corporation to expand production into a full floor of the former woolen mill where DEC was founded. "A lot of companies think they expand as a consequence of orders," he told the other members of the Digital board of directors. But orders, he argued, actually come in as a consequence of expansion. They held their next meeting in the new space, an empty floor as big as two football fields. Standing in the middle of the room, they could barely see the windows at the ends. Nine months later, the floor was completely full of machines and people, returning a net profit of 15 percent after taxes. Digital continued to buy buildings and land in the area ahead of the time when they would be needed. Forrester's suggestion thus contributed to the development of the Route 128 industrial corridor outside Boston.

Forrester developed and tested more computer management models over the next decade, in arenas as diverse as manufacturing, city government, and medical research. His first book on corporate systemic patterns, *Industrial Dynamics,* came out in 1961. It was compared with the work of Galileo, Malthus, Rousseau, and John Stuart Mill.[34] But despite the persuasiveness of his method, Forrester realized that any widespread acceptance of system dynamics would be slow to arrive—even in corporations, seemingly the most favorable environment. Like Pierre Wack, he felt that mental models were so deeply embedded in managers' thinking that they could not imagine alternatives. Eventually, after a decade or more of regular computer use, the "authoritarian, socialist" bureaucratic mindset of modern corporations might dissipate.[35]

Part of the problem was his own personality. Jay Forrester had a superciliousness to match his brilliance. He was known for being a tough student advisor and stubborn in arguments; his stiff demeanor conveyed the impression, whether he intended it or not, that nobody else understood the truth about a system as well as he did. Implicitly, the entire field of system dynamics suggested that nobody should make policy decisions unless they understood the counterintuitive logic of nonlinear equations. Otherwise, they would never understand how systems, influenced by those dynamics, interacted in the real world.

In 1970, the real world invited Jay Forrester to use his system dynamics approach on an unprecedented scale. The invitation came from the Club of Rome, an informal society of business managers, academics, and political leaders. The Club's membership was international, entered through invitation only, and limited in its bylaws to one hundred people. They had organized themselves in 1968 to investigate what they called the world's *problématique humaine:* their feeling that world population, pollution, poverty levels, natural resource depletion, crime, international terrorism, and youth rebellion were all bound inexorably for crisis, and were also somehow interrelated. Could any of these problems be tackled in the long run without addressing the others?

Aurelio Peccei, the founder, didn't think so. He was the prime mover behind the Club, a sixty-two-year-old former Fiat executive, a longtime member of the Olivetti board, a former World War II anti-Fascist resistance leader, and the founder of ItalConsult, Italy's most prominent economic consulting firm.[36] Peccei had intended the Club to be a carefully selected group of people who could investigate the *problématique* and present the public with an approach to solving it. There was always a long waiting list to get into the Club, for the members included a variety of eminences and thinkers: Hassan Ozbekan, a Wharton professor who had prodded Peccei to start the Club; Eduard Pestel, president of the University of Hannover in Germany; Saburo Okita, head of the Economic Research Center, a private institute in Tokyo; and Carroll Wilson, who had been one of the first people appointed to the U.S. Atomic Energy Commission and was now one of the most respected and beloved members of MIT's faculty—a physicist who had spent the last few years researching the longtime effects of pollution.

Wilson introduced Jay Forrester as a new member at a Club meeting in Bern, Switzerland, in June 1970. The Club had been promised a $400,000 grant from the Volkswagen Foundation if they could propose a viable research project. Hassan Ozbekan, the Wharton professor, had written a preliminary proposal, but the foundation had rejected it; they had sent $40,000 instead, to finance another proposal. Now the sixty-odd members of the Club couldn't agree on how to proceed. As a result, the whole project was floundering. Forrester sat through the first day without saying anything, feeling self-conscious about being an "ugly American" in this international gathering. Then, at 6 P.M., someone mentioned that Volkswagen would cancel the grant unless the Club could show they had a satisfactory methodology.

"Excuse me," Forrester said, "I think I have the methodology you are looking for." He explained briefly and invited them to visit MIT and see for themselves. Nobody seemed to hear him. He settled back in his seat until another lull in the conversation, when someone remembered him and asked him to elaborate. "This isn't something I can cover briefly," Forrester said, and once again invited them to visit—but either for two full weeks, he added, or not at all, because it would take that long to understand.

They agreed to come three weeks hence. Suddenly, Forrester had only days to organize a massive conference. On the flight going home, he began to muse about what he would show them. He began scribbling out a design for a model of the *problématique;* before long, his diagrams occupied nine empty coach seats. On the following Saturday, the Fourth of July, Forrester worked until eleven at night, converting his equations into a computer model (which he named "World").[37] By the time the Club of Rome members arrived in mid-July, his model was virtually complete.[38] Forrester's graduate students quickly painted it onto a white bedsheet, which covered one wall of the MIT classroom where the group met.

Like all of Forrester's models, "World" was a computerized network of interrelated policies, all affecting each other over time, as the model evolved. When "population" rose, for example, that caused "demand for goods and services" to rise, which increased "employment" and "capital investment," which allowed "population" to rise still further. A cycle was in place, pushing "population" continually higher, unless other forces intervened. There were many such interrelated cycles in the model, and they all came alive when researchers "ran" the simulation. A researcher could enter in a scenario of zero population growth, or of rapid population growth, along with various policies for economic development and agricultural production. Then the model would churn out its calculations and simulate the fate of the world over the course of two hundred years. The model was not intended to be accurate in local detail, but the plausibility of its relationships were confirmed later by research that the Club funded.

As soon as the Club first saw the model at MIT, there was flak—especially from Hassan Ozbekan, the project's own director. He resigned in protest after a stormy confrontation in Forrester's office. "You're selling out!" he said, meaning that he did not trust a technique based on a computer simulation. Then the Volkswagen Foundation trustees, apparently unwilling to send $400,000 to the United States, reduced the size of the grant to $240,000. The Club of Rome wanted Forrester to drop all his other work and devote the next year to refining, testing, and reporting on the model, but he refused; instead, he delegated the job to a team of MIT-based researchers.

The team was led by two postgraduates, around thirty years old, who were married to each other and had just finished a yearlong trip around Asia together. Their names were Dennis and Donella (Dana) Meadows. Dennis was lanky, long-faced, long-sideburned, slow-speaking, and cerebral; his previous system dynamics work had focused on the fluctuations of pork bellies in commodities markets.[39] Dana was talkative, a bit elfin in her features, and an avid writer. Her background was in biophysics and ecology. "I saw the world through the second law of thermodynamics," she later said.

They had stepped forward as volunteers to claim the project, and Forrester did not object. He completed his model, now called "World 2," and produced a book, *World Dynamics*, that he felt "had everything necessary to guarantee there would be no public notice." It had forty pages of equations and dealt with issues decades in the future. He doubted it would even get reviewed, but it garnered notices in the London *Observer*, *The Christian Science Monitor*, *The Wall Street Journal*, and *Fortune*. The notices were generally receptive; they focused on the message that the model seemed to substantiate, based primarily on the interrelationships between economic growth, pollution, and the consumption of resources. If unchecked and unmodified, industrial civilization would overshoot its ecological and population limits—and painfully collapse.

That was the nature of exponential growth—growth which builds upon itself, faster and faster. It can lead to deep trouble that isn't *seen* as deep trouble until it's too late. In the final rendition of the model (now named "World 3"), the MIT researchers tracked five key variables: population, food production, industrial production, pollution, and the consumption of natural resources. If you looked at each of these growth patterns separately, they all seemed relatively easy to cope with, and some seemed like cause for celebration: the changes in industrial output suggested that the world's overall living standard would double by 1984.

But growth in each of the five key variables seemed to accelerate the growth of the others—to a dangerous degree. The modelers entered various proposed "fixes, such as technological investment, higher-yield agriculture, and higher prices," into the program. In every case, unless industrial growth in its current form leveled off somehow, the model led to calamitous decreases in population, and finally in pollution, as industrial civilization faltered. Even without a decline in natural resources (for instance, if low-cost nuclear energy replaced oil), industrial growth would still be stopped by the accelerated rise of toxic pollution.[40]

Dana Meadows didn't fully see the implications until a meeting at a resort outside Ottawa early in 1971 where the MIT team made a presentation to the Club of Rome. Listening to Forrester explain how limits to growth occur in other types of systems, such as corporations, Dana had a vision of the Asian countries she'd visited the year before. She'd seen places where local economies collapsed after the villagers burned up their forests for fuel. The same thing could happen to the world as a whole, she thought. With half an ear, she heard the Club of Rome members argue back. They were trying to solve every problem with economic growth. As she listened, it seemed to her that this fixation on growth—this "mental model," as Forrester called it—was a boastful, bullying, living thing, with its own malignant needs. It seemed to believe that, while the world's resources and pollution capacities were infinite, the wherewithal for a decent life was scarce. The only effective way to live well was to grasp and hoard. What civilization really needed, she thought, was the reverse: an attitude whereby the earth was seen as finite, but sharing was appropriate. If people managed their own endeavors more efficiently, there would be enough for everybody's real physical and emotional needs. Businesses would have to find ways to be innovative *without* the emphasis on growing—by providing better services and better goods. We'd need to start asking ourselves, she decided, what are we growing *for?* For whom? For how long? And at what cost?

Questions like these were gaining urgency. Not long before, in January 1969, 5,000 barrels of oil had burst through undersea fissures beneath a Union Oil Company drilling platform a few miles offshore, near the Santa Barbara coastline. It later came out that the U.S. Geological Survey had granted Union Oil an exemption from drilling regulations, allowing the company's technical crews to install a shorter-than-standard casing inside the well's hole. Moreover, the company's geologists had known in advance that the channel's frequent earthquakes made it vulnerable to seepage. But they cut corners and discovered only after the fact that they couldn't contain the damage. The eruption left behind an 800-square-mile oil slick, thirty miles of sludgy beaches, some memorable photographs of oil-slicked gulls, two years of lawsuits and investigations, and a permanently foul reputation for offshore drilling.[41]

Previous conservation movements had been created by a love for natural environments. But the environmentalist new wave was motivated by a keen sense of loss. People felt personally bereaved. They had seen forests lost to development, streams lost to pollution, rivers to dams, and beaches to oil spills. They blamed corporations; they blamed government. They did not want it to happen again. But they lacked any sense of how to prevent it.

At that meeting, Dana Meadows volunteered for the job of preparing a ten-page summary of the results of "World 3." Instead of ten pages, she turned in twenty, which (after comments and questions from various Club members) expanded to 110. Aurelio Peccei, who of the leading Club of Rome members was probably the most impressed with the project's results, finally took the Meadowses aside. "The technical report is fine, but what we really need is Dana's little memo as a book." It was published, under the title *The Limits to Growth*, early in 1972 and rapidly became a best-seller.

In April 1972, the economists began to hit back. The first major negative review appeared in the New York *Times*, written by a Harvard economist named Peter Passell and two Columbia University economists named Marc Roberts and Leonard Ross. *The Limits to Growth*, they said, was "empty and misleading": it was based on an "intellectual Rube Goldberg device," full of "arbitrary conclusions that have the ring of science" but were really "less than pseudoscience."[42] *Nature* and the *Economic Journal* were harsher still. Economists and economic writers turned on *The Limits to Growth* throughout America and Europe, setting off a firestorm that would inflame the debate about economic growth for another twenty years.

The popularity of the small book made it an easy target. But even if it had been nothing but technical documentation, *The Limits to Growth* would probably have been attacked. To leftist economists, it was a slap in the face to developing nations, who were trying to improve their standards of living. To rightist economists, the *Limits* argument for global-scale planning would pave the way for a domineering world government. Forrester (in his earlier book *World Dynamics)* had actually suggested that governments should restrict the supply of money available for investment, as a curb on industrial growth and to cut back on the "green revolution"—deliberately producing *less* food to discourage population growth.

The model treated the entire world as one place, said critics, ignoring the divisions between the industrialized North and the developing countries of Asia, Latin America, and Africa. (This charge was true.) The model didn't seem to recognize that when timber fuel ran out, it would be replaced by coal fuel; when copper ran out, it would be replaced by fiber optics. (This was false; the "World" model builders did recognize substitution, and built some into their calculations. But they also felt that there are limits to substitution.) Some space enthusiasts, like science fiction writer Jerry Pournelle, criticized the model for leaving out the resources that would come from colonizing other planets.[43]

Most damning of all to the critics was the lack of a pricing mechanism. The last drop of oil would cost the same as the first drop to come out of the ground. If true, it would have made the model patently ridiculous. This charge, however, was false. The price variable was present, but aggregated into other factors and covered so obscurely in the text that most readers overlooked it. It was just one more example of how a central factor to economists could seem trivial to engineers, and vice versa, in a way that made conversation about the issues impossible.

Finally, critics charged that the model left no choice but zero growth. This too was wrong. The Meadowses, Forrester, and Aurelio Peccei found themselves insisting, time and time again, that they wanted to change the *nature* of growth, to make it more responsive and intelligent. Moreover, like all scenario builders, they were not *predicting* the future. They wanted to open up debate. In the tradition of system dynamics modeling, producing a model was only the first stage. Then you brought the model into the open for critique and refinement. Instead, debate polarized. Either the *Limits* argument was sacrosanct, or it was demonic. Growth was either the culprit, or it should not be questioned at all.

A few corporate managers refused to ignore the questions raised by *The Limits to Growth*. Robert Rodale of the Rodale Press, Ted Turner (of the then-fledgling Turner Cable Network), and Robert Anderson, the CEO of Arco Oil, all made public statements supporting discussion. Anderson might have gone further—he had even written his own report on the subject—but the vice presidents at Arco banded together and asked him not to publish it. This was one of several incidents that led Forrester to decide that the *Limits to Growth* theory was far more threatening to people inside organizational hierarchies than to those who had already risen to the top.

Dana Meadows saw the same thing when she spoke at business gatherings—as she did dozens of times during 1972 and 1973. In her memory, all the conversations blended into one recurring exchange:

"You're telling me my company can't grow?"

"Well, you could always deliver higher quality or concentrate on improving services." Then she would look slyly up at them and ask, "And why does your business have to grow anyway?"

She never remembered any of the answers; to her, the answers sounded like babbling. Why did they need to grow? Because that was how they measured success. The more their company grew, the more profits they could claim they created, and the more opportunities they would be given to increase their bailiwick. It was like asking why they needed to breathe oxygen.

Willis Harman began to quote from *The Limits to Growth* soon after it came out. It was rational itself, but its conclusions meshed perfectly with his renunciation of rationality. The industrial world, built by engineers, was enmeshed in a reductionist way of thinking. People, *without even realizing it,* had fragmented their lives. They separated their work life from their home life, as if they were two different people. They solved their family and personal problems by tearing them into pieces. They shrank back when conversations led to areas which might cross cherished boundaries.

Those of us from literary and artistic backgrounds, who look for patterns of the whole as a matter of course, might find this insight commonplace. We might wonder what all the fuss was about. We couldn't appreciate the compelling force it held for the engineers, social scientists, and managers who all their lives had been taught to compartmentalize.

For one thing, there were dramatic implications for designing work flow. You could not look at one division or department or function without considering the ramifications of your work for everyone else in the company. Marketing and finance, operations and research, were all part of one huge system, and when you saw them as a system, you had to look out for all of them, instead of boosting one at the expense of another. That's why the world's problems, as shown in *The Limits to Growth,* were such a valuable metaphor. On the surface, they seemed intractable and incomprehensible.

But you didn't have to see *all* the pieces fully, or understand them in a mechanistic way, to be able to act effectively. You *could* develop a good enough understanding of the relationships between the pieces so that you could act compassionately and elegantly for the benefit of the system. That was powerful—and novel in corporate circles. It explained why, even as Willis Harman and Oliver Markley, the SRI engineers, grew increasingly extreme, they continued to find young engineers and managers willing to follow their lead. They had seen the sheer, pragmatic, exalting *usefulness* of system-centered, holistic faith.

PARZIVAL'S DILEMMA

"A HERETIC'S LIFE IS A LIFE OF LEARNING":
EDIE SEASHORE, CHRIS ARGYRIS, AND
WARREN BENNIS, 1959–79

The stories of the Knights of the Round Table, hybrids of Christian and Celtic tradition, inevitably incorporated heretical influences.[1] *Perhaps some of the influences traced back, through chains of song and sermon, to Pelagius himself. Pelagius had said that salvation depends on people's own faith and deeds, and his followers, through the centuries, faced an eternal dilemma. The stakes were too high for error. If we are damned for our actions, but don't know our actions' results, then how dare we act? And yet, how dare we refrain?*

Parzival, a mythical young knight, faced this dilemma at the turning point of his life. His story, written in verse by a twelfth-century German knight named Wolfram von Eschenbach, is the most gripping of all the courtly tales. Eschenbach may have been a heretic himself; some sources link him with the Cathars, the most durable of the forbidden sects.

Parzival is a Knight of the Round Table—a bumptious, un-schooled youth whose mother deliberately tries to keep him from becoming a knight, for fear that he will be killed. None-theless, he finds his way to Arthur's court and the most sol-emn quest imaginable—the quest for the Holy Grail. At the most pivotal moment in his travels, Parzival visits the castle of Anfortas the Fisher King, the keeper of the Grail. The king is borne on a pallet into the great banquet hall. He has been wounded by a spear in his groin. He cannot stand or sit. He can barely lie still. The room glistens with luxury and expecta-tion. It has been foretold that the spontaneous act of a knight's noble heart will cure the king. For his part, when he sees the prone figure surrounded by weeping attendants, Par-zival feels drawn to rise to his feet and cry out: "What afflicts thee, Uncle?"[2]

But Parzival holds his tongue. He has been taught that a knight refrains from asking too many questions.[3] It would be dishonorable and improper. The festivities continue, albeit with a melancholy air, for by keeping still, Parzival has missed his chance to heal the king. Behind his politeness was the uni-versal fearful desire, spawned in all of us by civilized manners: the desire to figure out the rules and be safe, to know ahead of time whether our action will damn us. Parzival had worked all his life to master the knightly training. He couldn't leave all that training behind—could he?

Parzival awakes alone the next morning; all the residents of the castle have vanished. He spends the next five years lost and ashamed. Eventually, he finds his way back to the castle and heals the king—which, as Joseph Campbell pointed out, represented a dramatic shift for medieval mythmaking: at last, salvation could take place not just by being chosen but by persevering in our muddled way toward the aspirations we know are right. Every act is Pelagian in its intent, full of grace, and yet every well-intentioned act produces bitter consequences, just as the Augustinians warn. Given that harsh reality, Wolfram counseled his readers, there is only one course to follow. Lean toward the good. Turn your mind to humility. Deepen your own understanding, so that when called upon to say, "What afflicts thee, Uncle?" you can confidently rise to the occasion.[4]

▼▼▼

In the 1960s, as organization development burst out into large mainstream companies, its practitioners faced their own version of Parzival's dilemma: how did they know when it would be right to act? This had never been a problem in the past. The founders of National Training Laboratories, as purveyors of a vehicle of uncommon power (the T-Group), had always kept that power under strict control. The elaborate gauntlet of mentors that researchers had to pass to become fellows at NTL made the group dynamics community as fiercely protective of its secrets as a medieval guild. But then Douglas McGregor had published his book *The Human Side of Enterprise* and made the secrets visible. Robert Blake and Jane Mouton had commercialized them with the "Grid" system. Other NTL regulars had set up their *own* consulting operations, so that by the early 1960s, a nascent profession of "organization development" specialists and "human potential" advocates already existed. They sold T-Groups, and other forms of group dynamics, as a set of methods to help develop and nurture the "human resources" of the firm. After all, weren't the employees assets just as much as the capital investments, equipment, and receivables which showed up on the balance sheets?

If you were an OD practitioner during those years (or, in the language of the profession, a "process consultant"[5] or an expert on "team building"), you would become a coach to a team, sitting in on their meetings as they deliberated investment decisions or customer problems. You would help them talk safely about dangerous subjects, encourage them to build up trust, and continually bring to their attention their own behavior as a clue to deeper personal attitudes, the culture of their company, and how the two fit together.[6]

You might film the team's sessions, just as the T-Groups had been recorded, or let half the team watch the other half discuss its work in a simulated "fishbowl." You might conduct surveys: On a scale of 1 to 5, were the team members clear or uncertain about the team's purpose? Did they feel free to speak or were they cautious and guarded? Then you would feed back the anonymous results, in a package, to the team. In short, you would explicitly engineer all the types of conversation that in preindustrial vernacular village life had flowed naturally through the well-worn channels of custom. But in the formal ambiance of corporate culture, those channels did not seem to exist and managers could not manage their relationships on their own.[7]

As an OD consultant, Parzival's dilemma was built into the nature of your job. Your most fundamental premise came from Kurt Lewin: to understand a system, you must try to change it. You *had* to intervene. You had to stand up and ask, "What afflicts you, Uncle?" Yet your paycheck or consultant's fee came straight from the old established system that you were trying to change. And your entire discipline of T-Group practice was only twenty years old. T-Groups seemed to work fine in the rarefied hotels where executives went for off-sites. But inside the organization's own walls, who knew how easily they might backfire?

There are hundreds of people whose stories could be told here as part of the continuing story of NTL. But three practitioners in particular stand out. Between them, they encapsulated the influence that NTL would have on the rest of the culture. Each started out to change the world, and each ran up against Parzival's dilemma. Each had to find a way to act, balancing a new understanding against the old orthodoxy, while the potential for mistakes grew ever higher. Each found a different resolution: a different way of muddling through.

All three of them would eventually become famous, at least in organizational circles. Edie Seashore would be known as the matriarch of the organization development field, the NTL president-cum-house-mother who lived next door to the Bethel campus, and the co-designer of the most innovative effort to achieve organizational diversity in management history. Chris Argyris would be known as the theorist who found a way for managers to reconcile their imperfect behavior with their professed ideals. And then there was Warren Bennis—lecturer, professor, essayist, university president, author of prominent books on leadership, dreamer of grand visions, and the only NTLer to actually take the helm of a large organization and try to reshape it from the top.

There was a lot of joy in the work of organization development. If you were good at it, you could not only earn a living but could design a life for yourself with far more verve and flexibility than the humdrum work lives of most of your clients. You could help heal organizations—and, better still, you wouldn't have to *work* in one.

Consider the life of Edith Whitfield Seashore. She was, by many accounts (including her own), the most popular trainer in NTL's history. She was a vivacious, fast-talking, auburn-haired Jewish woman from a New York City suburb, who had gone to Antioch College, participated in student politics, met college president Douglas McGregor, and turned her life around to follow his example. McGregor had recommended her to NTL in 1950, just as she was leaving her senior year at Antioch College. That summer, in exchange for T-Group training, she bartered her time—putting together course materials and running contests on the golf course. She was not only the youngest person on the NTL grounds in Bethel but one of only two women staff members. And yet, among all those pompously earnest middle-aged men, she naturally fit in. She had the NTL gift for speaking plainly without offending; and she also had an uncanny ability to attract friendship. When she got home in the fall, Edie Whitfield was surprised to receive a call from Lee Bradford himself, the director. He had barely spoken to her during the summer. "We'd like to have you back next year," he said.

"That's wonderful," she replied. "I loved it up there."

"It's obvious you did." He mentioned a survey they had conducted, asking everyone at Bethel to name the people with whom they felt sympatico. "You were the star," Bradford said, "the one person whom everyone related to most."

For the next nine summers, she cultivated that role. She co-trained with nearly every established group leader on the premises, while men moved on to lead T-Groups after a year or two of co-training. Finally, one of her co-trainers, a psychologist and writer named Jack Glidewell, admonished her not to come back "until they can accept you as a trainer. You're too good to keep apprenticing."

By that time, she was based in New York, working as a consultant, specializing in the areas that seemed appropriate for women: nonprofits, religious groups, and the wives of CEOs. With each new client, like the handful of other consulting women in business in the early 1960s, she fought a constant subliminal battle to be accepted as a professional. Each time, she discovered how the NTL training gave her a Houdini-like ability to find her own way out of the trickiest situations.

Once, assigned to meet with the Hebrew Congregations of New York, she found herself at the head of a table of twenty viciously funny rabbis, all from different congregations and levels of orthodoxy, all arrogant as only successful religious leaders can be—bickering over the design of their next conference, except when they were making jokes about this woman who was supposedly going to help *them* talk together. There's only one edge I've got here, she told herself. I can see their process, and they can't.

"Listen," she finally said. "You're not doing anything but putting each other down. Does that happen just because I'm around, or does it happen all the time?"

"Well, it happens all the time," one of the rabbis said.

"Does it get you where you want to go?"

The rabbis looked at each other. This kind of feedback was the simplest technique a consultant had. But it worked. They stopped bickering. They started designing the session. The chief rabbi took Edie to lunch and became a good friend of hers thereafter. When she married, the rabbis of New York chipped in and planted a tree in Israel in her honor.

Through dozens of such encounters, bit by bit, she built up a following of loyal clients. Most men couldn't get away with displaying a compassionate attitude to the people they worked with. But men seemed to naturally assume that Edie was compassionate, even when she merely felt callous and sardonic. She also discovered what a generation of women consultants were apt to discover a decade later: men would make advances, but women with an independent role could easily handle it. As a consultant, she was neither dominated like a secretary or a clerk nor threatening like a junior executive. And she had leverage of her own; she could always resign, and her clients would have to explain to their bosses and colleagues why they had alienated Edie Whitfield, the great consultant.

Other aspects of being a woman were harder to deal with. She was never voted in as an NTL fellow, despite years of close involvement with the labs. Instead, in 1959, when Lee Bradford finally offered her a full-time job, it wasn't to lead T-Groups, but to be the office manager at NTL's Washington headquarters. Her consulting practice was just then taking off. "Lee, it's too late," she replied. "You trained me too well. I'm more trained than anyone else NTL has ever sent out into the world."

She got married in 1961 to another NTLer, one year younger than herself, named Charlie Seashore. Charlie's grandfather and father were both influential psychologists, but he wasn't taken as seriously as he might have been, because he perpetually clowned around. He was tall, rangy, and known for his tolerant cheer; he wore Western clothing and a constant grin. He proposed, more or less, by accident. Other boyfriends had hinted, or demanded, that she should put them through graduate school and then stop working. Charlie, on an early date, raised a wine glass and said, "If you were to marry me, you could work and travel as much as you please."

"I accept," Edie said.

"Wait a minute," he said. "That was only a hypothetical statement."

"Yes," she said, "but it's too late. I've already accepted."

In 1963, Edie was finally voted in as an NTL fellow. Bradford called her to give the news himself. Several board members had resisted to the end, he said, because she was a woman and had no Ph.D. (She found graduate school too boring to get one.) "We didn't get through with that board meeting until three in the morning," he told her. "Finally we decided that it wasn't our choice anyway. You were a symbolic figure of where NTL was going to go." Now, he said, he was calling because she was the first candidate this year "to be unanimously approved by your colleagues."

Seashore was laughing. "It doesn't surprise me," she told Bradford. "They all trained me. They'd *better* come through. Otherwise, they'd have to ask themselves what *they* did wrong!"

And Edie was, just as Bradford said, a forerunner of NTL's destiny. Organization development was, increasingly, to be a woman's game: not just because human resources and facilitator positions were lower-status slots (which they were) but also because women seemed to have a knack for keeping a conversation going well. (This stereotype would eventually dwindle, but not for another thirty years.) In the meantime, Edie benefited; her consulting business took off during the 1960s. Even having children didn't deter her; she applied her relentless drive to the tough task of coordinating nurses, babysitters, clients, and colleagues. She gave a dinner party the night before one of her children was born; when sudden trips called her to California or Europe, she paid her babysitters to come along. "I really was out to show that you could have it all," she recalled later, and she was, in fact, setting a pattern. It was frenetic, but a consultant mother's life was easier than the lives of women struggling to rise within corporations. It was a charmed life, and yet it went on within the context of a professional umbrella—the NTL community—that was beginning to fall apart.

As early as 1957, the center began to unravel at NTL.[8] Every year, more of the trainers slipped out for visits or sabbaticals to the new, looser encounter group centers in California such as Esalen or the Western Behavioral Sciences Institute in San Diego, where personal growth was expected to be part of the purpose of the T-Group, body work was an integral part of therapy, and understanding group power-dynamics was less and less important. More and more, the western influence trickled back to Bethel and the other NTL gatherings. It became normal to touch, and then to hug, the other people in your T-Group. The oak tables gave way to soft chairs without tables, then to cushions on the floor. On the West Coast, they were taking off their clothes and taking psychedelics; in the East, they never went that far, but they did invite business executives to crawl around on the floor, in the dark, bumping into each other in an effort to experience each other freshly.[9]

NTL trainers also began to employ the techniques of self-hypnosis. Instead of merely talking about their "preferred vision," stolid corporate engineers and school administrators were now encouraged to visualize every aspect of it, as if it hung in the air before them. If they couldn't master visualization, they could attend training sessions where the leader handed them a lemon and told them to acquaint themselves with every minuscule detail of the pitted, sour fruit. Then they'd all throw their lemons into a pile in the center of the room. "Go get your lemon," the trainer would say. Each participant's citrus stood out from its fellows as clearly as a lover's face. And there was, in fact, a valuable lesson here. If you could learn to recognize your lemon in a crowd by moving past your ordinary preconceptions, then consider how much you could see in the people around you, or in your own aspirations, if you gave yourself the time to really look.[10]

"I can remember working with a group in the Connecticut mountains," a long-standing trainer named Kathy Dannemiller recalled years later. "We were rocking this man. He was about fifty or sixty years old and I was holding his head. He was bald. When we rocked someone, at some point we'd say, 'Let go. You can let go now'—meaning that they could let themselves move into heavy-duty emotional release. At that moment, I leaned down and kissed him, and I suddenly saw two tears come out of his eyes, which were closed. He opened them and looked up at me and said, 'Was that you that kissed me?' I said yes. He said, 'I think that was the first kiss I ever felt.' That was the kind of experience we had with T-Groups, and why we kept coming back to them—because we had buried our emotions and perceptions so deeply as children of the Depression and the war."

But the looser the T-Groups grew, and the more they were oriented to "therapy for normals," the harder it was for the core academics of NTL to keep track, let alone control, of what the sessions contained. Standards at Bethel remained relatively strict, but other T-Groups, held around the country under a variety of auspices, far outnumbered the offerings from Bethel. Even if Lee Bradford, NTL's director, had had the funds and staff to enforce strict standards (which he didn't), he didn't have the heart. After all, this *was* the sixties; the world seemed to need to loosen up. And the old dream of the NTL triumvirate, to build a cadre of "change agents" who would reform organizations everywhere from the inside, now looked like it would finally come true.

The downside of the NTL dream first came to public light around 1963. That year, Cornell University brought Chris Argyris together with George Odiorne for a debate on the value of T-Groups. Odiorne was the popularizer of "management by objectives," a system in which managers set their own quarterly goals (under the direction of their bosses, of course). In theory, this helped them remain attuned to the organization's overall needs; in practice, managers soon realized that the important task was looking good on the report forms, no matter how good or bad their performance was in reality. Odiorne knew and revered Douglas McGregor, and management by objectives had been influenced by some of the NTL "visioning" practices.[11] But Odiorne was also out for blood at this meeting. He scoffed at group dynamics in business as a hypocritical, unprovable, self-indulgent, and downright dangerous "con game." Its only purpose was to rake in corporate fees.[12]

To the *Business Week* writer who covered the event, the testimonials of managers in the audience made the strongest impression. One by one, they stood up to talk about how they had been pressed to reveal secrets, or humiliatingly identified as an S.O.B. The flood of complaints only abated when one of the speakers mused, "You know, whenever you say anything negative about [T-Groups], you're just proving [to your bosses] that you're sick." Suddenly, the realization dawned across the face of everyone who had spoken: who might have heard them?[13]

Argyris, in the meantime, was cast as NTL's defender. It was not a role he preferred; he had doubts about T-Groups himself. He deplored the way that they seemed to make people dependent on the trainers.[14] He had come to the debate hoping that Odiorne and he could mutually inquire about the T-Group's viability. Instead, he felt forced into the role of advocate for NTL's case—forced to argue that T-Group trainers were *not* sleazy con-men. He later remembered a particularly revealing moment at the end, when Odiorne pulled him aside. "Chris," he said, "you give me the word, and we'll take this act throughout the United States. We'll make a pile of money."[15]

Argyris didn't join Odiorne on the road; but the meeting, and other encounters like it, raised questions that would be central to his career, and ultimately to our understanding of how organizations change. Then thirty-nine years old, Argyris was a Yale professor of administrative science. Like Edie Seashore, he had grown up in a suburb of New York City. He had also spent several years as a child with his grandparents in Greece. He was bespectacled, dark-complexioned, and slender, with a narrow face that tended, almost despite himself, to break into a delighted grin when arguments grew hot, as if he was overjoyed at the chance to test himself. His voice was distinctively mild-mannered and reedy with a slight European tinge. His style of debate was analytical—indeed, his approach to life was passionately devoted to inquiry, reasoning, and theory. But he was drawn to the kinds of problems that most analytical people eschew, the riddles of human nature. In particular, why did people fail to live up to their own professed ideals? Why was so much human behavior so self-frustrating, particularly in organizations?[16]

In 1957, Argyris had published a book called *Personality and Organization*, in which he had demonstrated, with full academic rigor, that corporations *inevitably* turned their employees into infantile people. No matter how much the company's managers espoused self-reliance and resourcefulness, the mere presence of mature, independent-minded people felt threatening to the senior leaders of the enterprise. Not because they were vile individuals; most senior managers were reasonably decent people. But an authoritarian chain of command, by its nature, placed managers into a double bind. If they spoke up, they automatically fell into the role of challenging their superiors—which meant they couldn't play the political games that led to success. Or they could remain obeisant and give up their maturity, ultimately passing on their babyishness to the next generation (if only by running their families in an authoritarian manner). Thus the immaturity of organizations, Argyris posited, would endure into eternity.[17]

Hence the value to Argyris of a T-Group in business. The group confronted people with the direct record—Argyris called this the "data"—of their own conversations, so they could see how they had been locked into destructive ways of thinking and relating. Nobody could confront a group with its "data" the way Argyris could. He was fearless in the facilitator's role; he seemed oblivious to whether people might be offended or have their feelings hurt, as long as they were learning. Listening to the conversation, his eyes would brighten and intensify until he was like a bird of prey, perching at the edge of the table, alert to the nuance in every phrase. Then, suddenly, he would pounce.

"From your last remark," he would say to a CEO, surrounded by his loyal lieutenants, "it sounds to me like you don't trust this group." Then he would turn to the other managers: "Is that true? Does it sound like he doesn't trust you?"

If they insisted that he *did* trust them, Argyris would ask them exactly *which* part of the CEO's remark implied trust.

"Well, it wasn't that remark," they would say. And Argyris would ask them to nail down *some* remark, until they were forced to admit there *was* no trust there.[18] Around and around they would go, peeling off one layer after another of their pretense of trust, while Argyris sat watching, stoking the conversation like a fire, never raising his voice, never losing his bemused smile, and never letting go. "Five minutes into a conversation," a close colleague of his later recalled, "he'd have anyone that he was talking to back up against the wall and fighting for their life with the kind of accusation about how they contradicted themselves a moment ago. He was always right. But he never backed off."

The healthier that corporate people claimed their company to be, the more effective Argyris seemed to be in bringing their deep, intractable problems to the surface. He regularly offered to pay all his own consulting fees and expenses if the company turned out to be healthy; a Yale alumnus had set up an endowment to underwrite the offer. No company ever took up the challenge. He also insisted on a rule that allowed either himself or his clients to cancel the consulting contract with only fifty seconds' notice; but, by the same rule, the other party could demand four hours to have the decision explained. Nobody ever canceled a contract with Argyris, no matter how angry he made them. No doubt the thought of those four hours, satisfying Argyris' relentless pursuit of the data, was too excruciating.

And yet . . . Argyris had to admit that many T-Group projects were ending badly. He had become entangled himself in 1964 with NTL's most visible failure, a highly public project with the U.S. State Department. The oldest federal agency, State was known around Washington as the Fudge Factory. Foreign service officers spent most of their time engaged in infighting or holding each other to the letter of the abstruse mass of State Department regulations.

In 1963, as part of a reorganization effort that would actually require these foreign service officers to manage their embassies competently, the new Deputy Undersecretary for Administration at State, William Crockett, decided to bring in a team of OD specialists from NTL. The United States was sending rockets into space; why couldn't it make the State Department work right?[19]

At first, there were terrific results. The young foreign service officers, who had signed up during the Kennedy presidency and seriously believed in "asking what they could do for their country," were wildly enthusiastic. T-Groups seemed like the answer to the hidebound bureaucracy in which they found themselves snared. The sessions brought deeply hidden problems, like the misunderstandings between ambassadorial diplomats and civil service administrators, to the surface: first in argument, then in a kind of thoughtful, creative conversation between the two groups. "If we could bring this technique to Israel or Russia," mused the enthusiasts at State, "just think what we could accomplish!"

But that was before the power structure fought back. By 1965, the T-Group effort and its champions found themselves sabotaged from within. Foreign service officers began to spread rumors that Crockett was resigning; his superiors, including Secretary of State Dean Rusk, started to worry out loud that he was "out of control." Otherwise, why would he want to delegate authority? Staffers threatened to leak their stories of shattered morale to the press. Finally, Crockett accepted a job offer from IBM in early 1967. His replacement canceled all the NTL-related contracts.

But it was too late to stop Argyris, who was halfway through writing up the report on the project, which he had agreed to write as part of the deal.[20] It no longer mattered that the clients no longer wanted a report. An agreement was an agreement. When the report came out, describing the personnel policies that inhibited effectiveness at state, it was guarded more carefully than some top secret documents. Representative John Rooney, chairman of the House Appropriations Subcommittee, obtained a copy and held a hearing to denounce it. ("Who is this fellow Argyris?" he asked. "Has he ever worked for the State Department?")[21]

By the mid-1960s, such awful denouements were becoming sadly typical in NTL-inspired projects. First, there would be stellar success. In some companies, a meeting wasn't considered "important" unless it had its own "process consultant" sitting in, offering expert guidance on the flow, interjecting comments about honesty and fulfillment, and taking notes on big sheets of paper on the wall. But then the effects would wear off. Bullying managers who had learned to listen openheartedly began bullying again. Managers who had finally learned to speak up at meetings, and to care about their company's future as a whole, reverted back to being passive-aggressive bureaucrats.

Sometimes things got *worse* after the NTL effort. This particularly seemed to happen when a company began to use OD on a large scale, and the T-Groups were no longer held on a cultural island. At Bethel, trainers needed years of apprenticeship under their belt before they could lead a group. But in companies, the eager audience was so large—particularly when the CEO endorsed a T-Group program—that some OD people were impressed into leading groups after having been to only one or two themselves. Relatively inexperienced, and caught in the company's internal politics, they tended to prod and poke at any disputes that came up as if they were scabs needing to be brushed away. And all too often the wounds broke open.

It might take weeks of group sessions, for instance, before a manager was ready to describe how he hated his boss's micromanagement. But the facilitator, tensely aware of the boss's presence in the room, might interrupt the manager, mid-sentence, and turn to the boss: "Ralph, how do Sam's remarks make you feel?"

"Well, it makes me feel like I haven't been much of a friend," Ralph the boss might say, in the nurturing spirit of the session. And all eyes would turn back to Sam.

"Are you ready," the facilitator would inquire, "to ask Ralph if you can trust him as a friend?"

Sam would look dumbfounded at the consultant. In truth, the answer was no. Ralph *wasn't* his friend. Sam *didn't* trust him. But he could not *say,* "No, I'm not ready," while other managers were listening. The remark, and its implied insult of Ralph, would be remembered for years.

Nor could he assent. The words would stick in his throat. And if he got them out, he would never be able to protest again, for fear of hearing Ralph say, "But you *said* I was your friend." All the old abuses would continue, covered over by his acquiescence.

If he had any savvy at all, Sam would find a way out of the jam—probably by swallowing his pride and making a half-hearted show of friendship—but he'd never speak openly in that organization again. If he had no savvy, he might choose to speak honestly—and feel reprisals. The following Tuesday, Ralph might drop by his office: "I understand you don't have much faith in me. In that light, I guess we don't need you on my project." And if Sam snapped and displayed emotion anytime in a T-Group—if, for example, he burst into anger or tears when someone tore his personality to shreds—the notoriety would haunt him years later: "Can we trust this allocation to Sam, when we've seen how unstable he is?"

Nor could Sam escape by avoiding taking part in T-Groups at all; for then he would become known as someone who "couldn't communicate." Thus, in many companies, one of the key skills (along with finessing the performance appraisals, and the "management by objectives" meetings) was finessing the T-Group. Sam had to learn to act willing to expose his deepest feelings at any moment, and like he would be searingly honest, without actually saying anything to incriminate himself.[22]

In 1967 and 1968, as if in unplanned choreography, corporate people began to drop out of the NTL networks. Businesses everywhere stopped signing up for T-Groups; too many people within the companies had begun to complain about the abuses. At General Foods, one manager of a testing laboratory committed suicide after a T-Group session with engineers who worked with him. "Anyone who runs a testing laboratory is a bastard," they told him, "and you always have been."[23] He had been unstable before, but the episode demonstrated how incomplete the T-Group method was for its uses in business settings, and how unprepared NTL was—in the sense that it had no malpractice insurance. The manager's family sued both the labs and the company, but settled out of court.

Everyone at NTL saw this case as a wake-up call. To some, like Argyris and Ed Schein, it provided one more reason for reevaluating their practice. Others saw the solution as obvious: they weren't thinking big enough. To make an impact, NTL itself would have to change.

At age sixty-four, NTL president Leland Bradford was ready to quit. There were plenty of reasons to feel tired. Critics like Odiorne continued to appear.[24] Income was high, but expenses continued to rise, in part because the increased enrollments had prompted $250,000 worth of renovations to the old Victorian house up in Bethel.[25] Tensions from the outside world were seeping in. In the summer of 1968, NTL had its first racial confrontation, when a group of black leaders, in Bethel for a T-Group workshop, revolted against the staff and delivered a list of nonnegotiable demands to Bradford: set up a program to hire black trainers and include more people of color in NTL's governance. Bradford refused, but agreed, in time-honored NTL fashion, to talk through their concerns—which took the next three days. When the dust cleared, Bradford had agreed to design a program to train black facilitators, to set a goal for 15 to 20 percent black representation in most NTL programs, and to set up a community center in an urban setting. Going over these demands must have seemed deeply ironic to him; after all, NTL had been born at a race-relations conference. Saul Alinsky had known enough to step out of the way in Rochester and let black leaders like Franklin Florence emerge, but the NTLers had never recognized their own need to do the same.

Most pressing of all, Bradford was beset by medical problems, including a serious infection in his retina. He recognized that it was time to step down. At his suggestion, the NTL board sent everyone in the NTL community a ballot, with three candidates for the position as his successor. Nearly all the votes came in for Warren Bennis, the third of the central figures of this chapter. Bennis was more than a candidate. In that bleak year, he was the great hope of NTL, the pioneering leader who could finally push the labs to the lofty social role that its members still felt it deserved.

Bennis was forty-four. In a sense, he had been groomed for the NTL presidency all his life. He was one of the most prominent experts on social change in the world and one of the leading academic figures of his generation. He had a Ph.D. in economics from MIT's Sloan School, where he had been a professor of industrial management in Douglas McGregor's department. (Like Edie Seashore, he was an Antioch alumnus and a McGregor protégé since college.) He had participated in several key organization development consultancies, including the State Department project. In his current day job, Bennis was a college administrator: vice president for academic affairs at the State University at Buffalo. He also had a wide reputation as a pathfinding commentator—one of the few social psychologists who could write engagingly for the general public. His essays rang with references to Kafka, Thoreau, Japanese folk wisdom, and his own feelings, even as he dissected the theories of his fellow social scientists.

Warren was a compact man, handsome and energetic, with a resonant tenor voice, hazel eyes, a mouth that might have been painted into a portrait of Cupid, and thick brown hair that was rapidly turning white. He was effortlessly charming in person; among his friends he counted the psychologists Carl Rogers, Abraham Maslow, and Erik Erikson, the management writers Peter Drucker and Douglas McGregor, the composer Leonard Bernstein, and the columnist Eppie Lederer (better known as Ann Landers)—to list only a few whose names he dropped in his essays during the 1960s. He and his wife at the time, Clurie, had been gently lampooned by a Buffalo newspaper for the massive dinner parties they gave. When McGregor and Maslow died, Warren gave the eulogies at their funerals.

He seemed capable of anything. But he also had the plaintive air of an outsider. He had grown up lonely and withdrawn in the 1930s, a shy Jewish kid in the WASPish suburb of Westwood, New Jersey.[26] After serving in Europe during the war, in his early twenties, he had deliberately reconstructed himself into a sophisticated, soulful adult. (His most autobiographical essay, written in the 1990s, would be called "An Invented Life.") He cheerfully described himself as the sort of person (like Leonard Bernstein) who aspired to be not just liked but loved by every human being he met. Many of his friends knew that he also aspired to a greater role in the public sphere. He didn't want elected office. He wanted to set in motion a chain of events that would reshape the nature of political governance in America.

In collaboration with a sociologist from Brandeis University named Philip Slater, Bennis had published an audacious article, "Democracy Is Inevitable," in 1964 in the *Harvard Business Review*. Like Herman Kahn, they foresaw the Soviet Union collapsing—along with all other totalitarian regimes—even if the United States did nothing to defeat it. Democracy, meanwhile, would undergo a full-scale cultural change, a movement beyond government by political parties and interest groups. It would be a society of people engaging in "full and free communication, regardless of rank and power," relieving conflicts through consensus instead of power-bloc voting, expressing themselves emotionally, not just through accumulating wealth or brokering status. While this sort of democracy was inevitable, it was a little slow in arriving, and the two authors urged their readers to find ways "to give a little push here and there."

Now, with this job offer, Bennis had an opportunity to give a little push of his own. There was only one problem. For an institution of such potential influence, NTL was an unprepossessing enterprise. It gave courses around the world, but it had only two headquarters—the remote cul-de-sac in Maine and the dingy administrative office in Washington, D.C. It would be hard to change the world from either place. If Warren left Buffalo to take this job, NTL would have to expand—to match not just *his* stature but its own long-awaited destiny.

He laid out his idea before the executive committee, the twelve-man group in charge of NTL's affairs, on March 16, 1969. NTL, he proposed, should become an "International University for Social Change," with a new campus to be built somewhere near Washington. There would be a conference center where business managers would learn more effective teamwork, community developers would compare methods, and journalists would learn to cover the deep forces behind the everyday news. "I think we could really reach into government," he told the board. There would be a center for conflict resolution, sending crack teams of negotiators to tense locales like Yugoslavia and the Middle East. (A few years later, law professor Roger Fisher and some colleagues would develop a center much like that at Harvard University, called the Harvard Negotiation Project.) And finally, there would be a "small elite program" for advanced graduate work in social sciences, blending humanistic psychology with philosophy and law, "to work on utopias and how you build new communities."[27]

The university would be designed to give people the intellectual tools they needed to accomplish the tasks that the times seemed to be crying for: Ending the war in Vietnam and all wars. Stopping pollution and expanding the general level of quality of life. Banishing racism and sexism. And showing the managers of large bureaucracies—the giant mainstream corporations and government agencies that dominated society—how they too could contribute to making a better world. The NTL board members, listening to Bennis speak, could close their eyes and imagine cadres of sophisticated young peace soldiers fanning out into society—a living counterpoint to the American troops ravaging Vietnam and to the insular, arrogant technocrats of the CIA and the military-industrial complex. *These* soldiers would have skilled conversation, empathy, and small-group workshops as weapons; the same weapons that Mahatma Gandhi and other peacemakers had used so eloquently. The culture of America was crying out for those weapons to emerge on a large scale.[28]

But they could not think small, Bennis insisted. Building the university would require between five and fifteen million dollars. A million dollars must be raised right away, earmarked for an endowment. Years later, he marveled at his own naiveté. He imagined that on the first day he showed up for work, there should be a bank account with a million dollars in it, which the new school could immediately "cash in."

One of the first things they would do with that money would be to establish part-time endowed chairs for faculty members—and Bennis announced, with evident pleasure, that Chris Argyris was eager to join in. If *he* was enthusiastic, that was a major selling point. "Chris said to me," Bennis reported, "and I think he really believes it," that an endowed chair could pull him away from his Ivy League post. Yale wasn't moving quickly enough in group dynamics research for Argyris, Bennis said. "Chris has already committed himself to six months in 1971."

The executive committee immediately agreed to the plan. To show Bennis that the million dollars could be raised, they began recruiting financial pledges within a few days.[29] The fund-raising chore fell, as it happened, to Edie Seashore. She had never raised funds before, but she was doughty and irrepressible. And she had a hidden asset. As a woman, she had had to lead many workshops over the years with the wives of CEOs. Now she got on the phone to the husbands of her old trainees. "We're creating an institution," she told them, "where you could send people for the rest of your life."

Bennis, meanwhile, came through with a land grant from the father of one of his students at Buffalo. The father, a prominent Washington real estate broker, agreed to donate 175 acres near Dulles Airport, out in the Virginia countryside. He offered another 250 acres for a bargain-basement $40,000, which the board also agreed to buy. To sketch out a campus, Bennis recruited the innovative architect Jim Rouse, who had designed the planned city of Columbia, Maryland. Construction would begin as early as January. Bennis and his wife flew to Washington to look for a house.

At the same time, Warren was privately developing doubts. The previous year, in July 1968, he had dined with Michael Murphy, the founder of the Esalen Institute on the West Coast. Murphy was upset that night. *Life* magazine had just sent him an advance copy of their July 12 issue, with a big feature story on Esalen. Called

"Inhibitions Thrown to the Gentle Winds," it included sniggering, thinly veiled references to free love and photographs of nude workshop visitors slipping in and out of the institute's cliffside baths. "On the cover of the same issue," Bennis later recalled, "was another nude group—Biafran children who were dying of famine. It struck me that I didn't want to spend my life dealing with nude bathing."[30] Bennis agreed with Murphy that the article treated Esalen unfairly. But thoughts of irrelevance and self-indulgence continued to haunt him. NTL was much more conservative, academically grounded, and cautious than Esalen, but in the end wasn't it also guilty of the same self-centered irrelevance?

"I felt that NTL and T-Groups were never going to really make a difference," he said years later. "I didn't know quite why. Why weren't we having the impact of *The Organization Man* or Rachel Carson's *Silent Spring?*" The problem, he felt, was in the group process itself, which operated on such a tiny scale—ten or twelve people at a time—that it would never have much impact on large-scale problems like Biafra. It was a sobering thought for a dedicated idealist who had spent his life working with small groups and who was deeply interested in getting the most leverage from his talents.

Then there was the problem of money. Only $250,000 in pledges of Bennis' million had been raised,[31] and very little of *that* arrived in Bennis' cherished bank account. There wasn't even money to buy that land by Dulles Airport, whose owner was clamoring to close the deal.

And that one million had been intended as only a *starting* point. Moreover, NTL's efforts in the past to raise funds didn't inspire much confidence; its fund-raisers had always cost more in expenses than their efforts brought in. For its operating expenses, the institute depended on the money from training seminars—which had unexpectedly, precipitately dropped off. The organization had to take out loans to pay its staff salaries that fall.[32]

Privately, staff members and trainers complained that the organization was sliding downhill fast. Then the same people stood up in board meetings and said, "The organization is in great shape." This was a terrible warning sign, because people came to T-Groups to cure exactly that sort of duplicity. Many of the staff members seemed unenthusiastic or simply burned out. Many of the trainers seemed to assume that a prestigious faculty post was theirs for the asking or that Warren would take their side in the inevitable turf wars. Bennis saw that the new university could mire him in a self-defeating position—the visible symbol of a struggling enterprise, doomed to spending all his time begging, dealing with finances, negotiating between fractious factions that were fighting each other for scarce resources, and keeping the dream afloat. "Don't take the job if you're ambivalent," Argyris advised him. "The last thing in the world NTL needs is ambivalence."[33]

On November 14, he betrayed no ambivalence at all in a speech to the NTL board. "The mere fact," he told them, "that a place exists that is coinhabited by executives and revolutionaries, young and old, parents and their children, will be mind-blowing. . . . No one is going to be excited about the fact that master's degrees are given there. They are going to be excited because this is the place where people who are concerned about social change are coming and meeting and learning and teaching. I know dozens of professionals who would drop out of good universities, temporarily or permanently, to come to such a place, were it implemented in an uncompromising way."[34]

The board eagerly agreed to move forward. They spent the lion's share of the meeting deliberating over the name, torn between "The NTL University for Applied Behavioral Science" and "The University for Man." They leaned toward the latter, with its echoes of humanism, but they worried timidly, in those early days of feminism, how women might feel about it.[35] Lee Bradford, the departing president, felt "entranced" (his own word) by Warren's performance and by the knowledge that his little institute would evolve into a well-endowed, world-renowned institution.[36]

The trance continued for two more weeks. Then, on November 24, a terse telegram from Warren Bennis arrived on Lee Bradford's desk. It said simply that he was turning down the job for "personal reasons." At the NTL offices, the people who received it were so angry that they remembered it years later as an endless document, rambling on about the lack of support and the need to raise money in a lost cause. Edie Seashore later claimed that people at the NTL offices were so angry that no one could finish reading it. "Somebody handed it to me and said, 'Here—you see if you can make any sense out of it.'"

That was the end of the NTL university. No one but Bennis could have led it into being. Years later, there are still members of the organization who have never forgiven him. They hear his story told around the old house in Bethel—the man who let the dream die. And in the wake of his departure, even the old NTL fell into jeopardy. Lee Bradford, despite his health problems, had to postpone retirement. Corporate enrollments stagnated. The black caucus continued to raise objections and press for training. Bills piled up from renovations and other halfhearted projects begun in preparation for the renaissance that had been aborted. "I handled what I did very badly," Bennis would later say, "but I was absolutely correct in what I did." Indeed, it would have taken dedication on a demonic scale to bring that dream to life.

And if the NTL university could somehow have come to pass, how might that have affected the world? At best, it might have served as a galvanizing point, a place from which reform of the culture would have rippled out, like circles in a turbulent pool. Yet in the end something similar happened—but without the university and without anybody noticing. Members of the NTL community went underground. They fanned out into a thousand organizations and locales. By the mid-1980s, many of them had positions of minor influence. By the mid-1990s, they were entrenched in senior echelons of major institutions. This ultimately was Lee Bradford's legacy—a widespread influence more subtly powerful than any university could have been.

And yet, no matter how benevolent the end results, there was no getting around the fact that Bennis had let the NTL dream crash. Like Parzival the first time around, he had kept himself from looking up and saying, "What afflicts you, Uncle?" The 1960s were showing him, and perhaps millions of other people, that you cannot hold a grand dream unless you can sacrifice everything for it—

especially your ideas about what would be prudent. That's why no one can ever agree on the single moment when the 1960s ended. For each person, they ended at the moment when they realized they could no longer give over their private lives in the service of a grand dream. Once that moment has come and gone, your dreams never completely fade away. They linger, reproachfully reminding you of the betrayals you felt forced to make. You may wander for years, as Parzival did, waiting for another chance.

Through the early 1970s, NTL struggled along—barely paying bills, but still giving T-Groups. Lee Bradford resigned in 1971. The presidency passed to a relative outsider, a family therapist from St. Louis named Vladimir Dupre. Other associates, coveting the job, tried to undermine or resist him. Some kept envisioning NTL as a membership organization which would run occasional programs for its members, while others (including Dupre) saw it as a consulting firm that could focus on getting billings and clients. While they bickered, many of the OD jobs that had once naturally gone to NTL moved to outside consultants, including many of the former regulars. Each year, NTL's offerings shrank a little bit more and its debts mounted. In the awful summer of 1972, advance fees from the August sessions were used to pay the salaries in April. Then trainer salaries ceased entirely. Within a year or two, the institute had five dollars in outstanding debt for every dollar in assets. Where once they had looked forward to the inventiveness of their colloquy at Bethel, now trainers jetted in as closely as possible to the start of a T-Group and left as quickly as they could when it was over. There were still participants walking around Bethel in the summer heat, sitting under trees with their arms around each other, still living those magical experiences. But as a center, the place was rapidly withering away.

The only people who acted as if it was still vibrant were Edie and Charlie Seashore, who retained roles as trainer and administrator, respectively. As the official leadership of NTL fragmented, they increasingly took on the unofficial roles of leaders of the institute. It was ironic for Edie, because at the same time she was engaged in a revolt—a woman's revolt from within.

After all these years, there were now almost 500 members of the "inner circle" of NTL trainers—the "fellows" elected by their peers—but only a handful of them were women. In the early 1970s, during the era of consciousness-raising, a few women in the NTL inner circle began to compare notes. They had all, it turned out, experienced the same dynamics. Edie, Barbara, Billie, or Jane[37] would make a suggestion to members of the NTL nominating committee: "There are a lot of competent women out there. We ought to name more of them as fellows."

"Gee, that's terrific," the committee member would say. "Send us a list."

The list would be dispatched. Then, a few weeks later, the same committee member would say in a meeting, "It's too bad there are no competent women around to nominate."

And Edie, Barbara, Billie, or Jane would exclaim, "What about the lists we sent you?"

"What lists?"

By the time the women compared notes, they could count several sets of lists that had mysteriously disappeared. It wasn't conscious sabotage, they concluded, but it might as well have been. In some cases, they had colluded too, if only because it was nice to be labeled one of the few token "acceptable" women who had made it past the barrier.

They also realized, comparing notes, that being insiders did not prevent them from being demeaned. During a planning meeting, before a T-Group session, a woman would make a suggestion. No one would reply, but a few minutes later a man would make the same suggestion. Another man would chime in, "That's a great idea, Bill."

The woman who spoke would spend the rest of the meeting castigating herself: "Maybe I said it wrong." Or wondering if the men were deliberately trying to ignore her. But *these* men, dedicated to improving communication and understanding, couldn't be trying to undermine their peers deliberately, could they? Was NTL really a sexist male club that needed to be changed?

In 1973, a women's caucus emerged at NTL. At the same time, Edie Seashore and some of the other NTL regulars began to find themselves increasingly called on to handle gender and racial issues at companies. The first affirmative action programs, started in the mid-1960s as part of the short-lived corporate social responsibility movement, had indeed produced results: Ford, AT&T, Procter & Gamble, Polaroid, and a number of insurance companies now, as a result of their efforts, found themselves with growing numbers of black and women managers. A host of new problems erupted, problems that only techniques like group dynamics, with the ability to bring hidden feelings to the surface, could handle effectively.

In the back of their minds, the managers who hired these people no doubt expected them to be grateful—for these *were* groundbreaking efforts. Like all immigrants, the new black and women hires were expected to dig in, work hard, find ways to assimilate, and gradually melt into the existing ambiance of the company. In other words, as all immigrants find wherever they settle, the game was rigged against them. They were supposed to adapt as best they could, keep their noses clean and their bosses satisfied at all costs, and wait until the second or third generation to achieve equality.

Except that (even if you accepted this depressing premise about how the world ought to work) a corporation wasn't like a vernacular community, where you could settle into an enclave of fellow immigrants who watched out for each other. Frequently the person of color, or the woman, would be the only such person on their team. They were often expected to fail, but they could master the work easily enough. The hard part was learning to assimilate the constant belittling of their identity: "Stop moving your hands that way. Stop making those kinds of jokes. Dress like the CEO dresses. Act like the finance manager acts."

When everyone comes from a similar culture, its mores are learned from childhood, but (Edie Seashore and others began to realize) for women and members of ethnic minorities, corporate culture was thoroughly alien. (In a few years, a book called *Games*

Mother Never Taught You would appear, explaining to women how corporate life was based on conforming to attitudes that stemmed from the games boys played, games from which girls had been excluded.)[38] The pressure was immense. Black managers or women in line positions would get ulcers. Their hair would fall out. People from ethnic backgrounds would rage internally at the fact that they couldn't include their old Chicano or Japanese or Jewish or African heritage in their proposals or presentations. The newcomers would wonder: Will I ever find a place that's right for me? They would become aware, as only an outsider would become aware, of every slight detail of the prevailing ambiance of the white male organizational culture. At least, they *thought* of it as white and male. In reality, it was the "numbers" culture of corporate power—flavored most of all not by race or gender, but by the impersonal bouquet of industrial finance.

Because it was new to them, the newcomers could see, more clearly than anyone else, how the prevailing ambiance undermined the company's performance. Fred Miller, for instance, was a young black manager at the Connecticut General Life Insurance Company in Hartford in those years. He had gotten his job through the company's desire to integrate its management, and he would eventually go on to become one of Edie Seashore's consulting colleagues.[39] At Connecticut, he worked under a supervisor with a law degree, handling policies for inner-city gas station owners. When someone didn't pay the bill, Miller's supervisor would send them a long, legalistic dunning letter. The gas station owners couldn't understand the letters ("In fact," Miller recalled, "neither did I half the time"), so they ignored them and became credit risks. Every once in a while, when he couldn't stand it anymore, Miller would surreptitiously call the gas station owners to find out why they hadn't paid their bill and clean up the case. It was his way of asking Parzival's question: "What afflicts you?" But when Miller's bosses found out, he was reprimanded. Insurance managers were not supposed to call up customers directly. That wasn't culturally acceptable.

A man like Miller was trapped in the role of heretic, in a way that Ed Dulworth of General Foods and John Mulder of Kodak were not. They could choose whether or not to speak out. But people like Fred Miller and Edie Seashore felt they had no choice. "As a white man looking for upward mobility," Miller later recalled, "my supervisor knew that if he played by the rules he would be rewarded and be taken care of. I knew that I couldn't win by those rules. Even if I did everything right I would still be black. So to be successful, I had to break the rules. Fortunately, I was in a company where I *could* break a lot of rules. I was ordered to be fired twice while I was there. Both times, the president of the company rescued me because he saw that some rule-breaking was necessary for the organization's success, and he saw me as one of the few people who could do it effectively."

There are hundreds of similar stories from those years. Edie Seashore heard many of them in 1973, when AT&T hired her in the aftermath of a class-action suit before the Equal Employment Opportunity Commission. Twenty-six thousand women and minority managers, who had been routinely shortchanged in pay and benefits compared to white men, were awarded pay increases collectively worth $51 million the first year. Part of the deal included an agreement for training—originally, training for women and minority managers in the skills they needed to advance. But as Edie Seashore and other trainers from NTL soon recognized, the white men needed the most help. They might talk about tolerance and ethnic diversity, but if you looked at their actions, it was obvious: these new people were competitors who, like all competitors, must be blocked. The results were expensive. Corporations spent millions to recruit top-notch women and people of color, and then the new recruits left in frustration after a couple of years.

The new groups that Seashore and other NTLers established became known as "diversity" training, focusing on the advantages that the company as a whole had to gain from varied points of view.[40] Companies would be much better equipped, for instance, for approaching global markets. They would be more resilient, less bound by foolish strictures (like the custom of not phoning customers). Managers would be honed and sharpened by the need to make themselves understood across lines of race, class, ethnic group, and gender. But all of these advantages were unproven. There was no organization to point to which had been founded on principles of diversity, to show what could be possible. And it didn't seem likely that any such organization could exist, not in the near future.

In 1975, the National Training Laboratories finally went bankrupt. Creditors stopped underwriting loans. The NTL board, which consisted largely of executives from companies that still booked training programs, insisted that they sell off their assets and pay the debts. A "For Sale" sign was posted in front of the old Victorian house in Bethel. The board began to debate how they might avoid a lawsuit brought by their creditors. In desperation, Vlad Dupre, the president, looked for someone to rescue the labs. At least one of the people he contacted declined, but he found four volunteers: Edie Seashore, Barbara Bunker (one of the other NTL inner circle women), Hal Kellner (one of Seashore's partners in the AT&T awareness sessions), and Peter Vaill, a business professor at George Washington University who had only recently become an NTL trainer. Together, they resolved to reshape NTL into a model of a diverse, integrated organization. Since it was about to go under, they had nothing to lose. They called themselves "the four horsepersons."

"We had the best time!" said Edie Seashore years later. "We usually had our meetings over a weekend, or from eleven at night until two A.M. on the telephone. We were all juggling full practices." They knew that rebuilding NTL with diversity as the first principle would force them to experience the ups and downs of cross-cultural exchange for themselves, and they could draw on that experience in their client work. If (as Lewin had said) you couldn't understand a system without trying to change it, then the growing business of diversity consulting—probably NTL's best hope for steady work—depended on this "experiment."

First, the four horsepersons needed to convince the NTL board. They had a surefire argument: reforming the company would free the board members from their liability. They could resign without feeling that they had abandoned the enterprise. To show that the business acumen of these new "horsepersons" could be trusted, Edie Seashore and Peter Vaill flew out from Washington, D.C., to meet a key group of Houston-based board members for lunch. That in itself showed they weren't stuffy academics. They made a simple proposal: the four horsepersons would line up seventy-five former NTL members as volunteers. Collectively, they would donate $200,000 worth of time to the enterprise without pay. That, plus the facilities NTL owned, was enough to offer a year's worth of courses, which in turn would generate enough cash to begin paying off debts and bring some life back into the system.

When the board accepted their idea, the four horsepersons gathered in a hotel for an extended weekend. Their first task was to select which seventy-five people to invite to form the new organization. They decided that the group should be divided, more or less equally, among all four of the diversity "quadrants": white males, nonwhite males, white females, and nonwhite females. They went down the list of candidates in rapid-fire succession. Any one of the horsepersons had veto power. They were merely following the old NTL precedent of selecting new members through a vote of their peers, but they had turned the process upside down, in a way that brought the arbitrariness of NTL membership into sharp relief.

"We made a lot of people very angry," recalled Seashore. "The new members had to be people we thought would be committed to a new type of institution based on social justice. A lot of former NTL big shots were rejected. We crossed people off without even talking about it, as long as any one of us was willing to reject them. One of the people we rejected was a very close friend of mine. I told her that I didn't even remember who had vetoed her, because it all went by so fast. 'Who did you think you were—God?' she asked. And I said, 'That's exactly right.' It was a terrible experience at one level, because we had people's lives in our hands."

The following month, in November 1975, the sixty-five new members (ten of the invitees had declined) gathered at the same hotel to elect a board. This time they set up the quadrant system as a strict rule. One-fourth of the board members would be white men, one-fourth white women. Another fourth would be "men of color" (a category which included Asians, Native Americans, and Latin Americans), and another fourth would be "women of color." Balloting was secret, or sort of secret: members covered their eyes as they raised their hands to vote.

Edie was elected to the board, and then the board members elected her as president. In her youth, she had been the organization's token woman, its unofficial cheerleader; now she was leading a transition to a system where there would be no tokens. She agreed to the job as long as she could work part-time. A trainer named Elsie Cross, a black woman, was elected as NTL's "chair of the board"—another part-time position.

Within a year or two, NTL had recovered from its financial crisis. Some problems persisted, though, concerning qualifications. At NTL, new members were admitted only under a "cohort" system. For every white male trainer admitted, there had to be one white female, one male of color, and one female of color. White male trainers with impeccable academic credentials felt shut out; few of the minority and women trainers had Ph.D.s. (Edie Seashore herself did not have one.) Thus, the prevailing NTL attitude had to change. Theoretical debates about organizational behavior disappeared. Conversations rarely focused on peak experiences either; the day of the human potential movement was over, at least at NTL. Instead, trainers talked pragmatically. What techniques had been effective with clients? What were they learning about race and gender in companies? Occasionally, they talked about the most worrisome aspect of the cohort system. Was it, in effect, a quota system? Would it lead to less competent trainers being selected over more competent ones?

It was difficult to talk honestly about those sorts of questions, or any serious issues, in racially mixed groups. It took patience and the willingness to sit in a room where people exploded in anger at each other. In fact, the first retreat for the new NTL board, early in 1976, erupted in anger—not between the men and women in the room, which Edie had expected, or between the whites and blacks, but specifically between the white and black *women*. They had split over the design of the NTL programs: Should they focus first on sexism or racism? White women didn't see themselves as racist, but suddenly their racism was on the table. It took hours, painful hours, to sort out the different ways in which white and black women interpreted the same simple conversations. And if they couldn't overcome their misunderstandings with each other, what hope did they have for helping outsiders?[41]

Although the transition was painful, the four horsepersons succeeded in creating a new type of organization. They had finally forced NTL out of the paternalistic, elitist culture it had had before. Now it was the kind of democracy that Lee Bradford, Ken Benne, and Ron Lippitt had talked about but never had been able to achieve. Standing committees, for the first time in NTL's history, organized their own programs. Their decisions could no longer be vetoed by board fiat.[42] And if you attended an NTL meeting, you'd find yourself surrounded by people from every conceivable ethnic background, of both genders at every age, in all sexual orientations, wearing a wide variety of garments, and speaking in a broad range of accents and styles. Yet somehow they all seemed to be able to operate in synch. They had faced the tribulations that came from their differences and talked through them enough so that they understood each other. The new NTL approach would be a significant (and controversial) force in the organization change movement of the 1980s and 1990s.

However, to anyone who knew NTL's past, there was something bittersweet about the change. NTL had been born amid the Pelagian attitudes of people like Kurt Lewin, Douglas McGregor, and Lee Bradford. Human beings are innately good; racism and sexism somehow stem from social institutions. There must be a way to restructure society that could bring racism and sexism to the surface and wipe it away.

But the new NTL approach seemed Augustinian at heart. People are inherently racist and sexist, it seemed to say. Oppression is built into human nature. Organizations must be designed to contain, regulate, and manage the racist and sexist impulses of their members.[43] Many of the NTLers found ways to synthesize the Augustinian critique of oppression with the Pelagian spirit of T-Groups; they taught "communication" techniques that drew forth the basic goodwill and appreciation of diversity that existed in the hearts of most of their clients. Nonetheless, increasingly during the 1980s, some of the "diversity management" pioneers would be accused of using the encounter group to instill their own points of view in people—abandoning the attitude of inquiry that made the T-Group worthwhile in the first place.

Chris Argyris, in the meantime, took a different path after the plans for an NTL university collapsed. He resolved to investigate NTL's own lack of learning head-on. He was embarking on his own equivalent, perhaps, to the years that Parzival spent wandering, wrapped up in questions about his own capabilities and motives. Argyris, however, took on that burden not just for himself but for all his colleagues and peers.

His investigations into the effects of the T-Groups had led him there. He would watch an authoritarian executive change, heart and soul. The executive would return to his ordinary life with a new, more open way of speaking, a taste for hearing what others had to say, and even a warmer relationship with his family. It would last for six months or even a year. But then the company would hit a period of stress: a cutback in orders, a tricky labor negotiation, or some other crisis. And the executive would revert back to being a snapping, subordinate-blasting, self-righteous S.O.B., as if the T-Group had never happened. There was no theory to explain this reversion. "How come the good stuff doesn't last," Argyris asked himself, "and the lousy stuff seems to persevere?"

In 1971, after moving to Harvard University, he took part in a Ford Foundation-funded project on school leadership, and there he began to work on the puzzling lack of learning among professional experts, such as architects, psychiatrists, and educators. Why, when their techniques went awry, did they cling to them? Why did they struggle so hard to justify their own school of thought, instead of inquiring into possible solutions offered by their rivals?[44]

In collaboration with an MIT professor named Donald Schön, Argyris soon developed his "theory of action," which has been at the core of organizational learning practice ever since.[45] Without it, arguably, every attempt to change an organization for the better will fail, foundering on the hubris of both the insiders and the outside consultants. And yet it's very hard to put the theory of action into practice. To do so requires going on an internal Grail quest of your own—stepping back through your own mind's levels of abstraction, becoming increasingly aware of your own stumbling blocks and those of others, and continually building the capacity in yourself to stop the action and say to yourself, "What is keeping me from asking what afflicts the King?"

Argyris and Schön posited that each of us carries two sets of theories in our heads. Closer to the surface lies the "espoused theory": the principles and attitudes about the world that we wish to believe that we believe. Thus, an executive going through a T-Group would come out espousing Theory Y-style beliefs: that people are intrinsically interested in making a contribution and learning. When that executive returns to his company, he will pay lip service to those beliefs. He may send other people to training programs so they'll "get it" about Theory Y. He may even institute some new policies or take other actions that reflect this espoused theory. But since it remains at the level of espoused theory, it never goes very deep.

Then comes a moment of stress. Suddenly, the executive's actions are no longer guided by the espoused Theory Y. They are guided by whatever "theory-in-use" has operated all along—which could be Theory X, that people basically will not take any initiative unless prodded by the carrot and stick. Since theories-in-use have taken a lifetime to develop, they usually exist below the surface. A manager may loudly espouse egalitarian treatment of all people, regardless of status—but in the boss's presence, a quavering voice and sweaty palms may reveal a very different "theory in use" about authority. These tacit theories provide the constancy in our perceptions and our identities: in a sense, we *are* our theories-in-use about the world. Thus, if you want to change someone's behavior, you cannot affect it in the long run, Argyris and Schön stated, by changing their espoused theory. You must change their theory-in-use.

And that requires such deep probing that you cannot force the change. Someone must be willing to bring their deepest theories to the surface, to look closely at them, to test them against new experience, and to practice living as if their theories-in-use were already changing.

With the concept of theories-in-use, Argyris could explain the frustrations in his earlier consultations. For example, the State Department bureaucrats had held a theory-in-use that revealing their feelings and attitudes made them vulnerable. No T-Group could have overcome that. In some role-playing workshops he had facilitated for IBM's senior leaders in the early 1960s at Yale, he had seen the president, Thomas Watson, Jr., repeatedly try to provoke people to tell him critical or bad news. "I'm worried," he would say, "that IBM could become a big, inflexible organization which won't be able to change when the computer business goes through its next shift."

"It'll never happen, Tom," his direct reports would say. "This is a world-class organization, with world-class people." Yet when there was trouble at a factory, or in a design lab, at each step up the hierarchy another sliver of bad news would be extracted, until by the time it reached the top the debacle had gradually become wonderful.[46]

Now, looking back on it, Argyris could see how Watson was trapped by the theories-in-use of his own subordinates ("who were first-rate people," Argyris later recalled). IBM had been built on the unspoken theory that the most important result of a meeting was making sure everyone in it was pleased, particularly the boss.

In the 1970s, Argyris became one of the most controversial faculty members at Harvard. He had taken a twin post, half-time at the business school and half-time at education. In both domains his classes were arenas of conflict—between, on the one hand, himself and the future managers struggling with numbers, and, on the other, future therapists, counselors, and educators going for their "Master's of Saving the World" social work degrees. In one of his earliest education classes, Argyris was denounced for teaching at the business school. A student stood up and proclaimed, "As long as they're businessmen they're no damn good," and the class erupted in applause.

Argyris was deeply offended. The student might be right; businessmen might indeed be no damn good. But a statement like that should be based on data. So the next week, he opened the class by calling on a black student. "I'd like to ask you," he said, "about the concept of 'nigger.'" There was dead silence. "What is the meaning of that concept? How would you describe it? What are its properties?"

The student said, "Are you crazy, Professor?"

"This is being taped," Argyris said. (He taped every class.) "You can have the tape. But I want to know the answer." After a half hour's discussion, he summarized the main points the students had made: "The concept of 'nigger' treats a human being as part of a class stereotype. It shows no respect for what a human being can be. No matter whether you are a good black, a hardworking black, or a lazy black—if you're black, according to that concept, you are no damn good. Is that right?"

The class agreed. Argyris pressed the button on the other tape recorder and they heard the voice from the previous week: "as long as they're businessmen they're no damn good!" Then he clicked off the tape and asked, "Ladies and gentlemen, what's the difference?" And this time the class gave *him* a round of applause.

That week, the Black Student Caucus met to discuss whether to censure him. Argyris, hearing of the meeting, said he would love to attend. But the Caucus refused. Instead, two students came to him afterward to tell him that the group had censured him, but personally they felt he was right. "You have the courage that a lot of other faculty don't seem to have. And we need that."

"Thank you," said Argyris. "Now would you say that in public?"

"No," the students told him. "That would start another war."

That episode set the tone for his years at the school. He often opened classes by saying to his graduate students in counseling or social work, "A lot of what goes by the name of counseling theory, or caring and support, is incompetence covered up by love." When they protested, he offered to prove it from their own counseling cases. His awareness of conversational nuance was razor-sharp—and since it was based on a theoretical framework that he had developed himself, few people could challenge it. In courses filled with self-satisfied Harvard students, he systematically shattered their illusion that, simply by following their instincts, they were going to do good. In the process, he would work himself up to a fever pitch, dancing at the front of the room, occasionally forgetting where he was and bumping into the podium—then turning to look at it as if to wonder: what was *that* doing there?

Students tended to remember Argyris' classes for years; some with deep affection, others with the feeling of having been brutalized. Argyris knew, from his work with T-Groups, that an intervention is a kind of drug—an experience based on a dramatically powerful technique for changing relationships, reframing attitudes, and raising new feelings of identity. These interventionists would be going out into the real world. The quality of their reasoning would dominate every encounter. If they were made anxious when examining their own reasoning dispassionately, then they were like surgery students who fainted at the sight of blood. Maybe they should find another job. "We'd better make damn well sure," Argyris told his students, "that we have the highest possible commitment to increasing the knowledge about our impact." And in the process of articulating that impact, Argyris would become a kind of human lightning rod, sparking emotions among his students that ran from adulation to revulsion. Years later, some students (and some clients) would find they *still* kept arguing with the Chris Argyris in their minds.

There was much more to Argyris' and Schön's work; indeed, they have never stopped developing it, separately and together. They theorized about learning, borrowing from the epistemologist/anthropologist Gregory Bateson. Most everyday learning (which they called "single loop") merely allowed you to pick up new knowledge or skills. To change your theories-in-use you needed to apply "double loop" learning and be open to information about your own defensiveness and mental blinders. Argyris, in particular, devoted himself to developing practices by which people could systematically look at the "data" of their own behavior, bring their theories-in-use to the surface, find safe ways to talk about them, and gradually retrain themselves to operate with more appropriate ones. This practice went to the core of Parzival's dilemma. We each design our own future behavior, and the future behavior of our organizations, in ways that we are not fully aware of. That's why it was so important not just to recognize theories-in-use but to actively try to change them.

Argyris and the few students he trained in depth developed a way of speaking that treaded carefully around emotional land mines. It was almost precious, yet it seemed to get to the heart of the matter: "What is it that leads you to believe this?" Or "What exactly prevented you from bringing up that difficult issue?"[47] The conversations sounded stilted; they had to be, in order to slow down the thought patterns so participants could see how the design would work and how it might be changed. Learning that design would be a lifelong task.

And yet to have that language gave people a remarkable feeling of power. They were no longer hung up by the strictures of their own misunderstandings. They could challenge their bosses safely; they could lay their assumptions on the table, as if they were tangible, and talk through their differences.[48] People who worked with Argyris, particularly in his business consultations, began to look at the relationship between people's espoused theory and theory-in-use as a finance officer would look at a balance sheet. It was concrete, testable. You could diagram it, and the diagram would match reality. You could never capture all the complexity of human interchange, but neither could a balance sheet. Once people had the skills of double-loop learning, Argyris noticed, they never forgot them. Even if a new boss came into an organization and told everyone to drop the talk of "theories" and "inferences," the people retained the skills. T-Groups had never been able to accomplish that.

By the end of the 1970s, each of the three key NTL figures had come to a similar understanding. Edie Seashore (and the three other horsepersons) had built an organization that no one had thought was possible, on the foundation of acknowledging the categories in which life had placed people. Chris Argyris had developed a rigorous path for self-understanding, free of mysticism, and replicable even in the most numbers-driven industrial organization. And Warren Bennis, like Parzival, had seen firsthand how no action can exist without the risk of failure.

In 1971, two years after he dropped out of NTL, Warren Bennis was selected to be president of the University of Cincinnati. He deliberately sought the presidency of a large university because he wanted to put his knowledge about management—and his own capabilities—to the test. For the first time since his old mentor Douglas McGregor had held the presidency of Antioch College twenty-five years before, someone schooled in group dynamics and change-agentry would actually run a mainstream organization: not just as a consultant, but as the chief executive. In that sense, Cincinnati provided the first full-scale opportunity to show what the "Pelagians" could do.

UC was a commuter university of 35,000 students, standing on a hill half a mile from downtown. The university's board, under great pressure to conclude its search, had reluctantly hired Bennis; he was the least politically leftist candidate that the college search committee had found. Nonetheless, he once again proposed a flamboyantly lofty vision for a university's destiny. UC would be "the greatest urban university of the century."[49] Instead of an encumbered bureaucracy, it would be an exemplar of collaborative management. It would not just train social workers and police, but develop ways to revitalize schools and communities in Cincinnati's poor neighborhoods. New interdisciplinary programs would span UC's autonomous "colleges," which heretofore had been fierce rivals. Bennis was impatient to galvanize this parochial commuter college into a full-scale educational centerpiece.

His presidency lasted six years. It is considered by many Cincinnatians to be a low point in the university's history, and he is the only UC President Emeritus who has never been offered an honorary degree by the university trustees. Yet, in retrospect, he had a remarkably successful administration. He ensured the university's survival by moving it from its part-public, part-private status completely into the state university system, and he set in motion a shift toward urban relevance that still serves the university well, twenty years later. He merely failed to accomplish the NTL ideal: leading a new kind of institution that would, in turn, change society.

Warren was a thoroughly charismatic leader. He seemed to be everywhere; striding into the Student Union with a small entourage straggling after him, charming faculty members in his office, hosting a local TV talk show, or sitting down for lunch on the college lawn with a group of students. Seemingly immune to circadian rhythms, he would hold all-night staff meetings at his house or wake faculty members in the wee hours, phoning about an idea he'd had. He sent key staffers off to National Training Labs seminars. He brought old NTL friends like Chris Argyris and Edie Seashore to lecture on campus. He hired well-known figures like Neil Armstrong, the first man to step onto the moon, to teach on campus. He and his staffers drew map after map for reconceiving the flow of work in the university, sometimes commissioning plywood sculptures of the diagrams if they were too complex for two dimensions.

Perhaps the most successful of his many innovations was the "open door" policy.[50] Universities are profoundly authoritarian institutions; there is frequently no recourse against a recalcitrant bureaucrat, an inaccessible dean, or an exploitative and malevolent Ph.D. advisor. Now, students (and junior faculty members) could turn directly to him during specified hours. "My office looked like an old-fashioned Middle Eastern court for a while," Bennis recalled years later. "I would get heartsick at every session, at the real problems students were having." Some people just showed up to observe; one woman, who always brought her knitting, told Bennis that it was the most interesting show on campus. Bennis made no decisions on the spot, but always appointed a staff member to investigate and carry the message to the appropriate dean. Occasionally, the complaints were made public. "That's why it was threatening to the deans and vice presidents. I undercut their authority."

In short, he was exciting, vibrant, tanned, and cosmopolitan, a bit bohemian (his wife, Clurie, was photographed in sandals in the local newspaper)[51]—and unable to keep from ruffling feathers. The first serious sign of trouble came in 1973, when his new dean of the education school, Hendrik Gideonse, began taking care of his newborn son at work two days a week.[52] He simply didn't want to be an absentee father. (This was the same Gideonse who had been Willis Harman's client at the U.S. Education Office. Almost immediately, a secretary's mother phoned Warren Bennis' office to complain. "Why doesn't he get a baby-sitter like everyone else?" she said. "Why isn't he taking care of his duties?" A staff member forwarded the complaint on to Bennis, who taped it to a box of Pampers and sent it to Gideonse. But then the *Cincinnati Enquirer* got wind of the story, and sent a photographer to Gideonse's office. Suddenly, there was the baby in its bassinet in the morning paper, surrounded by Gideonse's shelves of books. United Press International, and then worldwide TV, picked up the story: a father who loved his child so much that he took the baby to work.

In Cincinnati, however, men were not supposed to take care of children. "My in basket," wrote Bennis, "has been flowing . . . with letters that urge his arrest or merely his immediate dismissal. My only public comment has been that . . . if Hendrik can engage in this form of applied humanism and still accomplish the things we both want done in education, then, like Lincoln with Grant's whiskey, I'd gladly send him several new babies for adoption. Nevertheless, Hendrik's baby is eating up quite a bit of my time."

This was just one of the irritations that seemed to bedevil Bennis. A professor complained the building temperature was sixty-five degrees. ("I suppose he expects me to grab a wrench and fix it," Bennis groused.) A group of students complained that two beloved trees had been cut to make room for a sign with a benefactor's name on it. (Bennis, despite his authority, couldn't find out who had authorized the trees cut. No one seemed to know.)[53] As he dealt with crisis after crisis, he felt his time and aspirations for the school drip away, bit by bit. "Routine work drives out all nonroutine work," he opined—thanks to an "unconscious conspiracy" that sent all problems up to his desk[54] and made sure that nothing substantive actually happened. No matter how hard he tried to be a leader, he couldn't lead. He was too busy managing.

And yet, anyone who watched Bennis noticed that he encouraged all communications to flow directly through his office. When his attention wandered away from a project, other people felt it had become a low priority; they waited for him to prod them again before resuming. Anyone could say anything to him without fear of reprisal, and watch him agree, but more often than not, people walked out of his office thinking they hadn't made a difference. He would just change his mind again when the next person walked in. It was as if Bennis himself was the chief unconscious conspirator.

Then, in 1974, the school was overwhelmed by a severe budget crunch.[55] Bennis embarked on a passionate lobbying campaign to merge the school into the Ohio state university system. This meant selling the idea to the legislators *and* winning a Cincinnati city referendum. He forced himself into the role of politician, making speeches and canvassing for support he would need to lobby the state legislature—and the deal went through! Five years before, he had refused the presidency of the NTL university because he didn't want to deal with financial scarcity. But at Cincinnati, the crunch became an opportunity for his greatest triumph.

Meanwhile, human relations—his area of expertise—was the source of his worst disaster. Torn between his desire to promote participative management and his need to be an authority figure, Bennis asked all the department heads to work out a budget plan together for the common good of the school. But consensus management was a pipe dream when people had to divide an ever-shrinking budgetary pie. The department heads and college deans all fought each other bitterly. They were especially outraged when Bennis cut special deals for some faculty members he considered particularly worthy. He organized faculty T-Groups, which might have helped, but they dissipated into apathy when people realized that some participants were acting as moles, going back to Warren and telling him what everyone had said.

Finally, the faculty voted to join a union and institute collective bargaining. Warren was stunned. "Why do you suppose they did that?" he asked one of his faculty supporters.

"They figured, in the final analysis," came the reply, "that was the only way they could get a fair share, because all the other claimants for money were closer to the front of the line."

Bennis had nothing against unions per se, but to the board of directors—with its roots in the established Cincinnati business community—there was no surer signal that he was out of control. When he stepped down in 1977, it was widely assumed that he had been forced out of the job.[56] His life, which had been so public for so many years, abruptly became private. His marriage broke apart. He settled first in Aspen, then lived on a houseboat in Marin County.

Bennis lived quietly, particularly after a heart attack in 1979. Then, in the early 1980s, he broke into the public eye again as a management author, with a series of popular books on leadership.

This preoccupation with leadership stemmed directly from his Cincinnati experience. Managers were people who do things right, he said, while leaders do the right thing. In other words, organizations needed people not just with "know-how" but also with "know-why." To be taken seriously as a person with "know-why," however, would require managing yourself—a point that Bennis had borrowed from a United Technologies Corporation ad in *The Wall Street Journal*.[57] *He was* tired. He no longer talked about his own experiences at Cincinnati much, but returned again and again to talk about other institutional leaders he had known (he interviewed dozens during the late 1970s and early 1980s). He would be a college professor and writer, but never again the same figure of authority, with the same potential for reshaping the world, that he had been in Cincinnati.

Certainly, Bennis deserved more credit than he ever got—from either the Cincinnati business community or the NTL community— for running an institution. He had invigorated the university, and saved it from almost certain dissolution. No one else at NTL ever took the same level of risk. But his strength was the reason for his failure: he was too preoccupied with his own learning. The result was an enterprise that couldn't help but be centered around Bennis himself, as if the university were an extension of the man. Nonetheless, in the end, taking the presidency of the university had been a thoroughly heroic action. Bennis had met Parzival's dilemma by choosing to act, and anyone who paid attention could know, henceforth, that the knowledge of change-agentry theory in itself was necessary, but not sufficient, for changing the world.

Bennis' last commencement speech to the students, in 1977, summed up the force that had propelled him into an active role, again and again, despite all of his mistakes. He quoted a long letter to the daughter of a friend. She had written him to ask for advice on what to do with the rest of her life. Should she stay out in the small Colorado town where she lived? If she moved to a city, wouldn't she get trapped in a dehumanizing workplace? Bennis scolded her (and, by extension, the students sitting before him). He knew her as a bold and gutsy young woman, yet every career she conceived for herself sounded dull, dreary, unimaginative.

What made her think, Bennis asked, that she could abandon work just because workplaces were dehumanizing? Did she think that one ordered one's workplace from a Sears catalogue? One built one's workplace, attitude by attitude, conversation by conversation. One built one's life by making a commitment to it, and being willing to be broken by that commitment.

> For many years [Bennis quoted from his letter to her], I believed in predestination. I believed that people were born, doll-like, wound up by the Master Toymaker, to "run down" over a period of time along a given course. Life, in that view, is a kind of maze. Not frightening exactly if you watch closely for the clues and have faith, but risky, thanks to "free will" (an extra little gear invented by the Toymaker to keep from getting bored).
>
> I can't remember when or why I stopped believing in pre-

destination. . . . I seem to have spent a good deal of my life trying to understand from failure and always believing that that's what we are really here for: to learn from ourselves and others, and some anticipation of failure has to be a part of that. But can you see the paradox? If learning is the center-piece of living, as I think it to be, how can we ever *really* fail unless we decide: "Choice is too dangerous, failure is some-thing we cannot handle or tolerate, and learning is only pe-ripheral to living"? If we come to that, then our shutters close off life.[58]

MILLENARIANS

A movement of fervent aspiration emerged during the last years of the twelfth century. In the mountains of northern Italy and southern France, disaffected preachers talked quietly of a golden era about to come, glistening with inevitability, in which the rich would share their wealth with the poor. Earth would return to the natural harmony of Eden. Most important of all, the ordinary people—not the established church—would make this happen themselves.

The church was disorganized in those years, and substitute churches emerged as alternatives in the streets. If you were sympathetic in Moravia, you might be led by the hand, on foot, to a commune of like-minded people in Cologne. There, you might take part in shared trances, imagining the world to come. You might take a vow of "voluntary *poverty," after which you would become a deliberately home-less pilgrim, living on alms, engaging wherever you went in a rootless, endless conversation about the values of the world.*

These millenarians came to be known as the "brethren of the free spirit" or (since many of their leaders were women) as the "beguines." They came from well-to-do backgrounds; they were widows and spinsters from merchant families, re-bellious artisans, younger scions of aristocrats, and youthful members of the clergy. They were articulate; as fast as their writings could be suppressed and burned, they turned out new tracts. They preached in common languages, not in Latin, and they taught the practices of the mystics, but their purpose was not to see God. They would become Gods themselves. Many of them felt that they should be ex-empt from the strictures of ordinary morality. For was not the church, the sovereign institution of morality, inherently corrupt? And would it not be swept away as the world changed?

Much of what the millenarians had to say has been dis-torted and lost, and they are known, largely through their critics' accusations, as dissolute, orgying, syphilitic thieves. Their influence could not have been all dreadful, however, for it endured four hundred years. There was a sweetness to their preachings and a sense of self-renunciation. New brethren of the free spirit emerged wherever there was discontent. They were a lot like some of the people you might meet in, say,

Northern California in the early to mid-1970s. You wouldn't know whether to marvel at their naiveté or to admire their prescience.[1]

▼▼▼

We have the same problem today looking back at the countercul-ture of the 1960s and 1970s. So much politically expedient criti-cism has surfaced in recent years that it is difficult to see its dreams, its contributions, and its excesses in perspective. Certainly, it incor-porated the naiveté of a children's crusade, the anti-intellectualism of a mob movement, and the recklessness of any revolt against the status quo. By all means, it encouraged sexual experimentation and the use of illegal drugs; perhaps it could be accused of invoking "antifamily" attitudes (although it was hardly a source of enthusi-asm for big government; counterculture people found most large government to be untrustworthy and overbearing). All of these ele-ments, *even if true,* were peripheral to the counterculture's essence. It was a movement of apostasy—of rebellion against the bitter im-personality of industrial culture and the split that this culture had driven between the human mind, body, and vernacular spirit.

Even rock and roll, when traced back to its roots, represented the fusing of vernacular spirit and an industrial beat. Rock was a tribal message translated into electric guitar—emerging in the densely populated homelands of Kongo, Dahomey, and Yorbaland, carried on slave ships to the West Indies, flavored by pagan rhythms from Celtic slaves sent to Haiti in Oliver Cromwell's time, transmit-ted into New Orleans as voodoo (an ecstatic series of rituals that Joseph Campbell compared to the mysticism of Gnostic heretics), expressed as jazz in New Orleans and blues throughout the South, recorded by black musicians in the 1920s and 1930s, copied in the 1950s by white singers like Elvis Presley, and danced out into the rest of the culture. The counterculture doted on rock (in all its various forms) because the music fused dance and body movement with thought and poetry. It gave voice to the spirit people felt: We must be free.[2]

Counterculture people renounced the bitterness of the industrial mainstream. They refused to strive, unless they could set the purpose of their striving. Some who dropped out never returned. But the most creative and vigorous members of the counterculture discovered that they could not simply renounce an old establishment. They had to create a new one. In the process, they gave birth to the notion of a secular millennium—a postindustrial, countercultural, ecologically aware attitude shift affecting every aspect of society.

To use a term coined by geneticist Richard Dawkins, the secular millenium is an intensely hardy "meme." A meme, says Dawkins, is a cultural element, such as an idea, that replicates itself, moving through conversation and media through cultural forms of natural selection, acquiring new traits as it evolves.[3] An observer, following the conversations of the time, could almost track the evolution of *this* meme, watching it incorporate ideas about "living cheaply," environmentalism, corporations, economic growth, technological change, scenario planning, and social responsibility as it traveled. It was influenced by Karl Marx (who also predicted a secular millennium) and the many Marxists in the counterculture of the 1960s, but it rapidly took on flavors that grated on the Marxists. It always included, for instance, a fiercely physical, body-oriented, tribal component and a related component of nature worship.

Always, the meme centered on the same basic idea. The dramatic industrial growth of the past hundred years had depended on a set of poisonous attitudes: literally toxic in the case of industrial wastes. These attitudes would have to change before any serious reform could take place. Many of the heretics of this book—Willis Harman, Oliver Markley, Dana Meadows, Herman Kahn, and the scenario planners at Royal Dutch/Shell—became carriers, in one way or another, even if they didn't believe in the meme on its own terms. Many times, as you will see, the millenarian paradigm was just plain wrong. It's easy to recognize its delusions in hindsight. But that didn't make it any less useful or any less significant. At the end of the 1970s, when its meanderings were more or less played out, the millenarian paradigm had left a valuable practical legacy, probably undreamt of by any of its progenitors. It established an image, perhaps the only reliable image so far, of the purpose corporations might best serve as the years unfold after 2000.

In 1959, if you were a college student positioned among the best and brightest of your peers, you might have wanted to become an engineer or physicist and contribute to America's landing on the moon. In 1979, you would set your sights on becoming an investment banker and a millionaire by forty. But in 1969, there were only two appropriate choices: to be an artist or to save the world. In both cases, like the genteel aristocrats of the British Empire, you weren't really supposed to think about money, overt status, or even achievement. Instead, as the mythologist Joseph Campbell began to tell his students at lectures, you were supposed to "follow your bliss"—follow the goals you felt called upon to pursue.

In the separate societies of Berkeley, Cambridge, the East Village, Austin, the Haight, the French Quarter, Ann Arbor, and college towns everywhere, the bottom dropped out of the primary currencies of the business world. Money had no cachet; security was for frightened conformists. Planning for the future—making the right decision, cultivating the right career—was meaningless. It meant consigning yourself to a life in prison: a life of making choices based on what someone else would tell you to do, gradually internalizing that tyrannical authority in your own mind.

To people who complained, in effect, "Stop the world; I want to get off," the counterculture replied, in effect, "You can." Millions of young people opted out of industrial society. They supported themselves on odd jobs and allowances from their parents. They lived three, four, or six to an apartment, choosing poverty because it made them free and because there was no loss of dignity in it. If you were bright, poverty was exalting. It meant (though nobody used this language) that you had found a way to reembrace the vernacular spirit that society had tried to discard. You could live in a utopian sphere where everyone was an aristocrat. You did not commute, learn to balance a checkbook, or buy a business suit. You experienced life at each moment and felt no need to poison the quality of the moment by preparing for the future. More often than not, your life was wildly creative and inventive, spurred not just by drugs, but by cameraderie and free time.

Counterculture people could afford to take their stance precisely because living was easy. Rents were cheap; the parks, the streets, and the love of fellow members of the tribe were all available for nothing. As Herman Kahn noted, it cost about $500 per year to live as a hippie in 1968, which meant that twelve young people could share a large house, each working one month a year in the post office and taking eleven off.[4] (Nobody actually *did* this; but it gave Kahn a nice, mythically apt image to use in speeches.) In the heyday of the hippie era, suffused with vernacular spirit, people acted as if sharing with each other, even with strangers, was the most natural thing in the world. "Free" stores and clinics opened in neighborhoods like the Haight-Ashbury of San Francisco and Cambridge in Massachusetts: distributing food, used clothing, emergency medical care, and dense mimeographed broadsides about the coming apocalypse.

They also took time to talk. The counterculture was rife with groups, clubs, cells, meeting grounds, and mutual enterprises—but devoid of authority. Living in the counterculture was like living in a great, community-wide T-Group. Nothing was decided except through drawn-out dialogues and consensus sessions. Anyone was, in theory at least, capable of raising an objection or changing the flow of activity. The hippies were as intensely Pelagian as the academics of the National Training Laboratories, but their Pelagianism came straight from the heart. They lived and breathed it, without having to cultivate a particular environment for it.

Admittedly, those who had money and success sometimes felt as if they were carrying the burden of the tribe. Rock musicians with record contracts were under constant pressure to distribute their largesse. The music was an expression of the crowd flowing through them, so didn't the rewards from that music belong to everyone? The San Francisco concert promoter Bill Graham often found himself in shouting matches with young would-be concertgoers who wanted him to stop charging money for music. "What does your father do? Is he a plumber? Well, I want my pipes fixed for free! Is he a baker? Well, I want my bread for free!"

In retrospect, the startling thing about the counterculture was the disconnect between production and consumption. How could so many smart people fail to see a link between the work people did, the investments they made, and the rewards they gained? Only a very few students understood the issues of infrastructure and the industrial economy. A Berkeley student of that era, who later became a management consultant, recalled being approached to join a radical group. "Don't talk to me," she told them, "until you have some indication of how you're going to get the fruits, nuts, and vegetables from California and Florida up to New York and Chicago. Until then, I haven't got time to listen. Don't tell me what you're going to blow up; this country works on distribution systems and networks."[5] But the radicals she talked to didn't know what she was talking about.

Most young people had this blind spot, perhaps, because they had lived their entire lives in a world dominated by the giant, all-nurturing postwar corporations—institutions that separated work and sustenance. Daddy produced; Mommy consumed. Children never went to the office, for there was nothing resembling day care there, even in offices with women managers. ("Someday," the writer Betty Harragan would later point out, "reactionary management may understand that the poor 'image' of business in the public opinion polls will never be successfully counteracted as long as children in their most impressionable, formative years grow up with the idea that a business work site is an unfriendly, repelling, and sinister place which refuses to accept them until they are over twenty years old."[6] Instead of going to work, children of the 1950s and 1960s went to school, where they learned that the rewards for their labor and achievement were never tangible. The reward was an empty grade, a classification of a rank in relation to your peers. What was the point of living a life measured by *that*?

* * *

At first, it seemed as if the counterculture would do without the market entirely and produce everything they needed themselves. Some tried; self-sufficiency was an organizing principle in many of the communes of the late 1960s and early 1970s. But as historian Fernand Braudel has pointed out, existence without a market is "the lowest plane of human existence, where each man must himself produce almost all he needs."[7] Only a few communards who tried that game, the purest of mystics and ideologues, managed to sustain themselves. The rest turned their communes into businesses (the Farm, in Summertown Tennessee, earned its income by publishing books about midwifery, ham radios, and their own experience). Or else they came running back to the city, creating institutions of their own.

The first urban countercultural businesses emerged in the early 1960s. A woman who called herself Magnolia Thunderpussy opened a restaurant at Haight and Stanyan streets in San Francisco in 1962. It was designed whimsically and flamboyantly, so that every meal was a theatrical experience. By the mid-1960s there were restaurants serving cheap whole-grain food; often, the bulk of their clientele consisted of regulars whose hair was too long and whose clothes were too ragged to fit in at ordinary restaurants.[8] Other hippies, traveling to Kathmandu or Amsterdam, brought back the fruits of the life they found there—for sale to local boutiques.

Counterculture people often learned the rudimentary skills of marketing and management by dealing such drugs as marijuana and LSD. They'd give away a free joint to a new customer—a time-honored sales promotion technique. Like the bootleggers of the 1920s, they had to learn the intricacies of bookkeeping, or else they would get swindled by their suppliers—or hurt by their customers. Around 1969, organized crime moved into the lucrative narcotics trade of neighborhoods like the Haight-Ashbury and the East Village. The hippies stepped away from selling dope; they parlayed their account-keeping and budgeting knowledge into new lines of work, unabashedly aiming their goods and services at the members of the "tribe."

By the early 1970s, most mainstream services had counterculture equivalents. There were clothing stores that mixed new and used clothing, head shops that sold posters and drug paraphernalia, and food co-ops with organic grains that customers scooped into their own jars from large wooden barrels. There were transient hotels, like the Head Inn in New Orleans, where for one dollar a night you could sleep in a sleeping bag on a rickety iron-grille balcony overlooking a French Quarter alleyway.[9] There were hippie bus lines, on which for thirty dollars (after waiting a day or two for the bus driver to be ready) you could ride in the back of a gaily painted van—drinking beer, smoking dope, and groping your fellow passengers all the way from San Francisco to New York. There were fervent experiments with electronic gear, solar panels, and Buckminster Fuller-inspired domes, experiments that begat sophisticated small manufacturing companies. And there were publishers of magazines and books rooted in rock and roll, which the mainstream publishers didn't imagine would sell.

At first, these new forms of commerce lacked infrastructure. Counterculture businesspeople hardly ever knew about each other; they rarely knew how to keep going. The large-scale information in conventional business publications—*The Wall Street Journal* and *Fortune*—was worse than useless to them. It suggested that the only way to succeed was to professionalize yourself, to enter school. As an alternative to *that* horrible fate, the counterculture began to invent its own infrastructure. Instead of slipping through the cracks in the mainstream, they widened the cracks into an extensive surface. Gradually, this alternative infrastructure (which, after all, depended on the mainstream shipping and telecommunications lines) infiltrated and assimilated its way into American business culture.

Consider, for instance, the history of the Erewhon Trading Company, which for a time was the largest natural-foods distributorship in the United States. It began when two Japanese-born teachers of macrobiotics, Michio and Aveline Kushi, began to sell food and books out of their home in Cambridge, Massachusetts. The Kushis had been countercultural even back in Japan in the 1950s. They had met at Maison Ignoramus, a macrobiotic institute based outside Tokyo that had been founded by a Japanese writer, a former expatriate (he had lived in Paris) and Zen scholar named George Ohsawa. Ohsawa, who had cured himself of tuberculosis (he claimed) through a diet of brown rice, miso soup, cooked vegetables, beans, and seaweed, argued that improper diets (and other personal imbalances) caused not just health problems and depression but social ills as well. Ohsawa also believed in world government and recruited the Kushis (among others) to travel abroad to promote the idea; in the United States they fell in love and eventually established a teaching practice in Cambridge, Massachusetts. They had hoped for serious students, but they seemed to attract hippies, who puzzled the Kushis by saying things like "Brown rice makes you high."

Yet although they were tempted to write off their counterculture students as disorderly, the restrained and disciplined Kushis admired their creativity and adventurousness, as well as their rebellious stance against the sicknesses (as they saw them) of industrial culture. "We felt it was our responsibility to guide them," Aveline Kushi later wrote, "and help them recover their health and dream in life."[10] And the Kushis adopted the countercultural ethic of self-sufficiency themselves: so much so that when they were prosecuted for practicing acupuncture without a medical license, Michio resisted hiring a lawyer because he did not believe in the legal system on principle.[11]

Macrobiotic diets involved staples that were hard to come by in a typical East Coast supermarket: brown rice, miso, tamari, and whole-grain barley. To help students procure the grains, the Kushis opened a small store, and one of their students, Paul Hawken, took over as the clerk. Hawken was only eighteen; he was a lean, handsome young man from California with a raspy voice; he had suffered all his life from asthma, turned to macrobiotics for relief, and then discovered how difficult it was to find them. In the mid-1960s, health-food stores were still predominantly antiseptic places, tinged with the medicinal odor of vitamins, staffed by women wearing white uniforms and hosiery, like nurses on night duty. They rarely carried organic rice or beans, and their staffers had no knowledge of the sources of their foods: What types of farms were they grown on? Did those farms use pesticides or other agricultural chemicals? These concerns, irrelevant by most standards, were of crucial importance in a discipline like macrobiotics, where every bite is designed as a component of the whole of one's life.

Although he had no business background—his ambition had always been to be a writer—the Kushis accepted Hawken as a partner. They renamed the business the Erewhon Trading Company—after Samuel Butler's classic utopia story, a favorite of their Japanese mentor, George Ohsawa. Soon Erewhon was grossing more than $300 per day (up from its original $25), and Hawken discovered that the natural-foods business had a supply crisis.

One day a student came into the store and said, "How do you *know* this oil from Hain is cold-pressed?" Hain was a family-owned concern, based in Los Angeles, that supplied many of new stores like Erewhon with canned and bottled groceries. Hawken defended his supplier, but his curiosity was piqued, so he wrote to the manufacturer. They wrote back saying that "cold-pressed" simply meant that the oil was processed at very low temperatures so that fatty chemicals, such as stearates, would be drawn off. Hawken knew that wasn't correct, and he was heartsick; he had unwittingly betrayed his customer's trust. He began investigating his other suppliers and discovered that many of the packaged products they sold had labels that were (unconsciously or deliberately) deceptive.

Angry at what he saw as the lies of intermediaries, Hawken began to visit family farms himself. He traveled throughout the country, persuading them to adopt organic farming methods by promising to provide a market for their grains. But in order to guarantee a large enough market, he also had to line up other natural-food stores to carry the grain. He did the same with small family-owned manufacturing firms, such as those who made soy sauce in wooden casks. Since he didn't know the "rules" of wholesaling, he naively experimented in ways that later turned out to shape the natural-foods business. Erewhon always labeled its bags of grain with the farmer's name, location, and growing practices. "We made it en-

tirely transparent," he later said. Because they eliminated the mid-
dleman, they could keep the prices down. Now Erewhon *really*
took off, and suddenly Hawken was the president of a burgeoning
international natural-foods wholesaling firm, with its own chain of
retail stores around New England.

One of the first things he realized, as early as 1967, was the
paucity of useful business information available to him. *The Wall
Street Journal, Fortune,* and the Harvard Business School classes he
sneaked into all confused him. They seemed to relate to some "official" world of business that had nothing to do with the enterprise
he had founded. Hawken—and most of his counterculture business
colleagues—had to invent the rules all over again. They redesigned
food labels using calligraphy or simple handwriting to give products an informal feel; they priced goods clearly ($5 instead of
$4.99) so the prices would be easy to add up. And they dealt with
questions of ethical loyalty that an ordinary grocery owner
wouldn't have thought about twice. For instance, the Kushis' macrobiotic regime was limited to a narrow channel—no cheese, few
sweeteners, no salty prepared foods, and most cooking in the Japanese idiom. But customers came into Erewhon's store off Newbury
Street looking for natural ice cream and organic honey. Should or
should not Erewhon stock nonmacrobiotic foods? Eventually the
store did, in part when Hawken's own eating habits broadened. By
1970, the business's purpose was itself; it no longer existed merely
to serve the Kushis' macrobiotic community, except perhaps
through its profits.

There was also the question of keeping employees involved.
Most of them were students of the Kushis. Often, they were former
hippies who wanted to kick drugs, straighten out their relationships
with their parents, and find meaningful work. There was always an
implicit assumption that a job at Erewhon was not just a job; like
the food you ate, it was integrated into your identity and life. Few
businesses could live up to that ideal, in part because there was no
good information around about how to design a business on that
model. McGregor's *The Human Side of Enterprise* might have provided a first step, but it was focused almost exclusively on very

large corporations. Businesses like Erewhon were a completely different type of creature.

Most counterculture businesses held, for example, that "process is our most important product." How they made a decision, and how they felt afterward, was—in the long run—as important as the content of the actual decision itself. Thus, at Erewhon, Hawken continually struggled between two imperatives. On one hand, he needed to make decisions fast, and oftentimes he felt that only he had the experience to make them. Only he had been to Japan; only he had built up the business from the beginning; and he really had confidence only in himself to sustain the business, particularly in a long-hair milieu where people talked regularly about dropping out. On the other hand, he believed strongly in the principle of consensus: "Decisions at Erewhon," he would later proclaim, "are almost always the consensus, if not the unanimous wish, of those people who have been there for a while."[12]

Erewhon was one of hundreds of distribution, information, or financial networks created during those years. There were even networks of networks, such as *The Whole Earth Catalog,* which began as a "truck store," carrying books and other essential goods to communes in the remote southwest. All of them maintained, in one way or another, the idea that business should be personal. As they cast about for ways to govern themselves without rigid hierarchies, many of them turned to group dynamics, or to the consensus management that some of them knew from left-wing organizing. By mainstream business standards, these operations tended to have endless meetings. But a few countercultural businesses learned, through trial and error, to make those consensus meetings work more effectively. They learned to hustle when they needed to; to say, "I can feel that there's ten minutes of steam left in us. If we're gonna get to the last two items on the agenda here, that's how much time we've got." They learned, in short, to put the purpose of the enterprise before their own immediate needs. The alternative, as in any enterprise, was to stagnate.

*　　*　　*

When a counterculture is forced to create its own infrastructure, sooner or later the mainstream culture catches on. When it happened to medieval millenarian preachers, they were turned over to the Inquisition. When it happened to Erewhon, the reaction was subtler. One day in 1972, Paul Hawken walked into Erewhon's original store on Newbury Street in Boston and found four executives from a supermarket chain measuring the floor space and tallying register totals. "They were trying to figure out our sales per square foot, which were phenomenally high for the food industry," he later wrote. "Hi, guys."[13]

Hawken and several of his fellow managers saw that they had reached the point where the business would move beyond its origins; it would no longer be the Kushis' business, but an entity with its own identity.[14] They also had an opportunity to try to build a big business with counterculture values—an intriguing challenge, because it had never been attempted. With all of this in mind, they arranged for private financing, more than a million dollars' worth, from sympathetic sources. (One source was the father of Ram Dass, the Harvard professor turned spiritual leader who wrote the hippie classic *Be Here Now.*)

While waiting for the contracts to be signed, Hawken arranged a bridge loan from a bank to finance the expansion they were planning. But then (as Hawken later told the story) the Kushis rejected the deal. They apparently realized that a transition into the mainstream world would remove their control over the business. But to Hawken, Erewhon's growth made that mainstream transition inevitable. He felt betrayed. At first, he tried to regroup: he mollified the bank and made severe cutbacks in growth. He began to push for an employee-owned structure, and when the Kushis backed out of that as well, Hawken resigned. A year later, he sold his interest.

The Kushis hired new presidents, and Erewhon kept growing. But now there was competition from new natural-food stores and distribution networks. Austerity measures became commonplace. In 1977, the Erewhon workers voted to join a union—an almost unimaginable step from the viewpoint of the days when Kushi was strictly a teacher and the workers were all his grateful students. In 1984, Erewhon went into Chapter 11 bankruptcy and was sold.

Although they retreated from counterculture purity, hippie businesses (like Erewhon) provided an innate, vibrant, living alternative to the stifling industrial system. Anyone can see this simply by walking down a neighborhood with counterculture influence—the Haight-Ashbury, Greenwich Village, Mount Adams in Cincinnati, or the equivalents in any city.[15] Then travel to a mainstream commercial neighborhood awash in chain stores. You will probably have to drive to get there, but get out of your car and stand for a while. You will see the oily waves of fumes rising from the pavement as cars rush past, the smirking visages of forty-foot-high copyrighted cartoon characters on chain-store signs, the occasional scrub trees in an odd planted corner of a parking lot, and the irritated, anxious, just-killing-time grimaces on the faces of passersby rushing to get across the street. Every detail will speak of subtle pressure to buy as much as possible, as quickly as possible, and move on to the next joyless purchase.

Counterculture neighborhoods, by contrast, are filled with color and conversation. Every shop is a recognition that the customer exists as an individual; every sign and signal is full of greetings and rendezvous. Many of the shops in such a neighborhood tweak the sensibilities of the people who walked by, in some good-natured way. (One neighborhood gallery in San Francisco painted the corner of a $20 bill in its doorway, prompting many passersby to try to pick it up—and then to follow their nose into the store.) Commerce has engaged itself into the vernacular life.

These days, the most successful chain stores try to incorporate some of that counterculture spirit. (Even the "R" of Toys R Us would have been inconceivable during the 1950s.) They operate with varying levels of success, and they have varying degrees of manipulativeness. But it is not possible to co-opt without also being co-opted, and the world of money, in the years since the 1960s, has been forced to incorporate some of the luster and spark of the world of counterculture dreams.

* * *

Government would *not* be the vehicle for changing the attitudes of industrial society. By 1972, the scenario planners of Stanford Research Institute—Willis Harman and Oliver Markley—were convinced of that. Every time a Washington agency asked them to look at long-term issues, the same pattern took place. The SRI scenario artists would come in with futures that contradicted the "official" future. Oil costs would grow high enough to change people's consumption patterns. Or crime and physical decay would spread in cities like New York to the point where subways, for instance, would be too dangerous to ride. "That can't happen," the agency would tell them. "Forget about it."

The final straw was a 1974 report prepared for the Environmental Protection Agency pesticide group. Several hundred pages long,[16] it detailed ten scenarios for the future of the Agency. Nearly all of them suggested the same pattern: public support for environmental regulation would decline, triggered by a reaction against the Earth Day "fanatics." Apathy might last twelve years; then, in the late 1980s, prodded by the long-delayed reemergence of climate problems, food shortages, health hazards, and forest losses—along with a possibly revitalized economy—environmental fervor would rekindle. This prediction would ultimately turn out to be right on the money, but the client never had a chance to find out. "Sorry," said the EPA chief who commissioned the report. "That's just not going to happen."

But there *were* SRI clients who were willing to listen—those from corporations. Harman and Markley, with their engineering backgrounds, found it easy to talk to these clients. Businesspeople tended to be direct and blunt. They had no interest in wasting time. Moreover, Willis Harman had become convinced that large multinational corporations—as the dominant institution in our society, the modern equivalent to the Holy Roman Empire, as he put it— would be profoundly important in the coming quarter century. If mainstream corporations learned to cope with the postindustrial imperative, so would the world. "It's very important for all the rest of us," he told his staff, "that business should know what it's doing when it goes through that change, so that it doesn't make wrong decisions and make it a much more traumatic thing."

To communicate this evocation of the millenarian meme, the SRI researchers borrowed the notion of a "paradigm shift" from Thomas Kuhn, the Princeton-based historian of science who had written *The Structure of Scientific Revolutions.* They were the first to adapt this idea—which was intended to describe specific types of breakthroughs in the experimental priorities of scientific communities—to mean that society as a whole would have to change its most fundamental beliefs. Before they were introduced to Kuhn's book, they had been toying unhappily with terms like "Zeitgeist change." The word "paradigm," with its vague connotations of learning and colloquy, conveyed the idea much better. The SRI futures group suddenly found itself leading the New Age movement, *and* the corporate change movement, in using this new term. They would bowdlerize it to such an extent that Kuhn himself, a stickler for precision, eventually would quietly renounce his own use of it.[17]

In 1972, the SRI futures group won a massive assignment to develop a full-scale overview of the millenarian meme. The assignment came from the Kettering Foundation, based in Dayton, Ohio—an educational foundation that had been started by Charles Kettering, the mercurial engineer who had invented the cash register, the electric automobile starter, and Freon. The foundation had recently been endowed with $6 million per year to look at the long-range future of education. Various SRI subgroups paraded their techniques before the Kettering staffers. Willis Harman was the only one who showed up without a flashy slide show or presentation. "We don't quite know *what* methods we're going to use," he said quietly. "But I know what question you're trying to answer, and it has to do with holism and learning to change people's belief systems." Soon afterward, Harman's team was asked to prepare a small presentation, which they delivered in a southern Ohio motel. In that confined room, with traffic whizzing past on the freeway outside, they told the Kettering staff that in the next few years the Western image of the purpose of mankind was about to change.

The resulting study, titled *Changing Images of Man*,[18] is still probably the most concise introduction to New Age concepts that has ever been produced. It enjoyed a wide pass-along photocopy circulation that continues today. As part of the research process, the SRI team held a series of conferences at which researchers, anthropologists, social scientists, and artists locked horns over fundamental social concerns, and many of their comments were incorporated into the paper's footnotes. The resulting effect is like being at a seminar where Margaret Mead, René Dubos, Elise Boulding, and Geoffrey Vickers whisper back and forth around you, taking issue with the basic message and with each other.

As its title suggests, the report missed one key influence—the changing role of women and the effects of that change on the culture. This was a grave lapse, for this was already 1973, the feminist movement was having an effect on the workplace, and many of the key contributors to *Changing Images of Man* were women. (All of the staff members who prepared the report, however, were men.) The absence of any feminist spirit, plus the academic tone of the prose, showed that the report itself was not a creation out of the new paradigm it hoped to foster. It was like a screed by monks, remaining in their old world, but looking ahead with longing to the moment of the flaming chariot that they knew would arrive.

The report asks us to consider what Chris Argyris might have called the theories-in-use of industrial culture: not the espoused values, but the values you could infer from observing social behavior. For instance, people in industrial society saw themselves as separate, conscious, fundamentally rational beings. The goal of life was material fulfillment—certainly much more than mental or spiritual fulfillment. Rational materialism was paramount: mystic experiences (including the SRI work with extrasensory perception or Harman's LSD-based mysticism) were automatically suspect.

But this dominant image of economic man, said the report, "no longer fits the physical reality."[19] Adam Smith's doctrine of the "invisible hand"—in which individual decisions, made for self-interest, add up to the common good—wasn't working; such decisions had produced a 4 percent annual growth rate in energy usage, a dramatic rate of environmental degradation, and an overall decline in civilization.

What should replace the invisible hand? Certainly not the hand of government control. That was already discredited. There was no way out of the dilemma unless society came to hold a new image of humankind. Then the report ticked off the characteristics of the new paradigm waiting to be born. There was a great deal to include.

- ▼ Systems: Jay Forrester's systems modeling and Harman's own systems background provided a foundation for seeing all global processes as interrelated. You could not, under the new paradigm, separate your personal decisions from the fate of the world.

- ▼ LSD and parapsychology research: Changing the international image of humankind would require having people experience for themselves the feelings of interconnectedness that came from LSD use or meditation and mysticism. (This was another form of the fallacy that T-Group leaders had fallen into: "If we could just get our leaders to try this new way of thinking, we could change the world.")

- ▼ Corporate social responsibility: In endeavors like Campaign GM, the SRI group detected a reframing of the legitimacy of mainstream economic institutions. Companies would have to become responsible to their constituents.[20] Corporate people would be among the spear carriers of this new ethic. There would be not one Galileo challenging conventional wisdom, but Galileos scattered all through society.

- ▼ An end to impersonality: All policy decisions, whether made by government or business, depend (said the report) on how people see themselves. Cultures that see people as "animated machines of physical parts" ignore religious growth and learning, but cultures that see people as primarily spiritual neglect the human needs for health, employment, and housing—while both of those cultures, if they see humans as detached from nature, tend to foster an exploitative ethic.[21] Counterculture people had shown how an alternative way of life might feel: suffused with a sense of interdependence, of mutual responsibility, where everyone would feel charged with the inherent wish to look out for each other.[22]

In short, thanks to the reductionist Cartesian mindset of the industrial era, people perceived their lives in terms of fragmented, isolated components. This would have to be healed in the postindustrial era. Humankind would no longer separate cause from effect, mind from body, economy from ecology, or work from love. To help articulate these ideas, Harman sought out Joseph Campbell—the charismatic Sarah Lawrence mythology teacher who had written *The Hero with a Thousand Faces* and, just recently, *The Masks of God.* Campbell had devoted his life to myth in order to understand, as he put it, "the rapture of being alive"—which meant, at least in part, devoting oneself as part of something greater than oneself. Harman and Campbell both believed that the individualism and rootlessness of the counterculture—the ethic of "do your own thing"—was dangerous. Campbell saw the desire for a "world without money" as just another form of materialism—a *different* set of empty totems to collect. Certainly, Campbell was known for telling people to "follow their bliss,"[23] but what he meant by that was the opposite of "doing your own thing." He meant finding the thing that compelled you, that required a lifelong sacrificial commitment, like the commitment to a marriage.

Campbell made several trips to SRI, to help put together the lengthy mythological history that opened *Changing Images of Man,* and his visits always seemed to end in heated political arguments. In the midst of composing a passage about communal renunciation during the Bronze Age, he would start arguing about antiwar demonstrators and how the counterculture was wrecking civilization.[24] A young staffer would counterattack: "No, Joe, the counterculture is exactly the people who have a strong sense of community values. It's the politicians who won't get us out of Vietnam, who are wrecking civilization." It reminded some onlookers of the battles in *All in the Family*—except that the words had twice as many syllables.

For Harman, like everything else, this battle ultimately came down to a matter of personal preference: "Some people really drop out and totally change the outward form of their lives. I eventually concluded that right living, for me, means being *in* the establishment, being more or less acceptable to it. But by no means would I be *of* it. My destiny seems to be to help it to change."

Not long after the study was finished, in 1975, Oliver Markley wrote an Op-Ed piece about it for the *New York Times*. One of the SRI board members, an officer of the Searle pharmaceutical company, was incensed enough to call the SRI president. "If I understand what this guy is saying," said the board member, "he's calling for the end of the industrial era! Is that how you let your people talk? What's going on over there?" A new policy statement followed a few weeks later: SRI employees could say anything they wanted to the media, as long as they made it clear they were not speaking for the institute. "Please keep in mind," the statement concluded, "that we cannot exist if we infuriate our clients."

At this point, the millenarian meme diverged. It split into several branches before coming back together as a synthesis. Thus, this chapter must follow several simultaneous threads. At SRI, the meme evolved into a marketing strategy, of all things—an attempt to make the counterculture into a package for SRI's clients to consume.

This probably would not have happened if Willis Harman had stayed. He had no objection to marketing strategies—he assumed that they were a useful way of transmitting the millenarian paradigm into mainstream culture, where it belonged. But they did not interest him, and he had no flair for them. After 1974, he spent less and less of his time with the futures group. Meetings went by without him; project leaders found their own clients and assembled their own staffs. He even avoided eating lunch with the staff. As often as not, he was gone from the offices, in meditation sessions out in the desert with Captain Al Hubbard, the Johnny Appleseed of LSD. He began to lecture about religion and spirituality and the new paradigms at dozens of conferences. When he did show up at SRI, he seemed increasingly authoritarian and snobbish; he wrote people off if they didn't seem to grasp the import of the new paradigm. And he had become blissfully vague about details. He announced a "plagiaristic ethos" for the futures group—people would no longer get individual credit for their ideas and writing. "The overmind," he said, "provides these ideas to be used by everyone." Since he was the most public figure, that meant it would all appear under his name.[25]

The futures group had always been footloose; now it became fragmented. In the end, the work of management fell to the assistant director of the group, a writer and analyst named Arnold Mitchell—a man who would, in a quieter way, carry the secular millennium meme to a much more explicit stage and eventually into a marketing strategy.

Arnold Mitchell was an old-timer at SRI; he held ID badge number 22, which he would jokingly brandish to demonstrate his seniority. (Badges, numbered sequentially from the earliest days, had gotten up to 11,000 by then.) More importantly, he had struggled all his life to resolve ideas about integrity, materialism, and privilege. He was tall, slim, handsome, shy, and genuinely devoted to the people he worked with. Friendship and collegiality were paramount values for him. His father was the economist Wesley Clare Mitchell, a founder of the New School for Social Research, chairman of the first President's Council of Economic Advisers, and a creator of the theory of business cycles. His mother was Lucy Sprague Mitchell, the founder of the Bank Street College of Education; a dormitory at the University of California at Berkeley had been named for her. She had also written an autobiography of her married life, in which exactly one sentence was devoted to her only child. It was a childhood tailor-made for producing someone determined to find an independent path.

Unlike his parents, Arnold Mitchell had no advanced degrees beyond a BA in English. In his youth, he had been a small-press poet, and he had stumbled into the nascent SRI at the moment they needed an editor to produce their first reports (in the late 1940s). Within the futures group, he had tackled the question of Social Indicators. If they really wanted society to change, how could they measure their success? How would they know they were making a difference? He wrote prolifically, always in pencil, and he took over Willis' role as mentor to the young, poetic policy analysts and scenario crafters of the futures group.

On Friday afternoons, whoever was in town from the futures group would meet at Arnold Mitchell's large house in Atherton. Being careful not to drink alcohol (because it dulled the visioning capacity), they would talk about their projects and the questions they needed to answer. After they agreed on a topic, Oliver Markley would bring them down to trance level and guide them through an off-the-cuff narration. One week, for research on the future of air pollution over the Los Angeles basin, they visualized an eyeball fifteen feet in diameter. Markley guided them inside it, and the eyeball flew off to an altitude of 10,000 feet. It sped ahead to the year 2000, then to the year 2025, and each member of the group saw in his mind the air lighten and clear. Clean air legislation might indeed be successful. The futurists did not have to worry about whether they were "really" seeing the air pollution of the year 2025. They merely needed to see what was plausible, what might spark their client, the Department of Transportation, toward more realistic decisions. None of the clients, of course, ever learned that their $100,000 reports had been partly researched through psychic visualization.

As meditation practice sometimes does, Markley's experiments took on their own momentum. When bicycling home one afternoon, he heard a voice inside his head: "Hello. I am Henri. I have something I'd like to show. Would you come with me?"

Still pedaling, Markley found himself taken (in a corner of his mind) to a wonderful jewel-like city hanging in the middle of space. He entered a building that looked like the Hollywood palladium, where a swarm of sentient creatures who looked like little white lights, separate yet united in a single conscious entity, greeted him telepathically from inside a coat-check window. When Markley asked where he was, the entity replied, "*You* would use a name like the 'Omniverse Center for Cultural Development.'" The Omniverse, Markley gathered, was the collection of all possible universes, at all possible times. He could explore any he chose. He asked, "What is the ratio of war to peace here?" He saw a panel of red and white lights, representing war and peace, respectively. About 30 percent of the lights were red. Always the futurist, Markley asked, "But what are the trends?"

After a long silence, a new voice, slow and almost mournful, replied from above his head, "We judge that your mind is not sufficiently developed to understand a valid answer to that question. But if you insist we'll find a way to answer it."

"I'm a guest here," Markley said. "Far be it from me to press."

A few days later, the group at Arnold Mitchell's included three staffers working on a scenario they called "The Man on a White Horse," in which technological crises, and a charismatic new Hitler brought the Western world back to the Dark Ages. This future might offer some valuable lessons for their client, the Department of Transportation, but they couldn't make it hang together plausibly. Markley felt drawn to guide his colleagues to the Omniverse Center. He didn't dare second-guess his intuition; he put on a cassette of his most powerful telepathy-enhancing background music: Bartók's Night Music for Strings, Celesta and Percussion.

Together, with Markley's smooth voice guiding them, they entered the city-sphere in the sky. They spent about a half hour there. When they opened their eyes back in Arnold's living room, the three people closest to the "White Horse" study were too emotionally moved to speak right away. All three had seen different versions of the same message: Charismatic villains could never be persuasive anymore. Because Hitler, Stalin, and Mao had provided such unavoidable lessons of the pitfalls of ideological totalitarianism, their examples could not be repeated on any large scale.

The staffers used that vision to rework their story line. Instead of a "Man on a White Horse," they suggested that a Gandhi-like figure might emerge, a religious leader speaking out against dissension. This became known at SRI as the "Apocalyptic Transformation" scenario. It eventually found its way into *Seven Tomorrows*, a book of scenarios published in 1980.[26] One of the authors of that book was a staffer at SRI, Peter Schwartz, who a few years later would be invited to be Pierre Wack's replacement at Royal Dutch/ Shell. The second was philosopher Jay Ogilvy, who was leaving academia to come to work at SRI. The third was Paul Hawken, formerly of Erewhon, who was now living in the Menlo Park area. The three of them would become influential carriers of the millenarian meme into the global business community of the 1980s.[27]

Meanwhile, in 1976 and 1977, several SRI futures group members began to take the millenarian ideas more seriously—as a prescription for businesses. They had found an article by a mystic-ascetic writer named Richard Gregg, a Harvard-educated American who had studied and lived with Mahatma Gandhi. Gregg, writing in 1936, had borrowed the idea of "voluntary poverty" from the medieval millenarians and rechristened it as "voluntary simplicity." He advocated the ascetic life, not because it was spiritually more meaningful (although it was), but because it made life more effective. Voluntary simplicity meant "singleness of purpose, sincerity and honesty within, as well as avoidance of exterior clutter, of many possessions irrelevant to the chief purpose of life. . . ."[28]

The futures group members found they could translate this into terms they could sell to their clients. By now it was 1976: the era of limits. Oil prices had tripled from their previous levels and stayed high. Inflation was raging. It made sense for a shopper to consume with voluntary simplicity—to bring awareness and intelligence to *every* purchase. It would mean buying no junk, making each piece of property last, and cultivating natural elegance. Voluntary simplicity, as they saw it, was no longer something that only an ascetic might aspire to. It was a lifestyle choice. Businesses would have to learn to adjust, because voluntary simplicity represented the core of where the market was going.

One of the first expressions of the voluntary simplicity idea (though they didn't yet use the name) occurred in 1975, when SRI began to examine the future of cars for the Ford Motor Company. Peter Schwartz, Arnold Mitchell, and another researcher, Duane Elgin (the men who had unearthed the Richard Gregg article), soon began to look at the effect that the new energy environment was having on the values of car buyers. They predicted a slow but steady growth of a "frugal society"—a society compelled by ecological concerns and mobility of mind and spirit instead of fettered by the complexities of material possessions.[29] People would trade in their cars every five or ten years rather than every two. This meant that Ford's profit margins per car would be smaller, because large-size cars had larger margins. Auto dealers would shift from selling new cars to providing expert repair, service, and even upgrading. Certainly Japanese manufacturers would be a threat, but they didn't put this part of the prediction into writing.[30]

None of the SRI staffers knew that Henry Ford II had already heard this message from Ford's internal planners. He had come to SRI for a second (and, he hoped, a dissenting) opinion. His battles with his own charismatic "man on a white horse" lieutenant, Ford President Lee Iacocca, were moving into full swing. Iacocca argued that the company should produce more small, well-built cars, to provide better gas mileage during the crisis.[31] As long as he was fighting Iacocca, Henry Ford had to defend large cars (which even Iacocca had to admit provided the company with better margins). Peter Schwartz was allowed to make a brief presentation to "Mr. Ford" and his entourage. Ford listened stolidly, with the same bored, semi-contemptuous expression that he had shown during thousands of presentations in his lifetime. When it was over, Ford turned and spoke to his assistant.

"No," he said. "The Arabs are gonna go away. They'll be gone in a few years. And Americans ain't ever gonna want Jap cars." Then he turned and looked at Schwartz with his piercing blue eyes. "If they wanted 'em, we would do 'em, but Americans don't want 'em."

In meetings like that, you do not argue. You take it, with military bearing if possible. Never mind that, a year or two later, Ford would experience devastating losses, precisely because they couldn't compete with Japanese cars. Never mind that customers were ready—as SRI's research showed—for durability, energy efficiency, and quality. The futures group still didn't know how to get their message across.

* * *

Duane Elgin and Arnold Mitchell kept trying. They took the voluntary simplicity message on the road in 1977. They were joined by another young SRI recruit, a woman graduate from the Harvard Business School named Marie Spengler.

Marie Spengler, a fast-talking, bright, and attractive woman, presented quite a contrast to the burly and hirsute Elgin. Elgin was the most countercultural member of SRI; Spengler, the group's first feminist, believed in synthesizing the countercultural stance with the attitudes of conventional business. She had grown up in Berkeley, been the first in her family to go to college, and taken a job in the 1960s as a systems engineer for IBM. But although she came from a conservative background, Marie began to feel that she couldn't subscribe to the company's values. She couldn't devote her life to making money. Finally, in 1969, after a divorce, she took a negotiated settlement, left the company, and fled to Paris. After a stint in marketing there, she went to Harvard for an MBA, where she became disillusioned with the brand of business "magic" being taught there. Introduced by chance to a Willis Harman paper on "humanistic capitalism," she wangled plane fare to San Francisco (for an interview at McKinsey. Then she drove down to see Harman. He offered her far less than McKinsey had, but Spengler said, "I don't care about the money. I want to do this work. Not only that, but you *need* me. You're talking about transforming business culture, but you don't know how to talk to business."

She arrived just in time for Duane Elgin's report on voluntary simplicity to be produced. The report struck a nerve; it was the most popular report that SRI had ever produced. There were 500 or more requests for extra copies—a number so unprecedented that the marketing department at SRI decided to follow it up with a speaking tour. Suddenly, Marie Spengler, Duane Elgin, and Arnold Mitchell found themselves on a six-city tour. Their audience, primarily composed of businessmen and other SRI clients, would pay $500 or more per person per day to sit in an energy-wasting hotel, eating overpriced, cosmetically elegant food, and hear about the value of simple living. Elgin and Spengler would both remember those days clearly in future years, because they fell zealously into a love affair. Since it couldn't be revealed back at the office, only Arnold knew, and the three of them developed the close friendship that occurs among fellow conspirators.

Each had a role to play. Arnold was the "brawn" (although "brahmin" might have been a better term). The father figure of the group, he presented a dignified overview and carried the imprimatur of Stanford Research Institute. Marie was the "beauty": she came on like a sharp, well-dressed Harvard MBA, as if delivering a McKinsey marketing presentation. And then came Duane, the "beard" (years later, he remembered himself as the "beast"). He was the radical from Idaho, coming onto the stage in cowboy boots, without a necktie, in a sports jacket that he'd found in a thrift shop. He was the living example of voluntary simplicity, and while Arnold gave it respectability, and Marie made it seem profitable, he had come to advocate it for the sake of the listeners' souls.

They would speak for half a day, talking about the evolution of vernacular values and the demographic changes they implied. There were 5 million people practicing some form of industrial renunciation, but *75 million* with "simple" sympathies. That represented about half the U.S. population, and by 1987, ten years hence, they imagined it could be two-thirds of the country. To give these businesspeople a feel for the attitude, the program segued into a 35 mm slide show, accompanied by a recording of the Quaker spiritual "'Tis a Gift to Be Simple." Aerial views of tract homes dissolved into slides of farm communities; consumer goods, from high-tech kitchen equipment to cheap toys, were shown as addictive nemeses. These corny images came through, somehow, as a heartfelt repudiation of the growth that people in the room had devoted their lives to fostering. At the show's end, they sat silently, as if bewildered.

Then, after a coffee break, Marie and Arnold came back with the marketing implications. First-class durable products would sell. Shoddy, cheap stuff would not. Sturdy, natural-fiber clothing would overwhelm synthetics. Do-it-yourself stores would proliferate. Appliances and automobiles would have to become easy to repair; planned obsolescence would no longer sell. And leisure activities would be geared to country living. Tied up with this would be more of a market for services; far more money spent on travel and other experiences, instead of possessions; and an increasing willingness to pay for health prevention, instead of expensive cures. Consumption with a voluntary simplicity orientation hovered around $35 billion per year, they said, but by 1985 it could reach $140 billion, and $300 billion in the year 2000.[32]

After the first tour, Duane Elgin began to grow increasingly cynical about the value of their efforts. He passionately believed that the counterculture future would have to ripple out into the fabric of society. Someday, everyone would be like him—or they would perish. He had hoped that this series on voluntary simplicity would help businesspeople realize the same thing. Instead, somehow, the sublime millennial utopia of *Changing Images of Man* had devolved into a seminar to help companies market products to "simple-living people." He decided to change his own career. Henceforth, he would write directly for ordinary people, to help them unshackle themselves from the tyranny of the consumer culture. He would start, he decided, by writing a book based on his report. But his bosses at SRI refused to let the report out; it was, after all, a major cash cow for them. So Elgin resigned. He had had enough of preaching voluntary simplicity; he wanted to practice it.[33]

Marie and Arnold retained their close friendship with Duane, but they stayed at Stanford Research Institute. During the next six years, the voluntary simplicity project evolved into a "Values and Lifestyles Campaign": an attempt to divide the American consumer market into nine different categories, based upon the way they chose to live. Like voluntary simplicity, it would apply a commercial lens to personal aspiration, and it would ultimately be a key factor in reshaping marketers' attitudes during the mid-1980s. Meanwhile, Duane Elgin's hopes would not come to pass. Voluntary simplicity would never overwhelm the culture. The SRI researchers had misinterpreted survival strategies—people cutting back their purchases in the era of inflation—as lifestyle choices.

*   *   *

The most significant resistance to the millenarian meme came from the Hudson Institute's Herman Kahn. Kahn and his colleagues (most notably Tony Weiner and Barry Bruce-Briggs, two writers who had worked with him since the mid-1960s) had been brooding about the millenarian meme for years—ever since *Limits to Growth* had appeared. They resented the prominence and popularity that the Club of Rome-sponsored report had gained. It was more famous than any other future study, almost a household word—and, as Kahn and his cohorts saw it, a dangerous and offensive one.[34] In their view, Jay Forrester, the Meadowses, and the other authors had deliberately tried to lead society astray—if not maliciously, then at least recklessly. By basing a "crash and burn" future on a computer model of economic growth, the MIT modelers were encouraging people to shortchange their own collective aspirations.

Most importantly, Kahn said, the MIT modelers hadn't taken into account the natural way that postindustrial society would have to evolve. All of the problems that *Limits to Growth* foresaw—and *Changing Images of Man* spelled out—merely represented growing pains in a transition to a new millenarian age.[35] Like the "millenarian meme" future described by Willis Harman and his SRI colleagues, Kahn's millenarian ended in a utopia. But it would not require massive cultural change or a shift in attitude to get there. It would be an automatic result of technological innovation and the innate costs of life in industrial society. In short, having once explicitly described the "unthinkable" prospects of nuclear war, Kahn now offered a new "unthinkable" heresy—the prospect of an optimistic future.

Studying the long-range patterns of demographics, Kahn had discerned that by 1976, the growth of both population and gross world product would hit a point of inflection, after which it would start to decrease.

There might still be a long period of malaise, particularly if the antigrowth millenarians prevailed. But a new "belle epoque" would follow. The original *Belle Epoque* had lasted fifteen years: idyllic years of peace, rapid economic growth, free trade, and hedonism in Europe just before World War I. The second "belle epoque," ac-

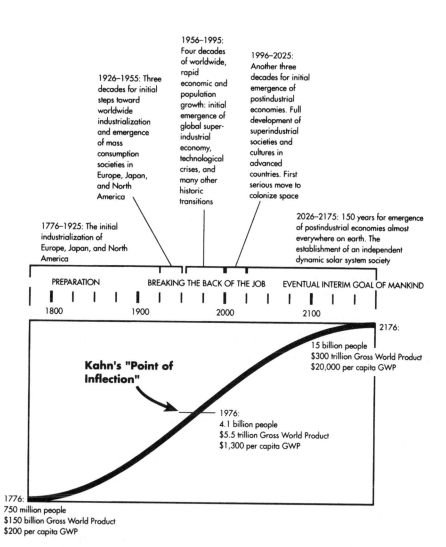

1956–1995: Four decades of worldwide, rapid economic and population growth: initial emergence of global super-industrial economy, technological crises, and many other historic transitions

1996–2025: Another three decades for initial emergence of postindustrial economies. Full development of superindustrial societies and cultures in advanced countries. First serious move to colonize space

1926–1955: Three decades for initial steps toward worldwide industrialization and emergence of mass consumption societies in Europe, Japan, and North America

1776–1925: The initial industrialization of Europe, Japan, and North America

2026–2175: 150 years for emergence of postindustrial economies almost everywhere on earth. The establishment of an independent dynamic solar system society

PREPARATION   BREAKING THE BACK OF THE JOB   EVENTUAL INTERIM GOAL OF MANKIND

1800   1900   2000   2100

Kahn's "Point of Inflection"

2176:
15 billion people
$300 trillion Gross World Product
$20,000 per capita GWP

1976:
4.1 billion people
$5.5 trillion Gross World Product
$1,300 per capita GWP

1776:
750 million people
$150 billion Gross World Product
$200 per capita GWP

**Gross World Product, Plotted Logarithmically, 1776–2176
(from Herman Kahn, *The Next Two Hundred Years*)**

cording to Kahn, had begun after World War II. Like the first, it was created by technological development. But unlike the first, this new "belle epoque" would not end in war.[36] Instead, it would evolve into a prosperous postindustrial society. "Two hundred years ago," he said, "mankind was everywhere poor, everywhere scarce, everywhere powerless before the forces of nature. Two hundred years from now, barring bad luck and bad management, mankind should be almost everywhere numerous, almost everywhere wealthy, almost everywhere in control of the forces of nature."[37]

The world, in Kahn's view, would be not like a global village, but like a global metropolis; the sort of place where people carved out intricate webs of relationships with others around the planet, living increasingly cosmopolitan and pluralistic lives, with the balance of power split not between the United States and the Soviet Union, but among five or six nations. The rise of multinational corporations would be a driving force in all this, "playing the central role," as Kahn put it, "in the development of an interdependent world economy." Despite their increasing power, Kahn poohpoohed the fears that multinational corporations would dominate the world; they would still have no sovereign authority or armed forces. "No one will kill or die for General Motors," he wrote.[38] But corporations would be intensive laboratories for productivity, because (thanks to global competition) the bureaucratic mind-set of current management would burn itself away.

Yes, Kahn agreed, the pollution issue was a harbinger of a potentially serious technological crisis; the way it was handled would have a tremendous effect upon society's evolution.[39] Yes, environmentalists *were* correct to mistrust the leaders of corporations and government; these institutions had been untrustworthy. And yes, the human race had indeed made a Faustian bargain with technology. But according to the Faust story, he reminded people, Goethe's hero "bought magical knowledge and powers that he was compelled to use, and then perforce he had to proceed to the next experience, the next project—or be forever damned."[40] Having started down the road of industrialization, humanity had doomed itself to finishing the course. Only technological progress could solve the problems that technological progress had created. To shrink back, for fear of "limits to growth," would make *Limits* a self-fulfilling prophecy.

Kahn's ideas would ultimately be used as grist for conservative ideology, but he himself was neither conservative nor liberal; like Whitman, he contained multitudes. On the liberal side, he agreed that *Limits to Growth* itself was a valuable cultural argument that needed to be made, for growth would have to slow down—but not so quickly, please. He wanted the rest of the world to catch up with America first.[41] On the conservative side, he used Irving Kristol's label of the "New Class" to brand liberal intellectuals and environmentalists, along with highly educated members of the media, law, management, and government professions, as effete, out of touch, dangerously self-serving people.[42]

The counterculturalists of the New Class were obsessed with environmental issues and other out-of-touch concerns, Kahn argued, because they were trying to protect their own privileged position in society, under the guise of helping society as a whole move forward.[43] He specifically attacked their Pelagian strain, which they had inherited from the likes of the National Training Laboratories. "Have you ever noticed a baby?" he would say to groups. "They're not known for tolerance, moderation. Babies will destroy the universe if they're empowered."[44] If the New Class was the class of heretics and reformers, then the Augustinians of the Silent Majority represented (in Kahn's words) a counterreformation. They included the growing number of people who belonged to fundamentalist and orthodox religions, but their bedrock concern was the defense of American square culture: Preserving marriage. Avoiding displays of public immorality. Keeping streets safe.

Kahn believed that the counterreformationists, the silent majority, were morally superior. But history was on the side of the New Class. For in a world leading to postindustrial society, everyone would be affluent and everyone would have a chance to be educated. Thus, the Silent Majority members would be the most impassioned American political force of the near future, because they felt themselves the most misunderstood. The New Class didn't see them clearly. No matter how obnoxious the dialogue Norman Lear wrote for his bigoted television bully, Archie Bunker, the character always tested as lovable. The Silent Majority recognized him as one of their own.

The two millenarian memes—Willis Harman's clash of paradigms and Herman Kahn's evolutionary utopia—now jumped the Atlantic. They became the basis for two new sets of scenarios among the planners of Royal Dutch/Shell. Dr. Gerrit Wagner, now the chairman of the Committee of Managing Directors, paved the way for this. In the inflationary years of the early 1970s, while managers everywhere shrank from the question of corporate social responsibility, he found himself attracted to the subject. Wagner was still avuncular, and still a bit rumpled, but he now had an international reputation. His intrepid diplomacy during the oil crisis had made him a well-known business figure in Europe.

Wagner had also been involved for five years in a series of international meetings and hearings, held by various United Nations commissions, aimed at defining a code of multinational corporate conduct. In these meetings, Wagner heard charge after charge about how multinational corporations had taken on the imperialistic role of colonial powers. They built factories where labor was cheap and regulations were few; they extracted natural resources without putting enough capital into the countries to spur growth; they used cartel tactics to boost prices of precious commodities like quinine;[45] and they propped up corrupt regimes with bribes.[46]

With the stubborn inquisitiveness of a Shell man, Wagner began to consider whether the critics were correct. The more he thought about it, the more convinced he became that companies like Shell had a social responsibility that went deeper than speeches and publicity efforts. Shell couldn't simply acquiesce to the demands of (for example) environmentalist groups who protested oil spills and offshore drilling. That would mean abdicating control of the company's destiny—he and the other managing directors would be thrown out by shareholders if they did. But there was a strategic imperative hidden, as if in code, within the environmentalists' messages. Shell's canny managers would have to learn to decode those messages. Moreover, if Herman Kahn was right—if multinational corporations would be the primary drivers of affluence and social values during the next two hundred years—then businesspeople would have to take seriously their role in developing the future. Otherwise, they wouldn't prosper; they'd be overtaken by companies that managed the social role effectively.

But how could you translate that sentiment into day-to-day policies? Wagner was a slow-speaking, thoughtful man, and he mistrusted Kahn's glib ebullience. Kahn presented only one future—the future *Kahn* liked—and hedged his specifics so much that it presented a very fuzzy image of the world. If Shell's planners had learned anything from their scenario triumph, Wagner mused, it was the need to paint any future image in specific detail. Thus, he set out to write a detailed Shell code of ethical conduct—one of the first of the ethical codes that many companies would adopt during the 1970s and 1980s.

Shell would feel "an interdependent responsibility," wrote Wagner (and his co-author, a Shell staff writer). The company would be responsible for keeping shareholder returns acceptable, the quality of products high, working conditions safe, wages fair, and environmental standards maintained. On the controversial issues of the 1970s, such as political payments to government officials, the code hedged a bit. Offering, paying, or taking bribes was "unacceptable," and there were always strong arguments against political payments, but Shell had to recognize that some cultures (such as Arab cultures) had enshrined them as regular practice.[47]

Now, when a Shell man felt pressure to step beyond the boundaries of his own ethics, he could refer back to the code. "I'd like to go along with this, but I can't, because I'm going to have to sign a statement at the end of the year that I have not cheated on my books."

At the same time, Wagner asked the Group Planning scenario people to study the future of social values. In any other year, the planners might have shrunk from such an audacious assignment. But this was 1974, and they were in the first flush of their success.

Throughout the operating companies around the world, Shell managers knew that *their* Group, alone among the major oil companies, had effectively anticipated the crisis.

Shell Française owned an old cloister on a mountaintop, one hundred miles north of Marseilles, in a town called Lurs. The windows looked out from a thousand-foot-high cliff onto a desolate, parched region called the Durance. The light was clear, like the light in Greece; the hillsides were barren below the tree line; and there was only one restaurant nearby. The next village was an hour's drive away, on winding, mountainous roads. Shell Française supposedly used the cloister for executive seminars, but the seminars must have been unusually austere. The rooms were the size of railway compartments, and there were no phones and few hot showers.

Retreats were common at Shell Française, but the Anglo-Dutch cultures of London and The Hague disapproved of them. So when eight planners rode down to Lurs in a minibus in May 1974, they traveled with the vague sense that they were doing something illicit. They knew that when Herman Kahn wanted to develop insights about, say, the future of economic growth, he would closet his Hudson Institute colleagues away for a week or more to hash out their ideas in detail. The Shell planners needed a similar period of collaborative "intense suffering," as Ted Newland called it.[48] This retreat would be particularly valuable because people tended not to congregate in groups at Shell Centre. With their 1973 scenarios, they had produced a seminal work together, but they still didn't really understand how each other thought and felt.

After their trip to Lurs, they did. For a week, from nine in the morning until eleven at night, the planners met at the big round table in the Lurs priory dining hall. Each of them had come with a subject to introduce: the world economy, the Arab nations, the Cold War, or the unpopularity of multinationals. Hans Dumoulin, a young Dutch engineer with a schoolmasterish temperament, had been trying to introduce the idea of environmental responsibility at Shell for several years. Nuclear power, he argued, would become socially unacceptable. Concern over acid rain would provoke laws forcing industries to reduce the sulfur emitted from their smoke-stacks. Gareth Price, a convivial man of Welsh descent, challenged the then-sacrosanct view that oil demand would keep growing. If the price of oil stayed high, that would force a slow shift to conservation measures and alternative fuels. Gradually, demand for oil could level off or even drop.

But would the price of oil stay high? Already, the conventional experts of the industry were saying that the price would soon collapse. OPEC, after all, was just a cartel, and cartels cannot sustain themselves. Herman Kahn predicted a fall in the price of oil as part of his "belle epoque" economic expansion scenario.[49] Managers in other industries, such as auto and electric companies, had come to believe that the energy crisis wasn't real. It was just the invention of wicked oilmen. Things would soon be back to normal.

But Pierre Wack and Ted Newland believed that the oil price would *not* drop, not right away. The price was like a soccer ball held in the air by jets of pressure. At that moment, all the significant pressure was coming from one direction: from OPEC, pushing the ball higher. No single oil-producing country had good reason to defy OPEC. (All it would take was one, and then OPEC's "power" would deflate.) As the planners shouted and wrestled in their monastic isolation, breaking out into at least one fistfight, they came to the conclusion that they could not present any credible scenario in which the price of oil fell soon.

Instead, they developed two geopolitical scenarios for a world of continuing rapids. They named their first scenario "Belle Epoque" after Herman Kahn's utopian future. Kahn had suggested that the "belle epoque" would come about naturally, but the Shell planners were not that optimistic. Their millennial future was a hybrid of those from Kahn and Willis Harman (whom they also knew; Pierre Wack had begun to make regular visits out to SRI's headquarters). To bring about a "belle epoque," everyone—governments and business—would have to take a "high road," acting beyond their selfish interests. There would be "effective political leadership," as Dumoulin later wrote, "in which governments understand and foster the process of wealth creation; the profit motive is recognized as natural and desirable, provided it is exercised responsibly."[50]

The Shell planners were short on details about how the high road might evolve, or precisely what policy changes would be required, but they knew that high economic growth was a key component. If it was high enough to create a middle class in developing countries, then it would drive other reforms, including environmental reforms. If not, then the result would be a "World of Internal Contradictions"—a phrase they also borrowed from Kahn, who had borrowed it from Karl Marx. Politicians and business leaders would continue to hunker inward, pursuing their own gains. In this world, wrote Dumoulin, "the work ethic is not that of 'makers and doers' but more that of 'takers and escapists'; the interest is in dividing the national cake rather than adding to it; increasing unemployment is absorbed in sinecure jobs; egalitarianism figures prominently; . . . as a result, one finds that investment is sluggish, industrial performance very disappointing and the world's economic motor is really not functioning on all of its cylinders."[51] The world would set off on a "low road" of self-interest, not much different from the crisis that SRI's planners had warned about.

All the planners felt an overwhelming sense of exhilaration at having wrestled these issues into something comprehensible. On the way back they began to talk excitedly about going into business on their own, freelancing scenarios to businesses. When the idea emerged, Napier Collyns, who was driving the minibus around a mountainous curve, could not resist turning around to his colleagues to exclaim his delight. "At that moment," Gareth Price later remarked, "we might have lost the whole study." Later, when they stopped for a drink, the place they found happened to be named the Café Belle Epoque.

Back home, the work at Lurs raised more questions than it answered. Most people at Shell, including most of the planners, believed that events had already taken them into the "World of Internal Contradictions"—and for a few years, that scenario served as a common bit of vocabulary for explaining the turbulent economics of the 1970s. The idea of a stable, long-lasting "belle epoque" was so ludicrous on second thought that the planners quickly changed the name.[52] Unfortunately, they had already prepared slides showing a "BE" scenario; they settled on "Business Expands."

In themselves, the scenarios were not very impressive. Many Shell managers (including Pierre Wack) saw them as a degeneration—a move to the murky arena of social change, away from strictly defined views of the oil industry. But for Ted Newland, the "Belle Epoque" and "World of Internal Contradictions" scenarios represented the beginning of a lifelong preoccupation. He saw that he could make a contribution to the world by defining a "high road" path that would genuinely lead to a prosperous world, as opposed to a "low road" of political strife. Once again, he was following Herman Kahn's example, but this time, he could be more influential. He, and several other Shell planners, intuitively felt that there was some kind of policy choice, which both governments and corporations could set in place, which might lead them to the high road.

Fortuitously, the planners were about to meet a man who would help define that policy choice—and reintroduce, in the process, the millenarian meme.[53] Amory Lovins was a staff member of the international environmental organization Friends of the Earth. He was twenty-seven years old, a third-generation American, the grandson of Ukrainian-born parents, and a lifelong prodigy. As a baby, he had been completely silent; then, at the age of twenty months, he had begun speaking in complete, grammatically correct sentences. "I didn't need to talk," he had explained to his parents. "Everybody did everything for me." He had pushed himself out of a sickly youth by joining (and then leading) mountaineering treks. He received his first patent, on nuclear magnetic resonance technology, at age 17, and in 1968, at age twenty-one, he became one of the first scientists to publish a paper about global warming.

Around the same time, Lovins dropped out of a physics program at Harvard after fighting with his professors (he wanted a more interdisciplinary curriculum). Applying to Oxford at age twenty-one for a student position, he had been appointed to the research faculty instead.[54] While there, in his spare time, he began his investigations into energy policy for Friends of the Earth. It was a natural convergence of the young researcher's interest in resources, climatology, and the vagaries of human culture and economics.[55]

The planners at Shell—indeed, everyone he met—found Lovins to be a captivating man. Slight and lean, he had the jerky, unworldly motions of a social misfit, along with black horn-rims and a thick shock of dark hair. His voice was oddly deep, and he spoke quickly. Like Herman Kahn (whose iconoclastic, polyintellectual background resembled his own), he was one of the few people who could reel off complex scientific theory and literary quotations with equal facility. He couldn't make small talk; his favorite epithet for himself was "techno-twit." But he was empathic. He knew how to listen closely to people, and resonate emotionally with them, while his posture remained stiff and his face never lost its bemused, distant smile. All of this gave him an endearing, Chaplinesque air, which he used to full advantage. For Lovins was also a missionary, a devotee to a cause. After a couple of years of energy studies, he now believed that the world was embarking on an economic and ecological disaster.

The disaster had to do with scale. At that time, the conventional wisdom of the electric power and oil industries followed the logic of the old "horse's tail" diagram that Shell planners had discarded. Demand for power would continue to burgeon, as it had since the 1950s, with the increasing use of air conditioners and other appliances. The industry's answer was massive construction: coal and nuclear plants. Dams. Heavy-duty transmission grids. And offshore drilling platforms, like the city-sized installation that Shell was building in the North Sea off the coast of Brent in Scotland.

Lovins insisted that this "hard path," as he called it, would self-destruct—not because of its ecological impact or the threat of terrorism and nuclear theft (although, he said, those problems were grave), but because of the immense amount of capital investment that a "hard path" investment, such as a drilling platform or nuclear power plant, required. Energy prices would keep rising to pay the capital costs. Demand would falter as prices rose, with the result that the income would not exist to pay back the investments. A scenario built around rising energy demand was actually a recipe for bankruptcy.

There were other reasons, too, why the hard path would fail. It was horribly inefficient. A white-hot nuclear reactor emitted immense amounts of wasted heat to produce a current of electricity that, in the end, heated a home to only 70 degrees. This was, to Lovins, inexcusably crude: "Like cutting butter with a chainsaw."[56] And then, every step along the way, more energy was squandered as it was converted from one power system to another. The world already had more energy than it needed, Lovins said. It simply had to stop squandering fuel in cars "that inefficiently convert oil into smog" and houses "that space-heat the outdoors." He compared the untapped potential of motor-vehicle fuel efficiency to a five-million-barrel-a-day oil field lying underneath Detroit.

As an alternative, he proposed an industrialized "soft path"—a redesign of the infrastructure of energy use with efficiency as an inherent quality, instead of tacked on as an afterthought. Factories might "co-generate" their own electricity as a by-product of the steam they already produced. Buildings everywhere would have solar panels and intensive insulation. Cars would be designed to get 100 miles to a gallon, and cities built and designed so routine trips required no car at all. The power grid itself might be decentralized—so that electricity might be produced in a small-scale neighborhood power plant or wind farm rather than in a massive nuclear plant 600 miles away. Instead of producing economic pressures and energy crises, this "soft path" would lead to decentralized businesses, increased renewable energy use, and independence from Arab or other foreign oil sources.

Though he knew nothing of Shell's scenario thinking, Lovins had hit upon his own version of Ted Newland's "low road" and "high road." If the country was serious about solar energy and efficient energy use, it would have to turn away from the low road: the "official future" of expanding nuclear, oil, and coal use. Investing in large-scale capital projects would consume the money, skills, attention, and time needed for the "high road": decentralized, distributed, small-scale systems.

At first, Ted Newland didn't recognize the parallels between his ideas and Lovins' thesis. Immersed in Herman Kahn's theory and his Royal Dutch/Shell experience, he (like most of the planners) viewed Lovins' ideas as extremist. Wack and Newland were both strong supporters of nuclear power, which they saw as a necessary component of international development. They regarded the antinuclear movement as an American indulgence, stemming from a nation that could afford to cut back one of its major sources of energy. Most other nations could not make that sacrifice.

But the planners also recognized the plausibility of energy efficiency as a force acting upon the world. Japan had already begun an intensive energy-efficiency program, based on a fervent desire to escape OPEC's stranglehold. If the rest of the industrial world followed suit, overcoming the inertia of its existing energy-wasting practices, the possibilities for decreasing energy demand were enormous. On the other hand, if energy demand continued to build steadily (as it had since World War II), then no supply could keep up. There simply wasn't enough money extant to buy the extra energy supplies—not when that money would also be required for the new buildings, vehicles, and factories that were supposed to *use* all that energy worldwide. Something would have to give.

In 1975, the Shell planners invited Lovins to visit their offices and spell out all of the calculations implicit in the soft path. He was delighted. To his compatriots at British Friends of the Earth, who said organizations like Shell were inherently evil and one shouldn't talk to them, Lovins replied, "On that basis one would hardly wish to talk to one's own government. Or anyone else's." Any major corporation, he believed, was an important reservoir of skills and resources, and progress toward the "soft path" would inevitably move faster through the "well-organized, profit-motivated, goal-oriented" private sector, especially as companies picked up experience.

Lovins was particularly pleased because Shell's planners were sophisticated, far more than most of the government people he had met. They were always looking for pragmatic measures that Shell could implement quickly, and they were bright, curious, and intellectually tough. They taught Lovins their methods for whole-system costing—calculating how the projected cost of a barrel of oil included everything from the wellhead to the gas pump. This was valuable for Lovins because it gave him a way to calculate the *real* costs, including all the hidden costs which power companies ignored, of electricity and heating. Even more useful to Lovins was the prodding he received from the Shell planners: to translate his tables of numbers into graphs that people could understand. He drew on Gareth Price's blackboard the two possible energy futures as he saw them: the conventional "hard path" and the millenarian "soft path."[57]

The "official future" (the "hard path," or dark gray line) showed the rising curve of energy as the conventional wisdom foresaw it. It would include no renewable energy, and shrinking

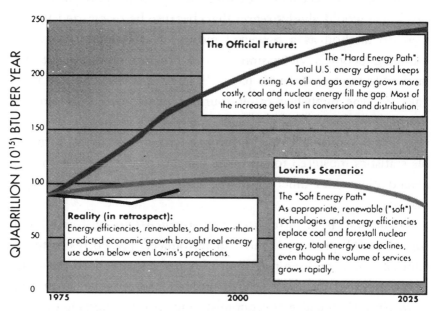

The Future of U.S. Gross Primary Energy Use, 1975–2025
(projected)

supplies of oil and gas, but coal and nuclear would fill the gap as world energy use soared. Under Lovins' "soft path," by contrast (the light gray line), total energy use would peak around the year 2000 and then gradually dwindle away. By 2025, the American power supply could come almost entirely from renewable sources, such as wind, passive solar, photovoltaics, biofuels, and hydropower. In addition, the carbon dioxide and other "greenhouse gases" that still threatened the biosphere in his view, would no longer be produced.

It was an audacious scenario, but it was analytically based and internally consistent. And some of the Shell planners found themselves agreeing with it. Gareth Price, for instance, had studied electrification in developing countries and come to the conclusion that no country outside the Persian Gulf could afford large-scale power plants. They would achieve their goals much more effectively with a grid of small-scale, decentralized power-generation systems.

During his visits to Shell Centre, Amory Lovins never met Pierre Wack. He would always regret that, because he recognized Wack's scenario method as a powerful means of storytelling, a way of changing people's viewpoints. The following year, he put that method to the test when his paper "Energy Strategy: The Road Not Taken?" was published (after fourteen revisions) in the eminent journal *Foreign Affairs*.[58] It was largely a scenario-style presentation of the "hard" and "soft" futures, with all of Lovins' formidable statistics mustered to show the dangers of the "hard path." To defend the values inherent in the "soft path," he quoted Willis Harman.

Lovins had been introduced to *Foreign Affairs* by Carroll Wilson, the MIT professor who had introduced Jay Forrester to the Club of Rome; and the reaction to Lovins' paper echoed the storm of protests that Forrester and his students had provoked with *Limits to Growth*. A cadre of economists and energy experts lined up to attack Lovins. This time, the most virulent were advocates of nuclear power from the electric and nuclear construction industries.

They accepted his recommendations for energy efficiency and solar power, but they would not accept his argument that society had to choose between the "soft path" and the "hard path."

Lovins battled with them in Senate hearings, in letters to the editor, and ultimately in scores of panel discussions and industry debates.[59] He argued that "those who have destroyed nuclear power have been its most avid promoters, who systematically mistook hopes for facts, advocacy for analysis, commercial zeal for national interest, expertise for infallibility, engineering for politics, public relations for truth, and the people for fools."[60] For the moment, he won few converts in industry; oil companies were generally more sympathetic than electric utilities. He was painted as a seductive self-aggrandizer, convincing even some utility industry people by manipulating their utopian fantasies.[61] The real battle, of course, was political. At stake was twenty years of investment, by government, industry, and big customers, in large-scale nuclear power plants. Those whose careers rode on the investment, and who believed in it (as Wack and Newland did), were damned if they would see that investment curtailed by a thirty-year-old punk with a pocket calculator.

Perhaps it would have been easier on Lovins if he'd chosen another phrase besides "soft path"—which to him simply meant benign and flexible. He didn't see its connotations of mushy thinking and the counterculture until faced with the accusations of his opponents. "I have nowhere said that a soft path is *easy*," Lovins said. "I have simply said that the problems are easier than if you don't take it."[62]

The debate on nuclear power continues today, even though no American corporation has been willing to invest in new nuclear energy plants since 1979. At the same time, the "soft path" remains unproven on a large scale. Here, we are not concerned with either proving or disproving Lovins' arguments about nuclear and solar energy, but in examining a less visible part of his philosophy: his sense of the purpose of corporations. For Lovins had a coherent vision of exactly how corporations could contribute to the millenarian future and what their role in that future might be.

His industrial critics (and some of his supporters) painted him as an advocate of voluntary simplicity. To achieve the gains he predicted, they charged, people would have to change their lifestyles. "It's true that much energy would be saved by ordering Detroit to manufacture only Volkswagens," snapped Dr. Ralph Lapp, an energy/nuclear consultant. "But the politics and socioeconomics of this conversion are formidable challenges to any society. Would Mr. Lovins practice what he preaches? Or would he continue to live a high-energy lifestyle with globe-circling jet plane travel?"[63]

But Lapp missed an important distinction. Lovins *was* pushing voluntary simplicity—not for consumers, but for *producers*. The ingrained corporate habits of oil, electricity, and transportation companies would all have to change drastically. The infrastructure of the energy grid would have to be reshaped, until energy efficiency was part and parcel of everyday life. The habit most in need of change was the tendency toward centralized control: the habit of investing in large-scale plants and factories, all owned and vertically integrated by a single megacorporation. Soft energy production would occur on a decentralized grid.[64] Ten years hence, there would be a useful model in the decentralized American telephone network, where hundreds of companies fit their equipment and services into a dynamic, ever-changing technological grid that no one company could control. But that model did not exist yet; American Telephone and Telegraph was still grimly fighting it. Nonetheless, there *was* a model extant, and it happened to exist within Royal Dutch/Shell itself.

Back in the 1960s, Shell's senior managers had prided themselves on their global, decentralized structure, with hundreds of operating countries around the world controlling their hiring and operations. But the traders at headquarters still directed the allocations of oil among companies. The decision to send barrels from Venezuela to

Argentina, for instance, had to pass for approval through an office in Shell Centre in London.

In 1971, André Bénard (who had just become managing director) proposed making the operating companies into truly independent entities. The Group had just been through the worst quarter in its history, the third quarter of that year. "We are excavating our own graves," he argued. The prices they charged operating companies for oil were often undermined by open market prices, over which they had no control, and which looked like they would fluctuate increasingly erratically. Instead of trying to keep up by frantically dictating prices and allocations from the central office, Bénard proposed letting the operating companies buy and sell oil freely from each other and from other oil companies, as if they had no common owners. Let them gain the flexibility that comes when every trading decision is separate, when no authority is in charge. Let the market be the authority. To coordinate the logistics, the managing directors set up a new trading firm, the Shell International Trading Company (SITC), as a kind of shared in-house commodities exchange.

Even as early as 1976, it was obvious that this experiment was wildly successful. In the turbulent years after the energy crisis, Shell's resilience was perhaps the single most critical factor in its success. It was especially apparent during the boycott, when other oil companies were hamstrung by their ties to the United States; but Shell France or Shell Italy could benefit from the agreements that their countries had made with OPEC. In the 1980s, drastic drops in the price of oil would show once and for all that, unprotected by the old international arrangements, the fuel from the earth was simply a commodity. By the late 1980s, oil men would look fondly back on the days when they could sign long-term contracts; when their money came from exploration and production, not from arbitraging and freight. Already in the mid-1970s, Wack and Newland and the other planners at Shell had begun to foresee this bitter denouement, and they would codify their insights in another set of scenarios in the early 1980s. In the meantime, however, the Shell International Trading Company existed as a harbinger of new corporate forms: a self-organizing system, which managed, without top-down controls, to flexibly and profitably respond to the turbulence of the new oil environment.

And self-organizing systems like SITC fit beautifully with the needs of the millenarian meme. Together, these two concepts would provide—as we'll see in the next chapter—an effective starting point for reconsidering corporate purpose.

THE RAPIDS

"THE PURPOSE OF A CORPORATION IS, AND ALWAYS HAS BEEN,
TO RECREATE THE WORLD":
TURBULENCE RIDERS, STRATEGY DESIGNERS, AND PROPHETS OF
MANAGEMENT CHANGE, 1974–82

The chattering crowd outside Notre Dame Cathedral heard a man pronounce from a burning pyre a curse on the Pope, the King of France, and all of their fourteenth-century world. The man at the stake, whose name was Jacques de Molay, was the fierce, elderly Grand Master of the sacred order of the Templars. His knights had been elite champions of the church all through the Crusades and its first line against the forces of Islam. But now the prevailing currents had turned against the Templars. They were accused of sorcery and devil worship; their property was confiscated. Despite his age, de Molay had been tortured and starved until he had confessed to desecrating sacred relics. Then, after recovering his senses, he had recanted his confession. And that, in turn, had led to his immolation. Burning at the stake was deemed appropriate for heretics only after they recanted.[1]

Perhaps the authorities should have found a way to keep de Molay from pronouncing his curse. Within a year, the King and Pope both died. First their houses, then their countries, fell rapidly into disarray. Noble families sank into debt, unable to command (or reward) the loyalty of peasants who had tilled their lands. Famine struck; shortages, unknown in earlier years, became commonplace. A bubonic plague spread through France. In former times, the plague would have sent people back to the stability and comfort of the church. But they could no longer trust the church. This was the age in which indulgences were offered for sale, church endowments were lent out at interest, and money stacked high in the countinghouses of monasteries. Two Popes existed, one in Rome and one in Avignon, scheming against each other, until the rivalries between the kings who supported them erupted into outright war.

Once, faith in the church had been as fundamental as faith in one's own existence. Now, faith in the church was the sign of a naif. The bedrock assumptions of society shimmered and collapsed. Memories seemed unreliable. When had things turned sour? No one quite knew. When had the estates collapsed? Where had the wealth gone? No one could say. They knew only that the channels that had guided behavior for a millennium had shifted. People felt themselves carried forward at accelerated speeds toward unknown calamity, with no way to halt or go back. God, or the Fates, had turned up the frenzy of existence, defying the human race to keep up, always push-

ing the pace one notch further than a reasonable person could tolerate.

In a time like that, who dares say what they want out of life? And yet, who dares keep silent?[2]

▼▼▼

It would have been startling, back in 1964 or 1965, to see how the decade of the 1960s is regarded by management writers today. In our eyes now, the 1960s were a doomed golden age, when managers and labor (in particular) could feel cushioned by years of peace and a booming economy. Even former counterculture people look back on those years as an intensely protected period, a time when they felt secure enough to reinvent their lives. But it didn't seem so cushioned at the time. People writing about the 1960s during that decade seemed, almost without exception, to take an apocalyptic tone, as if the world were about to crash and burn itself out of existence any moment.[3]

The only thing that people seemed *un*prepared for was what actually happened: twenty-five years of steady, anxious turbulence. This was the curse of the Jacques de Molays of the 1960s: the heretics who had been scapegoated and ignored, either by the corporations who had hired them or by the apocalyptic critics of the corporations. As a nation, we were prepared for the collapse of capitalism or its hegemony—but not for the kind of rolling, choppy, uncertain economic growth that struck different components of society in turn with prosperity and calamity, so that no component could ever remain secure. We were prepared for a battle over the direction of government, but not for an intensely pluralistic society, in which government was no longer the primary engine of governance, having ceded that role to corporations and interest groups. We were prepared for race war, but not global interconnectedness, where economies were held in thrall to the imperatives of bond and currency markets. We were prepared for giant corporations to become public enemies, but not for them to adopt an ambiguous role as public enemy *and* social contributor.

Most of all, we were not prepared for the speed of transactions to accelerate once again. In the 1400s, as you may recall from Chapter 1, a business transaction might take eleven years to complete. Families dominated business, simply because business moved too slowly for individuals to master it. In the 1930s, a transaction took a week, or a quarter, or perhaps a couple of years to complete, and individuals created their own large-scale enterprises. They threw away the vernacular ties of family and community. Now, in the 1970s and 1980s, we lived in a world where a transaction took only a few seconds to complete; or if it took more than a few months to fulfill an order, that was a sign that something was wrong. As a culture, we were not prepared for the ways in which this speedup would allow the vernacular spirit, the spirit of the counterculture, back inside the belly of the industrial beast.

The heretics of this book, in one way or another, anticipated that change. Eric Trist and his collaborator Fred Emery had seen it coming as early as 1967, when they began to write about the "salience of a turbulent environment." Levels of interdependence, complexity, and uncertainty were rising so rapidly that traditional institutional forms would not be able to keep up. Thoroughly new types of institutions would have to be created.[4] In the early 1970s, Pierre Wack and the other planners at Royal Dutch/Shell began to speak of the impending era as "The Rapids." In May 1975, based in part on their deliberations at Lurs, they described a medium-term future in which two seemingly contradictory economic trends—inflation and deflation—were *both* predetermined. Prices would rise, but demand would fall. Several scenarios were possible with these forces extant, but all of them carried one basic message. The managers at Shell, they said, would *never* be able to return to a life where they could follow the easy answers of straight-line predictions like the Unified Planning Machinery.[5]

Everywhere, the rules of the game changed after 1973. First to fall was the sense of legitimacy that business leaders enjoyed. They had been criticized from the left, sure, but they had always been respectable in the mainstream—they had, after all, *defined* the mainstream.

Then came the energy crisis of 1973–74. The easiest villains to pillory were oil and energy companies—and, implicitly, the profligate economy that oil companies encouraged.[6] In April, Washington's ascetic consumer advocate, Ralph Nader, began accusing the oil companies of fraud. None of them had increased their refining capacity during the earlier shortages of 1972. Had they deliberately held back their capacity—creating an illusory crisis—to force up the price? Were they trying to squeeze out smaller, independent distributors who sold gasoline without a monopoly's brand name?[7] Or was the oil shortage a blatant effort to undermine environmentalist opposition? Most damningly, nearly all the oil companies announced dramatic profit jumps—in many cases, record-level net earnings—in the last quarter of 1973.[8]

Unfortunately for their own cause, the senior executives of American oil companies were all terrible spokesmen. Early in 1974, Senator Henry Jackson subpoenaed them to testify, in televised hearings, before the special investigations subcommittee of the Senate.[9] The executives spent the sessions staring stoically at Jackson, stiffly enduring his charges of "obscene profits," and offering only hazy answers to his questions. The Nixon Watergate tapes had shown that a blustering, vicious, foulmouthed spirit lurked behind the presidential image. It was easy to perceive the same mean spirit behind the stolid grimaces of the oil executives in the hearing room, particularly when Ralph Nader's earnest face appeared next on the television screen.

The only candid executive at the Senate hearings was Harold Bridges, the president of Shell Oil—Royal Dutch/Shell's isolated American subsidiary. Bridges wryly pointed out that he and the others would be much more cogent and forthcoming if the senators interviewed them separately, instead of in a lineup with their chief competitors. The public might think of them lumped together as a conspiring cartel. ("They're like Siamese twins," Nader said in December. "They don't have to meet furtively. They know exactly what they are doing without meeting.")[10] But the executives themselves were all excruciatingly aware of their long-standing rivalries and differences, as well as the antitrust laws that kept them from communicating freely.[11]

The calumny trickled down, in various ways, to the middle-level oil supply managers who actually had handled the pressure of the oil crisis.[12] They had worked around the clock, performing miracles with computers and shipping schedules, sneaking oil into the countries most hurt by the embargo, deciding (on the spur of the moment) which contracts to defer, and countering government threats and protests. "We were being attacked in the press every day," the head of Gulf oil supply later told Daniel Yergin. "We had to . . . tell old friends that we were cutting them back, and go around the world explaining the supply/demand balance."[13]

The more heroic their efforts, the more unsung they were—even in their own companies. In the macho oil cultures of Houston and Rockefeller Center, you were supposed to keep your travails secret and never blow your own horn. Senior oil company executives might have forestalled some of the public protest if they had explained exactly where, and how, they intended to reinvest their windfall profits. But oilmen didn't feel like opening up publicly. They felt that the public (and particularly the press) had put them under siege. "One little smirk or crack on the *Tonight* show," said an oil company CEO at a series of meetings convened by the Conference Board in 1975,[14] "biases the opinions of millions of Americans." The wife of another oil CEO said, "It makes me sick to watch the evening news night after night and see my husband and the efforts of his industry maligned."[15]

By that time, other industries were facing similar crises of confidence. They were startled to discover, in the post-Watergate and post-Nader era, that their own hidden practices would no longer get a free ride. It came to light that food-packing companies sold cyclamate-laden fruit abroad, after the Food and Drug Administration banned it in the United States.[16] It was discovered that Mc-Donnell Douglas managers suppressed their own engineers' warnings of cargo door defects and (in the public interpretation) thus murdered 346 people in a plane crash in Paris.[17] In early 1975, a fifty-three-year-old man named Eli Black smashed his office window with an attaché case and leaped forty-four floors to his death on a Manhattan street. He was the president of the United Fruit Company. Within a few days came the revelation of a $2.5 million bribe that United Fruit executives had given the government of Honduras. The bribe was particularly damaging because the managers had listed it as a business expense on United Fruit's tax forms—an equivalent, perhaps, to listing the expenses from dealing cocaine as a tax deduction.[18]

"Nobody gives a damn about us," said a CEO at the Conference Board meetings. "Not the government, not the consumers, not our workers."[19] Executives, used to the adulation of people who worked for them, couldn't understand what people saw who looked at corporations from the outside: the trappings of hierarchy and stiff competition for perks, the peculiarly sensual rapport between executives and their secretaries, the fear that pervaded every conversation (even senior executives were terrified of cutting loose with what they really thought), and the results: shoddy products, pollution, and planned obsolescence. Like Richard Nixon, executives wanted the world to understand them, but revealed nothing of themselves. Like Nixon, they wanted to be trusted, but tended to have little faith in anyone else. Like the head of a household whose ignored wife has filed for divorce (a situation that probably described many of their private lives as well), they couldn't understand what had gone wrong.

They blamed university professors who'd never had to meet a payroll.[20] They blamed the so-called public-interest lawyers (like Ralph Nader) who proclaimed idealistic aspirations; after all, they knew firsthand about the idealistic aspirations of their own lawyers. (At one meeting, the CEOs considered a suggestion to recoup their lost honor by writing up a code of ethics for themselves. "You mean," snapped a voice across the room, "one that would work as well as the Bar Association's?"[21]) They blamed the environmental movement and the sinister influence of books like *Limits to Growth*.

Most of all, they blamed the press. They had never lived in a climate where business journalism was so routinely harsh to private interests. They had never seen harsh news stories cause so many stock prices to plummet. Why couldn't reporters write those glowing paeans to capitalism and progress that the CEOs remembered from their own college days? Obviously, because skewering big business sold newspapers. Rawleigh Warner, Jr., the chairman of Mobil Oil, grumbled in a business newsletter article that while Texaco's net earnings had gone up 57 percent between 1970 and 1973, the *Washington Post*'s net income had risen 160 percent.[22]

Of course, if a man like Warner had invested any of his analytical skills in studying the newspaper business, he would have realized that the surges in the *Post*'s profit had more to do with the demise of its rival, the *Washington Herald,* and its expansion into the suburbs than with any of its antibusiness exposés. Nor did most CEOs have any concept of the real forces that drove the media's antibusiness attitudes. They didn't understand the culture of writers and creative people, who had always been the outsiders in their dealings with management. In many interviews with a news reporter, a tough businessman, feeling put on the spot, would follow his instincts. "You know," he would say, "if you print that, it will end up hurting the interests of your own newspaper's corporation." That was a standard tack in the business world—a man-to-man reminder of the realities of the larger picture. But to reporters, who revered the "Chinese Wall" that protected the editorial staff from interference by advertisers, that sort of remark smacked of intimidation. They retaliated by letting more and more cynicism creep into their stories.

By all conventional standards, the cynicism should have eased up after 1975. Price controls had been lifted. Richard Nixon had resigned. His successor, Gerald Ford, had done no visible harm to the economy. Even the OPEC leaders had relented a bit; they had quietly withdrawn the oil embargo, and the price had slipped back down, closer to normal. Yet the rapids had continued. If anything, inflation and recession had gotten worse. Consumer demand had fallen rapidly, in part thanks to the cumulative effect of scare stories and in part thanks to the unofficial tax that OPEC's surcharges placed on just about every purchase. The auto industry, building and construction, and iron and steel—the industries paying the highest wages—suffered the most intense declines.[23] For the first time since World War II, profits and returns failed to live up to the levels that managers had expected all their lives. Since a manager whose reality did not match his projections was a manager who had lost control, a generation of corporate people suddenly found themselves facing the visage of a trickster in their balance sheets.

It was the last place they expected to find one. Managers ran through every trick they knew, every conventional device for controlling purchasing, operations, or marketing, and every approach that made sense, and yet the balance sheet projections refused to play along. The numbers even failed for the most prominent masters of numbers management. Even Harold Geneen—the CEO of International Telephone and Telegraph who had built his conglomerate through an unparalleled command over the numbers—seemed thrown, lost, and a bit confused by the fact that some of ITT's ventures were failing. In a no-growth economy, ITT's strict requirements for return on investment made the managers of its divisions jittery. They didn't have the leeway to build a business slowly; they had to produce fast results at the expense of future revenues. But their manic anxiety didn't work. ITT's profits actually declined in 1974 and 1975. Geneen, like many other corporate leaders, responded to the crisis with a wave of firings and bonus cutbacks.[24] The shock waves rippled past ITT, where they were intense, to the rest of American business. If Harold Geneen couldn't make a large, diversified corporation work, who could?

As the world spun further out of control, the fascination with control in conventional management circles intensified. Ostensibly, the goal of managers was still to return value to shareholders. But to anyone who looked closely, a more dominant "theory-in-use" was guiding managers' behavior. If they could make it through the rapids and come out the other side (they believed), there would be clear sailing again. The sooner they found the right hook, switch, or technique, the sooner they could return to the orderly, predictable world where they knew how to function, where they experienced the joy of effortlessly being winners at their work. From the bottom of their hearts, they did not want to hear that the rapids were here to stay.

When our intuitions fail, we yearn for strategy. Thus, in the mid-1970s, the idea of building a corporate strategic plan, with its echoes of Napoleon, Clausewitz, and Sun Tzu, evolved into an irresistible management fashion. Simultaneously a heretical fad and the epitome of conventional management wisdom, the discipline of strategic planning had its roots in business school. But the most significant progenitor of the idea was a renegade engineer turned consultant named Bruce Henderson, the founder of the Boston Consulting Group. BCG was second after McKinsey—not in size, but in the more important figure of revenues per consultant. BCG's young Harvard and Stanford MBAs were paid almost as much as McKinsey's, and they fit the same mold: clean-cut, sharp, highly analytical, and willing to work impossible hours. Within that mold, however, Henderson encouraged a kind of quirkiness, even rebelliousness—he himself was not an MBA, but a former engineer— that made BCG a little more interesting to work for.[25]

Henderson began his career as a heretic himself; in the mid-1960s, he recognized, when nobody else did, the value of learning to a company's bottom line. He unearthed a discovery called the "learning curve." It dated back to Curtiss Aircraft in the 1920s; a factory manager discovered that when a work team stayed on the line long enough to double their experience, costs dropped by 20 percent. During the last three years of World War II, Curtiss used the learning curve to design a remarkably effective and inexpensive production schedule.[26] But once the war's production demands ended, the learning curve fell out of fashion.

Then Bruce Henderson resuscitated it. In the mid-1960s, he helped Texas Instruments use it to miraculously keep cutting the prices of its semiconductor chips and electronic calculators. As prices fell, more people bought the devices, which pushed production levels up, which meant that TI learned more about production—which dropped costs still further. Even the billing procedures and advertising budgets grew more efficient as people in those departments learned to cope with greater numbers of products. To emphasize that it wasn't just a shop-floor phenomenon, Henderson renamed it the "experience curve." He said it was as real as the law of gravity, and he proved that by plotting the curve in client after client, in industries ranging from beer making to turbines to farming to retail stores to polyvinylchloride chemistry.[27]

He also discovered that the learning curve and market share fed each other. When a company dominated its competitors, it produced more products, which sent it faster along the experience curve. The rich really did get richer in Henderson's world. In theory at least, Coke learned better than Pepsi; GM, more effectively than Ford; Texas Instruments, faster than Hewlett-Packard, which was moving rapidly up behind it with its own calculator line.

While his sharp young protégés wandered around the world teaching the experience curve, Henderson began a range of studies in the early 1970s. These were prodded by Union Carbide, a company that always seemed, against its managers' own will, to be thrust into periods of introspection. Its two great competitors, Du Pont and Dow, had each carved out a niche for themselves. Du Pont, with its highly evolved technological laboratories, had a knack for developing new high-growth businesses. Dow's managers focused instead on their core product—low-cost, basic chemicals that they sold to other companies. "We can't compete with either," a Carbide manager said to Henderson. "Where the hell *can* we compete?"

Henderson's analysis was startling. All three chemical companies (plus Monsanto) had lost money by giving in to the irresistible temptation of undermining their best-performing divisions. They seemed unable to distinguish among the potentials of their various semiautonomous divisions, so they bled away their profits on lost causes.

With his Carbide study fueling his thinking, Henderson developed a simple management framework that made it possible for any manager to think like Harold Geneen. Henderson would have been horrified at the comparison, but it was apt. The tool became

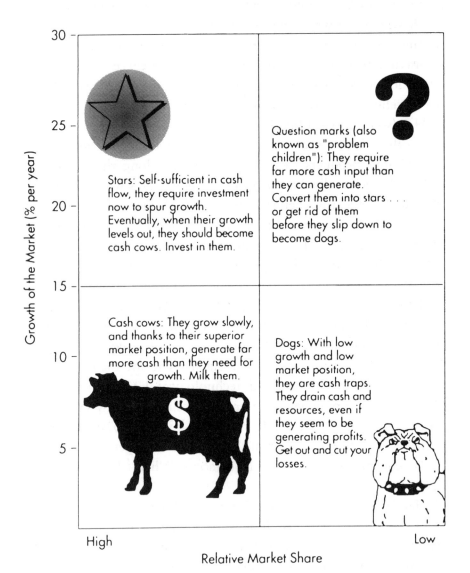

Stars: Self-sufficient in cash flow, they require investment now to spur growth. Eventually, when their growth levels out, they should become cash cows. Invest in them.

Question marks (also known as "problem children"): They require far more cash input than they can generate. Convert them into stars . . . or get rid of them before they slip down to become dogs.

Cash cows: They grow slowly, and thanks to their superior market position, generate far more cash than they need for growth. Milk them.

Dogs: With low growth and low market position, they are cash traps. They drain cash and resources, even if they seem to be generating profits. Get out and cut your losses.

Growth of the Market (% per year)

30 —
25 —
20 —
15 —
10 —
5 —

High   Low

Relative Market Share

The Boston Consulting Group's "Growth-Share Matrix"

popular around 1973—ironically, just as Geneen's ITT was sliding downhill—and it rapidly became a fixture in business decision-making practice. It was called the "growth-share matrix."

To use the matrix, you thought of your business as a portfolio of separate product lines. Every one of them fit into one of these compartments. Its placement depended on how much the market was growing (for instance, the market for American photocopiers was growing fast, while the number of American car buyers was stagnant) and on the amount of market share (for instance, in those years General Foods had the dominant market share for "semi-moist" dog food like Gravy Train). Ultimately, every product line had one of two destinies, symbolized in the bottom two quadrants. Either it would mature into a cash cow, yielding rewards to the bottom line for years or decades, or it would become a dog—hanging on tenaciously, barking for attention, and draining the vitality of the organization.

Thus, the job of a manager was controlled ruthlessness. A good portfolio manager shunted investment among the cash cows, stars, and question marks according to the rules that the matrix implied. It was worth borrowing money to keep a star shining, because a star might end up dominating its market niche. Was your product a cash cow, earning a rate of return on assets of at least 25 percent? Then milk it—keeping your investments carefully monitored, so you can draw cash out of it for years. Investing in a question mark required care. It might be a great opportunity or it might simply mean throwing money into a business that would never dominate its industry enough to jump onto the learning curve.[28]

As for the dogs, Henderson said, discard them—unsentimentally and fast. As the country moved into the Jimmy Carter presidency (which began as a question mark, became a star and then dwindled out into a dog), the growth-share matrix and the Boston Consulting Group became wildly popular—particularly with younger, more aggressive managers. The growth/share matrix bequeathed an era of highly intense competitiveness. Even if the market was expanding, a focus on market share made everyone act as if they were in a zero-sum game. Every automaker tried to be General Motors;

every consumer products company sought to be Procter and Gamble, on the assumption that only the leaders in a particular market segment would survive. Consumers, after all, routinely flocked to the biggest brand names; upstarts had an uphill battle at the grocery store. The purpose of a business, if you believed in market share, was not providing a service, making a good product, or even generating profits, but dominating a niche and seeking chinks in your competitors' armor. Customers were the battlefield that corporations trampled on as they fought.

Madison Avenue loved the growth-share matrix. In most large companies, this sort of war meant an increase in advertising, and—since market share depended on the largest mass audiences possible—the medium of choice was national broadcast television. In 1976, American television advertising expenditures hit an all-time high: a peak of $25 *trillion* dollars. Nearly all of that money went to the big three, NBC, CBS, and ABC, or their affiliates.[29] It was seen at the time as an indication that the industrial world was pulling out of its slump. Prosperity might be coming back.

But the eerie bicentennial boom of 1976 didn't last long. All it really meant was that the finance way of thinking had overtaken all decision-making functions of American enterprises.[30] In the past, managers bought and sold assets because they needed those assets to produce and sell their wares. Now, the profits would come increasingly from buying and selling assets in themselves: from acquiring stars and selling them as more profitable cash cows, before they were milked out.

The stage was now set for the great managerial event of the late 1970s and early 1980s: the realization, by mainstream American managers, that they did not have the answers. In 1978, Chrysler lost $205 million. This was enough, after a decade of ups and downs, to prompt the car company to apply for its famous bailout.[31] The following year, managers at the Ford Motor Company saw their projected $600 million profit turn into a $500 million loss.[32] Then General Motors experienced a calendar-year loss of $763 million, its first loss in sixty years.[33] General Electric, Kodak, Xerox, General Foods, and many other companies all saw their market share drop precipitously—if not to Japanese competition, then to smaller firms in the West.[34]

Corporate heretics, at this stage, were a glum group. Their strategies for boosting performance had failed or were ignored. Only a few companies, such as Procter & Gamble, continued to move forward. (P&G, by now, was implementing its technician system, still ruthlessly kept secret, in plants throughout Europe and South America.) Before anything more could be done to improve corporations, the message of the heretics would have to be heard in the central bastions of the numbers—in places like the Harvard Business School.

In 1979, two members of the operations management department at Harvard Business School—a section of the school that had been gradually losing status, through the 1960s and 1970s, to the finance-oriented departments—found themselves thrown together in Vevey, Switzerland, for the summer. They were William Abernathy, the HBS resident expert on auto manufacturing, and Bob Hayes, known for applying operations research to the assembly line. Both men were in their late forties; both had backgrounds in industry (Du Pont/General Dynamics and IBM, respectively) before coming to Harvard. Both were considered conventional, easygoing men—neither would have been considered a heretic (although Abernathy was known for his rapid-fire, stream-of-consciousness, wide-ranging conversation).

Hayes had just spent two years researching the differences in management styles between European and American multinationals. He had started with the idea that, since Europeans tended to speak more languages, they should have an easier time with cultural diversity; Americans, on the other hand, should clearly have the technological edge. But they didn't. Hayes visited a tiny machine tool manufacturer in southern Germany, a company of thirty or forty people. Sophisticated Americans barely understood computer-aided manufacturing software, but this firm was using it on a daily basis and getting remarkably resilient at quickly producing custom-made tools. It wasn't just Germany; he began to see signs of sophisticated machine tools coming from Czechoslovakia, Switzerland, Hungary, and Japan. The more he looked, the lower his morale fell.

Finally, while teaching a class to European businessmen, someone asked him why American productivity had declined so drastically during the past ten years. He hauled out the standard answers: organized labor, government regulations, the oil crisis, and the attitudes of the baby boomers. His students looked at him with polite amusement. "We have all those factors here," one of them said, "and *our* productivity is increasing."[35]

Confused and shaken, Hayes began taking regular hikes with Abernathy, who had just arrived in Vevey. Abernathy was going through a similar set of shocks. He had come to compare the European auto industry with the Detroit Big Three. Seeing the same stagnation, they began comparing notes and eventually settled on the only explanation that made sense to them: the core of the business "magic," the reliance on numbers that had made American business so powerful, was now hamstringing them.

Consider, for instance, what happens when a manager becomes dependent on return on investment. Managers who used it as their primary yardstick would always give a higher ranking to the projects that got good ROI figures. Those projects would get the bulk of investment. In theory, that meant the company would prosper— fewer "dogs" and more "stars" would be supported. (Hayes and Abernathy singled out the growth-share matrix as a particularly pernicious influence.) In practice, a dependence on ROI meant that risky initiatives, long-term projects, and anything driven by a manager's personal aspiration or care would be shoved into the background. The companies would no longer risk; they would no longer pursue. For the first time, their goals had shrunk to pursuing return on investment to shareholders, at the expense of all other purposes or objectives, *and the entire American economy was suffering as a result.*

That October, Hayes wrote up their ideas in a lead article for the *Harvard Business Review.* The reaction was intense. It is still the most requested reprint in the history of the *Harvard Business Review,* and it divided the business school. There was vitriolic criticism. Some came from economists who claimed there *was* no productivity decline, no loss of American competitiveness, no American malaise. And there was a great sigh of relief from a surprisingly wide group of managers, who said that yes, somebody finally had articulated what they had felt for the past few years but hadn't been willing to say out loud.

Hayes and Abernathy had tapped into a growing feeling of shame, in fact, among business school academics, who felt they had to take some of the blame for the virulent wave of hostile mergers that was beginning at that time. No doubt the authors could have taken their protests further, but Hayes and Abernathy were more concerned about validity and research than about making a public splash. The next popularizer of similar ideas didn't have that inhibition.

Tom Peters has always been an excitable man. His speeches, as many observers have noted, are like a stump preacher's rants. He works himself up until his voice rises and falls, his arms wave, and his eyebrows waggle with the force of moral invocation. In ordinary conversation, he is much calmer and more mannered, but there is always the fidgety sense of constant churning within him. His weight fluctuates, too, but when he is thin he resembles the actor Harrison Ford. To some extent, Peters cultivates the image of himself as an excitable man; he has been known to introduce himself to other managerial authors by writing, "I just read some of your work, and I *went berserk!*"[36] In a world of staid management consultants and academics, including most of his former colleagues at McKinsey, this has given him an edge.

If they had known what they were getting, it's doubtful that McKinsey, with its clipped, sharp, staid young overachievers, would ever have hired him. In fact, they never had a chance to test him as they would an ordinary associate. He lasted only eighteen months, paying his dues, before being swept up into the project that would make him McKinsey's most famous alumnus.

He had joined McKinsey, as a thirty-two-year-old Stanford Business School graduate, in 1974. McKinsey, for the first time in its history, was irritated by a competitor. Their traditional role, as the slavishly devoted, impeccably sophisticated, clinical psychologists of the consulting world, had been preempted by the Boston Consulting Group. Clients who switched because of Bruce Henderson's growth-share matrix were defecting, essentially, because they thought BCG was *smarter*—an insult that could not be ignored. Thus, in 1977, McKinsey's managing director initiated two new research projects. The first was an effort to come up with principles for strategic management and beat BCG at its own game.

The other project was a minor spin-off: an effort to find out what was going on in the practice of management worldwide. Peters, perhaps because of his Stanford MBA, perhaps because he wasn't urgently needed for any billable assignment, or, more likely, because he was based in San Francisco, was tapped for the project. Though he was an extremely junior consultant from a small, eccentric office, he had virtually a free hand at first. He had an unlimited travel budget and (as he saw it) an unparalleled chance to talk firsthand with people whom he had read about at Stanford, people whom "McKinsey couldn't have found with a Hubble telescope on their own." He went first to Scandinavia, which was one of the hotbeds of the sociotechnical movement. In the United States, the sociotechnical movement had evolved into a series of programs called "Quality of Working Life." There were projects underway at both Ford and General Motors plants, and there were several annual conferences a year where the cognoscenti gathered (including many of the veterans of the Gaines Topeka plant). But the movement as a whole was uninfluential in the States; only in Norway and Sweden were whole industries being revamped around the principles of self-governing work teams. Peters interviewed Einar Thorsrud, Eric Trist's old friend and a former Nazi resistance leader, who was applying the principles of self-government to work teams on Norwegian oil tankers. He visited the shop floor at Volvo, where teams of technicians were taking over the work flow. He talked to fifty or sixty people in Scandinavia and Britain. And instead of falling into despair, like Hayes and Abernathy, he fell in love (his own phrase) with the ideas.

It was not easy to communicate that infatuation to his bosses back at McKinsey. Peters' initial reports were rebuked as irrelevant. Worse still, he seemed unable to stop making snide remarks about strategic planning, which was regarded, at McKinsey now, as their primary weapon against BCG. Fortunately for Peters, there was a sympathetic soul in the San Francisco office: Robert Waterman, Jr., a McKinsey consultant since 1963, who had spent the last few years successfully turning around a disastrously performing McKinsey office in Australia. Waterman was a natural foil for Peters; he had a gift for speaking plainly, in a subdued and reasonable way that raised controversies without raising hackles. He was a crackerjack networker and an avid reader, who kept pumping Peters for all the source material he'd gathered. And he instigated a week-long session in San Francisco in 1978, so he and Peters, along with business professors Anthony Athos and Richard Pascale, could turn these peculiar ideas into in-house training materials. That Monday, Athos and Pascale came up with what eventually became known around McKinsey as the "Seven-S" framework.[37]

McKinsey people shared the congenital weakness that consultants everywhere had for frameworks: something to sketch on the board and, in a trice, show how everything fit together. The four bottom S's represented the "soft" management concerns of skills, style, staff, and shared values—domains that McKinsey traditionally ignored. At the top were the conventional McKinsey concerns: structure, strategy, and systems. With this model, a consultant could talk about any subject that came to mind, even something related to nurturing people or building teams, and it would still manage to "look McKinsey."

For a hidden network of sympathetic "excellence" people was emerging within the firm. By any outside criteria they were hardly countercultural; they wore the standard black suits with white shirts, and if they held unusual political opinions, they were careful not to espouse them. But they all had worries about the quantitative strategic approach. They had heard McKinsey consultants tell clients, "It's very important *not* to understand too well the products you make, because you can't allow yourself any kind of passionate attachment to them." They had seen declining performance (much as Hayes and Abernathy had) in the companies that took strategy to heart. As they compared notes, and then talked quietly about their hidden fears and hopes, the same question continued to arise again and again. If it *wasn't* the strategy, then what *was* it that made some McKinsey clients continually succeed while others continually failed?

The "excellence" name emerged when the managing director of the San Francisco office—who was emphatically skeptical of this "Seven-S stuff"—nonetheless asked Tom Peters to fill in on a client presentation (to Dart Industries in Los Angeles) when their original material died in a computer crash. "Excellence is something everyone likes," the managing director said. "Why don't you do something on that?" Peters wrote up a small paper based on his research and gave a wildly successful speech. Suddenly, his report began circulating around McKinsey. Hearing of it, Royal Dutch/Shell, Siemen, and PepsiCo all asked for presentations—which bombed. But today each of the three companies has managers who take credit for "starting Tom Peters on the path to *In Search of Excellence*."

Actually, if any single company could take credit, it would be Hewlett-Packard. To prepare for their Shell speech, Peters and Waterman went to interview John Young, the president there. They asked a question that McKinsey had never asked before: "What do you do to promote excellence at your company?" Startlingly enough, Young told them, and introduced them (as he had once introduced Michael Maccoby) to other managers for further interviews. Then Peters and a research associate went to 3M, IBM, P&G, Frito-Lay, and a dozen other firms, collecting stories from vice presidents, plant managers, and team leaders. They learned about the way managers kept memos to one page, set up ad hoc projects, cultivated suggestions from their customers, or pursued hundreds of other innovations.[38]

While Waterman accentuated the positive, Peters took his drive from the negative. Another McKinsey consultant, Alan Kennedy, invited him to meet a group of renegade executives at Xerox. This was before Xerox's celebrated turnaround in the early 1980s, but the ground was already fertile for change. Peters would sit with the engineers and managers over beers in Rochester, talking about how screwed up the company was, and how they had to change their management methods. As he wrote up his results, he targeted every word, in his mind, to those idiots who were running Xerox.

In 1980, still feeling competitive with BCG, McKinsey hired its first-ever public relations officer, who engineered a piece in *Business Week* with Peters' byline. Suddenly Peters was a celebrity, deluged with requests for speeches, flying off the handle chaotically onstage, delighting crowds, making his McKinsey colleagues suspicious and resentful—and getting a book contract with Harper & Row. The advance was for $5,000: a respectable sum, considering that the subject was management.

Originally, Peters and Waterman each intended to do a book. But neither man found it easy to get started, until Peters was involved in a car accident in 1981. Confined to his home, he finally began drafting. At McKinsey, he felt more and more isolated, and acted more and more obstreperous, until several months before the book's final deadline, Waterman asked him to quit McKinsey, if only for his own good. To help make the exit smooth, Waterman negotiated a deal in which Peters would get to keep his royalties. Nobody thought they would amount to much, and the first printing was slated for only 10,000 copies. The book appeared in October 1982, hit the best-seller list in April 1983, and went on to sell five million copies.

In Search of Excellence was, on the surface, a validation of American management ("It all but had the frigging flag on the cover of the damn thing," Peters said), but at its heart it was a powerful indictment. Everything the book lauded and praised was a departure from the corporate norm. It was a paean to the ideas of the heretics. (Chris Argyris, Douglas McGregor, Warren Bennis, Abernathy and Hayes, and Peter Vaill were cited.) More importantly, it took its insights from the people on the job who were struggling to implement them. It quoted Sam Walton saying that his best ideas came not from highly paid staff or consultants, but from his clerks and stock boys.[39] It recognized upstart companies like Apple (which was then only three years old), and quoted Steve Jobs describing how he succeeded by "hiring great people" and creating an environment where they could "make mistakes and grow."[40]

Certainly, Peters was already turning his act into shtick, and during the years to come, managers would see exactly how difficult it was to follow his precepts. Certainly Peters and Waterman were Manichaean—every story in their book represents a purported struggle between corporate good and pure evil, with little in between. Later there would be a backlash, when some of the praised companies, such as Atari, Revlon, and General Foods, were scorned as poor performers or takeover targets.[41] Nonetheless, to reread *In Search of Excellence* now, 15 years after its publication, is to be impressed by its cheerful candor and roar of genuine feeling—especially considering the tepid, overblown business books that would follow through the 1980s.

Right at the beginning, Tom Peters and Bob Waterman invoked the magic "paradigm shift" that Willis Harman had championed ten years earlier. They declared "disturbers of the peace" and "fanatical champions" to be the most vital people in the enterprise, and they attacked the fundamental tacit principle of scientific management: "If you can read the financial statement, you can manage anything." They also attacked the continual drive for growth at all costs.

Unlike Willis Harman, Peters and Waterman were insiders, and, more important, the world was ready to hear them. The Age of Heretics as outside gadflies or covert double agents was over. Henceforth, the heretics would be able to move out into the open.

The Age of Heretics has moved into another phase since then. The tribulations and experience of corporate heretics laid a foundation for the mainstream institutional reinventions of the last fifteen years—in quality, in customer responsiveness, in the ability of managers to communicate effectively, and in the capacity of organizations to learn. Where once a few people within the company had dared to say, "The emperor has no clothes," now the corridors of many large organizations are thronged with people shouting that message, each with a different set of garments to promote. In many companies, no one clamors more loudly for a reshuffling of corporate power than the CEO—the person who has spent his career as the beneficiary of that power. Thus, the influence of the heretics of this book broadened and deepened, in one way or another, through the 1980s and 1990s:

▼ The practices of "team building," "search conferences," and "shared vision" are direct descendants of Kurt Lewin's ideas and the people of National Training Laboratories—the "Pelagians" of Chapter 2.

▼ The practice of self-managing work teams, probably the most successful factory-floor innovation of the 1980s, stems from the work of the "reformists" of Chapter 3—Eric Trist, Charlie Krone, Lyman Ketchum, Ed Dulworth, the industrial democracy researchers of Scandinavia, and many others who have been part of the "sociotechnical systems" movement. Without the sociotech experience, organizations would not have been prepared for either the quality movement or reengineering, the two most prevalent management fads of the late 1980s and early 1990s. Charles Krone and his family of associates probably pushed the ideas furthest, and with the most ambiguous results. A group of them attempted to transform Pacific Bell in 1987, only to be forced out by the Public Utilities Commission after some employees complained. They demonstrated, in a way that will resonate for a long time to come, the care that is needed in trying to extend a small success onto a large organization.

▼ Many of the "protesters" of Saul Alinsky's organization (Chapter 4) are also operating now in the corporate arena; they base the work on not just the principles, but the spirit of grassroots organizing.[42] Another thread extends from shareholder protests against various watchdog groups—some of which, like the Coalition for Environmentally Responsible Economies, have found ways to raise critical public concerns so that managers can act on them responsibly.

▼ The "mystics" of Royal Dutch/Shell (Chapter 5) have had increasingly visible influence. Shell continues to use scenario planning to this day, as do a growing number of other organizations. It is *most* successful when it leads managers to see the blinders that they have unconsciously adopted over years at the same firm. Pierre Wack and Ted Newland were both involved in a large-scale scenario-planning process that helped South Africa prepare, as a nation, for the peaceful overturning of apartheid and the rise of Nelson Mandela to the nation's presidency.

▼ It is more difficult to assess the influence of the "lovers of faith and reason," the Peter Abelard counterparts, of Chapter 6. Today, Willis Harman is the president of the Institute for Noetic Sciences, where he continues to promote research into paranormal science and other hopefully paradigm-shifting activities. He has also been the prime mover behind the World Business Academy, an organization of businesspeople who want to talk seriously about values. Jay Forrester's techniques of "system dynamics" have continued to expand into a worldwide academic and professional discipline. They became a vital component of the learning organization movement ("systems thinking" is the fifth of Peter Senge's "five disciplines"[43]); and there is extensive experimentation going on today using system dynamics in grade-school education.

▼ The three heroes of "Parzival's Dilemma" (Chapter 7) each have had great influence. Warren Bennis' well known writing and speaking on leadership continued through the 1980s. Edie Seashore and the "four horsepersons" of NTL inaugurated a form of diversity consulting whose effects are still being played out on the corporate stage. Chris Argyris' influence is probably the deepest of the three. His theory and practice immerse managers in a culture with a new set of rules, where people feel free to question themselves and each other without fear of reprisal.

▼ Finally, from the counterculture (the "millenarians" of Chapter 8) came an image of corporate purpose as we move into the next century.

* * *

You might believe that the purpose of corporations is power, pure and simple; they are as deliberately totalitarian as the state in George Orwell's *1984*.[44] Or perhaps you believe that the purpose of corporations is return on investment—the accumulation of wealth for shareholders, and the use of that measure as a score of managers' performance. Either view suggests that corporations are dangerous, psychopathic structures, cut off from any sense of purpose that will allow them to survive in the long run. Consider the dangers, in a turbulent environment where transactions are instantaneous, of the view that corporations exist primarily to provide ROI.[45] To be sure, return on investment is important—for the same reason that a score is important in any game. It provides a signal of your effectiveness. But no one plays a game solely for the score, and when ROI becomes a business's purpose, then its managers have delegated authority to the numbers. They send an implicit message to customers: "We depend upon you merely for our revenues. We're willing to make a buck off your back in any way we can." They sour relationships with employees, by letting them know that any rhetoric about "all being in this together" will be empty rhetoric. They drain away the vernacular spirit that nurtures the people of the firm.

Shareholders themselves should also be wary of a company that puts its purpose in their hands. When a company sends the message, through its communications to stock analysts, that it will do anything necessary for short-term capital (typically meaning that it will slash costs and lay people off frantically), that ensures that the capital it raises *will* be short-term—ready to switch to any other company that promises to slash costs more. Sooner or later, a company that is built around this purpose will falter. Its competitive advantage will wither away, since *any* enterprise can dedicate itself to returning investment on capital—merely by reinvesting it.

Finally, the belief that the purpose of a corporation is return on investment is the root cause of excessive legislation. If a company is not credited with ethical capability—if its fundamental purpose makes it basically socially irresponsible—then government will feel obliged to set enough rules to rein the company in. The company's ability to act with impunity, like that of any irresponsible creature, will be increasingly limited.[46]

Any heretic who tries to argue this case—even the CEO—will face a difficult battle. Every force associated with the corporation, even the victims of short-term policies, will line up on the side of return on investment as the ultimate purpose of the firm. The compelling value of simply keeping score, to try to stay in the game and survive at all costs, will overwhelm all other concerns. That is why you cannot make any long-lasting change in a corporation without an alternative image of what its purpose should be.

If not return on investment, then, what purpose *should* a corporation have? What are corporations for?

It might seem ridiculous, at first, to answer that question by saying, "They are here to remake the world." But that has been their purpose all along, ever since the days of monasteries, ecclesiastical universities, and joint-stock companies. A corporation has always been an artificial vehicle, with powers bestowed upon it by the state, which could act independently, through which men and women could wreak large-scale change at little risk to themselves.

Corporations have become powerful because they work. They work because of the power of large-scale business methods. As Peter Drucker has noted, most of the outside protest against corporations exists not because they are failures, but because they are successful. We who are their neighbors, or who consume their products, or who live in their world, want them to act with similar success on behalf of the whole of humankind.

Without the full-hearted participation of corporate interests, no efforts to make the world better can succeed, because corporations are responsible for infrastructure—not just the networks of telecommunications and transportation, but the distribution, commerce, energy, and financial infrastructures that determine the quality of life in general, inside and outside the commercial world.

A typical executive of a multibranch bank in a city is often put in the position of consolidating branches. He or she must decide which neighborhoods will lose a branch and a local source of funds. This is typically done by people who have little knowledge of the local area. They don't know the people, and they don't know how to judge the risks. There is an enormous opportunity, therefore—in both social and bottom-line terms—for a bank that had made a systematic effort to find and cultivate officers from heretofore neglected neighborhoods. A manager who knew the area would know how to spur investment, building a priceless kind of loyalty and a business that would last for decades. Neither government nor social agencies could engineer this type of revitalization without a corporation's involvement.

Paul Hawken proposes a similar step in his idea of "green utilities": private companies set up with a government-guaranteed profit floor to manage wildlife refuges, oil-drilling areas, or other examples of public "commons" where resources are limited. As utilities, they would have the built-in incentive to push conservation and efficiency. Along these lines, Amory Lovins has helped power utilities develop "fee-bate" and "nega-watt" programs. Just as Bruce Henderson told Black & Decker that they didn't sell drills, but holes, Lovins has repeatedly told oil and power companies that they didn't sell energy. They sold comfort and transportation: "warm houses and cold beer," as he had put it back in the 1970s. Under his guidance, in the 1980s, energy companies began to pay for weather stripping and to help customers replace inefficient refrigerators; those were less expensive measures than building new power plants. Adding "nega-watts" to their palette also allowed energy utilities to become much more flexible. They could let commodity prices (like the oil price) fluctuate, and their supply options were flexible enough to pick up the slack. It became much easier to make their margins.

Initiatives like these would require managers to operate with concern for matters outside their conventional boundaries. A few farsighted managers are beginning to realize this. At Procter & Gamble, for example, a packaging recycling manager named Thomas Rattray is one of the leading theorists on how plastics recycling infrastructure should evolve. Plastics recycling is economically unfeasible today because of the expense of sorting and processing the varied types of jugs, jars, and containers. Rattray argues that the basic problem stems from the multitude of organizations involved: industrial chemical firms like Du Pont and Union Carbide, waste management firms like Browning-Ferris and WMX, manufacturers like his company, state and local governments, environmental groups, small-scale recycling and sorting outfits, small independent industrial plastic processors and refabricators, and "mom and pop" garbage collectors throughout the nation.

But suppose these different firms could come together to redesign the overall sorting process, from the curbside collection to the final meltdown (so they don't undo and redo each other's labor). Rattray calculates they could lower the cost of recycled plastic by half a cent a pound. At the same time, they could collaborate on redesigning packaging to make more use of recycled plastic, and they could apply such simple frugalities as shipping plastic in flake form instead of as pellets. All of these measures would require unprecedented cooperation, often between companies that have traditionally seen each other as rivals.[47]

For the first time, such cooperation is plausible. Decision making in future years will be increasingly decentralized, as computer links lead to networks of aligned, self-determining teams, acting to mutual purpose within a larger corporate structure.[48] We are beginning to hear, from experiments in modeling and neural network flow, that decision making in this form is more effective and robust. We can also expect that many of the technological constraints on manufacturing will disappear. Already it is possible to shift an automobile assembly line from making Chevrolets to making Buicks in a matter of minutes. We can imagine a time when factories that make Fords on Monday make Chevrolets on Tuesday . . . and refrigerators on Wednesday. If such a time ever came to pass, economies of scale would be meaningless, and disputes about job flight wouldn't matter. Factories would be located near their customers, designed to fit into human habitats without intruding or polluting; and semiskilled, expensive workers would be more in demand, tapped to continue learning on the assembly line, than their un-skilled counterparts.

Managers of environmental affairs already know what the in-dustrial infrastructure could look like in fifty years. Smokestack pollution could be almost nonexistent. Either it will have been re-duced through techniques of reshaping industrial processes, or its by-products will be reused as input to some other industrial pro-cess, where one factory's waste is another's raw material. Factories could coexist side by side with neighborhoods where people live, without the concerns about pollution that currently shadow every industrial site.[49]

If the industrial infrastructure does not move to such an ap-proach, it cannot sustain itself. But imagine what it would take to move there—in human terms. Executives would have to think about goals that do not immediately accrue profits to shareholders. Companies would have to become leaders: presenting a picture of life in the next millennium to citizens who have no reason to trust corporations but who have been waiting for someone to credibly present that picture. Companies would also have to be open and responsive enough, internally and externally, to live up to the trust that consumers then place in them.

Gradually, companies would give up their previous source of security: the control they had over production. Some companies (as Lovins suggests) would become more like banks, providing money to fund projects. Others would evolve into contracting agencies, assembling teams of people to meet a particular need at will. Others would find their real power comes from being distribution and trading systems, as Royal Dutch/Shell discovered with its in-house commodities exchange. Still others would survive as purveyors, pri-marily, of a brand name. Everything else might be contracted out, *except* the judgment about what quality is good enough to be called "Charmin" or "Phillips" or "Sony." Companies will learn that there is more to gain from brokering—from providing expertise where needed, and quality control, and the reliability of a brand name, but not needing to dominate every aspect of production. There is more to lose from running roughshod over community values—whether in Kansas City, New Delhi, Caracas, or anywhere else—and more to gain from trying to serve a vast variety of people and link them into burgeoning global channels.

Corporations, in short, will discover they can no longer profit by controlling the market. They can only profit by participating. But when you *don't* own the means of production, you're thrown back on other forms of loyalty. You can no longer compel people and other institutions to follow. You must win their trust and cooperation; you must listen to the heretics. Sooner or later, business managers will have to recognize this. They will have to take a responsible political role, and face squarely their role as prime movers.

How will a manager have to behave in this environment? Managers are fortunate: they already know the value of renunciation, devotion, and service. They would have to cultivate their intellectual curiosity and their willingness to consider, as Herman Kahn put it, the "unthinkable." They would have to learn, on their own terms, the value of pushing not for continual growth, but for continual *choice*—the continuous evaluation of the value of what they do together, the value that Buckminster Fuller called "know-why."

Vernacular values suggest that any community must be mutually responsible; people in a community take care of each other. But what does that mean in the case of a corporation? Does it mean that the corporation looks out only for long-term employees? Only for all employees? Or for customers, neighbors, suppliers, and potential members of these groups? What is the extent of these responsibilities? These are not abstract questions; they go to the heart of a corporation's essence. There are no clear answers; like Parzival, we can only discover the answer *after* we act. Heretics, in corporations, instigate this type of all-important, experimental, "learn-by-doing" action.

These days, the greatest asset that heretics have is that there are so many of them. They exist in every organization, balancing the imperative to do good works with the imperative to keep their jobs and keep earning a living. They have been daunted, but not thoroughly disheartened, by the waves of "downsizing" that emerged in the last decade. Their greatest aspiration is to bring their work lives in tune with their personal hopes and dreams. They want to earn a paycheck, and yet accomplish their own goals. And they recognize that they can only do it by changing the systems of the world around them, one piece at a time. Perhaps a corporation exists, in the end, precisely for its heretics. Perhaps its purpose, in the long run, is to help people expand their souls and capabilities—by providing venues within which people can try things on a large scale, to succeed and fail and thereby change the world.

ACKNOWLEDGMENTS

Harriet Rubin, editor at Doubleday/Currency, initiated this book. It emerged from a series of articles she commissioned me to write in 1989. She has been a steadfast, wise, and supportive editor during the six years that I have spent on this project.

Joe Spieler, literary agent, has been a friend and business partner since 1986. His support, suggestions, and insight were crucial to making this book real.

Janis Dutton has been an ongoing conscience, as well as a research administrator. She has repeatedly helped organize, coordinate, and manage the gruesome, mammoth tasks of keeping the book's research going and I've learned a great deal from working with her. Eric Brush, Max Stoltenberg, Chris Haymaker, Benjamin Florer, and Tom Fritsch also provided research help.

At Doubleday, the book benefited dramatically from the time and involvement invested by Lauren Osborne. It also benefited from conversations with former Doubleday editor Janet Coleman. I have also been glad to know, and to work with, Michael Ianazzi, Jennifer Breheny, and Laurel Cook, and I appreciated the impeccable copy editing of Jack Lynch.

Tape transcriptions were a key part of this book's research. Judi

Webb handled the bulk of the transcribing, particularly since 1991, with savoir faire, dignity, and aplomb. Before that, I depended on the work of Ronna Herman and Esther Shear. Laura Tawater provided some transcription and much encouragement and spark. Deborah Bowles took the author photograph.

I wish to single out several people for the time they spent guiding me through the unfamiliar terrain of the material herein.

Napier Collyns saw the potential value of this book in its earliest stages and has been a constant source of perspective, cheer, and insight. Without Napier's help, the sections on Royal Dutch/Shell could never have been researched, and much of the rest of the book would lack verve. His and Pat Collyns' support gave me the confidence to continue even during bleak moments. Napier has probably never been acknowledged in print for his role as a godparent to significant books, including *The Fifth Discipline, The Art of the Long View, Living Without a Goal,* and *The Prize.* This book is a definite addition to the list.

Donald N. Michael, social psychologist and author, has been a key influence and good friend throughout my research. He has continually prompted me toward thoughtfulness, comprehensiveness, and rigor. He has also been a colleague, counselor, collaborator, and mentor to many of the people and events described in this book. He counseled Warren Bennis about the NTL presidency; he oversaw Willis Harman's project for Hendrik Gideonse; he was one of Pierre Wack's remarkable people; he is a member of the Club of Rome, and was a colleague of Eric Trist's. In early drafts, Don's name kept popping up; ultimately I was forced to remove most of the references for simplicity's sake, but that does not diminish his significance.

Dick Beckhard's name was also cut for the sake of narrative simplicity. Any comprehensive history would include him as a key innovator and cofounder of organizational development (beginning in the early 1950s), as well as a close associate of Douglas McGregor, a professor in the MIT organizational behavior program, and an ongoing mentor and guide to many people in the field. (For example, he employed Edie Seashore during the early

1960s.) He provided a living link between the "change agentry" of the 1950s and '60s and the "learning organization" work of the 1980s and '90s. He also took great pains to help me better understand the NTL, P&G, and General Foods histories.

Milt Moskowitz introduced me to the subject of corporate social responsibility, which no one knows better. He edited the newsletter *Business and Society* in the 1960s and early 1970s. In more recent times, he has become known as the instigator of the *Everybody's Business* series of almanacs, on which I depended during my research. He should write a history of his own observations someday.

My *Fifth Discipline Fieldbook* and MIT "learning history" colleagues—Charlotte Roberts, Rick Ross, Peter Senge, Bryan Smith, Michael Goodman, Nina Kruschwitz, and George Roth—all made a point of helping me understand and express the value of corporate heresy. Martin Elton, Will McWhinney, Ken Wessel, Tom Gilmore, Beulah Trist, Mary Wilson, and Michael Brower all went far out of their way to help me understand the sociotechnical/open systems body of work—the work of Eric Trist, Charles Krone, and others. Diana Smith, Grady McGonagill, Bill Joiner, and Robert Putnam welcomed me into a better understanding of Chris Argyris' work and the theory of action in practice. Bill Isaacs, Lawrence Wilkinson, Doug Carmichael, V. Shannon Clyne, and Tom Johnson showed me what a corporation was. Clare Crawford-Mason, coauthor of *Quality or Else,* introduced me to the quality movement and deepened my knowledge of the corporate change terrain. James C. Davidson went over the facts about Royal Dutch/Shell with me repeatedly; without our correspondence, that section would be far more awry. Phil Mirvis, on a parallel trail, made me feel I wasn't alone. David Bradford contributed images to this book, and insights and knowledge about NTL. Ed Dulworth and Lyman Ketchum worked persistently to articulate their story. Marc Sarkady provided a vital sense of the linkage between seemingly unrelated areas of the terrain. Pierre Wack and Ted Newland hosted me and contributed generously of their time and insight. Edie and Charlie Seashore also hosted me, and took a strong and valued interest in the project, as did Edgar Schein. Oliver Markley served as a Dantean guide to the caverns and byways of futures research. Ken Krabbenhoft shared his knowledge of mysticism and his passion for understanding religious practice. J. Baldwin broke into his own book schedule for a critically important talk with me about the counterculture. Larry Frascella, in a conversation in 1989, showed me that there would be an audience for this book.

The information in this book was drawn from interviews and correspondence with a large number of people. In many cases, their interest, encouragement, and extra effort meant a great deal to me personally. They include Billie Alban, Hank Alkema, Jackie DeMoss Allen, Michael Allen, Brad Allenby, Roy Anderson, Chris Argyris, Michael Assum, Douglas Augstrom, Nancy Badore, Edward Baker, Paul Banas, Joan Bavaria, Peter Beck, André Bénard, Warren Bennis, Dave Berlew, Robert Blake, Auriol Blandy, Peter Block, Irving Bluestone, Lee Bolman, Joan Bragan, Ren Breck, Bill Brenneman, Mike Brimm, Juanita Brown and David Isaacs, Barry Bruce-Briggs, Rinaldo Brutoco, Jim Burch, Frank Burns, Ernest Callenbach, Bill Campbell, Pat Carrigan, Stanley Carson, John Catenacci, Tom Chappell, Dan Ciampa, Liane Clorfene-Casten, Nancy Cole, Eliza Collins, Nancy Couch, Bob Craig, Philip Crosby, Kathy Dannemiller, Kathy Davis, Arie de Geus, Leslie Deighton, Chris Desser, Joe Doyle, Hans Dumoulin, Betty Duval, Charles Eberle, Amy Edmundson, Max Elden, Duane Elgin, John Elkington, Don Ephelin, Werner Erhard, Mitchell Fein, John Filer, Jeffrey Fine, Larry Fink, Franklin Florence, Jay Forrester, Michael Foster, Susan Frank, Winston Franklin, Milton Friedman, Shelley Gallup, Robert Gass, Jeffrey Gates, Clark Gellings, Peter Gibb, Hendrik Gideonse, Larry Good, Charles Grantham, Ian Graham-Bryce, Michael Gruber, Lynne Hall, Harold Haller, Betty Harragan, Robert Hargrove, Willis Harman, Sidney Harmon, Roger Harrison, Jim Harney, Jerry Harvey, Cliff Havener, Paul Hawken, Denis Hayes, Sally Helgesen, Hazel Henderson, Ed Henneman, Jim Henry, Harvey Hornstein, Mark Horowitz, Thomas Hout, Sanford Horwitt, Huey Johnson, Bill Joiner, Walter Jolson, Jane Kahn, Mark Kamin, Rosabeth Moss Kanter, Jeff Kaplan, Charlie Kiefer, Jim Knight, Frank Kontely, Don LaFond, Dutch Landen, Jeff Litwin, Paul and Janice Long,

Amory Lovins, Vic Lowe, Michael Maccoby, Alice Tepper Marlin, Bruce MacDonald, Jane Mansbridge, Leon Martel, Mike McCurdy, Norm McEachron, Jack McKittrick, Dana Meadows, Dennis Meadows, Douglas Merchant, D. R. Miller, Frederick Miller, Kelly Blake Morgan, Laura Nash, Thomas Naylor, Larry Nichols, Barry Oshry, Michael Owen-Jones, Ken Oye, Richard Pascale, Bill Paul, Claude and Sandy Pelanne, Myron Peskin, Stanley Peterfreund, Tom Peters, Neil Pickett, Darryl Poole, Elsa Porter, Don Povejsio, Gareth Price, Wendy Pritchard, Robert Putnam, Rafael Ramirez, Dick Raymond, Charles Reed, Jim Richard, Margaret Rioch, Mickie Ritvo, Vickie Robin, Jeremy Robinson, Sylvan Robinson, Alan Rodda, Joe Roeber, Mitch Rofsky, Steven Roselle, Leo Rosten, Joel Schatz, Peter Scholtes, Peter Schwartz, Robert Schwartz, Will Shutz, Eric Siegel, Wayne Silby, Herm Simon, Mary Sinclair, Max Singer, R. G. H. Siu, Diana Smith, J. Andy Smith, Benson Snyder, Basil South, Marie Spengler, Carl Spitzer, Lowell Steel, David Sternlight, Myron Stolaroff, Jim Stone, Harris Sussman, Karel Swart, Lee Swenson, Norman Thomas, Noel Tichy, Bill Torbert, Jack Trainor, Hugh Tranum and Sam Nalbone, Beulah Trist, Alexander Trowbridge, Peggy Umanzio, Peter Vaill, Kees van der Heijden, Bill Veltrop, Doug Wade, Gerrit Wagner, Tom Wagner, Richard Walton, Robert Waterman, Paul Weaver, Anthony Weiner, Edith Weiner, Marvin Weisbord, Margaret Wheatley, Dr. Norman White, Ian Wilson, Brian Yost, Rene D. Zentner, Sam Zimmerman, and others.

I am very grateful for the help, guidance, and friendship (or all of the above) which the following people have rendered to this project: George Agudow, Steve Baer, Linda Baston, Hilary Bradbury, Stewart Brand, John Brockman, Rinker Buck, David Burnor, Red Burns, William Calvin, Brian Clough, Ferris Cook, Sheryl Erickson, Jim and Marylin Evers, David Ferguson, Alan Fertziger, Herb Florer Jr., Graham Galer, Lorrie Gallagher, Tracy Goss, Alan Gussow, Ed Hamell, Tom Hargadon, Sally Helgesen, Anne Herbert, Sue Miller Hurst, Ivan Illich, Jody Isaacs, Peter and Trudy Johnson-Lenz, Adam Kahane, David Kantor, Lisa Kimball and John Cooney, Bryan Kreutzer, Bill Leigh, Steven Levy, Nan Lux,

Pamela McCorduck, Gregory Meyding, Irving Mintzer and Amber Leonard, Marc Mowrey, Jacqueline Mouton, Nancy Murphy, Kathleen O'Neill, Patricia Phelan, Michael Phillips, Patti Poore and Bill Breen of *Garbage,* Vincent Potenza, Ruthann Prange, Tim Redmond, Howard Rheingold, Alan Richardson, Hank Roberts, Joyce Ross, George Roth, Harry Schessel, Dan Simpson, Ellen and Bruce Singleton, John Sumser, Lee Swenson, Robert Tannenbaum, Ann Thomas, Langg Tomura, Martin Turchin, John Wallis, Alan Webber and Bill Taylor of *Fast Company,* Bob Weber and Dave Mason and others of Northeast Consulting Resources, Diane Weston, Fred Weiderhold, and Linda Zarytski. I am sure that there are other people significant to me and this project—whose names I have overlooked in the heat of finishing the manuscript after five years of work.

I benefited from aid from BNA films, the University of Cincinnati Rare Documents Library (Kevin Grace), Block Petrella Weisbord, the Buckminster Fuller Institute, *Processed World Magazine,* the River inquiry conference, the WELL writer's conference (Thaisa Frank, Joe Flower, and many others), the New York University Interactive Telecommunications Program, many people at CoOp America, the Wayne State University Archives of Labor and Urban Affairs (Thomas Featherstone), the NTL Archives at the University of Akron, Antiochiana at the Antioch College Library (Nina Myatt), the MIT Museum, the MIT Center for Organizational Learning, Global Business Network, the Institute for Noetic Sciences, Point Foundation and the *Whole Earth Catalog,* and libraries at Miami University, New York University, the Work Research Unit (ACAS, British Government), the University of Cincinnati, MIT, the University of Dayton, Harvard Business School, George Washington University, and Columbia University.

I want to acknowledge several people whom I interviewed or talked with about this project, who passed away during the period of research, but who were often in my thoughts: Dr. W. Edwards Deming, Tom Mandel, David Miller, Calvin Pava, Dr. Joseph Smith, Carol Townsend, Eric Trist, and William C. Williams.

My parents, Dr. Julius Kleiner and Irene Slovak Kleiner, have been a constant source of help, guidance, and encouragement. I would also like to thank Edward Kleiner for his understanding and support, as well as Regina Weisman, and Max and Helen Kleiner, for their longstanding interest. I wish to express much appreciation and gratitude to Dr. Linda Heusser, Dr. Calvin Heusser, Benjamin Florer, and Herb Florer III.

Finally, I wish to acknowledge gratitude, admiration, and love for my wife, Faith Florer, to whom the book is dedicated. It has been a central part of her life for the past six years. I am proud and happy to be a central part of her life. In a thousand great and small ways, she has shown how much she cares about the quality of the work, and the happiness of its author.

TO THE READER

This book, while it is extensively fact-checked and historically accurate to the best of my ability, makes no attempt to be comprehensive. Many, many people who deserve coverage are omitted from these stories, only for the sake of coherent narrative. Personally, I don't subscribe to the "great person" theory of history, but focusing on a few people makes it much easier to tell the story.

My model is not typical business journalism, but the mythic literature of destiny and integrity. Myth holds its characters to a higher ethical standard than they can possibly fulfill, and yet shows us how to love them when they slip. Or, at least it forces us to recognize that slippage is inevitable. All of the characters in this book are real people, with lives outside these pages. If any of them have been misinterpreted here, that responsibility is mine.

I welcome comments from readers, particularly because I am researching a follow-up book, tentatively titled *The Hour of Reconstruction*. This will cover the history of "what happened next": the evolution of the movement to change corporations, from 1976 to the present day. I can be reached at: Art Kleiner, PO Box 943, Oxford OH 45056; or by email at <art@well.com>.

NOTES

Note: References to sources in the Bibliography contain only the author's name (and, if necessary, the title).

EXECUTIVE SUMMARY

1. A paraphrase of a comment made by Don Michael.

MONASTICS

1. John P. Davis, p. 82.

2. Peter Drucker, *The Concept of the Corporation*, 1946, 1972, New York: John Day, pp. 15–21; Drucker, *Adventures of a Bystander*, pp. 264–65; George Wise, *General Electric's Century*, unpublished manuscript, p. 10.

3. Illich, *CoEvolution Quarterly*, Summer 1980, pp. 30, 41.

4. Braudel, *The Wheels of Commerce*, pp. 120–23.

5. The details on math come from Heilbroner's wonderful first chapter in *The Worldly Philosophers*.

6. Illich elaborates on this point in his book *Gender*, 1982, New York: Pantheon.

7. Heilbroner, pp. 34ff.

8. Elin Smith helped me see this, partly in E-mail and partly in her article "The Vindication of Karl Marx," *Whole Earth Review*, 74 (Spring 1992), p. 86.

9. For example, Commodore Vanderbilt. See Gordon, pp. 222–30, 281–85, 372–75.

10. Galbraith, Chapters 5 and 6, particularly pp. 107–8.

11. Jeffrey Burton Russell, *Witchcraft in the Middle Ages*, 1972, Ithaca, NY: Cornell University Press, pp. 5–6.

12. This story, often told by Pierre Wack, was written up by Schwartz, p. 120.

13. Thomas Johnson, "Accounting and the Rise of Remote-Control Management: Holding Firm by Losing Touch," unpublished paper. Also Johnson and Kaplan, pp. 9–10, 21–25, 32–33.

14. Johnson, "Accounting and the Rise of Remote-Control Management."

15. Drucker, *The Practice of Management,* p. 30.

16. Fligstein, p. 140.

17. Gary R. Brown, "The Business That Could Not Fail," *Audacity,* Summer 1995, p. 46.

18. The pivotal chapter of Sloan's memoir, *My Years with General Motors,* is called "The Development of Financial Controls," and it concerns his successful efforts to use Brown's formulas to get GM's famous automobile divisions (Buick, Chevrolet, Pontiac, Cadillac, and Oldsmobile) under "control." The company had been buffeted by the business turndown of 1921, and Sloan had vowed it would never happen again. It never did, because the financial controls ensured that division heads, no matter how much rivalry they felt toward each other, would not work at cross-purposes. One division would not be profligate with expenses while another was counting pennies.

19. To use just four examples from Jae K. Shim, Joel G. Siegel, and Abraham J. Simon, *The Vest-Pocket MBA,* 1986, Englewood Cliffs, NJ: Prentice-Hall.

20. See, for example, Al Ries and Jack Trout, *Marketing Warfare,* 1986, New York: McGraw-Hill.

21. Moskowitz, Levering, and Katz, *Everybody's Business,* 1980 edition, p. 825. They quote from Anthony Sampson, *The Sovereign State of ITT,* 1973, Stein and Day.

22. Robert J. Schoenberg, *Geneen,* 1985, Warner Books, p. 259.

23. I'm getting a surprising amount of this from the evocative chapter "The Numbers" in Geneen, *Managing.* Quote is from p. 194.

24. This example comes from *Customs in Common,* E. P. Thompson, New York: New Press. Distributed by W. W. Norton, 1991.

25. Alvin Toffler talks at length about this in *The Third Wave,* 1980, New York: Morrow, particularly in the chapter "The Invisible Wedge," p. 37. Toffler takes a lot of his historical understanding from Fernand Braudel, *Capitalism and Material Life.*

26. Robert Crumb, "Why Oh Why Oh Why Am I the Hell in Detroit?" *Motor City*, No. 1 (April 1969), reprinted in *The Complete Crumb Comics*, Vol. 6: *On the Crest of a Wave*, edited by Gary Groth, 1991, Seattle: Fantagraphics Books.

27. Braudel, *The Perspective of the World*, p. 629.

28. Fuller, *A Grunch of Giants*, p. 2. Also *Everything I Know*, Vol. 5, tape 27A, counter 1842.

29. Fuller, *Everything I Know*, Vol. 5, tape 27B, counter 1907ff.

30. E. J. Kahn, "We Look Forward to Seeing You Next Year," *The New Yorker*, June 20, 1970, p. 49.

31. Crystal, p. 187.

32. William H. Whyte, *City*, 1988, New York: Doubleday, pp. 291–93.

33. Maccoby, pp. 249–50. Also Erich Fromm and Michael Maccoby, *Social Character in a Mexican Village: A Sociopsychoanalytic Study*, 1970, Englewood Cliffs, NJ: Prentice-Hall. Ivan Illich's ideas about the value of the vernacular influenced Fromm, Maccoby, and this book.

34. Maccoby, p. x.

35. Whyte, *The Organization Man*.

36. Maccoby's research was based on his work on *Mexican Villages* with Erich Fromm. See Fromm and Maccoby, *Social Character in a Mexican Village*, p. 68. It was based on Erich Fromm, *Man for Himself*, 1947, New York: Rinehart.

37. Maccoby, p. 147.

38. This quotation and the one above are from Doug Carmichael, a psychoanalyst who worked as one of Maccoby's researchers. He was also the researcher who noticed the "hero factor" at the end of the chapter.

39. Maccoby, pp. 200–1, 220–23.

PELAGIANS

1. Rees, especially pp. 1–19, and Christie-Murray, pp. 87–92.

2. I would like to acknowledge people who were significant in NTL, Tavistock, and organization development history but whose stories I do not have room to include as I would like in this chapter and Chapter 7: Billie Alban, Alex Bavelas, Dick Beckhard, David Berlew, Harold Bridger, Werner Burke, Robert Chin, Jim Clark, Kathy Dannemiller, Morton Deutsch, Jack Glidewell, Roger Harrison, Jerry Harvey, Robert Kahn, Rensis Likert, Gordon Lippitt, Alfred Marrow, Elizabeth Menzies, Mickie

Ritvo, Will Shutz, Herb Shepard, Robert Tannenbaum, John Weir, Tommy Wilson, and many, many other people.

3. Kenneth D. Benne, "The Processes of Re-Education: An Assessment of Kurt Lewin's Views," in Bennis et al., *The Planning of Change,* 3rd ed., pp. 315–16.

4. The play was produced in 1948. The movie came out in 1957; based on a book by Richard Bissell *(Seven and a Half Cents),* directed by George Abbott, choreographed by Bob Fosse, and released by Warner Brothers, it starred Doris Day and John Raitt.

5. "A person and his psychological environment, Lewin insisted, are dynamically one field," Marrow wrote in a biography of his mentor. "They should never be treated as separate entities. From early childhood, social facts—especially the sense of belonging to particular groups—are among the most fundamental determinants of the child's growing world, for they shape his wishes and goals and what he considers right and wrong." Marrow, *The Practical Theorist,* p. 110.

6. See, for example, Kurt Lewin, *A Dynamic Theory of Personality: Selected Papers,* translated by D. K. Adams and K. E. Zener (1935, New York: McGraw-Hill Book Company), p. 66ff.

7. Lewin may have been the first modern researcher to articulate the idea of "creative tension," the valuable stress that stems from simultaneous awareness of aspiration and current reality, and pulls people forward toward their goals. See Robert Fritz's "structural tension" *(The Path of Least Resistance,* 1989, New York: Fawcett-Columbine) and Senge's "creative tension" (Senge, pp. 150–55), as well as Marrow, *The Practical Theorist,* pp. 30–32.

8. Weisbord, pp. 83–84, describes how Lippitt and Lewin coined the name "group dynamics" in 1939 and how originally Lewin meant "groups of forces" rather than "groups of people"—but came to change his approach.

9. K. Lewin, R. Lippitt, and R. K. White, "Patterns of Aggressive Behavior in Experimentally Created Social Climates," *Journal of Social Psychology,* 10 (1939), pp. 271–79. Also see Lippitt and White.

10. Lippitt and White, p. 25.

11. This statement of Benne's first principles is adapted from a line in Hirsch.

12. Lippitt, p. 116 and elsewhere.

13. Ironically, neither of the two original sponsors, the Connecticut

State Interracial Program and the National Conference of Christians and Jews, ever sponsored a T-Group again.

14. Bradford, p. 48.

15. For the first few years, from 1947 to 1950, funding came from the Office of Naval Research and then from the Carnegie Foundation.

16. Bradford, p. 81.

17. Eventually "Group Dynamics" was dropped.

18. Bradford's memoirs, Appendix, p. 167.

19. Bradford, p. 73.

20. David Bradford, son of Leland, communication with the author.

21. Some of this sequence comes from "Trainer-Intervention: Case Episodes," by Leland P. Bradford, in *T-Group Theory & Laboratory Method,* edited by Leland P. Bradford, Jack R. Gibb, and Kenneth D. Benne, 1964, New York: John Wiley & Sons, p. 136. I also drew from Spencer Klaw, "Two Weeks in a T-Group," *Fortune,* August 1961; Alfred Friendly, "Where Bosses Let Down Their Hair," Washington Post, November 27, 1966; and "What Makes a Small Group Tick," *Business Week,* August 13, 1955.

22. These lectures would cover, for example, the theories of Wilfred Bion, Jacob Moreno, and Eric Trist. Much of the group dynamics work at NTL was deeply influenced by the Tavistock Institute of Human Relations. See Weisbord, pp. 146–49, and Back, pp. 62–64.

23. Seashore, Seashore, and Weinberg, pp. 4–11.

24. There are many different versions of this story, with many people credited. Sometimes it's newsprint from a print shop. In one version, it was a butcher shop and the paper was butcher paper; in another, it was the Bethel Citizen. Weisbord, p. 100, says it actually happened at the Connecticut workshop in 1946.

25. Excerpt from Maslow's journal, in *Abraham H. Maslow: A Memorial Volume,* compiled with the assistance of Bertha G. Maslow, 1972, Belmont, CA: Wadsworth, p. 92. Maslow labeled T-Groups a "peak experience" on p. 52 of the same volume. Carl Rogers wrote similarly about T-Groups in *Carl Rogers on Encounter Groups,* 1970, New York: Harrow Books.

26. Friendly, "What Makes a Small Group Tick."

27. "An O.D. Expert in the Cat Bird's Seat," interview with Warren Bennis by Campbell Crockett and Ron Boyer, in *Journal of Higher Education* (Ohio State University), 1972, p. 395.

28. Friendly, "Where Bosses Let Down Their Hair."

29. McGregor was the founder of the industrial relations program at MIT's School of Economics and Social Science (the Sloan Business School had not yet been created).

30. Warren Bennis suggested this point.

31. Some of this charge is represented in Charles Hampden-Turner, "An Existential 'Learning Theory' and the Integration of T-Group Research," *Journal of Applied Behavioral Science,* No. 4, pp. 367–86; reprinted in Robert T. Golembiewski and Arthur Blumberg, *Sensitivity Training and the Laboratory Approach,* 1970, Itasca, IL: F. E. Peacock. It also appears in *Carl Rogers on Encounter Groups.* William H. Whyte opened *The Organization Man* with an attack on the leaderless groups of NTL (p. 54).

32. Edgar H. Schein, *Brainwashing,* 1961, Cambridge: Center for International Studies, MIT.

33. Edgar Schein, "The Academic as Artist: Personal and Professional Roots," an unpublished paper, October 1990; and Edgar H. Schein, "Management Development as a Process of Influence," *Industrial Management Review,* May 1961.

34. Edgar H. Schein, "Management Development as a Process of Influence," *Industrial Management Review,* May, 1961.

35. Standard Oil of New Jersey, descended directly from John D. Rockefeller's original oil company, had a surfeit of names. Its chief brand, sold in the East, was Esso, named after the letters "S" and "O." Antitrust suits had forced it to use the brand names Enco and Humble elsewhere. Its own managers called it Esso, while oilmen at other companies called it Jersey. Eventually, in 1972, all these identities would be gathered together under the name Exxon.

36. See, for example, Geohegan, pp. 52–53.

37. Iris Lynn Neill Hicks, *Forgotten Voices: Women in Organizational Development and Human Resource Development,* Ph.D. dissertation, University of Texas at Austin, 1991. University Microfilms #9128249, pp. 65–86.

38. Blake and Mouton, *Diary of an OD Man.*

39. This episode takes place in Chapter 8, "Headquarters Intervenes," in *Diary of an OD Man,* p. 63.

40. *Diary of an OD Man,* p. 10.

41. Robert Blake and Jane Srygley Mouton, *The Managerial Grid,* 1964, Houston: Gulf Publishing Company, p. 10.

42. This observer was Dick Beckhard.

43. All of this comes from Blake and Mouton, *Corporate Excellence Through Grid Organization Development.*

44. Robert R. Blake, "Memories of HRD," in *Training & Development,* March 1995.

REFORMISTS

1. Tavistock was a complex organization, composed of a psychiatric clinic (associated with the British Health Service) and a separate, but related, research institute. Two influential psychoanalytic figures at Tavistock were Melanie Klein and Wilfred Bion. See Weisbord, p. 146; and H. V. Dicks, *50 Years of the Tavistock Clinic* (London: Routledge & Kegan Paul, 1970).

2. Schein, *Organizational Psychology,* pp. 60–61.

3. The concept of "open systems" comes primarily from the work of Eric Trist. See Trist, *The Evolution of Socio-technical Systems,* 1981, Toronto: Ontario Quality of Working Life Centre; Trist, "Culture as a Psycho-Social Process," paper T.1059, self-published, 1950 (for the Symposium on the Concept of Culture arranged by the Anthropological Section of the British Association for the Advancement of Science), revised 1967 (for the Celebration Book for Sir Frederic Bartlett's Eightieth Birthday); Weisbord, p. 150; F. E. Emery and E. L. Trist, "Socio-technical Systems," in C. W. Churchman and M. Verhulst, editors, *Management Science, Models and Techniques,* Vol. 2, 1960, New York: Pergamon, pp. 83–97, reprinted in Emery.

4. The stories about Norwegian work teams come from several people who knew Einar Thorsrud or heard him speak. Also see Weisbord, p. 165. However, one knowledgeable source, Max Elden, discounts the story as I have told it here.

5. The resulting paper was called "The Causal Texture of Organizational Environments," *Human Relations,* 18 (1965), pp. 21–32, reprinted in Emery, p. 241.

6. Ludwig von Bertalanffy, "The theory of open systems in physics and biology," *Science,* vol. III (1950), pp. 23–29, reprinted in *Systems Thinking,* edited by F. E. Emery (London: Penguin Books, 1969), p. 70. Also D. Katz and R. L. Kahn, "Common Characteristics of Open Systems," from *The Social Psychology of Organizations,* Chapter 2, Wiley, 1966, pp. 14–

29. The ovum example comes from Katz and Kahn. (They talked specifically about sea urchin ova.)

7. Weisbord, p. 62.

8. Wren, p. 127.

9. The story that follows is partly based on, and complementary to, the story told in Waterman, pp. 36ff.

10. At least four different people, in various versions of the story, are credited with first introducing the sociotechnical techniques into P&G: Charles Eberle, Dave Swanson, Phil Willard, and John Anderson. In crediting McGregor with helping design the Augusta plant, I'm choosing to follow the account given by Waterman. Others at P&G say that McGregor did little more than make speeches. It is certain that Dick Beckhard, who worked closely with McGregor, and taught with him at MIT, was closely involved in consulting on the design of Mehoopany.

11. The quote about "navel examining" comes from Charles Eberle, who managed the Sacramento plant in the early 1960s. He later promoted the technician system throughout Procter's international system.

12. Downy at first; the Biz assignment was added soon after the plant started up.

13. Waterman, pp. 47ff.

14. David Jenkins, *Job Power: Blue and White Collar Democracy*, 1973, New York: Doubleday, pp. 231–35. Also correspondence from Michael Brower.

15. Many people associated with the "T-Group" movement had settled at UCLA, such as Robert Tannenbaum, Jim Clark, Richard Walton, and some prominent psychologists including Carl Rogers and Abraham Maslow, who were exploring the idea of humanizing business. Finally, there was a large sociotechnical contingent there, spearheaded by an organizational sciences professor named Lou Davis, who brought Eric Trist in from the Tavistock Institute in 1966. O.D. and Sociotechnical movements, once linked through Trist's friendship with McGregor, had now fallen apart, and only at UCLA, when the P&G contingent arrived with curiosity about both schools of thought, did the two groups of professors (whose offices were down the hall from each other) discover they had much to talk about.

16. Bennett, p. 77.

17. Krone, pp. 364ff.; "Seminar by Charles Krone of the International Development Organization," in *Massachusetts Quality of Working Life Center* newsletter, Vol. II, No. 6, June 1977, p. 6; and Waterman, p. 64.

18. Krone, "Open Systems Redesign," p. 366. Social psychologist Karl Weick describes a theory similar to Krone's "flower theory": The most satisfying thing any of us can get out of work is not money, but "the removal of equivocality." A pile of component chemicals is highly "equivocal"; it can be made into many different products. It's satisfying to make that lump more specific, by turning it into detergent, and more satisfying still to make a bottled product from start to finish, continually improving the process for yourself. That's why mechanized processes dehumanize, and why workers seek money in compensation. See Weick, pp. 75–76.

19. Lyman Ketchum, "A Case Study of Diffusion," in Davis, Cherns, and Associates, p. 140.

20. The "plant manager" job in Kankakee had the title "operations manager." This was the company's way of distinguishing between Post's four "big" plants (Battle Creek, Hoboken, Dover, and Kankakee) and the smaller ones.

21. Quaker Oats Company, U.S. Naval Reserve, Safeway Stores, Staley Milling Company (a small feed manufacturer), and then General Foods.

22. "If we want workers to work . . . willingly and well, we must give them the right to think. . . . We must welcome the expression of their thinking and let management decisions be influenced by it. We must even delegate some decisions directly to the workers; for instance, decisions on all phases of safety, on some or all phases of house rules and discipline, on many phases of technological changes . . . There must be an increasing supply of the facts, which have been the exclusive property of management because only management needed them for its thinking." Alexander R. Heron, *Why Men Work*, 1948, Stanford, CA: Stanford University Press, p. 175.

23. The champion of the study, Jack Shipman of the Post division's market research department, was given the same treatment for his career that Lyman Ketchum got.

24. This story is told in Havener, 1994, pp. 30–41. Havener is the former General Foods manager who proposed the package redesign for Biscuits and Bits and shortly thereafter left the company.

25. They were advised in this by Dick Walton.

26. The planning group included: Ketchum, Dulworth, Don Lafond (see later in chapter), Robert Mech, and Phil Simshauser. Mech and Simshauser took jobs at Topeka as managers.

27. *Topeka Organization & Systems Development,* internal General Foods document, October 24, 1969.

28. Other key corporate champions at GF were Art Larkin and Ross Barzelay.

29. Jim Stone, letter to the author.

30. David Jenkins, "Democracy in the Factory: A Report on the Movement to Abolish the Organization Chart," *Atlantic Monthly,* April 1973, p. 78. (Figures on p. 80.)

31. Brimm, p. V-7.

32. Brimm, p. V-5.

33. Brimm, p. V-31.

34. Brimm, p. V-51.

35. Brimm, p. V-53.

36. Brimm, p. X-5.

37. Brimm, p. X-5.

38. Brimm, pp. VII-17.

39. Kanter and Mirvis, pp. 116–17.

40. Walton, pp. 70ff; particularly see pp. 71–74. Also see *Work in America,* Report of a Special Task Force to the Secretary of Health, Education, and Welfare, 1973, Cambridge: MIT Press.

41. The stereo equipment magnate Sidney Harman, whose company, Harman-Kardon, also made automobile mirrors, had instigated a "quality of working life" program for a plant in Bolivar, Tennessee. He would eventually become an undersecretary in the U.S. Department of Commerce. There were full-fledged projects going on at Corning, Polaroid, Texas Instruments, and General Electric, as well as at Volvo in Sweden.

PROTESTERS

1. The heretic's speech is adapted from "A Vindication of the Church of God," circa 1250, in "The Catharist Church and Its Interpretation of the Lord's Prayer," in Wakefield and Evans, pp. 592ff.

2. This line comes from "A Debate Between Catholics and Heretics," in Wakefield and Evans, pp. 189ff.

3. Some of this material is influenced by Joseph Campbell, *In Search of the Holy Grail: The Parzival Legend.*

4. This statement is a quote from V. Shannon Clyne, who (in conversation) offered this definition of corporate purpose: "A corporation's pur-

pose is to maximize shareholder wealth, defined as the *present discounted value of all future profits*. In other words, the longer a shareholder has to wait for future profits, the less they are worth." Communication with the author.

5. I acknowledge that this inquiry is the basis of "stakeholder theory," as set out in R. Edward Freeman, *Strategic Management: A Stakeholder Approach*, 1984, White Plains, NY: Pitman Publishing. I have not written about stakeholder theory in this book, because it seems like a nonheretical way of evading the issues raised in corporate responsibility. I agree with the arguments made by Sternberg, pp. 51–53.

6. Moskowitz et al., 1980 ed., p. 410.

7. Arthur L. Whitaker, "Anatomy of a Riot," *Crisis*, January 1965, pp. 20–25; quoted in Sethi, *Business Corporations and the Black Man*, p. 68.

8. Sethi, *Business Corporations and the Black Man*, pp. 67–68.

9. Horwitt, p. 456.

10. Horwitt, p. 453.

11. Horwitt, pp. 451–52.

12. Alinsky, p. 91.

13. Horwitt, p. 457.

14. Alinsky, p. 138.

15. Horwitt, p. 465.

16. Having picked the acronym, they selected its component rhetorical parts: "Freedom, Integration, God, Honor, Today." "God" was Alinsky's own last-minute suggestion, and "Integration" was later changed to "Independence." Horwitt, p. 461.

17. Sethi, *Business Corporations and the Black Man*, p. 76.

18. Alinsky, p. 102.

19. Sethi, *Business Corporations and the Black Man*, p. 52.

20. Horwitt, p. 489.

21. Much of this comes from Sethi, *Business Corporations and the Black Man*, pp. 11–12 and pp. 26–27.

22. Sethi, *Business Corporations and the Black Man*, p. 50.

23. Horwitt, p. 492. Sethi, *Business Corporations and the Black Man*, p. 35.

24. Sethi, *Business Corporations and the Black Man*, p. 22.

25. Sethi, *Business Corporations and the Black Man*, p. 35.

26. Alinsky, p. 178.

27. The most prominent crusader in these protests was Lewis Gilbert. See Talner, p. 5.

28. Peter Drucker, *The Unseen Revolution: How Pension Fund Socialism Came to America,* 1976, New York: Harper & Row. In the end, the prevalence of pension fund investment has diffused ownership and made it more difficult for either managers or shareholders to take control of an enterprise.

29. Floyd Norris, "As Magellan Makes Big Bets, the Risks Rise," New York *Times,* December 11, 1994, section 3, p. 1.

30. Interviewed in Editors of *Institutional Investor,* p. 33.

31. See, for instance, Robert Sobel, *The Rise and Fall of the Conglomerate Kings,* 1984, New York: Stein & Day.

32. Sethi, *Up Against the Corporate Wall,* p. 124, quoting John Kifner, "21 Churches Withhold Proxies to Fight Kodak Rights Policies," New York *Times,* April 7, 1967.

33. Horwitt, p. 497, and Alinsky, p. 173.

34. Horwitt, p. 498.

35. Sethi, *Up Against the Corporate Wall,* p. 126.

36. *Rules for Radicals,* p. 175.

37. Vogel, pp. 48–55.

38. "Nader Panel Rebuffed by GM on Plea to List Customer Demands," *Wall Street Journal,* March 6, 1970, p. 14.

39. Kanter and Mirvis, p. 113.

40. After the strike described here, some of the young leaders of the United Auto Workers had begun to look seriously at changing the structure of the assembly line. Those labor leaders, particularly Irving Bluestone and Don Ephelin, would find themselves, later in the decade, at the center of the labor movement's dilemma over the "quality of working life": Was the ability to improve the plant worth fighting for? Or should a union stick to grievances and wages? Bennett Kremen, "Lordstown—Searching for a Better Way of Work," New York *Times,* September 9, 1973, section 3, p. 1.

41. Barbara Tuchman, *The March of Folly, From Troy to Vietnam,* 1984, New York: Knopf, p. 62.

42. Dan Cordtz, "Henry Ford, Superstar," *Fortune,* May 1973, p. 285.

43. Whiteside, p. 9.

44. Whiteside, p. 164.

45. Whiteside, pp. 25–29.

46. Peter F. Drucker, *The Age of Discontinuity*, 1967, New York: Harper & Row, pp. 203–4.

47. Donald E. Schwartz, "The Public-Interest Proxy Contest: Reflections on Campaign GM," *Michigan Law Review*, January 1971, p. 426.

48. Talner, p. 14.

49. E. J. Kahn, Jr., "We Look Forward to Seeing You Next Year," *The New Yorker*, June 20, 1970, p. 40.

50. Talner, p. 20.

51. *Business and Society*, January 7, 1969, pp. 2–3.

52. Vogel, p. 176.

53. Not just to me. Note Eggert's sympathetic (to Friedman) article, pp. 12–15.

54. Milton Friedman, "The Social Responsibility of Business Is to Increase Its Profits," *New York Times Magazine*, October 4, 1970, p. 32.

55. Horwitt, p. 533.

56. Alinsky, pp. 190–96.

57. Brown, "Change, Challenge, and Community," p. 7. Fred Ross and Ed Chambers, two of Alinsky's longtime associates, deserve credit here.

58. Brown, "Sí, Se Puede—Yes, It Can Be Done!"

MYSTICS

1. Kenneth Krabbenhoft, "Reading the Mystics: Allegories of Body, Garden and Temple in the Classical Literature of Western Mysticism," unpublished manuscript.

2. *A History of the Royal Dutch/Shell Group of Companies*, 1988, London: Royal Dutch/Shell Group Public Affairs.

3. Doug Wade, taped interview with Ted Newland, held on Friday, May 13, 1994, at Cybard, France; internal document for Shell Group Planning, p. 1.

4. In 1966, the Seven Sisters sold 90 percent of the world's petroleum. Three were remnants of the old John D. Rockefeller monopoly: Standard Oil of New Jersey (Esso, Enco), Standard Oil of California (Chevron), and Mobil. Two were large companies with roots in Texas: Texaco and Gulf. A sixth company, British Petroleum, owed its heritage to the long-standing relationship between Britain and Persia (it was previously called Anglo-Iranian). Royal Dutch/Shell was the seventh.

5. "The Seventh Sister," *Forbes*, November 15, 1972.

6. P. D. S. Hadfield, "From Scenarios to Strategy," 1990 Top Management Forum, Managing in the 1990s; Crafting and Implementing Strategy in a Changing Global Environment, Paris, June 13–14, 1990. The drawing is adapted from J. S. Jennings, *The Energy Outlook: Its Implications for Upstream Oil and Gas,* paper delivered at the Energy Policy Seminar, Sanderstolen, Norway, February 9, 1989, Fig. 5.

7. Hamilton, pp. 9, 104. Also Yergin, Chapters 21–28. Six-Day War: Sampson, pp. 209–11.

8. P. W. Beck, "Strategic Planning in the Royal Dutch/Shell Group," 1977; presented to the Conference on Corporate Strategic Planning, Institute of Management Science, New Orleans.

9. Yergin, pp. 65–69.

10. Higdon, esp. pp. 134–48. The story of the Shell job is on p. 143. Shell hired McKinsey after a successful restructuring of Cia. Shell de Venezuela in 1956; John Loudon, then the chairman, had the initiative to bring them in, and Hugh Parker was the leader of the McKinsey team at the time.

11. In 1994, Royal Dutch/Shell's managers decided to dismantle part of this system, eliminating the "region" part of the chart of command, while still keeping the separate operating companies and the "function" hierarchy.

12. Kahn, *On Thermonuclear War,* p. 19; James R. Newman, "This is . . . ," review of *On Thermonuclear War* in *Scientific American,* March 1961; Kaplan, p. 228.

13. "I am one of the 10 most famous obscure Americans," profile of Herman Kahn by William A. McWhirter, *Life,* December 6, 1968; also Kaplan, pp. 57–61, 220.

14. Wade/Newland, p. 8.

15. An alternative history for the term has it coming from military uses, through the OSS to RAND. I prefer this story, which comes directly from Leo Rosten.

16. Kahn and Weiner, Chapter 4: "Post-Industrial Society in the Standard World."

17. Tony Weiner phrased this point in *The Year 2000* this way: "Our own Standard World, adumbrated throughout the volume, reflects our own expectations, of course, and we have tried to make these explicit as much as possible" (p. 8).

18. "Herman Kahn's Thinkable Future," *Business Week,* March 11, 1967, p. 116.

19. H. J. Alkema and E. V. Newland, "Increased Efficiency of the Use of Energy Resources," Shell International Petroleum Company, given at the Institute of Petroleum Summer Meeting at Harrogate, June 5–8, 1973. Copyright the Institute of Petroleum, 1973.

20. In the 1980s, Rothschild would be accused by Tory backbenchers—but never with substantiation or much credibility—of being a member of Kim Philby's spy ring. See "Lord Rothschild: Biotechnologist and Businessman," obituary, *Financial Times,* March 22, 1990, p. 11.

21. Wade/Newland, pp. 2–3.

22. Wade/Newland, p. 3.

23. G. I. Gurdjieff, *Meetings with Remarkable Men,* written in the 1940s; published in 1957. American edition, 1963, New York: E. P. Dutton.

24. In 1986, Bénard would become a co-chairman of the Channel Tunnel Project to link France and England. He published the first serious article on scenario planning in the *Harvard Business Review:* "World Oil and Cold Reality," November/December 1980, p. 91.

25. In framing this narrative, I have not been able to give full credit to the contributions of other significant members of the Planning Department: Cor Kuiken, Harry Beckers, Doug Wade, Gareth Price, Napier Collyns, and others. As Jimmy Davidson wrote (in correspondence with the author), "It would be grossly unfair . . . to give the impression that everything flowed from Wack and Newland, or that they were the [sole] leaders . . ." This is also a good place to acknowledge Karel Swart, a managing director whose support was critical to Shell's scenario planning team.

26. Hamilton, p. 100; Sampson, pp. 274–85; Yergin, pp. 583–85.

27. Gerrit Wagner, Karel Swart, and André Bénard are the three managing directors about whom I can say this with assurance.

28. Pierre Wack's exact words are forever lost, but these, taken from a speech given years later and from Gerrit Wagner's and his own recollections, are similar to what he said that September morning. The speech was "I find by experience . . ." (see the Bibliography). Another version of this speech saw print as Wack, "Scenarios: Uncharted Waters Ahead."

29. Yergin, pp. 594–95.

30. *Scenarios for 1973 Planning Cycle,* Group Planning, 1973, p. 10.

31. Pierre Wack, "Scenarios: The Gentle Art of Re-Perceiving Reality:

One Thing or Two Learned While Developing Planning Scenarios for Royal Dutch/Shell," 1984, Harvard Business School Working Paper #9-785-042, p. 28.

32. *Scenarios for 1973 Planning Cycle,* Group Planning, 1973, p. 12.

33. From his letter to Pierre Wack, September 24, 1985.

34. *Scenarios for 1973 Planning Cycle,* Group Planning, 1973, p. 24.

35. Originally, the planners had wanted to suggest a price of $12, but had moved it down to $10 before the presentation.

36. This concept of "rents" dates back to the nineteenth-century economist David Ricardo. See Yergin, p. 432.

37. Gerald Clarke, "What Went Wrong?", *Time,* December 10, 1973, p. 49.

38. Wagner's letter to Pierre Wack, September 24, 1985.

39. Mohamed Heikal, *The Road to Ramadan,* 1975, London: Collins, p. 167, quoted in Yergin, p. 597.

40. Jeffrey Robinson, p. 148.

41. Jeffrey Robinson, p. 146.

42. The "lime and Coke" story is told in Yergin, p. 602, and Sampson, p. 18. My account is based on comments from André Bénard, who showed Sampson his original notes of the meeting but disputes some of that version. (The man in his pajamas, Bénard says, came from Iraq, not Kuwait; and Yamani never placed a call to Baghdad.) The detail of the dates from Saudi Arabia is described here for the first time; thanks to Bénard, it's my own addition to the record about "one of the most critical encounters in the history of oil," as Sampson puts it.

LOVERS OF FAITH AND REASON

1. This account comes from several sources, but I relied most heavily on Nigg, p. 158. I also used the account of Abelard in Will and Ariel Durant, *The Age of Faith,* 1950, New York: MJF Books, and Etienne Gilson's *Heloise and Abelard,* translated by L. K. Shook, 1963, Ann Arbor: University of Michigan Press.

2. For example, Stafford Beer, as quoted in Richardson, pp. 170–71.

3. Robert E. Shannon, "Operations Research and Mathematical Modelling," in Lester R. Bittel, editor, *The Encyclopedia of Professional Management,* 1978, New York: McGraw-Hill, p. 810.

4. Wren, p. 473. Also *Encyclopaedia Britannica*'s entries on "Opera-

tions Research" (written by Russell L. Ackoff) and "Systems Engineering" (written by H. W. Bode), in *Encyclopaedia Britannica*, Macropaedia Vols. 13 and 17, 1980, Chicago: University of Chicago Press.

5. Gelber and Cook, pp. 64–74.

6. This was part of the international "Jesus as Teacher" movement; see Gelber and Cook, pp. 42–55; Stolaroff, *Thanatos to Eros*.

7. Lee and Shlain, pp. 87–88, 96–117, etc.

8. Lee and Shlain, pp. 6–19, etc.

9. Lee and Shlain, pp. 48–51; Gelber and Cook, pp. 79–86.

10. Lee and Shlain, p. 198.

11. The Sequoia Seminars later became known as the Beyond War Foundation.

12. Auden, "The Labyrinth," in *Collected Poems*, Edward Mendelson, ed., 1976, New York: Random House, p. 9.

13. Lee and Shlain, p. 18n.

14. Gibson, p. 5.

15. Gibson, p. 184.

16. Gibson, pp. 88, 99–100, 102, 108.

17. Royce, Bill, "A History of Strategic Management and Planning at SRI," 1985, Internal SRI report.

18. "SRI Pulls Hard on the Growth Reins, *Business Week,* March 25, 1967, p. 106.

19. Other advisors to Gideonse and his Project included Syracuse University futurist Michael Marien, and Don Michael, then at the University of Michigan.

20. Russell Rhyne, "Projecting Whole-Body Future Patterns—The Field Anomaly Relaxation (FAR) Method," Menlo Park: Stanford Research Institute Educational Policy Research Center, 1969, p. 32.

21. Rhyne, p. 35.

22. O. W. Markley, "Alternative Futures: Contexts in Which Social Indicators Must Work," EPRC Research Note 6747-11, February 1971, supported by the National Center for Educational Research and Development, prepared for a session on social indicators for the American Statistical Association, Detroit, December 27–30, 1970, contract OEC-1-7-071013-4274, pp. 3–6. Also the Rhyne paper just described, but this gives a more effective overview of what the group was doing.

23. Educational Policy Research Center, Progress Report, June 1, 1971–September 1, 1971, contract OEC-1-7-071013-4274.

24. Oliver Markley, "The Omniverse Center for Cultural Development, and Other Noetic Technologies for Global Consciousness and Personal/Planetary Transformation," presented at Open Heart, Open Mind: the 4th annual conference of the Institute of Noetic Sciences, San Diego, CA, July 17, 1995.

25. Jay Forrester, "From the Ranch to System Dynamics: An Autobiography," in Bedein.

26. Linda Runyan, "40 Years on the Frontier (History of Computing)," *Datamation,* March 15, 1991, p. 34.

27. David Warsh, "Reaping the Whirlwind," Boston *Globe,* August 10, 1986, p. 79.

28. This story has been described to me in two ways: once (by Forrester) as being about General Electric, the other (by Dennis Meadows) as being about Sprague Electric, makers of electrical components such as resistors and capacitors.

29. Richardson, p. 129.

30. These numbers come not from General Electric's actual experience, but from Forrester's computer simulation of their case.

31. Adapted from Forrester.

32. Forrester, pp. 22–35.

33. Forrester, pp. 49–50.

34. Conversation with Peter Senge, referring to reviews of *Industrial Dynamics* by University of Chicago physicist John Platt.

35. Jay Forrester, "A New Concept of Corporate Design," Industrial Management Review, Vol. 7, No. 1, Fall 1965, p. 5; and Jay Forrester, "Reconsidering 'A New Corporate Design,'" 1993, manuscript copy; written for William Halal, Ali Geranmayeh, and John Pourdekinad, editors, New York: Wiley.

36. Claire Sterling, "Club of Rome Tackles the Planet's 'Problématique,'" Washington *Post,* March 2, 1972, p. A18, and Patrick O'Keefe, "A Warning on Man's Big Problem," Washington *Evening Star,* March 2, 1972, p. A3.

37. The model is described in full in Jay W. Forrester, *World Dynamics,* 1971, Cambridge: Wright-Allen Press; currently available from Productivity Press, Portland, OR.

38. Markley says that it looks like the main variables there were based on the 1954 book *The Challenge of Man's Future* by Caltech geochemist Harrison Brown.

39. Dennis L. Meadows, *Dynamics of Commodity Production Cycles,* 1970, Cambridge: Wright-Allen Press. The other members of the team were Jörgen Randers and William W. Behrens III.

40. Meadows et al., *The Limits to Growth,* pp. 129, 140.

41. Art Kleiner, "Flexing Their Mussels," *Garbage,* Vol. 4, No. 4, July/ August 1992, p. 48.

42. Review of *The Limits to Growth, World Dynamics,* and *Urban Dynamics,* by Peter Passell, Marc Roberts, and Leonard Ross, in *The New York Times Book Review,* April 2, 1972, section 7, p. 1.

43. Jerry Pournelle, "Computing at Chaos Manor: The Hunt for Bad Sectors," *Byte,* June 1, 1989, p. 119.

PARZIVAL'S DILEMMA

1. Hermann J. Weigand, "Trevrezent as Parzival's Rival?" in *Wolfram's Parzival: Five Essays,* edited by Ursula Hoffman, 1969, Ithaca, NY: Cornell University Press, pp. 149–51. Also see Nigg, p. 185.

2. "Woe's me that he did not inquire! For him I still feel sorrow dire," in *The Parzival of Wolfram von Eschenbach,* translated by Edwin H. Zeydel and Bayard Quincy Morgan, 1951, Chapel Hill: University of North Carolina Studies in the Germanic Languages and Literatures, p. 127, Book 5, Verse 240, line 3. The question is finally posed much later: "What afflicts thee, Uncle dear?" p. 328, Book 16, Verse 795, line 29.

3. "Abandon boorish breeding. From too much questioning refrain . . . ," in *The Parzival of Wolfram von Eschenbach,* p. 89, Book 3, Verse 171, lines 17–18.

4. My rendition of Parzival owes a tremendous amount to the explications of Joseph Campbell. I found two Campbell renditions of this story: in *Reflections on the Art of Living* and in *In Search of the Holy Grail* (see the bibliography).

5. Schein.

6. "The [conventional academic] group dynamics research was very static in its emphasis on experiments, and the classic Sherif studies on intergroup conflict studied outcomes more than process. What I think I and others have argued for, all these years, is more careful attention to the ongoing dynamics of what went on between people and in groups, and the moment-to-moment consequences of small bits of behavior." Edgar Schein, in a letter to the author, June 1995.

7. These details come from Marvin R. Weisbord, "Team Work: Building Productive Relationships," in W. Brendan Reddy and Kaleel Jamison, editors, *Team Building: Blueprints for Productivity and Satisfaction*, 1988, Washington, DC: NTL Institute. It was adapted in turn from Weisbord, *Productive Workplaces*, pp. 297–310. The questions "on a scale of 1 to 5" come from Roger Harrison, "Role Negotiations," in W. Burke and H. Hornstein, editors, *The Social Technology of Organization Development*, Washington, DC: NTL Institute/Learning Resources.

8. The date 1957 is suggested by Robert Blake, who describes the first pivotal clash between the "power and authority" people and the "morale and cohesion" people at NTL as occurring that year. Gradually, the morale and cohesion people shifted West. Robert R. Blake, "Memories of HRD," *Training & Development*, March 1995.

9. John A. Byrne, "Executives Latch On to Any Management Idea That Looks Like a Quick Fix," *Business Week*, January 20, 1986, p. 52.

10. This "lemon game" was invented by Jon Klee, a member of the NTL staff.

11. The MBO system was originally conceived by Peter Drucker, using the ideas of Douglas McGregor, Ron Lippitt, and others. Odiorne expanded upon Drucker's ideas and developed the "MBO" package, which persists in many companies today. Odiorne describes his system concisely in "Objectives, management by," in *The Encyclopedia of Professional Management*, 1978, New York: McGraw-Hill, pp. 781–87. Also see George Odiorne, *The Human Side of Management: Management by Integration and Self-Control*, 1987, Lexington, MA: Lexington Books/University Associates, p. xii.

12. For his argument, see George Odiorne, "The Trouble with Sensitivity Training," *Training Director's Journal* (American Society for Training and Development), 1963.

13. "Yourself as Others See You," *Business Week*, March 16, 1963.

14. Chris Argyris, "On the Future of Laboratory Education," *Journal of Applied Behavioral Science*, 3, Summer 1967, pp. 153–83; Chris Argyris, "T-Groups for Organizational Effectiveness," *Harvard Business Review*, 42, (March 1964), pp. 60–74, especially pp. 68, 71; Argyris, *Interpersonal Competence and Organizational Effectiveness*, pp. 232–33, 250–54.

15. This story was recounted by Argyris. I couldn't check it with Odiorne, who had passed away.

16. Chris Argyris, "Looking Backward and Inward in Order to Contribute to the Future," essay distributed directly by Argyris, p. 51.

17. Argyris, *Personality and Organization.*

18. Chris Argyris, *Management and Organizational Development, The Path from XA to YB,* 1971, New York: McGraw-Hill, p. 120.

19. Bennis, afterword to *Making Waves in Foggy Bottom,* p. 77.

20. Argyris, "Some Causes of Organizational Ineffectiveness Within the Department of State."

21. Marrow, *Making Waves in Foggy Bottom;* see pp. xiii, 3, 7.

22. This episode is based on a training session witnessed by the author in 1993; OD veterans have commented that it is representative of problematic interventions since the 1960s.

23. Back, pp. 220–21.

24. Bradford, p. 178.

25. Hirsch, p. 88.

26. Bennis, *An Invented Life.*

27. "NTL Executive Committee Meeting," March 16, 1969, in Bradford, pp. 341–42.

28. David Bradford suggests this point in a letter to the author, 1995.

29. Bradford, p. 184.

30. Jane Howard, "Inhibitions Thrown to the Gentle Winds," *Life,* July 12, 1968.

31. Conversation with Bennis. In his memoirs (p. 185), Lee Bradford writes that they received pledges for the full million.

32. Hirsch, p. 89.

33. After taking part in a two-day meeting at Bethel, where they could see both the attitudes of NTL's existing staff and Warren's own ambivalence, both Chris Argyris and Don Michael advised him to decline the job.

34. Warren Bennis, "Development of a Dream: A New International University for Social Change," speech given at NTL board meeting, November 13–14, 1969, in Bradford, p. 346.

35. Hirsch, pp. 85–86.

36. Hirsch, p. 95.

37. Edie Seashore, Barbara Bunker, Billie Alban, and Jane Moosbrucker were four of the most prominent NTL trainers who were women.

38. See Harragan.

39. Miller is now president and CEO of the Kaleel Jamison Consulting Group, Inc.; he was also to become an NTL board member. Connecticut

General is now called CIGNA. Some of this story comes from Frederick A. Miller, "Forks in the Road: Critical Issues on the Path to Diversity," in Cross et al., p. 115.

40. Clare C. Swanger, "Perspectives on the History of Ameliorating Oppression and Supporting Diversity in United States Organizations," in Cross et al., pp. 13–14; Sonny Kleinfield, *The Biggest Company on Earth,* 1981, New York: Holt, Rinehart and Winston, pp. 205–6.

41. Charles N. Seashore and Beverly R. Fletcher, "The White Male Category at the Intersection of Race and Gender," in Cross et al., p. 157.

42. Hirsch, p. 109.

43. See, for example, Mark Chesler, "Organizational Development Is Not the Same as Multicultural Organizational Development," in Cross et al., p. 240. I make the point raised here in an exploratory vein. I hope to report more thoroughly on the aspirations of "diversity training," as well as its effects and the issues it brings to the surface, in future work.

44. See, for instance, Donald A. Schön, *The Reflective Practitioner: How Professionals Think in Action,* 1983, New York: Basic Books, pp. 18–20.

45. Schön taught urban studies and education at MIT. Although his contribution to the "theory of action" was equal to that of Argyris, he was less concerned with the application of that theory in organizations.

46. This is written up in Argyris, *Interpersonal Competence and Organizational Effectiveness,* p. 5.

47. For more on this, see Robert Putnam, "Conversational Recipes," p. 260, and Philip McArthur, "Opening Lines," p. 263, in Senge et al.

48. For some examples, see Senge et al., particularly "Skillful Discussion at Intel," p. 392; "Creating a Learning Lab—and Making It Work," p. 554; "The Ladder of Inference," p. 242; and "The Left-Hand Column," p. 246.

49. Richard L. Gordon, "Warren Bennis: New President Looks Beyond U.C. Campus," *Cincinnati,* November 1971, p. 32.

50. Mark Edinberg, "Dr. Bennis's Open Office Hours," social psychology paper for Dr. L. Lansky's class, University of Cincinnati, December 13, 1971.

51. Rosemary Davis, "UC's New First Lady Arrives," *Cincinnati Enquirer,* September 1, 1971.

52. Some of this story is told in Bennis, *The Unconscious Conspiracy.*

53. Warren Bennis, "Reflections on Six Impatient Years," *Cincinnati Horizons,* June 1977; Nancy Foy, "Bennis breaks out of his Ivory Tower," *The London Times,* August 20, 1973, p. 20.

54. Warren Bennis, ". . . Only Connect . . .", speech at American Group Psychologists Association annual meeting, New York City, February 18, 1974.

55. Susan Yohe, "UC money crisis may mean end to some programs," *Cincinnati Post,* April 19, 1973.

56. In conversation, Warren Bennis claims that he resigned on his own volition. He was tired. He didn't want the responsibility any longer. And it was a good time to leave, since the merger with the state system had just been completed. Other sources suggest strongly that he was forced out. However it happened, it happened abruptly—so much so that the university had to clean out his books and papers from his offices. Most of them are still in the school's library.

57. The ad was placed by United Technologies Corporation, and quoted in Warren Bennis and Burt Nanus, *Leaders,* 1985, New York: Harper & Row, p. 22.

58. Commencement Address, University of Cincinnati, August 26, 1977.

MILLENARIANS

1. Cohn, pp. 53–57, on peasant life, and Malcolm Lambert, *Medieval Heresy: Popular Movements from Bogomil to Hus,* 1976, New York: Holmes & Meier.

2. This story is told, with power and force, in Ventura.

3. Richard Dawkins, *The Selfish Gene,* 1976, 1989, Oxford: Oxford University Press, p. 206; Dennett, *Darwin's Dangerous Idea,* pp. 342–46.

4. Herman Kahn, "Forces for Change," in Kahn, *The Future of the Corporation,* p. 127.

5. This story was recounted by Lynne Hall.

6. Harragan, p. 305.

7. Braudel, *The Wheels of Commerce,* p. 59.

8. Art Kleiner, "Renegades of Retail," *San Francisco Bay Guardian,* October 15, 1986.

9. Paul DiMaggio, *The Hitchhiker's Field Manual,* 1973, New York: Macmillan, p. 161.

10. This story is told in Kushi, especially pp. 185–86.

11. Kushi, p. 192.

12. Richard Warren Eivers, "From Alternative to Big Business: The Story Behind Erewhon's Unionization," *New Age Journal,* November 1978; also "Erewhon: High Hopes, High Standards—and Low Profits," *New Age Journal,* July 1982. Also interviews with the Kushis in *Meetings with Remarkable Men and Women,* from the editors of *East West,* 1989, Brookline, MA: East West Health Books.

13. Paul Hawken, *Growing a Business,* 1987, New York: Fireside/Simon & Schuster, p. 48.

14. Eivers, "From Alternative to Big Business," p. 31.

15. Kleiner, "Renegades of Retail."

16. Duane S. Elgin, David C. MacMichael, and Peter Schwartz, *Alternative Futures for Environmental Policy Planning, 1975–2000,* October 1975, prepared by Stanford Research Institute, Center for the Study of Social Policy, for the Environmental Protection Agency, Office of Pesticide Programs, Strategic Studies Unit, EPA-540/9-75-027.

17. Thomas Kuhn had posited "paradigms" as a shared set of agreements about what types of examples and scientific puzzles were worth paying attention to. A "paradigm shift," as Kuhn saw the concept, was a focused, narrow-scale change whereby a community changed its views of what exemplars or examples were acceptable.

Norman MacEachron, currently at SRI International, first introduced the "paradigm" idea to the futures group there. As Don Michael has noted, when Willis Harman, and then other writers such as Joel Barker and Hazel Henderson, began to use the term, they were actually talking about broad-based, vague shifts of attitude—hardly the same thing. See Thomas Kuhn, Postscript to *The Structure of Scientific Revolutions,* 1970, Chicago: University of Chicago Press, p. 177.

18. Harman et al., *Changing Images of Man.*

19. *Changing Images of Man,* p. 58.

20. *Changing Images of Man,* pp. 71–72, 255.

21. *Changing Images of Man,* p. 4.

22. *Changing Images of Man,* p. 75.

23. Joseph Campbell, with Bill Moyers, *The Power of Myth,* 1988, New York: Doubleday, pp. 5, 117–21.

24. *Changing Images of Man,* p. 23.

25. Don Michael recalls saying, "Willis, as long as we are recognized for our own work on *this* plane, then I want to be credited!"

26. Hawken et al., pp. 107–25.

27. See, for example, Hawken, *The Ecology of Commerce, The Next Economy,* and *Growing a Business.* Also Schwartz, *The Art of the Long View,* and James Ogilvy, *Many Dimensional Man,* 1977, New York: Oxford University Press; and *Living Without a Goal,* 1995, New York: Doubleday/Currency. Schwartz and Ogilvy would later become partners, with Napier Collyns, Stewart Brand, and Lawrence Wilkinson, in Global Business Network.

28. Richard Gregg, "Voluntary Simplicity," *Visva-Bharati Quarterly,* August 1936; reprinted in abridged form in *CoEvolution Quarterly,* Summer 1977, p. 20.

29. Elgin et al., pp. W-36, W-47.

30. Elgin et al., pp. W-33–W-49.

31. Collier and Horowitz, pp. 379–81.

32. Duane Elgin and Arnold Mitchell, "Voluntary Simplicity," *CoEvolution Quarterly,* Summer 1977, p. 6.

33. Elgin's book became *Voluntary Simplicity: Toward a Way of Life That Is Outwardly Simple, Inwardly Rich,* 1981, New York: Morrow.

34. Kahn et al., *The Next 200 Years,* p. 4.

35. Herman Kahn, *The Prospects for Mankind One and a Year 2000 Ideology,* Croton-on-Hudson, NY: Hudson Institute, Report #H1-1648/4-D, August 1, 1972, p. 4-D.

36. Kahn and Bruce-Briggs, *Things to Come,* pp. 30, 44.

37. Herman Kahn, Governor Jerry Brown, and Amory Lovins, "The New Class," *CoEvolution Quarterly,* Spring 1977, p. 8.

38. *Things to Come,* p. 60.

39. *Things to Come,* p. 219.

40. *The Next 200 Years,* p. 164.

41. Kahn, *World Economic Development,* especially the first few chapters.

42. "The New Class," p. 10.

43. "The New Class," p. 11.

44. "The New Class," p. 17.

45. Morton Mintz and Jerry S. Cohen, *America, Inc.: Who Owns and Operates the United States,* 1971, New York: Dial Press, p. 342.

46. Wagner, p. 117.

47. "Royal Dutch/Shell Group of Companies Statement of Business Principles," reprinted in Wagner, pp. 121ff.

48. Wade/Newland, p. 8 (see note 3, chapter 5).

49. *World Economic Development*, p. 285–88.

50. Hans DuMoulin and John Eyre, "Energy Scenarios: A Learning Process," *Energy Economics,* April 1979, p. 78.

51. DuMoulin and Eyre, p. 78.

52. DuMoulin and Eyre, p. 77.

53. As Napier Collyns points out, Shell's planners met Lovins through Dennis Gabor, the Hungarian physicist who had just won the Nobel Prize for inventing the hologram. They had contacted Gabor as part of their search for an expert on energy efficiency. Gabor said he was too old to help, "but I've met this young man who knows the answers to all of your questions."

54. Many of these details come from Chip Brown, "High Priest of the Low-Flow Shower Heads," *Outside Magazine,* November 1991, p. 58. Also John R. Emshwiller, "Amory Lovins Presses Radical Alternatives for Fueling the Nation," *Wall Street Journal,* March 16, 1981, p. 1.

55. Chip Brown, p. 58.

56. Introduction to Lovins' article in *Not Man Apart,* Friends of the Earth, Autumn 1976. The "butter with a chainsaw" line, often attributed to Lovins, was first said by Doug Kelbaugh, a professor at the University of Washington. Chip Brown, p. 60.

57. This diagram is adapted and simplified from Amory B. Lovins, "Energy Strategy: The Road Not Taken?" *Foreign Affairs,* October 1976. It was later updated in Amory B. Lovins, "An Historical Footnote," 1991, Rocky Mountain Institute.

58. Lovins, "Energy Strategy."

59. "The New Class," p. 22.

60. Lovins, letter to the Manchester *Union Leader,* date not available (but sometime after October 1976).

61. This is a paraphrase of a speech made by Carl Goldstein, assistant vice president of the Atomic Industrial Forum, at the AIF-SVA International Workshop, "Nuclear Power and the Public," Geneva, Switzerland, September 26–29, 1977.

62. "Setting Business Straight on Energy Priorities," interview with

Amory Lovins by Stephen G. Michaud and Donald Ediger, *Business Week,* December 5, 1977.

63. "Lapp vs. Lovins," in Hugh Nash, editor, *The Energy Controversy: Soft Path Questions and Answers, by Amory Lovins and His Critics,* 1979, San Francisco Friends of the Earth, p. 93.

64. Douglas Foster, "The Calculator Kid," *Mother Jones,* February–March 1978, p. 49.

THE RAPIDS

1. Tuchman, pp. 43ff.

2. Tuchman, p. 34.

3. Just a few examples: Servan-Schreiber's *The American Challenge;* Mark Gerzon's *The Whole World Is Watching;* Paul Ehrlich's *The Population Bomb;* the SDS Port Huron statement (reprinted in Paul Jacobs and Saul Landau, *The New Radicals,* 1966, New York: Vintage); and many more. Henry Mintzburg offers a similar comment in *The Rise and Fall of Strategic Planning,* p. 204.

4. See especially F. E. Emery and E. L. Trist, "The Causal Texture of Organisational Environments," *Human Relations,* 20 (1967), pp. 199–237.

5. Wack, "Scenarios: Shooting the Rapids."

6. Gerald Clarke, "What Went Wrong," *Time,* December 10, 1973, p. 49.

7. "Big Oil—Under Pressure, *Newsweek,* December 17, 1973, p. 79; Ralph Nader, "It's a Gas," *New Republic,* December 14, 1973, p. 16.

8. Sampson, pp. 318–19.

9. Yergin, p. 657.

10. "Big Oil—Under Pressure," p. 79.

11. Robert Sherrill, *The Oil Follies of 1970–1980,* 1983, New York: Anchor/Doubleday, p. 217.

12. Yergin, p. 621.

13. Yergin, pp. 621–22.

14. Leonard Silk and David Vogel, *Ethics and Profits: The Crisis of Confidence in American Business,* 1976, New York: Simon & Schuster.

15. Vogel, pp. 110–11.

16. Robert L. Heilbroner, "Controlling the Corporation," in Heil-

broner et al., *In the Name of Profits,* 1972, New York: Doubleday; p. 192. Heilbroner cites *The Wall Street Journal,* February 11, 1971.

17. Russell Mokhiber, *Corporate Crime and Violence,* 1988, San Francisco: Sierra Club Books, pp. 163–70.

18. Frederick D. Sturdivant, *The Corporate Social Challenge: Cases and Commentaries,* 3rd ed., 1985, Homewood, IL: Richard D. Irwin, pp. 127–29.

19. Vogel and Silk, p. 178.

20. Vogel and Silk, p. 117.

21. Vogel and Silk, p. 221.

22. Rawleigh Warner, Jr., "On Becoming 'A Controversial Issue of Public Importance,'" *Conference Board Record,* August 1974, p. 3. Quoted in Vogel and Silk, p. 113.

23. Office of Technology Assessment Project Staff, *Technology and the American Economic Transition: Choices for the Future,* 1988, U.S. Office of Technology Assessment, OTA-TET-283, p. 175.

24. Schoenberg, pp. 303–8.

25. Henderson, pp. 3–4.

26. Michael Rothschild, *Bionomics: The Inevitability of Capitalism,* 1990, New York: H. Holt, pp. 178–79. The factory manager who discovered the curve was Theodore P. Wright.

27. This curve is modeled after the pages of *Competing Against Time,* by George Stalk and Thomas Hout, 1990, New York: Free Press, pp. 6–8.

28. Bruce D. Henderson, *Henderson on Corporate Strategy,* 1979, Cambridge: Abt Books, p. 82.

29. "The World of 1976: A Time of Healing, a Return to Growth," slides by Lawrence Wilkinson, Global Business Network, Emeryville, CA.

30. Fligstein, particularly Chapters 7 and 8.

31. Robert Reich and John D. Donahue, *New Deals: The Chrysler Renewal and the American System,* 1985, New York: Viking/Penguin, p. 90.

32. Weaver, pp. 84–85.

33. Keller, p. 68.

34. Pascale, pp. 18–19; Mintzburg, p. 103.

35. Leslie Wayne, "Management Gospel Gone Wrong," *New York Times,* May 30, 1982, section 3 p. 1; Robert H. Hayes and William J. Abernathy, "Managing our way to economic decline," *Harvard Business Review,* July-August 1980.

36. This is from a letter to Peter Vaill.

37. Peters and Waterman, p. 10.

38. Peters and Waterman, pp. 150, 127, 132.

39. Peters and Waterman, p. 246.

40. Peters and Waterman, pp. 286–87.

41. See, for instance, "Who's Excellent Now?" in *Business Week,* November 5, 1984, pp. 76–88; Daniel Carroll, "A Disappointing Search for Excellence," *Harvard Business Review,* Vol. 61 (December 1983); 78–88; or the most in-depth survey, *Redefining Excellence,* by Arabinda Ghosh, 1990, New York: Praeger.

42. See Juanita Brown, "Sí, Se Puede"; also Brown and Isaacs, in Senge, et al., p. 511.

43. Senge, *The Fifth Discipline.*

44. See, for example, Shorris, *Scenes from Corporate Life.*

45. This segment is based on material written with Bryan Smith, published in *The Lost Chapters of the Fifth Discipline Fieldbook,* 1994, Oxford, OH: Fifth Discipline Fieldbook Project, and then in *The Systems Thinker,* 6, No. 3 (April 1995).

46. This point borrows from a statement made by Libbi Lepow in the River inquiry conference, September 1995.

47. Art Kleiner and Janis Dutton, "Time to Dump Plastics Recycling?" *Garbage,* Spring 1994.

48. Charles Handy calls this the "Shamrock" corporation, because there is no single center. See Handy, p. 72.

49. See, for example, Hawken, *The Ecology of Commerce,* pp. 61–67; or Hardin Tibbs, *Industrial Ecology,* 1993, Emeryville, CA: Global Business Network.

ⒷIBLIOGRAPHY

It would take a full-sized volume to list the written sources I perused in researching this book (and its sequel to come). This bibliography, with brief annotations, represents my informal guide to the books that spurred me on or changed my thinking, and the sources I think readers might find most useful if they chose to follow up.

Alinsky, Saul, *Rules for Radicals,* 1971, New York: Random House. An autobiography/manifesto, in which Alinsky's voice comes through terrifically strong. Makes you wish you could have known him.

Argyris, Chris, "Some Causes of Organizational Ineffectiveness Within the Department of State," Center for International Systems Research Occasional Paper #2, published by the U.S. Department of State, Washington, DC, 1966. If this booklet had a mouth, butter would not melt in it. See Chapter 7.

———, with Roger Harrison, *Interpersonal Competence and Organizational Effectiveness,* 1962, Homewood, IL: Dorsey Press/Richard D. Irwin. Argyris explores (and reproduces dialogue from) high-level management teams in a large mid-1960s corporation (IBM).

———, *Personality and Organization,* 1957, New York: Harper & Row. How organizations infantilize or eject the people who work for them.

———, and Donald Schön, *Theory in Practice: Increasing Organizational Effectiveness,* 1974, San Francisco: Jossey-Bass. The explanation of theories-in-use versus espoused theories and how they affect managers' learning.

Back, Kurt, *Beyond Words,* 1972, New York: Russell Sage Foundation. A full, in-depth history of NTL, encounter groups, and all the dilemmas and conundrums that emerge as people try to put them into practice.

Beck, P. W., "Strategic Planning in the Royal Dutch/Shell Group," 1977; presented to the Conference on Corporate Strategic Planning, Institute of Management Science, New Orleans. A tourist's guide to Shell's globally unified but disparate management structure.

Bedein, Arthur G., *Management Laureates: A Collection of Autobiographical Essays,* 1991, Greenwich, CT: JAI Press. Chris Argyris, Robert Blake, and Jay Forrester all wrote autobiographical essays for this book.

Bennett, J. G., *Is There "Life" on Earth? An Introduction to Gurdjieff,* 1973, New York: Stonehill; 1989, Santa Fe, NM: Bennett Books. The most accessible introduction for novices (like myself).

Bennis, Warren, *An Invented Life: Reflections on Leadership and Change,* 1993, Boston: Addison-Wesley. I appreciate Bennis' writings about himself, particularly in this retrospective collection of his most powerful essays.

———, *The Unconscious Conspiracy: Why Leaders Can't Lead,* 1976, New York: AMACOM. Essays written during the time of student protest, Watergate, and Bennis' presidency at the University of Cincinnati. Fascinating glimpses of Bennis' own personality and priorities.

———, Kenneth Benne, and Robert Chin, editors, *The Planning of Change,* 1st and 3rd eds. New York: Holt, Rinehart and Winston, 1961 and 1976. One of the nice things about these collections of early OD articles is the strange feeling of anarchy they evoke; you can see Bennis and Chin creating the first texts of their field (of organization development) and reveling in the freedom to do so.

Berry, Wendell, *What Are People For?* 1990, Berkeley, CA: North Point Press. Cogent essays that argue against the premise of *Heretics*—that corporate reform is a worthy activity. Large remote enterprises, he says poetically, are inherently corrupt.

Bittel, Lester R., editor, *The Encyclopedia of Professional Management,* 1978, New York: McGraw-Hill. All conventional management practice is laid out in this gargantuan book, which served as a constant reference.

Blake, Robert, and Jane Srygley Mouton, *Corporate Excellence Through Grid Organization Development: A Systems Approach,* 1968, Houston: Gulf Publishing Company. Provides the overview to the "Managerial Grid" system that shows how it is supposed to work when followed all the way to the end.

———, and ———, *Diary of an OD Man,* 1976, Houston: Gulf Publishing Company. A wonderful memoir of two years of harrowing consultation at the Bayway refinery, as described in Chapter 2.

Bradford, Leland P., *National Training Laboratories: Its History, 1947–*

1970, 1974, Bethel, ME: NTL Institute for Applied Behavioral Science. Bradford's memoirs are a rich vein of ore about the man and the institution; the book also is a mini-archive in itself, including many of the pivotal documents in NTL's history. Whenever I describe how "NTLers" saw things, particularly in the early years, I am probably relying on something in this book.

———, Jack R. Gibb, and Kenneth D. Benne, editors, *T-Group Theory & Laboratory Method,* 1964, New York: John Wiley & Sons. Nitty-gritty T-Group practice, almost enough to run one as it was run in the late 1950s.

Brand, Stewart, editor, "The New Class," a meeting transcript with Herman Kahn, Amory Lovins, and Governor Edmund G. Brown, in *CoEvolution Quarterly,* Spring 1977, p. 8. A conversation between two prodigies (three, if you count Jerry Brown), that still rings with insight two decades later.

Braudel, Fernand, *The Wheels of Commerce* (Vol. 2) and *The Perspective of the World* (Vol. 3), from *Civilization and Capitalism, 15th–18th Century,* translated by Siân Reynolds, 1967–83, Berkeley: University of California Press. These were the two more useful volumes, for my purposes, of Braudel's classic three-volume history of the age when vernacular culture first faced off against the predecessors of industrial culture. Others seem to read these books from front to back; I dive into them, and surface several hours later, having gone back in time.

Brimm, Michael, *Analytical Perspectives in Organizational Behavior: A Study of an Organizational Innovation,* 1975, Cambridge: Harvard University, School of Business, Department of Business Administration. An in-depth, wonderfully written guide to day-to-day life at the Topeka plant. It contains both a Marxist and a sociotechnical critique; Brimm was trying to show how a researcher's point of view influences the conclusions.

Brown, Juanita, "Change, Challenge, and Community: Walking the Life-work Path," and "Sí, Se Puede—Yes, It Can Be Done! Merging the Best of Two Worlds," 1995, Mill Valley, CA: Whole Systems Associates. Two beautifully written essays describing how Alinsky-style techniques translate into modern corporate practice.

Callenbach, Ernest, *Ecotopia: The Notebooks and Reports of William Weston,* 1975, New York: Bantam. Originally a news report about sewage, this became one of the few viable postwar utopian novels. It portrays a society much like the dreams of Californians in the 1970s: the internal-combustion engine was outlawed, and babbling brooks flowed down San Francisco's Market Street. *Ecotopia*'s most engaging quality is the portrait that Callenbach provides of the golden young people of the counterculture, living the vernacular spirit that American culture had beaten down. I believe that a few hours with this novel would be worthwhile for any manager: particularly the chapter, near the end, in which Callenbach (a former OD consultant) describes Ecotopian corporations—collaborative enterprises owned by the participants.

Campbell, Joseph, *In Search of the Holy Grail: The Parzival Legend* (cassette recording), 1989, 1990, HighBridge Productions; and *Reflections on the Art of Living: A Joseph Campbell Companion,* selected and edited by Diane K. Osbon, 1991, New York: HarperCollins, p. 71. My version of Parzival borrows from the explications of Joseph Campbell. Campbell has written and spoken several renditions of this story; these are not the most scholarly, but the most evocative.

Christie-Murray, David, *A History of Heresy,* 1976, London: New English Library. Probably the most complete overview; a Baedeker of everyone who challenged the ideas of the Christian church from within.

Cohen, Peter, *The Gospel According to the Harvard Business School,* 1973, New York: Doubleday. Diary of a sorcerer-in-training, rife with anecdotes, angst, student protest, and soul-searching.

Cohen, Sam, "Smartest Guy in the Army," *Army Magazine,* January 1984, p. 35. A short, thoroughly engaging profile of Herman Kahn the person, by one of his oldest and closest friends.

Cohn, Norman, *The Pursuit of the Millennium: Revolutionary Millenarians and Mystical Anarchists of the Middle Ages,* 1957, 1981, New York: Oxford University Press. After being swept up in Cohn's dramatic account of waves of "free spirits," beguines, proto-anarchists, true believers, and flagellants, I saw echoes of them all in our time.

Collier, Peter, and David Horowitz, *The Fords: An American Epic,* 1987, New York: Summit Books. Nice group biography with lots of rich detail about the Fords and their company. Lots of heresy stories.

Cross, Elsie Y., Judith H. Katz, Frederick A. Miller, and Edith W. Seashore, *The Promise of Diversity;* 1994, New York: NTL Institute/Irwin. Forty authors talking directly to the reader about their diversity work. I have found no better overview, and I base most of what I wrote about diversity in Chapter 7 on reactions to points made in this book.

Crystal, Graef S., *In Search of Excess*, 1991, New York: Norton. The best book extant on corporate corruption, by someone who understands it from the inside out—a compensation consultant who can write, and who turned defector.

Davis, John P., *Corporations*, 1961, New York: Capricorn Books. Originally published in 1897, it traces the corporation back to the monastery and on into the ecclesiastical university and beyond. I have a great affection for this book, as if Davis were a beloved former professor.

Davis, Louis E., Albert B. Cherns, and Associates, *The Quality of Working Life*, 2 vols., 1975: New York: Free Press. Like Zager and Rosow, a collection of key papers in the Quality of Working Life movement.

Dennett, Daniel C., *Darwin's Dangerous Idea*, 1995, New York: Simon & Schuster. A valuable introduction to evolution, memes, and heresies.

Drucker, Peter, *Adventures of a Bystander*, 1978, New York: Harper & Row. A wonderful, inspiring book of portraits that gives face and voice to the twentieth century.

———, *The New Realities*, 1989, New York: Harper & Row. I borrowed gratefully from Drucker's description of the "Great Divide" that struck society around 1973. Much of the curiosity that fed my research stemmed from a desire to fill in the gaps of the story told here.

———, *The Practice of Management*, 1954, New York: Harper & Row. I taught myself the content of conventional management with this book, much as managers probably did when it first came out.

Eccles, Robert G., and Nitin Nohria, with James D. Berkley, *Beyond the Hype: Rediscovering the Essence of Management*, 1992, Cambridge: Harvard Business School Press. The closest I've seen (besides Drucker) to a guide to the meaningful concepts that lie forgotten beneath ordinary business practice.

Editors of *Institutional Investor*, *The Way It Was: An Oral History of Finance, 1967–1987*, 1988: New York: Morrow. Exactly what the subtitle says, with no attempt to provide Cliff Notes for novices. Great glimpse of an alien culture.

Eggert, Jim, "A Liberal's Guide to Milton Friedman," *CoEvolution Quarterly*, Summer 1979. Rollicking.

Elgin, Duane, *Voluntary Simplicity*, 1981, New York: William Morrow. Portrait of the vernacular undertow.

———, Arnold Mitchell, M. W. Reynolds, Peter Schwartz, and J. W. Waters, "The Impact of Sociocultural Changes upon the Automobile Industry, 1975 to 2000," Appendix W in *Long-Term Outlook for the United States Auto Industry,* November 1975, prepared for the Ford Motor Company by the Stanford Research Institute, Accession #L 34611, pp. W-36 and W-47. The fabled report that Henry Ford II snubbed. See Chapter 8.

Emery, F. E., editor, *Systems Thinking: Selected Readings,* 1969, New York: Penguin. A series of important papers from the late 1960s, applying principles from biology and cybernetics to organizations. How they struggled.

Fairtlough, Gerard, *Creative Compartments: A Design for Future Organisation,* 1994, London: Adamantine Press. A Shell planner explains three key forms of corporate governance—market, clan, and hierarchy—and their implications.

Fligstein, Neil, *The Transformation of Corporate Control,* 1990, Cambridge: Harvard University Press. The most insightful contemporary corporate history I have read. Among the pleasures is his analysis of the changing impact of three great subcultures—manufacturing/engineering, marketing, and finance—on the standard corporate culture. If my book is a history of corporate heresy, his is a brilliant history of the culture that the heretics sought to undermine.

Forrester, Jay, *Industrial Dynamics,* 1961, Cambridge: MIT Press; currently published by Productivity Press of Portland, OR. Most accessible (to me) of Forrester's books, and not just an introduction to systems modeling but also to management thinking.

Friedman, Milton, "A Friedman Doctrine: The Social Responsibility of Business Is to Increase Its Profits," *New York Times Magazine,* October 4, 1970, p. 32. See Chapter 4.

Fuller, R. Buckminster, *A Grunch of Giants,* 1983, New York: St. Martin's Press; 1995, Buckminster Fuller Institute, Santa Barbara, CA. One of Fuller's last books, it is a polemic venting against the banker/pirates/corporations and how they distorted civilization.

———, *Everything I Know: 42 Hours with Buckminster Fuller,* January 20, 1975, Vol. 5, published by the Buckminster Fuller Institute, Santa Barbara, CA. Listening to these tapes clarified my understanding dramatically; people say Fuller is hard to follow in audio, but I hung on effortlessly, riveted.

Galbraith, John Kenneth, *The New Industrial State,* 1967, 1971, Boston: Houghton Mifflin. Galbraith wrote (incorrectly, in my view) that corporate power stemmed from the effectiveness of group decision making. But he gave a clear picture of the assumptions of scarcity behind corporate power, and the way that power overrode all other concerns, inside and outside the organization.

Gelber, Steven M., and Martin L. Cook, *Saving the Earth: The History of a Middle-Class Millenarian Movement,* 1990, Berkeley: University of California Press. Tells what happened to the Sequoia Seminars (later the Beyond War Foundation) before, during, and after their intersection with Willis Harman.

Geneen, Harold, with Alvin Moscow, *Managing,* 1984, New York: Doubleday. I did not understand the "numbers" until I read this book. Geneen declined to be interviewed for this project. However, knowing the ghostwriting process, I suspect that Geneen's voice in the book, resonant with respect for people and orneriness, is true to his character.

Geohegan, Thomas, *Whose Side Are You On? (Trying to Be for Labor When It's Flat on Its Back),* 1991, New York: Farrar, Straus, Giroux. My favorite guide to the labor movement, written by a street poet in labor-union-lawyer's clothing, full of regrets and howling outrage, and sensible political proposals that, alas, will never be followed.

Gibson, Wendell B., *SRI: The Founding Years (A Significant Step at the Golden Time),* 1980, Los Altos, CA: Publishing Services Center. A kind of yearbook that gives a strong impression of SRI as it was and later yearned to be.

Gordon, John Steele, *The Scarlet Woman of Wall Street,* 1988, New York: Weidenfeld & Nicolson. The emergence of American capitalism, seen through the deeds of the heroes (Vanderbilt) and villains (Drew, Fisk, Gould) of the railroad wars of the nineteenth century.

Gregg, Richard, "Voluntary Simplicity," *Visva-Bharati Quarterly,* August 1936; reprinted in abridged form in *CoEvolution Quarterly,* Summer 1977, p. 20. The original statement that Duane Elgin of SRI found (Chapter 8).

Halberstam, David, *The Reckoning,* 1986, New York: Morrow. Intertwined history of the decline of the U.S. auto industry, the rise of the Nader counterculture, and the emergence of Japan. W. Edwards Deming said that Halberstam was a "great man" for writing this book.

Hamilton, Adrian, *The Price of Power,* 1986, London: Rainbird. Documentary source of oil industry history, admired by Shell scenario planners.

Handy, Charles, *The Age of Unreason,* 1989, London: Business Books, Ltd. Views of the organization of the future, described in the style your uncle might use during a long car ride to a job interview.

Harman, Willis, et al., *Changing Images of Man:* Policy Research Report #4. Prepared for the Charles F. Kettering Foundation, Dayton, OH 45429. Contract URH (489)-2150. O. W. Markley, Project Director. Prepared by Joseph Campbell, Duane Elgin, Willis Harman, Arthur Hastings, O. W. Markley, Floyd Matson, Brendan O'Regan, and Leslie Schneider. May 1974, Menlo Park, CA: Stanford Research Institute. The great millenarian manifesto, described in Chapter 8.

Harvagan, Betty Lehan, *Games Mother Never Taught You,* 1977, New York: Warner Books. This unsentimental "bible" for women entering corporate life nailed the numbers culture down cold.

Havener, Cliff, with Margaret Thorpe, *Discovering the Lost Spirit of Business,* 1994: Forest Lake, MN: Growth Resource Group, Inc. *Value Based Business,* an unpublished manuscript by Cliff Havener (the former General Foods manager who proposed the package redesign for Biscuits and Bits and shortly thereafter left the company).

Hawken, Paul, *The Ecology of Commerce: A Declaration of Sustainability,* 1993, New York: HarperBusiness. Hawken begins to envision a "restorative economy," and thus articulates—for the first time—the ecologist's view of what the value of large mainstream corporations can be. I turned here for answers to the question "What are corporations for?"

———, James Ogilvy, and Peter Schwartz, *Seven Tomorrows: Towards a Voluntary History,* 1980, 1982, Covelo, CA: Yolla Bolly Press; New York: Bantam, pp. 107–25. Probably the finest single flowering of the SRI scenario approach.

Hayes, Robert H., and William J. Abernathy, "Managing Our Way to Economic Decline," *Harvard Business Review,* July–August 1980. See Chapter 9.

Heilbroner, Robert, *The Worldly Philosophers: The Lives, Times, and Ideas of the Great Economic Thinkers,* 1953, 6th ed. 1986, New York: Simon & Schuster. A wonderful history of economic thinking, whose first chapter deeply influenced my first chapter.

Heller, Joseph, *Something Happened*, 1974, New York: Knopf. Artist's eye view of the pathologies, power plays, and heartbreak of the world of the "numbers."

Henderson, Bruce D., *The First Ten Years—Remembered, or How BCG Became a Group*, 1973, Boston: Boston Consulting Group, pp. 3–4. Compelling memoirs.

Hicks, Iris Lynn Neill, *Forgotten Voices: Women in Organizational Development and Human Resource Development*, Ph.D. dissertation at the University of Texas at Austin, 1991. University Microfilms #9128249. Includes cogent, informative, lively biographies of Jane Mouton and Edie Seashore.

Higdon, Hal, *The Business Healers*, 1969, New York: Random House. So few books about management consultants are attempted, let alone published; the chutzpah and liveliness of this one were refreshing.

Hirsch, Jerrold, *A History of the NTL Institute for Applied Behavioral Science, 1947–1986*, Ed.D. dissertation, Boston University School of Education, 1986. University Microfilms #8615320. A great, readable dissertation, where I first learned that the National Training Lab's story was a story worth telling.

Horwitt, Sanford, *Let Them Call Me Rebel*, 1989, New York: Alfred A. Knopf. An incisive, compassionate biography of Saul Alinsky by an associate/writer/journalist.

Hunt, Morton, *The Story of Psychology*, 1993, New York: Doubleday. The reference I used for basic information about psychologists.

Illich, Ivan, "Vernacular Values," *CoEvolution Quarterly*, Summer 1980, p. 22. Published, in edited form, in Illich, *Shadow Work*, 1981, Salem, NH: Marion Boyars, Inc. Illich's surveys of the shadow side of industrial culture are the greatest antidotes I know to the corporate/professional mind-set. This essay is a history of the centuries-old battle between "subsistence," preeconomic, preindustrial life, and the urge to control and professionalize all human activity.

Johnson, H. Thomas, *Relevance Regained*, 1992, New York: Free Press. The book of denunciation and renunciation (see *Relevance Lost*). A heretic steps out on a limb.

————, and Robert S. Kaplan, *Relevance Lost: The Rise and Fall of Management Accounting*, 1987, 1991, Cambridge: Harvard Business School Press. Building upon historian Alfred Chandler, Johnson and Kaplan get to the bottom of the story of the "numbers," how they evolved, and how they eventually deceived the managers who depended on them. Kaplan used this book to springboard "activity-based cost management," which Johnson later denounced.

Kahn, Herman, *On Thermonuclear War,* 1960, Princeton: Princeton University Press. This is fascinating because it preserves Kahn's lecture style, and it presents a range of scenarios for disasters that never happened.

———, *World Economic Development: 1979 and Beyond,* 1979, Boulder, CO: Herman Kahn. Written four years before his death, it weaves together the arguments from all Kahn's books and provides the most accessible framework to his utopian futures and the facts behind his reasoning. It would be a good component of anyone's liberal education.

———, editor, *The Future of the Corporation,* 1974, New York: Mason & Lipscomb. This set of conference proceedings represents Kahn's only direct statement on corporations as entities, and he doesn't have much to say. But the people he invites do—particularly Peter Drucker on the responsibility of managers to the world at large.

——— and Anthony J. Weiner, *The Year 2000,* 1968, New York: Macmillan: Herman Kahn and Barry Bruce-Briggs, *Things to Come (Thinking about the Seventies and Eighties),* 1972, New York: Macmillan; Herman Kahn, William Brown, and Leon Martel, *The Next 200 Years,* 1976, New York: Morrow. Herman Kahn's trilogy of glances ahead, each with a different co-author. See Chapter 5.

Kanter, Donald L., and Philip H. Mirvis, *The Cynical Americans: Living and Working in an Age of Discontent and Disillusion,* 1989, San Francisco: Jossey-Bass. The legacy of heretics, says this book, is shattered expectations and defeated idealism. Nowhere to go but up.

Kaplan, Fred, *The Wizards of Armageddon,* 1983, New York: Simon & Schuster. Authoritative, nicely written history of the RAND Corporation and nuclear strategists.

Keller, Maryann, *Rude Awakening,* 1989, New York: Morrow. One of the most eloquent writers on the automobile industry.

Ketchum, Lyman D., and Eric Trist, *All Teams Are Not Created Equal,* 1992, Newbury Park, CA: Sage. How (and how not) to create a "Topeka" of your own, by two key heretics from Chapter 3.

Krone, Charles G., "Open Systems Redesign," in W. Warner Burke, editor, *Contemporary OD: Conceptual Orientations and Interventions,*

1975, La Jolla, CA: University Associates. Later republished by University Associates as *New Technologies in Organization Development.* This, to my knowledge, is Charlie Krone's only published written work.

Kuhn, Thomas, *Structure of Scientific Revolutions,* 1962, 1970, Chicago: University of Chicago Press. A heretical book, with almost nothing to do with *this* book, except through an accident of history described in Chapter 8.

Kushi, Aveline, with Alex Jack, *Aveline: The Life and Dream of the Woman Behind Macrobiotics Today,* 1988, Tokyo and New York: Japan Publications. Straightforward autobiography by Paul Hawken's ex-partner (who mentions him exactly once in the book, by my count).

Lee, Martin A., and Bruce Shlain, *Acid Dreams,* 1985, New York: Grove Press. Classic story of the early days of LSD, full of colorful characters like Al Hubbard.

Lewin, Kurt, *A Dynamic Theory of Personality: Selected Papers,* 1935, New York: McGraw-Hill. Back to the source.

Lippitt, Ronald, *Training in Community Relations,* 1949, New York: Harper & Brothers. Nearly all the direct description of the Connecticut workshop, including all of the dialogue I used, comes from Ron Lippitt's authoritative write-up.

———, and Ralph K. White, *Autocracy and Democracy: An Experimental Inquiry,* 1960, New York: Harper & Brothers. This is the story of the "boys' club" experiments in which Lewin, Lippitt, and White demonstrated how completely organizational structure determines behavior. They knew how to conduct an experiment in those days.

Lovins, Amory B., "Energy Strategy: The Road Not Taken?" *Foreign Affairs,* October 1976. This was expanded later into Amory Lovins, *Soft Energy Paths: Toward a Durable Peace,* 1977, San Francisco: Friends of the Earth International. Influential analysis of the choice America faced (and faces) for its energy grid.

Maccoby, Michael, *The Gamesman,* 1976, New York: Simon & Schuster. Described in Chapter 1. As fascinating to read as an anthropological study, which in fact it is.

Manchester, William, *The Glory and the Dream,* 1972, Boston: Little, Brown. This history of the United States from Roosevelt's era to Nixon's inspired the form of *The Age of Heretics.* I can think of no better model for a comprehensive history.

Mansbridge, Jane J., *Beyond Adversarial Democracy,* 1980, 1983, Chicago: University of Chicago Press. Shows how NTL-inspired modes of governance and conversation actually operated in a real-life counterculture "Help-line," and leaps from there to compelling insights about how to create political organizations that engage constituents.

Marrow, Alfred, *Making Waves in Foggy Bottom,* 1974, Washington, DC: National Training Laboratories. A brief, to-the-point narrative history of the fateful State Department intervention in Chapter 7.

———, *The Practical Theorist: The Life and Work of Kurt Lewin,* 1969, New York: Basic Books. A loving history by a student and collaborator.

McGill, Michael, *American Business and the Quick Fix,* 1988, New York: Henry Holt. Acerbic survey of forty years of management fads, notable for the way it portrays business' love-hate relationship with "the numbers."

McGregor, Douglas, *The Human Side of Enterprise,* 1960, 1985, New York: McGraw-Hill. The classic. See Chapter 2.

McWhinney, Will, *Paths of Change,* 1992, Newbury Park, CA: Sage Publications. McWhinney's system, a sort of developmental path for change agents, is well worth studying for anyone who wants to move beyond a pilot project to influence an organization on a large scale.

Meadows, Donella H., Dennis L. Meadows, and Jörgen Randers, *Beyond the Limits,* 1992, Post Mills, VT: Chelsea Green Publishing Company. Twentieth anniversary recap of *Limits to Growth.* I find this the most valuable of the *Limits* books because the authors, all three of whom were around at the beginning, have had a chance to consider the implications over time.

———, ———, ———, and William W. Behrens III, *The Limits to Growth,* 1972, Washington, DC: Potomac Associates. See Chapter 6.

Michael, Donald N., *On Learning to Plan—and Planning to Learn,* 1973, San Francisco: Jossey-Bass, 1996, Alexandria, VA: Miles River Press. Don Michael's explication of the ways in which planners can effectively set themselves up as nonexperts—if they can only see past their own predilections. A lodestar for judgment.

Mintzburg, Henry, *The Rise and Fall of Strategic Planning: Reconceiving Roles for Planning, Plans, Planners,* 1994, New York: Free Press. As Tom Peters says: "A shockingly, tightly ordered, tightly argued 25 years of the history of the ups and downs of strategic planning around the world." Depicts strategic planning as a vain desire for control of the uncontrollable. Mintzburg is an authoritative advocate of intuitive management. Like its subject, this book is a bit forbidding to outsiders.

Moore, J. L., *Writers on Strategy and Strategic Management,* 1992, New York: Penguin. Nice overview of strategic theorists such as Bruce Henderson and others.

Moore, James, *Gurdjieff: The Anatomy of a Myth,* 1991, Longmead, Shaftsbury, Dorset, and Rockport, MA: Element Books. A well-written biography.

Moskowitz, Milton, editor, *Business and Society: A Biweekly Report on Business and Social Responsibility,* collected issues from July 2, 1968, to December 27, 1974. This newsletter summed up just about everything going on in social responsibility with indefatigable passion and commitment.

————, Robert Levering, and Michael Katz, *Everybody's Business: The Irreverent Guide to Corporate America,* 1980, New York: Harper & Row; 1990, New York: Doubleday/Currency; and Milton Moskowitz, *The Global Marketplace,* 1987, New York: Macmillan. Engaging field guides to the histories and personalities of large mainstream corporations. Probably the most dog-eared, tattered, well-used books in my office.

Mowrey, Marc, and Tim Redmond, *Not in Our Backyard: The People and Events That Shaped America's Modern Environmental Movement,* 1993, New York: Morrow. Compelling stories of the people in the modern environmental movement.

Nigg, Walter, *The Heretics,* edited and translated by Richard and Clara Winston, 1962, New York: Alfred A. Knopf. Nigg was a minister and professor at the University of Zurich, who conceived of his subjects, medieval heretics, as mythic creatures adrift amidst the clash of colossal forces.

Pascale, Richard Tanner, *Managing on the Edge: How the Smartest Companies Use Conflict to Stay Ahead,* 1990, New York: Touchstone. Clearest indictment of American management on its own terms, because it combines detailed reporting (Ford, GE, GM, Honda) with a solid understanding of "the fallacy of straight-line thinking."

Peters, Thomas J., and Robert H. Waterman, Jr., *In Search of Excellence,*

1982, New York: Harper & Row. Less a book than an event, this is still a very good book. See Chapter 9.

Phillips, Michael, *The Seven Laws of Money*, 1974, Menlo Park, CA: Word Wheel Books; New York: Random House. The great counterculture money book; describes the ways to think about one's life with money, with great zest, good humor, and Taoist wisdom.

Rees, B. R., *Pelagius: A Reluctant Heretic*, 1988: Suffolk, Eng.: Boydell Press. Pelagius remains the most compelling heretical figure in my eyes, and this is the most complete work I found on him; it's idiosyncratic but carries forward the story of Pelagian influence through the centuries.

Richardson, George, *Feedback Thought in Social Science and Systems Theory*, 1991, Philadelphia: University of Pennsylvania Press. Very technical, very engrossing history of all the strands of "systems thinking" and how they moved from engineering and cybernetics into politics and organizational change. I admire the depth of research and skill of distinction that went into this book.

Robinson, Jeffrey, *Yamani: The Inside Story*, 1988, London: Simon & Schuster. A British potboiler in that great Fleet Street style.

Robinson, Peter, *Snapshots from Hell: The Making of an MBA*, 1994, New York: Warner Books. Twenty-two years and 3,000 miles after *The Gospel According to Harvard Business School*, and nothing has changed.

Russell, Jeffrey Burton, *Dissent and Order in the Middle Ages*, 1992, New York: Twayne/Macmillan. A slim, elegant, thoroughly engrossing book that makes sense of the heretics' struggle, gives them a historical context, and draws the reader into their story.

Sampson, Anthony, *The Seven Sisters: The Great Oil Companies and the World They Shaped*, 1975, New York: Viking. Amazing feat, to be so thorough and readable on such a big topic so soon after the crisis happened.

Schein, Edgar H., *Organizational Psychology*, 1965, 1970, 1980, Englewood Cliffs, NJ: Prentice-Hall. Very solid, concise, and thoughtful overview of the theories of organizational behavior and the people who developed them.

———, *Process Consultation*, Vol. 2, 1987, Boston: Addison-Wesley. "But what do organizational change agents actually *do?*" This is the manual that most of them read—a guide for professionals to wielding the power of conventional OD, at its best, without doing damage.

Schoenberg, Robert J., *Geneen*, 1985, New York: Warner Books. Fascinating, in-depth, journalistic biography.

Schwartz, Peter, *The Art of the Long View*, 1991, New York: Doubleday/Currency. Scenario practice as Wack and Newland practiced it and as it evolved further at Shell and elsewhere, codified and described by an old SRI hand. I was a consulting editor on this book. I refer people here when they want to practice developing scenarios.

Seashore, Charles, Edie Seashore, and Gerald M. Weinberg, *What Did You Say? The Art of Giving and Receiving FeedBack*, 1992, North Attleborough, MA: Douglas Charles Press. You too can learn what they do in T-Groups and NTL skill sessions. A matter-of-fact book of conversational skill-building by very nice people.

Senge, Peter, *The Fifth Discipline*, 1990, New York: Doubleday/Currency. The preeminent manifesto of the "learning organization" movement, this book lays out five bodies of activity that are necessary for transforming organizational life. Provides introductions to the ideas of Chris Argyris, Jay Forrester, and the organizational change movement. I conceived of *The Age of Heretics* while working as a consulting editor on *The Fifth Discipline*, and wondering about the roots of its practices.

———, Art Kleiner, Charlotte Roberts, Rick Ross, and Bryan Smith, *The Fifth Discipline Fieldbook*, 1994, New York: Doubleday/Currency. Five authors and seventy contributors (including me) present recipes for practice, intended to bootstrap readers out of the need for recipes. This would be a good place to go to follow up on Alinsky (organizations as communities), Argyris, systems thinking, and shared vision.

Sethi, S. Prakash, *Business Corporations and the Black Man*, 1970, Scranton, PA: Chandler Publishing Company. I depended heavily on this for detail and context on the Kodak/FIGHT story.

———, *Up Against the Corporate Wall: Modern Corporations and the Social Issues of the Seventies*, 1971, Englewood Cliffs, NJ: Prentice-Hall. Sethi was watching, seemingly, at every crisis where corporations fought the public, including PG&E's notorious Bodega Bay nuclear plant battle (they lost), the first surgeon general's antismoking campaign, the Eastman Kodak/FIGHT story, Dow's fights with anti-napalm student protests, and Campaign GM. He conveys the sensibilities of all sides with thoroughness.

Shorris, Earl, *Scenes from Corporate Life,* 1984, New York: Penguin; originally published as *The Oppressed Middle,* 1981, New York: Doubleday. Shorris musters stories and political analysis to show that organizations are inherently totalitarian. Some of his stories are heartbreaking; for instance, the floor polish marketing director who sees his destiny soar, and then crash, all because they cut a few pennies per bottle from the production budget and inadvertently created a floor wax that turned to coarse grey film in cold weather.

Sloan, Alfred P., *My Years with General Motors,* 1963, 1990, New York: Doubleday/Currency. Robert Blake's favorite management book. I had not understood, until reading this, the drive, vigor, farsightedness, and incredible discipline of the pioneering industrial mind.

Sternberg, Elaine, *Just Business: Business Ethics in Action,* 1994, Boston: Little, Brown. This is a terrific, hardheaded book on the purpose of business and why simply "returning investment to shareholders" is not sufficient—because it doesn't protect the shareholders! It also contains the most cogent arguments against "social responsibility" and stakeholder theory, and for business ethics and whistle-blowing, that I have seen.

Stolaroff, Myron J., *Thanatos to Eros: 35 Years of Psychedelic Exploration,* 1994, Berlin: Verlag für Wissenschaft und Bildung. Heartfelt personal autobiography of one manager's experience with psychedelics, extrasensory perception, and personal growth.

Talner, Lauren, *The Origins of Shareholder Activism,* 1983, Washington, DC: Investor Responsibility Research Center, 1983. Plain and simple, the full story.

Tuchman, Barbara, *A Distant Mirror,* 1978, New York: Random House. Tuchman holds up a sharp mirror to the plague-ridden fourteenth century.

Vaill, Peter B., *Managing as a Performing Art,* 1989, San Francisco: Jossey-Bass. Very nice collection of heretical essays, all about learning to make better distinctions among the abstractions of management theory and practice.

Ventura, Michael, *Shadow Dancing in the U.S.A.,* 1985, Los Angeles: Jeremy Tarcher. Contains the essay "Hear the Long Snake Moan," about the slavery/African/Irish/voodoo/jazz roots of the counterculture, and several other fine essays.

Vogel, David, *Lobbying the Corporation: Citizen Challenges to Business Authority,* 1978, New York: Basic Books. A spirited, comprehensive guide to the shareholder protest/corporate social responsibility movement, which manages to convey the fervor that its members felt (and feel) and the stunned, grim resignation that the executives felt.

Von Eschenbach, Wolfram, *The Parzival of Wolfram von Eschenbach,* translated by Edwin H. Zeydel and Bayard Quincy Morgan, 1951, Chapel Hill: University of North Carolina Studies in the Germanic Languages and Literatures. I chose this translation because it was in verse.

Vonnegut, Kurt, *Player Piano,* 1952, New York: Delacorte. Vonnegut worked at General Electric's "Works" during the late 1940s or early 1950s. This novel portrays corporate engineering culture vividly and effectively.

Wack, Pierre, "Scenarios: Uncharted Waters Ahead," *Harvard Business Review,* September–October 1985, and "Scenarios: Shooting the Rapids," *Harvard Business Review,* November–December 1985. Republished as *Scenarios: The Gentle Art of Reperceiving,* "Strategic Planning in Shell Series No. 1," Shell International Petroleum Group Limited, Group Planning, London, February 1986. Those interested in scenarios as useful tools should follow up with Wack's own writing. These clearly written, but dense and oracular reports reward study.

———, "I find by experience . . . ," transcription of a Wack lecture to a Harvard Business School MBA course in Country Analysis and Scenario Planning, 1985, printed in the *Harvard Business School Magazine,* 1985. A document with Pierre Wack's voice intact.

Wagner, G. A., *Business in the Public Eye: Reflections on the Ethics of Business,* translated by Theodore Plantinga, 1982, Grand Rapids, MI: Wm. B. Eerdmans. Meditations on ethics by a thoughtful Shell managing director.

Wakefield, Walter L., and Austin P. Evans, *Heresies of the High Middle Ages,* 1969, 1991, New York: Columbia University Press. A book of rants, exhortations, pleadings, condemnations, and other source documents.

Walton, Richard E., "How to Counter Alienation in the Plant," *Harvard Business Review*, November–December 1972. The ur-article about Topeka, translating its innovative story into a language aimed at conventional business academics.

Warsh, David, *Economic Principals: Masters and Mavericks of Modern Economics*, 1993, New York: The Free Press. Collection of insightful columns on economic personalities from the *Boston Globe*. Approves of Forrester.

Waterman, Robert, *What America Does Right*, 1994, New York: Norton. Why didn't more people pay attention to this book? If I were a working manager, I would get a great deal of inspiration from the examples given here.

Weaver, Paul H., *The Suicidal Corporation*, 1988, New York: Simon & Schuster. Great memoir by a former neoconservative writer whose ideals brought him to Ford at a crisis point. True to life about Ford and all companies.

Weick, Karl, *The Social Psychology of Organizing*, 1969. Boston: Addison-Wesley. Dense, illuminating theory of corporate design.

Weisbord, Marv, *Productive Workplaces*, 1987, San Francisco: Jossey-Bass. The first part is a set of in-depth profiles of Taylor, Lewin, McGregor, and Trist; the second part describes how Weisbord himself used their techniques and practices. One of the most valuable books in my library.

Whiteside, Thomas, *The Investigation of Ralph Nader*, 1972, New York: Arbor House. Straightforward journalistic recounting of Nader's trials with General Motors.

Whyte, William H., *The Organization Man*, 1956, New York: Simon & Schuster. Pathfinding excursion into the dark and bright sides of the corporate mentality.

Wren, Daniel A., *The Evolution of Management Thought*, 1972, New York: Ronald Press. A well-written snapshot of management thought as seen in 1972. I was surprised at how often I referred to it.

Yergin, Daniel, *The Prize*, 1991, New York: Simon & Schuster. Highly complete and readable narrative history of the coevolution of the oil industry and "hydrocarbon man." I depended on it as a model and a guide to the oil crisis.

Zager, Robert, and Michael P. Rosow, editors, *The Innovative Organization: Productivity Programs in Action,* 1982, New York: Pergamon Press. Reports on real-world Quality of Working Life and sociotechnical experiments, with critical details on key projects, in one semi-slim book.

INDEX